Charles Seale-Hayne Library
University of Plymouth
(01752) 588 588
LibraryandITenquiries@plymouth.ac.uk

SELF-RELATED COGNITIONS
in ANXIETY
and MOTIVATION

SELF-RELATED COGNITIONS
in ANXIETY
and MOTIVATION

Edited by

RALF SCHWARZER
Free University of Berlin

LEA LAWRENCE ERLBAUM ASSOCIATES, PUBLISHERS
1986   Hillsdale, New Jersey   London

Lawrence Erlbaum Associates, Inc., Publishers
365 Broadway
Hillsdale, New Jersey 07642

Library of Congress Cataloging-in-Publication Data
Main entry under title:

Self-related cognitions in anxiety and motivation.

Bibliography: p.
Includes index.
1. Anxiety. 2. Motivation (Psychology) 3. Self-
perception. 4. Self-evaluation. 5. Achievement
motivation. 6. Social interaction. I. Schwarzer,
Ralf.
BF575.A6S46 1986   155.2   85-20425
ISBN 0-89859-513-4

Printed in the United States of America
10 9 8 7 6 5 4 3 2 1

Contributors

Carole Ames, University of Maryland, Department of Human Development, College Park, MA 20742

Peter Aymanns, University of Trier, Fachbereich I, Fachgebiet Psychologie, 5500 Trier, Federal Republic of Germany

Ann Boggiano, University of Colorado, Department of Psychology, Boulder, CO 80309

Walter Braukmann, University of Trier, Fachbereich I, Fachgebiet Psychologie, 5500 Trier, Federal Republic of Germany

Arnold H. Buss, University of Texas, Department of Psychology, Austin, TX 78712

Charles S. Carver, University of Miami, Department of Psychology, Coral Gables, FL 33124

Martin V. Covington, University of California, Berkeley, Department of Psychology, Berkeley, CA 94720

Edward L. Deci, University of Rochester, Department of Psychology, Rochester, NY 14627

Sigrun-Heide Filipp, University of Trier, Fachbereich I, Fachgebiet Psychologie, 5500 Trier, Federal Republic of Germany

Carolyn M. Jagacinski, Purdue University, Department of Education, West Lafayette, IN 47907

John M. Levine, University of Pittsburgh, Department of Psychology, Pittsburgh, PA 15260

Herbert W. Marsh, University of Sydney, Department of Education, Sydney, New South Wales, 2006, Australia

Arden T. Miller, Morehead State University, Department of Psychology, Morehead, KY 40351

Richard L. Moreland, University of Pittsburgh, Department of Psychology, Pittsburgh, PA 15260

Larry W. Morris, Middle Tennessee State University, Department of Psychology, Murfreesboro, TN 37132

John G. Nicholls, Purdue University, Department of Education, West Lafayette, IN 47907

Paula M. Ponath, Middle Tennessee State University, Department of Psychology, Murfreesboro, TN 37132

Diane N. Ruble, New York University, Faculty of Arts and Science, New York, NY 10003

Richard M. Ryan, University of Rochester, Department of Psychology, Rochester, NY 14627

Barbara R. Sarason, University of Washington, Department of Psychology, Seattle, WA 98195

Irwin G. Sarason, University of Washington, Department of Psychology, Seattle, WA 98195

Michael F. Scheier, Carnegie-Mellon University, Department of Psychology, Pittsburgh, PA 15213

Ralf Schwarzer, Free University of Berlin, Institute of Psychology, 1000 Berlin 33, Federal Republic of Germany

Richard J. Shavelson, University of California, Los Angeles, The Rand Corp., Santa Monica, CA 90406

Sigmund Tobias, The City College, New York, School of Education, New York, NY 10031

Robert A. Wicklund, University of Bielefeld, Department of Psychology, 4800 Bielefeld, Federal Republic of Germany

Contents

Preface

Research on anxiety and motivation has witnessed substantial progress in recent years in developing innovative perspectives and applying advanced psychometric tools. The most important contributions were made by cognitively oriented psychologists who have related the information processing view to anxiety and motivation. The organized knowledge about oneself and the storage, processing and retrieval of information concerned with one's attitude and behavior strongly influences the way people think, feel and act. Therefore, self-referent thoughts play a major role as a cognitive component in anxiety and motivation.

It is the idea of this book to integrate different lines of thinking in the field of anxiety and motivation by relating both topics to self-focussed attention, self-concept and self-evaluation in achievement contexts as well as in social contexts.

In test anxiety research, for example, the separation of two components has proven useful: worry and emotionality. Worry can be understood as a self-related cognition which seems to be primarily responsible for performance impairment, whereas the emotionality, i.e. the perception of autonomous arousal, is less relevant for academic behavior. This distinction of a cognitive and an emotional component has been transferred fruitfully from state anxiety to trait anxiety research, and recently has been applied to social anxiety. In research on social anxiety an additional construct has gained popularity, that is, self-awareness as a necessary condition for embarrassment, shyness, shame, and audience anxiety. A state of public self-awareness is claimed to be a prerequisite of social anxiety.

In self-concept research there is a shift from traditional measures of self-esteem or "ideal self versus real self discrepancy" measures, to an information processing approach focusing on self-knowledge, ability cognitions, and self-efficacy and competence expectations.

Self-referent thought has also made an impact on research in achievement motivation. Drives and motives have been replaced by expectancies and self-regulatory actions. There is a revival of competence motivation in terms of cognitive control, attribution, and self-efficacy expectancy.

This book is addressed to scientists as well as to students in the fields of psychology and education. Those working in personality and social psychology will find it especially useful and the sequence of chapters can be adapted to individual preferences. However, the topic is relevant to clinical and educational psychology as well. I wish to express my thanks to the contributors to this volume for meeting the deadline and for the cooperation displayed in fashioning their chapters.

Ralf Schwarzer
Berlin, West Germany

1 Self-Related Cognitions in Anxiety and Motivation: An Introduction

Ralf Schwarzer
Institut für Psychologie, Freie Universität Berlin

The cognitive approach has strongly influenced most areas of psychology and education. Attitudes, emotions, and actions are greatly affected by conscious or semi-conscious processes as found in perception, memory, thought, and language. The processing, storage, and retrieval of information are basic elements in the regulation of behavior and, thereby, are precursors of habit formation and personality development. Emotions are viewed as being dependent upon cognitions, or as being constituted by cognitions, feelings, and arousal in a complex manner. This will be discussed further within the context of anxiety. Self-focused attention can be a starting point for more elaborated cognitions about oneself, such as attributions, self-evaluations, and expectancies in stressful or demanding situations. Motivated actions are strongly determined by self-related cognitions. This introductory chapter discusses some recent advances in research on social and test anxiety, coping, self-evaluations, and motivation. The following chapters, written by well-known experts in these fields, will deal with these and related topics in detail.

SOCIAL ANXIETY

Social anxiety can be defined as consisting of (1) negative self-evaluations, (2) feelings of tension and discomfort, and (3) a tendency to withdraw in the presence of others. This is a pattern of cognitive, emotional, and instrumental variables which may occur simultaneously, but need not. Shyness, embarrassment, shame, and audience anxiety are different kinds of social anxiety. *Shyness* is a general social anxiety applicable to a variety of social situations.

Embarrassment can be seen as an extreme state of shyness indicated by blushing. *Shame* occurs when one sees himself as being responsible for negative outcomes or for failing in public. *Audience anxiety* is characterized by a discomfort when performing in front of an audience (stage fright) which can lead to an inhibition of speech. This is closely related to test anxiety because the individual is afraid of being under the scrutiny of others. Both kinds of apprehension in face of tests and social interactions share this aspect of evaluation anxiety (Wine, 1980). Social anxiety is more general, whereas test anxiety can be conceived of as very specific with respect to written exams. In the case of oral exams and any other tests performed in public, test anxiety as well as social anxiety are adequate variables to be taken into account. Test anxiety researchers have usually neglected this social aspect or have defined test anxiety in a manner too broad to be of use.

Whether social anxiety can be subdivided into these four emotions has not been finally agreed upon. There may be more or fewer facets. Buss (1980) has made this differentiation popular, but now undertakes a conceptual change by conceiving embarrassment as part of shyness (Buss, this volume). Some authors don't make any distinction at all and prefer to accept social anxiety as one homogeneous phenomenon. In contrast, Schlenker and Leary (1982) conceive shyness and embarrassment as separate facets of social anxiety. This question requires further theoretical efforts. Table 1.1 shows a matrix of potential differentiations. It may be possible that some cells are empty, e.g., a trait of embarrassment may not exist.

Therefore, in the following discussion shyness as the most typical and well-understood social emotion is the focus of attention, representing social anxiety. It is useful to distinguish state shyness from trait shyness in accord with the widely accepted conceptualization of state and trait anxiety (Spielberger, 1966). The *state* of anxiety refers to the acute feeling in the process of emotional experiencing. The *trait* of anxiety refers to a proneness to respond with state anxiety in threatening situations. This proneness is acquired during the individual's history of socialization. Shyness is characterized by: public self-awareness, the relative absence of an expected social behavior, discomfort in social situations, an inhibition of adequate interpersonal actions, and awkwardness in the presence of others. Buss (1980) claims that public self-awareness is a necessary condition of any kind of social anxiety. In this emo-

TABLE 1.1
Potential Differentiation of Social Anxieties

	Shyness	*Embarrassment*	*Shame*	*Audience Anxiety*
State				
Trait				

TABLE 1.2
Components of Social Anxieties

COGNITIVE

> public self-awareness
> worry about social inadequacy
> self-preoccupation
> self-evaluation as a social being
> concern with one's public image
> perceived inability to cope with social demands

EMOTIONAL

> feeling of distress and discomfort
> perceived autonomic reaction, e.g., blushing
> tension

INSTRUMENTAL

> awkwardness
> tendency to withdraw from situations
> inhibition of gestures and speech
> absence of social activity
> disorganization of social activity

tional state the person's attention is directed to those aspects of the self which can be observed by others, like face, body, clothes, gestures, speech, or manners. At the trait level public self-consciousness is the respective variable. Persons high in public self-consciousness are prone to perceive themselves as social objects and tend to think and act in front of an imaginary audience. The direction of attention to the self can be understood as a mental withdrawal from the social situation at hand, leading to a decrement in social performance. Self-related cognitions are part of the complex emotional phenomenon of shyness or social anxiety in general (see Table 1.2).

The anxious individual worries about his social performance, is concerned with his public image, perceives inability to cope with social demands, is apprehensive of behaving inadequately, permanently monitors and evaluates his actions, and is preoccupied with himself as a social being. The emotional component refers to the feelings of distress, discomfort, tension, and the perception of one's autonomic reactions in the presence of others. For example, blushing when experiencing embarrassment, and being aware of it, can lead to a vicious cycle (Asendorpf, 1984). The "emotional component" can be seen as a "quasi-cognitive component" because it deals with information processing of feelings and arousal. Finally, the instrumental or action component refers to awkwardness, reticence, inhibition of gestures and speech, a tendency to withdraw from the situation, and the disorganization or absence of social behavior. Both shy and polite people can be very similar in behavior but differ in cognitions and feelings: non-shy, polite individuals are relaxed and calm, and direct their attention to the situation, whereas shy individuals do not. These three components have to be inserted in each cell of Table 1.1 and require a cell-specific theoretical elaboration.

Causes of shyness can be theorized in different ways. Schlenker and Leary (1982) propose a self-presentational view: Shyness occurs when someone desires to make a favorable impression on others but is doubtful of the desired effect. Embarrassment occurs when something happens which repudiates the intended impression management. There may be a discrepancy between one's own standard of self-presentation and one's actual self-presentation. When such a discrepancy is expected, shyness will result, and when it is actually perceived, embarrassment is experienced. This can be seen as a two-stage process at the state level of social anxiety. A person who expects to fall short in impressing others will be shy. If this anticipation becomes true, the person is embarrassed. Buss (this volume) mentions a number of other potential causes for shyness, such as feeling conspicuous, receiving too much or too little attention from others, being evaluated, fear of being rejected, a breach of privacy, intrusiveness, formality of social situations, social novelty, and so forth. With respect to common stress theories social anxiety depends on the appraisal of the social situation as being ego-threatening and the appraisal of one's own inability to cope with it.

The development of shyness can be traced back to two sources (Buss, this volume). The "early developing shyness" appears in the first year of life and is better known as stranger anxiety or wariness. Novelty, intrusion, and fear of rejection are the immediate causes. Since there are no self-related cognitions at that time, this is a fearful shyness, whereas the "later developing shyness" can be regarded as a self-conscious shyness. It first appears in the fourth or fifth year of life and is associated with acute self-awareness and embarrassment. Both kinds of shyness contribute to the complex phenomenon of shyness during the individual socialization process. Fearfulness as an inherited trait and public self-consciousness as an environmental trait may be two sources of trait shyness, which attains its peak degree during adolescence (Buss, this volume). Low self-esteem and low sociability may be two additional causes. In a field study with 94 college students, we obtained satisfactory correlations between shyness on the one hand and, on the other self-consciousness (.39), audience anxiety (.39), general anxiety (.36), other-directedness (.36), and self-esteem (−.62) (Schwarzer, 1981). These may be rough indicators of trait associations.

There are few measures designed to assess trait social anxiety. As in test anxiety research, separate worry and emotionality scales have been constructed (Morris, Harris, & Rovins, 1981). However, these scales do not distinguish shyness from embarrassment, shame, and audience anxiety. Additionally, the specific shyness scale of Cheek and Buss (1981) does not provide a separation of cognitive and emotional components. Evidently there has been a lack of operationalization compared to the obvious increment in theoretical efforts during the past few years. A complex measure of social anxiety which satisfies the needs of the present approach should consider the four kinds of social anxiety and the state-trait distinction (Table 1.1) as well as the three components (Table 1.2), and also provide as many subscales. The distinction between a cognitive and an emotional component bears treatment implications: Self-related cognitions could be modified by a restructuring and attention training, whereas tension and nervous feelings could be treated by systematic desensitization.

TEST ANXIETY

Anxiety can be defined as "an unpleasant emotional state or condition which is characterized by subjective feelings of tension, apprehension, and worry, and by activation or arousal of the autonomic nervous system" (Spielberger, 1972, p. 482). Test anxiety is a situation-specific state or trait which refers to examinations. As mentioned above, this may be confounded with social anxiety when the test is taken in public or when social interactions are part of the performance to be evaluated. Test anxiety theory has a long tradition which makes it one of the most studied phenomena in psychology (Morris & Ponath, this volume; Tobias, this volume). However, as paradigms shift in our general psychological thinking, this has a strong impact on the investigation of specific phenomena, too. The cognitive approach to emotions and actions has given rise to new concepts which are fruitful in understanding and explaining the subjective experience of anxiety in specific situations. The first four volumes of the new series *Advances in Test Anxiety Research* demonstrates the far-reaching consequences of cognitions of the worry type for our scientific knowledge (Schwarzer, Van der Ploeg, & Spielberger, 1982, Van der Ploeg, Schwarzer, & Spielberger, 1983, 1985).

Tests are mostly regarded as general academic demands in schools or in higher education, but also can be conceived of as highly specific demands, as discussed in mathematics anxiety (Richardson & Woolfolk, 1980) or sports anxiety (Hackfort, 1983). Such demands, if personally relevant for the individual, can be appraised as being challenging, ego-threatening or, harmful (Lazarus & Launier, 1978). The appraisal of the task as ego-threatening gives rise to test anxiety if the person perceives a lack of coping ability. This second kind of appraisal is most interesting for the study of *self-related cognitions.* The individual searches for information about his specific competence to handle the situation. The coping resources looked for could be one's ability to solve the kind of problem at hand or the time available and the existence of a supportive social network (see B. Sarason, this volume). Perceiving a contingency between the potential action and the potential outcome and attributing this contingency to internal factors is most helpful in developing an adaptive coping strategy. This confidence in one's ability to act successfully can be called self-efficacy (Bandura 1977). A lack of perceived self-efficacy leads to an imbalance between the appraised task demands and the appraised subjective coping resources, resulting in test anxiety, which inhibits the ongoing person-environment transaction and decreases performance. This is a case of cognitive interference (I. Sarason, this volume). The individual's attention is divided into task-relevant and task-irrelevant aspects. The presence of task-irrelevant cognitions can be regarded as a mental withdrawal (Carver & Scheier, this volume). People who cannot escape from an aversive situation physically because of social constraints or lack of freedom to leave, do so by directing their thoughts away from the problem at hand. Task-irrelevant thoughts can be divided into self-related cognitions (like worry about one's inability or failure) on the one hand and those which are totally unrelated to the task (like daydreams) on the other. This mental withdrawal from the threatening demands equals the test anxiety component which debilitates academic performance. The perception of discomfort and tension is the other component. Autonomic arousal may accompany this state or trait but need not. Mental withdrawal is maladaptive in a specific situation because it contradicts any kind of problem-centered coping action. However, in the long run there may also be a certain adaptive value because the person may learn to distinguish such situations from those which are easily manageable and, therefore, avoids selecting inappropriate situations or too difficult tasks.

There are many causes which make a person test anxious. The individual's history of success and failure combined with an unfavorable attributional style (Wine, 1980) and no supportive feedback from parents, teachers, and peers may lead to a vicious cycle which develops a proneness to scan the environment for potential dangers ("sensitizing"), to appraise demands as threatening, and to cope with problems in a maladaptive way.

The assessment of test anxiety has to consider these theoretical advances and, therefore, requires measures for separate components. Such a satisfactory measure for example is the Test Anxiety Inventory (TAI) by Spielberger (1980) which is now available in several languages (see Schwarzer & Kim, 1984). Another new instrument, called "Reactions to Tests," is introduced by I. Sarason in this volume.

SELF-FOCUS, COPING AND PERSISTENCE

Self-related cognitions and anxiety bear some implications for the motivation process and the task accomplishment. Very often it is stated that self-focus distracts from task-focus, that attention capacity used for self-deprecatory rumination reduces the attention capacity necessary for problem solving, and that the worry component is mainly responsible for performance decrements. On the other hand it is also said that under certain circumstances anxiety may facilitate performance. This whole motivational process is very complex and requires consideration of variables like situation appraisal, prior experience, task frustration, task difficulty, outcome expectancy, attributional style, effort, coping resources, and persistence (Anderson, Horowitz, & French, 1983; Bohrnstedt & Felson, 1983; Krantz 1983; Kulik, 1983; Murphy & Moriarity, 1976; Paulhus, 1983; Schwarz & Clore, 1983; Weiner, 1980, 1982, 1983).

There is no sufficient empirical evidence which lumps all these variables together and gives a clear answer to the question of when the motivational process starts, how it works, and what kind of action and outcome it produces. However, some partial theories and empirical findings shed light on the complexity of the phenomenon, as shown by several contributions in this volume. First, I will speculate on situation appraisals as related to repeated failures and their impact on anxiety, coping and persistence. Second, I will discuss recent deliberations on self-focus and self-efficacy.

Anxiety, despondency, disengagement, and helplessness are complex motivational states and traits based on a certain amount of exposure to stressful events or demands. The perception of contingency between one's actions and the outcomes as well as the attribution of this contingency are key concepts in the understanding of why people exert effort and how long they persist with tasks (Bandura 1977, Heckhausen 1980, Seligman 1975). Experiencing no contingency between one's action and outcome and, further, attributing this failure to a lack of ability, may lead to anxiety or helplessness. The resulting motivational state is dependent on previous experience with the same kind of demands. If failure is repeatedly experienced, some form of helplessness is more likely to occur or is more dominant than anxiety. These motivational states can be either task-specific or subject matter-specific. Also, the same level of anxiety can be facilitating for one person and debilitating for another. The expectancy of coping with the problem at hand makes the difference (Carver & Scheier, 1981).

The developmental causes underlying negative motivational states or traits can be theorized as follows (Schwarzer, 1981). The initial question is how students process information in academic settings. If the environmental demands are highly self-relevant, that is, personally stressful, they can be appraised as a challenge, a threat, or a loss of control (Lazarus & Launier, 1978). This cognitive appraisal need not be exclusive in content. However, the question is which cognition is the dominant one within the set of appraisals. The first unexpected failure might cause challenge to be dominant. If this happens repeatedly, the person will feel more threatened than challenged, but will still persist with the task. Later, when the next failure is already expected with a high degree of likelihood, the person will experience loss of control, feeling less threatened because the loss is certain. This theoretical model of the development of cognitive appraisals is depicted in Figure 1.1.

The x-axis in Figure 1.1 represents the number of failures or the amount of non-contingencies. Challenge decreases and loss increases from one point in time to the next. Threat first increases and then decreases with continuing experience of failure. The highest degree of threat is located where there is complete uncertainty about the next outcome. This whole model is built only for the special case of continuous failure, whereas in natural environments intermittent success would be more likely.

Cognitive appraisals lead to emotions and behavior. Challenge leads to curiosity, exploration, and productive arousal. Threat leads to anxiety, and loss of control to helplessness or depression. With respect to the intersections of the curves in Figure 1.1 and the emotions derived from cognitive appraisals, four stages can be distinguished (see Table 1.3).

Stage I

This is the reactance stage (Brockner et al., 1983; Wortman & Brehm, 1976). The person is challenged by one or several failures, but still has confidence in his or her ability to cope with the demands. High self-efficacy is combined with productive arousal and the tendency to explore the nature of the task.

Stage II

When failures mount, threat surpasses challenge appraisal, and anxiety becomes the leading emotion. This combination of anxiety with productive

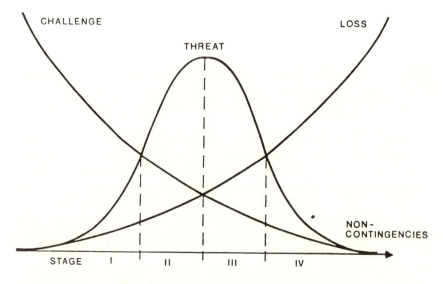

FIG. 1.1   Development of cognitive appraisals.

TABLE 1.3
Stage Model of Motivational States and Traits[1]

Stage	Cognition	Emotion	Persistence/ Effort
I	1. Challenge	Curiosity Exploration	High
	2. Threat	Productive arousal	
II	1. Threat	Facilitating anxiety/ emotionality	High
	2. Challenge		
	3. Loss		
III	1. Threat	Debilitating anxiety/ worry	Low
	2. Loss		
	3. Challenge		
IV	1. Loss	Helplessness	Low
	2. Threat		

[1]From Schwarzer, Jerusalem, & Stiksrud, 1984.

arousal can be called "facilitating anxiety," because the person is still self-reliant and persists with the task. The emotionality component would be higher than the worry component in anxiety.

Stage III

At the culminating point there is complete uncertainty about the next outcome. The threat appraisal will be combined with less challenge and more loss of control. This is called "debilitating anxiety," because self-related cognitions distract from the task. The person worries about the performance, is afraid of another failure, has self-doubts and is no longer confident of his or her competence.

Stage IV

Finally, loss of control is dominant, replacing the appraisal of threat. The student becomes helpless and gives up trying. The next failure is almost certain.

There is some empirical evidence supporting this model (Schwarzer, Jerusalem, & Stiksrud, 1984). The relationship between coping and self-focused attention is discussed in detail by Filipp, Aymanns, and Braukmann (this volume).

Self-focus often is contrasted with task-focus, implying that the direction of attention is the major determinant of task persistence and accomplishment. However, studies by Carver and Scheier (1981, this volume) have proven that this dichotomy is too simple and misleading. At the trait level a high degree of self-consciousness makes the person prone to a high frequency of self-focused attention. At the state level self-focus can be induced experimentally by the presence of a mirror or any other technical device which gives feedback of one's face, voice, or behavior. Also it can be induced naturally by anxious arousal. The person perceives bodily changes like increased pulse rate, blushing, sweating, and so forth, which leads to self-focus and interruption of the on-going action. (It remains unclear, however, if either self-focus or interruption come first.) Self-focus, then, facilitates performance for low–anxious people and debilitates performance for high–anxious people. This important statement in the work of Carver and Scheier raises the question of anxiety definition. If one equates anxiety with perceived arousal there would be no disagreement with the statement. But if anxiety is defined as a cognitive set of worry, self-deprecatory rumination, and negative outcome expectancy combined with emotionality, then their statement would be questionable. Carver and Scheier redefine anxiety as a coping process starting with self-focus. Self-focus leads to an interruption of action and provokes a subjective outcome assessment. At this point the authors claim the existence of a "watershed" with respect to the content of the self-focused attention: This state of self-awareness leads some people to favorable and others to unfavorable outcome expectancies. The first group will shift to more task-focus, invest more effort, show more persistence, and will attain more success. The second group will withdraw from the task mentally and will be preoccupied with self-deprecatory ruminations. Therefore they will invest less effort, be less persistent, and will probably experience failure. The first can be defined as a low–anxiety group, the second as a high–anxiety group.

A feedback loop makes the high anxious persons more prone to perceived discrepancies and interruptions of action by arousal cues. The key variables in this model are self-focus and outcome expectancies. Worry, here, is not the primary cause of performance decrements, it is only one element in a maladaptive coping procedure based on mental withdrawal and unfavorable expectancies. Self-focus gives way to a cognitive process where one's own coping ability is under scrutiny.

The notion of outcome expectancy or "hope versus doubt" is similar to Bandura's (1977, 1982) concept of *self-efficacy*. This can be defined as a perceived action-outcome contingency attributed to one's ability. In our own model this is called "competence expectancy" (Fig. 1.2).

This construct of perceived self-efficacy or competence expectancy could possibly be defined as part of anxiety. Bandura (1983) postulates an "interac-

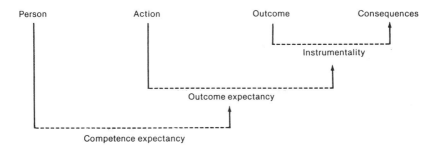

FIG. 1.2   Hierarchy of expectancies (Schwarzer 1981).

tive, though asymmetric, relation between perceived self-efficacy and fear arousal, with self-judged efficacy exerting the greater impact" (p. 464). For him perceived self-efficacy and anxiety are different concepts with the first one being more influential for performance prediction. However, his definition of anxiety is not a cognitive one. Instead, it is something like fear or perceived arousal, in other words: he refers to nothing but the emotionality component when talking about anxiety. Therefore his findings indicating a superiority of self-related cognitions over "anxiety" is in line with those who claim the same hypothesis for the worry component of anxiety. The question raised by the findings of Bandura (1983) and Carver and Scheier (this volume) as well as many others seems to be a matter of definition: which theoretical concepts described in the process of coping should be subsumed under the heading of anxiety? I prefer a broad conceptualization and suggest use of variables like perceived self-efficacy (hope versus doubt), self-deprecatory rumination (worry), and mental withdrawal (escape cognitions) as constitutive cognitive elements of anxiety as a state and as a trait. Subdividing anxiety into more than the usual two components is in line with the findings of Irwin Sarason (this volume), Helmke (1982), and Stephan, Fischer, and Stein (1983). Conceiving anxiety as a multi-faceted construct of course requires adequate measures designed to assess each facet separately. Other variables discussed above such as situation appraisal, self-focus, attributional style, effort, persistence, and performance are not part of this construct but are part of the related process of motivation and coping with situational demands.

SELF-EVALUATION AND MOTIVATION

Perceived self-efficacy can be acquired by direct, indirect, or symbolic experience (Bandura 1977): Mastery of tasks provides information about one's capability of handling specific kinds of problems: observing similar others performing well on a task leads to an inference of the same capability in oneself; being convinced verbally to possess the necessary coping strategies may also be sufficient to perceive oneself as competent. Self-evaluation of past or future performance creates a motivational basis for further actions (Weiner, 1980, 1982, 1983). However, the process of self-evaluation is co-determined by a variety of circumstances which have to be considered. Not all situations are evaluative in the same sense. Feedback by parents, teachers, and peers is the most prominent situation where cues are available to be transformed into the self-concept. If these cues occur in public, the person is "on stage" and may be motivated to reduce discrepancies between the public image inferred by the feedback and the desired public image. Strategic self-presentation could lead to acception, neglect, or rejection of the feedback. Failing on a task in a private environment is less harmful because the person is "off-stage" and can easily distort the outcome by use of several kinds of self-serving biases. Evaluating oneself too positively may strengthen one's self-esteem and may make one less vulnerable to depressive disorders (Alloy & Abramson 1979, Lewinsohn, Mischel, Chaplin, & Barton 1980). Realistic self-evaluation may be unfavorable for one's mental health. On the other hand, illusions of control may lead to an underestimation of academic demands and may seduce people to select overly difficult tasks resulting in unexpected failures. Distortions of reality seem to be characteristic for highly self-reliant persons. In two experiments (Schwarzer & Jerusalem 1982) students working on an intelligence task were given fictitious feedback and statistical interactions were found between self-esteem and success versus failure. It turned out that high self-esteem students attributed their presumable success to their ability but did not attribute presumable failure to a lack of ability.

The dominant goal structure of the achievement setting is another co-determinant of self-evaluation processes (Ames, this volume). If classes are competitive the students judge their outcomes with respect to their reference group, whereas in an individualistic goal structure they refer to their previous outcomes. In the first, ability is the preferred attribution factor, in contrast to effort in the second context. Social comparison is primarily directed to one's competence or self-worth. Attempting to make progress without comparison to others requires effort. Success of a cooperative group requires combined efforts and shared beliefs in group mastery, possibly by social comparison to other groups.

The implicit goal structure of a learning environment has some similarity with the type of involvement as described by Nicholls, Jagacinski, and Miller (this volume). An ego-involvement situation implies an interest in one's ability level. This can only be inferred from a normative perspective. Problems that only few persons can solve are difficult tasks, and success in solving them indicates a high competence level (Nicholls & Miller, 1983). Social comparison is seen as a strategy for information search, competitiveness is one motivational consequence of ego-involvement. A task-involvement situation, on the other hand, implies an interest in mastery. The person wants to solve a problem because of its challenging nature or because he likes to monitor his own progress in coping with increasing task difficulties. This is similar to the "intrinsic pleasure" in White's (1959) theory of competence motivation. Succeeding with high effort evokes positive emotions such as pride. In an ego-involving situation, however, succeeding with low effort evokes positive emotions. The reason is that ability as a capacity can be optimally demonstrated by investing high effort. This implies that someone who tries hard and fails must be incompetent. A strategy to prevent such a public image is to invest low effort. In case of failure this would be attributable to low effort without doing any harm to one's sense of self-worth. In case of success, however, this could be attributed to high ability which causes positive affect – a point strongly made by Covington (1983, this volume) and Nicholls et al. (this volume).

Ego-involving situations (Nicholls) and competitive goal structures (Ames) are nearly identical theoretical concepts involving ability attributions and social comparisons. But a task-involving situation does not equate individualistic goal structure. A mastery approach is criterion-referenced, that is, one's outcome is compared to an absolute or task-immanent standard, whereas the individualistic structure seems to be based on self-evaluations over time as stated in the theory of temporal comparison processes (Albert 1977). It is therefore useful to distinguish at least three reference norms: criterial, individualistic, and social, which play different roles in self-evaluation processes and bear different motivational implications. This does not mean that the one is associated with *more* motivation than the other, but the cognitions and emotions involved are not the same. A new systematic approach to evaluative cognitions is made by Levine and Moreland (this volume) who have distinguished between social and temporal comparisons as well as type of comparison. This culminates in a three-dimensional heuristic model capable of including most of the cases mentioned in the previous literature (see Messe & Watts, 1983; Tabachnik, Crocker, & Alloy, 1983).

Cognitive evaluation theory (Deci & Ryan, this volume) claims that ego-involvement and task-involvement are specific phenomena which can be embedded in a broader context. Environmental and internal events are divided into informational, controlling, and noncontingent events. Informational events outside or inside the person provide effectance-relevant information and can be equated to task-involvement. Controlling events like rewards or deadlines (outside or inside the person) impose pressures and restrict the freedom of action and choice. This can be equated to ego-involvement where one feels the need to behave in compliance with certain demands or to create a favorable public image. Rewards are usually perceived as controlling and therefore reduce intrinsic motivation. Noncontingent events where actions and outcomes are perceived as independent lead to helplessness or to amotivation. Only informational events provide the basis for self-determination and intrinsic motivation. In the process of self-regulation two directions can be distinguished: self-determination characterized by freedom, and self-control characterized by self-imposed pressures. Both, self-determination and self-control are motivating, the first intrinsic, and the second extrinsic. This can be traced back to childhood and has considerable impact on the personality (see Deci & Ryan, this volume).

The student's motivational orientation towards specific tasks is influenced by the way teachers administer reward contingencies and give evaluative feedback (Meyer 1984; Boggiano & Ruble, this volume). Controlling strategies of teachers produce a learning environment of extrinsic motivation which is prone to be oriented to a competitive goal structure. In such classes poor performers have to suffer more from low self-esteem and test anxiety than in the opposite kind of environment. The focus is on one's competence in relation to others. Self-related cognitions are centered on information-seeking about ability while the interest in the nature of the task may decrease.

The academic self-concept is based on an individual's history of evaluative feedback and self-related cognitions in learning environments (Marsh, Relich & Smith, 1983; Marsh, Smith & Barnes, 1983). It is clearly separated from a social, an emotional, and a physical self-concept (Shavelson & Marsh, this volume). The acquired and organized knowledge about oneself as a learner — which is the meaning of "academic self-concept" — has a more or less strong belief in one's competence as its core. Future research should find out if ability and effort as attributional trait components of self-concept are developed by the long-term experience of controlling versus informational contingencies and/or by the steady exposure to competitive versus individualistic goal structures. The finding that a math concept and a reading concept are subfacets of academic self-concept includes the notion that at lower levels of the hierarchy more specific and less stable self-related information is processed, stored, and retrieved. It still has to be investigated whether ability and interest are already separated at this level.

Research on anxiety and motivation profits from taking the perspective of social psychologists working on self-awareness and self-definition (Carver & Scheier, 1981; Wicklund & Gollwitzer, 1982, Wicklund, this volume). Cognitive processes about oneself in relation to others are a key factor for understanding and explaining human emotions and actions in a variety of experimental and natural settings. People are concerned about their public image and their competence as defined within a reference group and strive to enhance their sense of self-worth.

REFERENCES

Albert, S. Temporal comparison theory. *Psychological Review,* 1977, *84,* 485–503.
Alloy, L. B., & Abramson, L. Y. Judgment of contingency in depressed and nondepressed students: Sadder but wiser? *Journal of Experimental Psychology,* 1979, *108,* 441–485.

Anderson, C. A., Horowitz, L. M., & French, R. D. Attributional style of lonely and depressed people. *Journal of Personality and Social Psychology,* 1983, *45,* 127–136.

Asendorpf, J. Shyness, embarrassment, and self-presentation: A control theory approach. In R. Schwarzer (Ed.), *The self in anxiety, stress, and depression.* Amsterdam: North Holland Publ. Co., 1984.

Bandura, A. Self-efficacy: Toward a unifying theory of behavioral change. *Psychological Review,* 1977, *84,* 191–215.

Bandura, A. Self-referent thought: A developmental analysis of self-efficacy. In Flavell, J. & Ross, L. (Eds.), *Cognitive social development.* New York: Cambridge University Press, 1981.

Bandura, A. Self-efficacy determinants of anticipated fear and calamities. *Journal of Personality and Social Psychology,* 1983, *45,* 464–469.

Bohrnstedt, G. W., & Felson, R. B. Explaining the relations among children's actual and perceived performances and self-esteem: A comparison of several causal models. *Journal of Personality and Social Psychology,* 1983, *45,* 43–56.

Brockner, J., Gardner, M., Bierman, J., Mahan, T., Thomas, B., Weiss, W., Winters, L., & Mitchell, A. The roles of self-esteem and self-consciousness in the Wortman-Brehm model of reactance and learned helplessness. *Journal of Personality and Social Psychology,* 1983, *45,* 199–209.

Buss, A. H. *Self-consciousness and social anxiety.* San Francisco: Freeman, 1980.

Carver, C. S., & Scheier, M. F. *Attention and self-regulation: A control-theoory approach to human behavior.* New York: Springer, 1981.

Cheek, J. H., & Buss, A. H. Shyness and sociability. *Journal of Personality and Social Psychology,* 1981, *41,* 330–339.

Covington, M. V. Anxiety, task difficulty and childhood problemsolving: A self-worth interpretation. In H. M. van der Ploeg, R. Schwarzer, & C. D. Spielberger (Eds.), *Advances in test anxiety research* (Vol. 2) (pp. 101–110). Lisse/Hillsdale: Swets & Zeitlinger/Erlbaum, 1983.

Hackfort, D. *Theorie und Diagnostik sportbezogener Ängstlichkeit.* Köln: Deutsche Sporthochschule, 1983.

Heckhausen, H. *Motivation und Handeln.* Heidelberg: Springer, 1980.

Helmke, A. *Schulische Leistungsangst — Messung und Diagnose.* Konstanz: Unv. Diss., 1982.

Krantz, S. Cognitive appraisals and problem-directed coping: A prospective study of stress. *Journal of Personality and Social Psychology,* 1983, *44,* 638–643.

Kulik, J. A. Confirmatory attribution and the perpetuation of social beliefs. *Journal of Personality and Social Psychology,* 1983, *44,* 1171–1181.

Lazarus, R. S., & Launier, R. Stress related transactions between person and environment. In L. A. Pervin & M. Lewis (Eds.), *Perspectives in international psychology* (pp. 287–327). New York: Plenum, 1978.

Lewinsohn, P. M., Mischel, W., Chaplin, W., & Barton, R. Social competence and depression: The role of illusory self-perceptions. *Journal of Abnormal Psychology,* 1980, *89,* 202–212.

Marsh, H. W., Relich, J D., & Smith, I. D. Self-concept: The construct validity of interpretations based upon the SDQ. *Journal of Personality and Social Psychology,* 1983, *45,* 173–187.

Marsh, H., Smith, I. D., & Barnes, J. Multitrait-multimethod analyses of the Self-Description Questionnaire: Student-Teacher agreement on multidimensional ratings of self-concept. *American Educational Research Journal,* 1983, *20,* 333–358.

Messe, L. A., & Watts, B. L. Complex nature of the sense of fairness: Internal standards and social comparison as bases for reward evaluations. *Journal of Personality and Social Psychology,* 1983, *45,* 84–93.

Meyer, W.-U. *Das Konzept von der eigenen Begabung.* Bern: Huber, 1984.

Morris, L. W., Harris, E. W., & Rovins, D. S. Interactive effects of generalized and situational expectations on the arousal of cognitive and emotional components in social anxiety. *Journal of Research in Personality,* 1981, *15,* 302–311.

Murphy, L. B., & Moriarty, A. E. *Vulnerability, coping, and growth.* New Haven and London: Yale Univ. Press, 1976.

Nicholls, J., & Miller, A. The differentiation of the concepts of difficulty and ability. *Child Development,* 1983, *54,* 951–959.

Palys, T. S., & Little, B. R. Perceived life satisfaction and the organization of personal project systems. *Journal of Personality and Social Psychology,* 1983, *44,* 1221–1230.

Paulhus, D. Sphere-specific measures of perceived control. *Journal of Personality and Social Psychology,* 1983, *44,* 1253–1265.

Richardson, F. C., & Woolfolk, R. L. Mathematics anxiety. In I. G. Sarason (Ed.), *Test anxiety.* Hillsdale: Erlbaum, 1980.

Schlenker, B. R., & Leary, M. R. Social anxiety and self-presentation: A conceptualization and model. *Psychological Bulletin,* 1982, *92,* 641–669.

Schwarz, N., & Clore, G. L. Mood, misattribution, and judgments of well-being: Informative and directive functions of affective states. *Journal of Personality and Social Psychology,* 1983, *45,* 513–523.

Schwarzer, C., & Kim, M.-J. The development of the Korean Form of the Test Anxiety Inventory. In H. M. van der Ploeg, R. Schwarzer, & C. D. Spielberger (Eds.), *Advances in test anxiety research* (Vol. 3). Lisse/Hillsdale: Swets & Zeitlinger/Erlbaum, 1984.

Schwarzer, R. *Streß,* Angst und Hilflosigkeit. Stuttgart: Kohlhammer, 1981.

Schwarzer, R. (Ed.). *The self in anxiety, stress, and depression.* Amsterdam: North Holland, 1984.

Schwarzer, R., & Jerusalem, M. Selbstwertdienliche Attributionen nach Leistungsrückmeldungen. *Zeitschrift für Entwicklungspsychologie und Pädagogische Psychologie,* 1982, *14,* 47–57.

Schwarzer, R., Jerusalem, M., & Stiksrud, H. A. The developmental relationship between test anxiety and helplessness. In H. M. van der Ploeg, R. Schwarzer, & C. D. Spielberger (Eds.), *Advances in test anxiety research* (Vol. 3). Lisse/Hillsdale: Swets & Zietlinger/Erlbaum, 1984.

Schwarzer, R., van der Ploeg, H. M., & Spielberger, C. D. (Eds.). *Advances in test anxiety research.* (Vol. 1). Lisse: Swets & Zeitlinger, 1982.

Seligman, M. E. P. *Helplessness.* San Francisco: Freeman, 1975.

Spielberger, C. D. (Ed.). *Anxiety and behavior.* New York: Academic Press, 1966.

Spielberger, C. D. Conceptual and methodological issues in anxiety research. In C. D. Spielberger (Ed.), *Anxiety: Current Trends in Theory and Research* (Vol. 2). New York: Academic Press, 1972.

Spielberger, C. D. *Test Anxiety Inventory. Preliminary professional manual.* Palo Alto: Consulting Psychologist's Press, 1980.

Stephan, E., Fischer, M., & Stein, F. Self-related cognitions in test anxiety research: An empirical study and critical conclusions. In H. M. van der Ploeg, R. Schwarzer, & C. D. Spielberger (Eds.), *Advances in test anxiety research* (Vol. 2) (pp. 45–66). Lisse/Hillsdale: Swets & Zeitlinger/Erlbaum, 1983.

Tabachnik, N., Crocker, J., & Alloy, L. B. Depression, social comparison, and the false-consensus effect. *Journal of Personality and Social Psychology,* 1983, *45,* 688–699.

Van der Ploeg, H., Schwarzer, R., & Spielberger, C. D. (Eds.). *Advances in test anxiety research* (Vol. 2). Lisse/Hillsdale: Swets & Zeitlinger/Erlbaum, 1983.

Van der Ploeg, H., Schwarzer, R., & Spielberger, C. D. (Eds.). *Advances in test anxiety research* (Vol. 3). Lisse/Hillsdale: Swets & Zeitlinger/Erlbaum, 1984.

Van der Ploeg, H., Schwarzer, R., & Spielberger, C. D. (Eds.). *Advances in test anxiety research* (Vol. 4). Lisse/Hillsdale: Swets & Zeitlinger/Erlbaum, 1985.

Weiner, B. *Human motivation.* New York: Holt, Rinehart & Winston, 1980.

Weiner, B. The emotional consequences of causal ascriptions. In M. S. Clark & S. T. Fiske (Eds.), *Affect and cognition. The 17th Annual Carnegie Symposium on Cognition.* Hillsdale: Erlbaum, 1982.

Weiner, B. Some methodological pitfalls in attributional research. *Journal of Educational Psychology,* 1983, *75,* 530–543.

White, R. W. Motivation reconsidered: The concept of competence. *Psychological Review,* 1959, *66,* 297–333.

Wicklund, R. A., & Gollwitzer, P. M. Symbolic self-completion, attempted influence, and self-depreation. *Basic and Applied Psychology,* 1981, *2,* 89–114.

Wicklund, R. A., & Gollwitzer, P. M. *Symbolic self-completion.* Hillsdale: Erlbaum, 1982.

Wine, J. D. Cognitive-attentional theory of test anxiety. In I. G. Sarason (Ed.), *Test anxiety* (pp. 349–385). Hillsdale, N.J.: Erlbaum, 1980.

Wortman, C. B., & Brehm, J. W. Responses to uncontrollable outcomes: An integration of reactance theory and the learned helplessness model. In L. Berkowitz (Ed.), *Advances in experimental social psychology* (Vol. 8) (pp. 277–336). New York: Academic Press, 1976.

2 Test Anxiety, Worry, and Cognitive Interference

Irwin G. Sarason
University of Washington

Most writers agree that anxiety is an important aspect of human life, but there is wide disagreement about its definition. Typically it is discussed as being such a complex experience as to make scientific investigation difficult or impossible. If there were such a thing, perhaps the modal definition of anxiety would be in terms of an unpleasant emotional state or condition marked by apprehension. Spielberger (1972) defined anxiety as "an unpleasant emotional state or condition which is characterized by subjective feelings of tension, apprehension, and worry, and by activation or arousal of the autonomic nervous system" (p. 482). More recently, Leary (1982) offered this definition of anxiety: "Anxiety refers to a cognitive-affective response characterized by physiological arousal (indicative of sympathetic nervous system activation) and apprehension regarding a potentially negative outcome that the individual perceives as impending." (p. 99). The problem is that many of the terms in these definitions have low inter-writer reliability. For example, how much agreement is there about what an emotional or affective state is; what objective feelings of tension are; and what the referents are for the concepts of activation and arousal?

In addition to the reliability problem, the illustrative definitions refer to yet another problem that confronts the anxiety researcher: the multiple aspects of the concept. To use the concept empirically requires a component analysis of its ingredients in order to formulate testable hypotheses. The main focus of this paper is the cognitive component, most particularly the worries people experience. I describe research findings suggesting that this component, which is relatively unambiguous and can be assessed quantitatively and reliably, plays a significant role in one important class of situations, those in which people perform and are evaluated. I also describe a new instrument, Reactions to Tests, that was designed to aid in an analysis of several frequently mentioned components of test anxiety.

THE COGNITIVE PERSPECTIVE

There is increasing evidence that cognitive processes play important roles in both maladaptive and adaptive behavior. A person's train of thought and mental set can be viewed as either assets or vulnerability factors that interact with characteristics of situations to produce adaptation or maladaptation. For example, in anxiety disorders, precipitating events elicit or magnify underlying personal preoccupations (such as fear of negative consequences) and give rise to uncertainty about outcomes, hypervigilance, and concern over potential dangers. The anxious individual continuously scans situations for potential danger signals. In looking for these signals an individual might not pay adequate attention to the task at hand.

While it has often been said that distortion of reality characterizes psychotics but not neurotics, considerable evidence now indicates that disorders of thinking, less gross and more limited than in psychosis, are important features of anxiety disorders. People with these disorders are prone to think in extreme terms about certain types of situations, such as those in which personal danger is a possibility, although a quite remote one. An unexpected noise in the house could be burglars breaking in and the noise of children playing in the street could give rise to visions of a hit-and-run accident. The anxious person is prone to anticipate rejection, humiliation, and deprecation by strangers as well as friends. These expectations of harm can result in high levels of bodily mobilization for danger.

Although all people from time to time question their personal capabilities to perform particular types of tasks, anxious individuals tend to become overly preoccupied with such thoughts. Saying such things as "I don't know what to do now" or "I'm dumb" can be self-defeating if the person really has the wherewithal to handle the situation. High levels of anxious self-preoccupation interfere with the perception and appraisal of events and lead to errors in estimating the possibility of danger, loss (of love, job, money, reputation), and probability of attaining goals. Research in both naturalistic settings (e.g., Deffenbacher & Deitz, 1978), and laboratory evidence (e.g., Marlett & Watson, 1968; Sarason & Stoops, 1978), suggests that cognitive interference, often in the form of worry, is a key factor in lowering the performance of highly test-anxious people.

STRESS AND SELF-PREOCCUPATION

While writers may differ in their explanations of how people come to terms with their worries, there is unlikely to be disagreement about the fact that worries are a universal category of thoughts. Although there may be wide individual differences in the frequency and correlates of worries and their levels of accessibility to awareness, we all know what worries are and can recognize them in ourselves and often in others. Worries are distressing preoccupations and concerns about impending or anticipated events. Whereas depressed people tend to be preoccupied with the past, the worries of those who are anxious tend to be future oriented.

The concept of stress is useful in a cognitive analysis of worries. Stress can be understood in terms of perceived performance demands, a person's awareness of the need to do something about a given state of affairs. These demands are evoked by situational challenges and can lead to either task-relevant or task-irrelevant cognitions. From this point of view, the most adaptive response to stress should be task-oriented thinking which directs the individual's attention to the task at hand. The task-oriented person is able to set aside unproductive worries and preoccupations. The self-preoccupied person, on the other hand, becomes absorbed in the implications and consequences of failure to meet situational challenges. Anxious people worry about their perceived personal incompetence and possible difficulties they may be called upon to confront. Their negative self-appraisals are unpleasant and, because they are self-preoccupying, they detract from task concentration. Since many anxious people describe themselves as being tense and feeling that something terrible will happen, even though they cannot specify the cause of their worry, these self-preoccupations are likely to create cognitive interference that precludes an orderly, task-oriented approach to situational requirements.

The situational challenges to which people react may be either real or imagined. It seems clear that an understanding of the effects of stress and the prediction of behavior must take into account (1) an individual's perceptions of the nature of a challenge and his or her ability to meet it and (2) the self-preoccupations that influence these perceptions (Sarason & Sarason, 1981).

While this paper is primarily concerned with worry evoked by evaluational situations, it is important to place worry in its proper context and remember that people can be preoccupied about a variety of topics. Very little is known about the cognitive processes involved in preoccupation. Sometimes the preoccupation may have a long range problem solving focus. For example, when Crick and Watson were pondering the structure of the DNA molecule they were probably preoccupied. Sometimes preoccupations do not seem to be oriented toward problem solving. Many of these might be described as generalized or specific worries. A person might spend a great deal of time thinking about the general problem of nuclear war, world food shortages, inflation, whether a vicious dog might suddenly appear to block the path home, or whether he or she has learned enough to pass the next exam in a psychology course. Personality characteristics and social background influence the content of self-preoccupations. For example, an anger-prone person or an anxiety-prone person may have quite different thoughts in particular situations. Cognitive preoccupations, whatever type they happen to be, may interfere with the veridical perception of environmental cues, their interpretation, and decisions about responses to them.

TEST ANXIETY

In some ways, the study of test anxiety might be taken as a prototype for anxiety research because the evaluational role of the test is its most important aspect. Test anxiety is a personal and social problem for several reasons, not the least of which is the ubiquitousness of taking tests. Test anxiety is not simply an unpleasant experience for the affected individual. It both plays a role in personal phenomenology and influences performance and personal development. Indices of test anxiety reflect the personal salience of situations in which people perform tasks and their work is evaluated.

Many studies have shown that test anxiety is inversely related to performance in a wide variety of evaluational situations such as college entrance and course examinations. Some recent findings obtained at the Navy Submarine School, Groton, Connecticut, illustrate the significant role test anxiety plays in relation to performance (Sarason, Potter, & Sarason, 1983). The subjects were 247 Navy Submarine School students who had taken the Armed Services Vocational Aptitude Battery (ASVAB) and the Test Anxiety Scale (TAS). The ASVAB is a well standardized test used to classify and predict the performance of U.S. military personnel. Both the ASVAB and the TAS were significant predictors (p < .001 and p < .006 respectively) of Submarine School students' grade point averages. At each of three levels of aptitude (high, middle, and low ASVAB scores), students high in test anxiety obtained lower grades. Correlational analyses showed that the ASVAB accounted for 18.6% of the variance in GPA when used alone, while test anxiety alone accounted for 13.13% of the variance. The correlation between ASVAB and TAS was − .33 and the two measures together accounted for 24.2% of the total variance. Thus, the ASVAB plus the TAS did a significantly better job (25% better) of predicting Submarine School grades than did the ASVAB alone.

A relationship between test anxiety and performance could come about either because (1) persons low in ability become anxious about the need to confront situations that produce failure or, at least, relatively poor performance or (2) anxiety somehow prevents full use of personal wherewithal. While each of these directions of influence makes sense, perhaps the more challenging one is the second, since it is completely expectable that failure situations are aversive and likely to lead to hopelessness, helplessness, and feelings of inefficacy.

Evidence of a negative correlation between test anxiety and performance in evaluative situations has led to a wide variety of experiments aimed at evaluating hypotheses about the processes that may be involved. Experimental evidence has added to knowledge about the deleterious influence of high levels of test anxiety on information processing and performance. There is considerable evidence that the performance of highly test-anxious individuals on complex tasks is detrimentally affected by evaluational stressors (Sarason, 1972a, 1972b, 1975). The less complex, less demanding the task, the weaker this effect is.

An example of an evaluational stressor used in laboratory studies is achievement-orienting instructions that either inform subjects that some kind of evaluation of their performance will be made or provide some other rationale for the importance of performing well. A study carried out by Sarason and Stoops (1978) illustrates the experimental approach to test anxiety. The investigation comprised a series of three experiments concerning subjective judgments of the passage of time. After being given either achievement-orienting or neutral instructions, subjects waited for an undesignated period of time before performing an intellective task. The experiments were aimed at providing information about the way individuals differing in anxiety fill time. It was predicted that, in the presence of achievement-oriented cues, time would pass more slowly for high than for middle and low TAS scorers. When these cues are not present there should not be a significant gap in estimates of time duration among groups differing in test anxiety. Furthermore, the effects of an achievement orientation should be as noticeable while the individual is waiting to perform as during performance itself.

The results showed that individuals for whom tests are worrisome experiences (high TAS subjects) tend to overestimate, to a greater degree than do other subjects, both the duration of the performance evaluation period and the time spent waiting for the evaluation to take place. Sarason and Stoops' highly test-anxious subjects performed at significantly lower levels than did low or middle scorers when emphasis was placed on the evaluational implications of performance. Furthermore, highly test-anxious subjects under the achievement-orienting condition experienced levels of cognitive interference that were significantly higher than those of subjects in other conditions, including highly test-anxious subjects who performed under neutral conditions.

The available evidence suggests that there usually is more to test anxiety than simply a history of failure experiences. Test-anxious people process their objective successes and failures in distinctive ways and their anxiety is related importantly to how they, and significant others in their lives, evaluate their test-taking experience. Every teacher can think of bright, successful students who, contrary to what one would expect, spend inordinate amounts of time worrying about whether they can meet the next academic challenge they must face.

An important factor related to performance is attributional style, or the way in which responsibility for outcome is typically assessed. In a recent experiment, Türk and Sarason (1983) studied the performance of subjects differing in test anxiety, assessed by the TAS, as a function of a prior success or failure experience and the subject's assignment of responsibility for the performance level achieved. Half of the subjects began the experiment by working on either insoluble or easy anagrams. For each difficulty level, the subjects were given either achievement-orienting or neutral instructions. All subjects were asked to check "passed" on their test if they solved three of the five anagrams and "failed" if they solved fewer than three problems. (All the subjects who worked on the easy anagrams "passed.") They then filled out a questionnaire that dealt with causal attributions. The questionnaire asked the subjects about the extent to which they interpreted their anagrams performance as being due to ability, effort, luck, and task difficulty. Attributions were made on a Likert-type scale of 7 points. In the next phase of the experiment all subjects worked on a series of moderately difficult anagrams.

Following the failure condition, the high TAS group performed at a lower level than did all other groups in the experiment. This is consistent with previous work on test anxiety. Following the success condition, the high TAS group performed at a higher level than did all other groups. When the subjects were categorized on the basis of their causal attributions, subjects who made internal attributions on the failure task (e.g., "I'm not good at solving problems.") had poorer subsequent performance on the anagrams regardless of their TAS score. Following the success condition, the best performing group consisted of high TAS subjects who made internal attributions (e.g., "I'm an intelligent person."). This study illustrates the need to know more about the effects of success experiences on subjects differing in test anxiety and the antecedents and correlates of positive as well as negative attributions. Positive attributions might be particularly effective with highly test-anxious people because they counter the worrying and preoccupation that is characteristic of anxiety.

Goldberg (1983) correlated test anxiety, assessed using the total score of the Reactions to Tests (to be described below), with the Attributional Styles Questionnaire (ASQ) (Peterson et al., in press), which yields scores for causal attributions regarding both good and bad (desirable and undesirable) events. She found that highly test-anxious subjects tend to attribute successful task performance to external factors (e.g., "It was an easy test.") and unsuccessful performance to internal factors ("I don't have good aptitude."). She also found that test anxiety is positively correlated with scores on the Fear of Negative Evaluation scale (Watson & Friend, 1969). Thus, highly anxious individuals worry about what other people think of them and attribute bad outcomes to "personal helplessness," while low test-anxious individuals tend to attribute their successes to personal competence and their failures to external factors. In other words, attributions to long-lasting pervasive causes rather than temporary situational factors are reversed for success and failure in the two groups.

These differences in attributional style that seem to characterize high- and low-anxious subjects may be related to different types of cognitive activity that occur prior to and during the evaluational session. There is now considerable evidence that highly test-anxious subjects in situations that pose test-like challenges perform at relatively low levels and experience relatively high levels of task-irrelevant thoughts (such as self-deprecating attributions). In non-test situations, groups at different test anxiety levels show either smaller or no differences in performance and cognitive interference. This type of evidence led Wine (1971, 1982) to an attentional interpretation of test anxiety, according to which people at high and low levels of test anxiety differ in the types of thoughts to which their attention is directed in the face of an evaluative stressor. Consistent with this interpretation are the results of Ganzer's (1968) experiment which showed that, while performing on an intellective task, high test-anxious subjects made many more irrelevant comments than did low test anxiety scorers. A high percentage of these comments were self-deprecatory. Various researchers have found that high are more likely than low test-anxious people to be preoccupied with and blame themselves for their performance level, feel less confident in making perceptual judgments, and set lower levels of aspiration for themselves (Sarason, 1980).

THE COMPONENTS OF ANXIETY

Despite its usefulness, the concept of anxiety may be so complex as to obscure important processes. It may also have too much excess meaning, and therefore be misleading. An approach that would reduce these problems is one that deals more explicitly with the scope of phenomena that seem to pertain to anxiety.

One heuristic distinction relevant to the study of anxiety is the distinction between worry and emotionality (Deffenbacher, 1977, 1978; Kaplan, McCordick, & Twitchell, 1979; Liebert & Morris, 1967; Morris, Davis, & Hutchings, 1981). Worry refers to the cognitive side of anxiety (preoccupations, concerns); emotionality refers largely to a person's awareness of bodily arousal and tension. In their reviews of the literature on the worry-emotionality distinction, Deffenbacher (1980) and Tryon (1980) showed that while worry and emotionality are correlated, only worry is related to performance decrements in the presence of an evaluational stressor. Worry and emotionality, like anxiety, are concepts. They may or may not be unitary. An additional useful step would be to define more reliably the various types of reactions people have when placed in evaluational situations.

There is a sizeable body of evidence consistent with the idea that proneness to self-preoccupation, and more specifically, worry over evaluation, is a powerful component of what is referred to as test anxiety. If, as several studies suggest, the most active ingredient of test anxiety is self-preoccupation, there are some important and practical implications for assessment. While both general and test anxiety are usually defined as complex states that include cognitive, emotional, behavioral, and bodily components, most anxiety measures reflect this inclusive definition by yielding only one global score. Wine (1982) has pointed out that it is not immediately obvious how to identify the active or most active ingredients in this complex and has suggested that test anxiety might fruitfully be reconceptualized primarily in terms of cognitive and attentional processes aroused in evaluational settings.

In order to assess separately several components of a person's reactions to test situations, an instrument, Reactions to Tests (RTT), has recently been created (Sarason, 1984). It consists of four factor analytically derived scales:

Tension ("I feel distressed and uneasy before tests")
Worry ("During tests, I wonder how the other people are doing")
Test-Irrelevant Thought ("Irrelevant bits of information pop into my head during a test")
Bodily Reactions ("My heart beats faster when the test begins").

While these scales are positively intercorrelated, the correlations seem low enough to justify comparisons among them concerning their predictive value.

In preliminary studies, the RTT was related to performance on a difficult digit-symbol task under evaluative conditions. The Worry scale was more consistently related to performance and post-performance reports of cognitive interference than were the other scales. The Tension scale approached the Worry scale as a predictor of performance.

The RTT has been related to physiological measures obtained during a test-taking situation. Burchfield, Sarason, Sarason, and Beaton (unpublished study) recently examined the relationship of the RTT to physiological indices gathered while college students worked on items of the type found on intelligence tests. Both the Tension and Worry scales were significantly correlated with skin conductance (GSR) and finger tip temperature changes during performance. There were no significant correlations with EMG changes. Interestingly, the Task-Irrelevant Thinking and Bodily Reactions scales were unrelated to all physiological change measures. More studies dealing with relationships among components of test anxiety, performance variables, and physiological measures are needed.

THE ASSESSMENT OF COGNITIVE ACTIVITY

Beyond specifying the components of test anxiety, another needed step is assessing the characteristics and effects of self-preoccupying thoughts. Efforts to assess the thoughts and ideas that pass through people's minds is a relatively new development. Cognitive assessment can be carried out in a variety of ways (Kendall & Korgeski, 1979). Questionnaires have been developed to sample thoughts in a particular set of circumstances, for example, after an upsetting event has taken place. "Beepers" can be used as signals to subjects to record their current thoughts (for example, their concerns) at certain times of the day (Klinger, Barta, & Maxeiner, 1981). There are also questionnaires to assess the directions people give themselves while working on a task and their personal theories about why things happen as they do.

Anyone who has taken exams knows that worrying about one's level of ability, failure, and what other students might be doing interferes with effective performance. While thoughts that reflect worry have undesirable effects, thoughts that are task-relevant are helpful. The Cognitive Interference Questionnaire (CIQ) was developed by Sarason and Stoops (1978) to assess retrospectively the degree to which people, after working on tasks, report having had thoughts of various types including those that interfere with concentration on the task. These task-irrelevant thoughts were negatively correlated with performance, particularly among highly test anxious students.

In a recent study (Sarason & Basham, unpublished paper), subjects were given the RTT, then a series of general information questions, and finally, a three part modified version of the CIQ, called the Thought Occurrence Questionnaire (TOQ). The first part of the TOQ asks about thoughts related to the task just performed. The second part asks about thoughts not related to the task. The third part is a single item asking about the degree to which the subject's mind wandered while working on the task. Scale II of the RTT, the Worry scale, correlated most highly with Part 1 of the TOQ. Scale III of the RTT, Task Irrelevant Thoughts, correlated most highly with Parts 2 and 3 of the TOQ. These findings suggest that the scales of the RTT can be used to predict the type and degree of interfering thoughts that actually occur in an individual in an evaluative situation.

REDUCING COGNITIVE INTERFERENCE IN EVALUATIONAL SITUATIONS

Worry is unmistakably an attentionally demanding cognitive activity. Can anything be done about a person's proneness to this type of self-preoccupation? The study by Türk and Sarason (1983) described earlier suggested that success experiences may be particularly beneficial in improving the performance of highly test-anxious people. One line of investigation in anxiety research has been concerned with the effects of pre-performance communications (Sarason, 1960; Sarason, Kestenbaum, & Smith, 1972). Reassuring and neutral instructions at the outset of an experimental session facilitate the performance of high test-anxious groups. Unfortunately, these same conditions may be detrimental for low test-anxious groups. For example, there is evidence that reassurance about the nonevaluative nature of a performance situation seems to lessen the effort of subjects low in test anxiety (Sarason, 1958).

Modeling of adaptive overt behavior and cognitions may be more generally effective than pre-performance reassurance in improving performance. Observational opportunities can provide a person not only with demonstrations of overt responses but, if the model "thinks through" problems and tactics aloud, covert ones as well. Observing a model prepare for a test situation can shape and reshape one's views and expectancies concerning oneself and others. Whereas exposure to models who have failure experiences has a negative effect on the performance of high test-anxious subjects, exposure to models displaying adaptive behavior plays a discernible positive role in facilitating learning and performance (Sarason 1972b, 1973). In one experiment, subjects differing in test anxiety were given the opportunity to observe a model who demonstrated effective ways of performing an anagrams task. Using a talk-out-loud technique, the model displayed several types of facilitative thoughts and cognitions. The major finding was that high test-anxious subjects benefited more from the opportunity to observe a cognitive model than did those low in test anxiety (Sarason, 1973). Cognitive modeling might have considerable potential in instructional programs as a means of demonstrating for students the differences between adaptive and maladaptive cognitions and the negative aspects of maladaptive attentional habits.

Another approach that might have as great or greater potential is developing short, pertinent, easily understood pre-performance instructions that direct subjects' attention to the importance of task-relevant thinking. In a recent experiment, 180 undergraduate students differing in RTT Worry scores worked on a difficult anagrams task in groups of 15-20 (Sarason & Türk, 1983). The subjects were told that performance on the anagrams task was a measure of the ability to do college-level work. After this communication, one-third of the subjects were given an attention-directing condition, one third were given reassurance, and a control group received no additional communication.

The instructions for the anagrams task were contained in the test booklet. The attention-directing and reassuring communications were given by the experimenter after the subjects had read the task instructions which included the achievement-orienting message. Subjects under the Reassurance condition were told not to be overly concerned about their performance on the anagrams. The experimenter made such comments as "Don't worry" and "You will do just fine." Subjects under the Attention-Directing condition were told to absorb themselves as much as possible in the anagrams task and to avoid thinking about other things. The experimenter said, ". . . concentrate all your attention on the problems . . .," "think only about the anagrams." and "don't let yourself get distracted from the task." High-Worry subjects under the control condition performed poorly compared to the other control subjects. High-Worry subjects in the Attention-Directing and Reassurance groups performed well. However, consistent with previous evidence, the study showed that reassuring instructions have a detrimental effect on people who are not worriers. Non-worry subjects in the Reassurance group performed poorly, perhaps because non-worriers take the reassuring communication at face value, that is, they take the task lightly and lower their motivational level. The performance levels of all groups that received the Attention-Directing instructions were high. The Attention-Directing approach seems to have all of the advantages of reassurance for high-Worry subjects with none of the disadvantages for low Worry subjects.

After the anagrams task all the subjects responded to the CIQ, which provided a measure of the number and type of interfering thoughts experienced in that particular situation. Cognitive interference at the end of the anagrams tasks was relatively low under the Attention-Direction condition for high- as well as low-Worry subjects. Similar to previous findings concerning highly test-anxious subjects, the high-Worry groups showed high cognitive interference under the control conditions.

The performance and CIQ scores were reanalyzed in terms of the other RTT scales, but none of these analyses revealed statistically significant results. The findings of this experiment support an attentional interpretation of anxiety and worry. They suggest that simply calling subjects' attention to the need for task-oriented behavior can have a salutary effect on their performance, with a reduction in instrusive thoughts.

CONCLUSIONS

If stress is viewed in a cognitive perspective as the need to respond to perceived situational demands, then worry and self-preoccupation over the inability to respond adequately would seem to be critical factors in performance. The test-anxious person experiences self-preoccupying worry, insecurity, and self-doubt in evaluative situations. These internal distractors lessen attention to the task at hand and contribute to relatively poor performance. There is growing evidence that, at least in evaluative situations, the problem of anxiety is, to a significant extent, a problem of intrusive, interfering worry-type thoughts that diminish the attention to and efficient execution of the task at hand.

Instructions emphasizing the evaluative nature of the task have been shown to increase the interfering thoughts of highly test-anxious subjects (Sarason, 1978). As we have seen, both cognitive modeling geared to task orientation and other easily applied training procedures emphasizing a task focus seem to be effective in reducing interfering thoughts. Thus, experimental manipulations can either increase or decrease the self-preoccupation of test-anxious subjects. The amount of self-preoccupation, in turn, influences performance level. These relationships are consistent with Geen's (1976, 1980) analysis of test anxiety as a narrower of the range of cues available to a person in a given situation. Worry over evaluation leads to thought patterns that interfere with attention to the range of situational cues. The wider the range of relevant cues in the situation, the greater the debilitating effects of cognitive interference.

While the general concept of anxiety has been researched extensively, many of the findings have been conflicting and confusing. Contributing to this confusion have been definitions of anxiety that are too broad with regard to both what it is and how it functions in affecting performance. Might the concept of anxiety be defined primarily or exclusively in terms of interfering worry and self-deprecation? Such a definition would be consistent with what we know about the relationships among test anxiety, self-preoccupation, and performance. It would, however, not be consistent with the widely held view that physiological arousal is a major component of anxiety in general and that the anxious response to stress involves hypermobilization of physiological resources. Perhaps the physiological aspects of anxiety need rethinking at least in relation to the test-type situations. For example, in an extensive literature review, Holroyd and Appel (1980) concluded that the cognitive aspects of test anxiety may be its most active ingredients and that no relationship has been demonstrated between test anxiety and physiological activity.

Can we conclude that the problem of anxiety, or at least the problem of test anxiety, is simply a problem of worry and interfering thoughts? By no means would it be reasonable at this stage in our knowledge. For one thing, we know very little about these interfering thoughts. For example, there is little data about where worries come from and what people do about them (Borkovec, Robinson, Pruzinsky, & DePree, 1983). Do persistent painful worries go underground, that is, become unconscious? To what extent are worries of which we are aware either in part or entirely symbolic of past worries that have been cognitively transformed? How are worries and other interfering cognitions related?

There is another reason for resisting any temptation to reduce anxiety to a collection of worries and off-target thinking: the fact that anxiety is a complex concept is not a sufficient reason to arbitrarily truncate it. However, its complexity is a sufficient reason to separate its components for investigation in order ultimately to put them together again in an effort to better understand the wide range of human experience.

The growing interest in the worry-emotionality distinction is a positive development in the delineation of the concept of anxiety. Nevertheless, it is important to recognize that there are pitfalls in operationalizing the two concepts being distinguished. For example, the Morris, Davis, and Hutchings (1981) Emotionality scale includes items that refer to both general tension level ("I feel panicky") and specific body reactions ("I am so tense that my stomach is upset"). The items in the Emotionality scale of Spielberger's Test Anxiety Inventory also refer to both general tension and bodily reactions. The bodily reactions items seem less ambiguous than the tension items. However, people who describe their reactions to tests in terms of general tension may or may not differ in their physiological reactions from those who emphasize their worries. Do the phrases "I am tense" and "I am worried" simply differ semantically, or do they refer to different phenomenological and bodily experiences? The Tension scale of the RTT may, to a degree, be a "semantic factor"; that is, a factor that reflects one way of saying things like "I get worried when I have to take a test."

To the extent that statements such as "I feel tense" are simply a way of saying, "I am worried," the distinction between worry and emotionality becomes blurred. While the concepts of emotions and emotionality are often discussed in terms of their physiological components, it would be a mistake to think of worry and emotionality as uncorrelated factors. The analysis of most emotional states in daily life almost requires identification of the thoughts that contribute to their arousal. It would be worthwhile to put on the anxiety research agenda further exploration of the inter-relationships among classes of cognitive and bodily processes, such as types of worries, level of actual autonomic arousal, and person's perceptions of their bodily states. Perhaps when we clarify the concepts of emotion, tension, and affect, that is, define them less ambiguously and use them less globally, we will be in a better position to come to grips with the problem of anxiety. A better understanding of worries and their relationships to behavior and bodily processes can contribute to the needed clarification.

REFERENCES

Borkovec, T. D., Robinson, E., Pruzinsky, T., & DePree, J. A. Preliminary explorations of worry: Some characteristics and processes. *Behavior Research and Therapy,* 1983, *21,* 9–16.

Burchfield, S., Sarason, I. G., Sarason, B. R., & Beaton, R. *Test anxiety and physiological responding.* (Unpublished study), 1982.

Deffenbacher, J. L. Relationship of worry and emotionality to performance on the Miller Analogies Test. *Journal of Educational Psychology,* 1977, *69,* 191–195.

Deffenbacher, J. L. Worry, emotionality and task-generated interference in test anxiety: An empirical test of attentional theory. *Journal of Educational Psychology,* 1978, *70,* 248–254.

Deffenbacher, J. L. Worry and emotionality in test anxiety. In I. G. Sarason (Ed.), *Test anxiety: Theory, research, and applications.* Hillsdale, NJ: Lawrence Erlbaum Associates, 1980.

Deffenbacher, J. L., & Deitz, S. R. Effects of test anxiety on performance, worry, and emotionality in naturally occurring exams. *Psychology in the Schools,* 1978, *15,* 446–450.

Ganzer, V. J. The effects of audience pressure and test anxiety on learning and retention in a serial learning situation. *Journal of Personality and Social Psychology,* 1968, *8,* 194–199.

Geen, R. G. Test anxiety, observation, and range of cue utilization. *British Journal of Social and Clinical Psychology,* 1976, *15,* 253–259.

Geen, R. G. Test anxiety and cue utilization. In I. G. Sarason (Ed.), *Test anxiety: Theory, research, and applications.* Hillsdale, NJ: Lawrence Erlbaum Associates, 1980.

Goldberg, S. A. *Cognitive correlates of test anxiety: Examination of the relationship among test anxiety, fear of negative evaluation, social anxiety, and attributional style.* Providence, RI: Unpublished Honors thesis, Brown University, 1983.

Holroyd, K. A., & Appel, M. A. Test anxiety and physiological responding. In I. G. Sarason (Ed.), *Test anxiety: Theory, research, and applications.* Hillsdale, NJ: Lawrence Erlbaum Associates, 1980.

Kaplan, R. M., McCordick, S. M., & Twitchell, M. Is it the cognitive or the behavioral component which makes cognitive-behavior modification effective in test anxiety? *Journal of Counseling Psychology,* 1979, *26,* 371–377.

Kendall, P. C., & Korgeski, G. P. Assessment and cognitive-behavioral interventions. *Cognitive Therapy and Research,* 1979, *3,* 1–21.

Klinger, E., Barta, S. G., & Maxeiner, M. E. Current concerns: Assessing therapeutically relevant motivation. In P. C. Kendall & S. D. Hollon (Eds.), *Assessment strategies for cognitive-behavioral interventions.* New York: Academic Press, 1981.

Leary, M. R. Social anxiety. In L. Wheeler (Ed.), *Review of personality and social psychology* (Vol. 3). Beverly Hills, CA: Sage, 1982.

Liebert, R. M., & Morris, L. W. Cognitive and emotional components of test anxiety: A distinction and some initial data. *Psychological Reports,* 1967, *20,* 975–978.

Marlett, N. J., & Watson, D. Test anxiety and immediate or delayed feedback in a test-like avoidance task. *Journal of Personality and Social Psychology,* 1968, *8,* 200–203.

Morris, L. W., Davis, M. A., & Hutchings, C. H. Cognitive and emotional components of anxiety: Literature review and a revised Worry-Emotionality Scale. *Journal of Educational Psychology,* 1981, *73,* 541–555.

Peterson, C., Semmel, A., von Baeyer, C., Abramson, L., Metalsky, G., & Seligman, M. E. P. The Attributional Style Questionnaire. *Cognitive Therapy and Research,* (in press).

Sarason, I. G. The effects of anxiety, reassurance, and meaningfulness of material to be learned on verbal learning. *Journal of Experimental Psychology,* 1958, *56,* 472–477.

Sarason, I. G. Empirical findings and theoretical problems in the use of anxiety scales. *Psychological Bulletin,* 1960, *57,* 403–415.

Sarason, I. G. Experimental approaches to test anxiety: Attention and the uses of information. In C. D. Spielberger (Ed.), *Anxiety: Current trends in theory and research* (Vol. 2). New York: Academic Press, 1972a.

Sarason, I. G. Test anxiety and the model who fails. *Journal of Personality and Social Psychology,* 1972b, *22,* 410–423.

Sarason, I. G. Test anxiety and cognitive modeling. *Journal of Personality and Social Psychology,* 1973, *28,* 58–61.

Sarason, I. G. Test anxiety, attention, and the general problem of anxiety. In C. D. Spielberger, & I. G. Sarason (Eds.), *Stress and anxiety* (Vol. 1). Washington, DC: Hemisphere, 1975.

Sarason, I. G. The Test Anxiety Scale: Concept and research. In C. D. Spielberger & I. G. Sarason (Eds.), *Stress and anxiety* (Vol. 5). Washington, DC. Hemisphere, 1978.

Sarason, I. G. *Test anxiety: Theory, research and applications.* Hillsdale, NJ: Lawrence Erlbaum Associates, 1980.

Sarason, I. G. Stress, anxiety and cognitive interference: Reactions to tests. *Journal of Personality and Social Psychology,* 1984, *46,* 929–938.

Sarason, I. G., & Basham, R. *Reactions to tests and general information.* Unpublished study. Seattle, WA: University of Washington, 1983.

Sarason, I. G., Kestenbaum, J. M., & Smith, B. R. Test anxiety and the effects of being observed. *Journal of Personality,* 1972, *40,* 242–250.

Sarason, I. G., Potter, E., & Sarason, B. R. *Test anxiety and ASVAB performance.* Unpublished study. Seattle, WA: University of Washington, 1983.

Sarason, I. G., & Sarason, B. R. The importance of cognition and moderator variables in stress. In D. Magnusson (Ed.), *Toward a psychology of situations: An interactional perspective.* Hillsdale, NJ: Lawrence Erlbaum Associates, 1981.

Sarason, I. G., & Stoops, R. Test anxiety and the passage of time. *Journal of Consulting and Clinical Psychology,* 1978, *46,* 102–109.

Sarason, I. G., & Türk, S. *Test anxiety and the directing of attention.* Unpublished study. *Seattle, WA: University of Washington, 1983.*

Spielberger, C. D. Conceptual and methodological issues in anxiety research. In C. D. Spielberger (Ed.), *Anxiety: Current trends in theory and research* (Vol. 2). New York: Academic Press, 1972.

Spielberger, C. D. *Test Anxiety Inventory.* Palo Alto, CA: Consulting Psychologists Press, 1980.

Tryon, J. D. The measurement and treatment of test anxiety. *Review of Educational Research,* 1980, *50,* 343–372.

Türk, S., & Sarason, I. G. *Test anxiety, success-failure, and causal attribution.* Unpublished manuscript. Seattle, WA: University of Washington, 1983.

Watson, D., & Friend, R. Measurement of social-evaluative anxiety. *Journal of Consulting and Clinical Psychology,* 1969, *33,* 448–457.

Wine, J. D. Test anxiety and direction of attention. *Psychological Bulletin,* 1971, *76,* 92–104.

Wine, J. D. Evaluation anxiety: A cognitive-attentional construct. In H. W. Krohne & L. Laux (Eds.), *Achievement, stress and anxiety.* New York: Hemisphere, 1982.

3 Anxiety and Cognitive Processing of Instruction[1]

Sigmund Tobias
City College, City University of New York

The effects of anxiety on learning from instruction have been frequently demonstrated. Despite the robustness of this effect the number of studies of anxiety in the educational research and educational psychology literature in the United States has been relatively modest in the last two decades (Tobias, 1979). An analysis of the 1983 program of the American Educational Research Association, for example, reveals only a single session devoted to test anxiety, and none to the more general topic of anxiety. This deemphasis of anxiety research is probably attributable to the paradigm shift to a more cognitive psychology. Recent attempts to reinterpret the construct of test anxiety entirely in terms of deficits in cognitive acquisition skills, to be reviewed in detail below, are consistent with this *zeitgeist*.

There are apparently national differences in interest regarding the relationship between test anxiety and achievement. Evidence of European activity in test anxiety research can be seen from the two volumes published by the European based International Society for Test Anxiety Research (Schwarzer, van der Ploeg, & Spielberger, 1982; van der Ploeg, Schwarzer, & Spielberger, 1983), from the convention of that Society in Leuven, Belgium, held in May, 1983 (also to be published in book form), and from the present volume. Eu-

[1]This paper formed the basis for an invited address at a conference on "Anxiety and Self-Related Cognitions" held at the Free University, Berlin, July, 1983. Preparation of this paper was partially supported by a grant from the Basic Research Program of the Army Research Institute for the Behavioral and Social Sciences. The views and opinions expressed are those of the author and should not be construed as official, or as reflecting the views of the Department of the Army or the U.S. Government.

ropean psychology was ahead of American psychology in displaying interest in existential psychology and in recognizing the importance of Piaget's contributions which led to a more cognitively oriented psychology. Perhaps the greater interest in anxiety among European researchers is a harbinger of things to come in American psychology as well.

There are signs that the deemphasis in American educational research and educational psychology regarding research on affect in general, and anxiety in particular, may be coming to an end. Activity in this area is seen by a conference on "Affect and Cognition" subsequently published in book form (Clark & Fiske, 1982). A recent conference at Stanford University on the topic of "Aptitude, Learning, and Instruction: Cognitive and Affective Process Analyses" to be published subsequently (Snow & Farr, in press), is another sign of interest in this field. At that conference Sarason (in press) reviewed the relationship of test anxiety to cognitive interference in learning. Finally, contemporary analysis of people's cognitive processing, to be reviewed below, provides evidence for interference by anxiety in the effective cognitive processing of instruction. It is, therefore, an opportune time to examine the state of knowledge regarding the effects of anxiety on the cognitive processing of instruction, and to attempt to suggest some new directions in this area.

RESEARCH MODEL

It may be useful to examine the recent research on anxiety in terms of a research model proposed following a review of the effects of anxiety on learning from instruction (Tobias, 1977, 1979). The model specifies the points at which anxiety can be expected to affect learning. It is assumed that: "Since learning is a process that is essentially cognitively mediated, anxiety can affect learning only indirectly by impacting on the cognitive processes mediating learning at various stages" (Tobias, 1979, p. 575). The model, depicted in Figure 3.1, arbitrarily separates the instructional process into the three classical information-processing components: input, processing, and output. The input component denotes presentation of instruction to students. Processing represents all the operations performed by students to encode, organize, and store input. Output encompasses students' performance on any evaluative instrument after instruction. Some possible indirect ways in which anxiety can affect instruction are indicated by the broken lines in Figure 3.1. It was hypothesized that there were three possible points at which anxiety can affect learning from instruction most prominently: (1) preprocessing, (2) during processing, and (3) after processing and just before output. Empirical support for the model is briefly reviewed below.

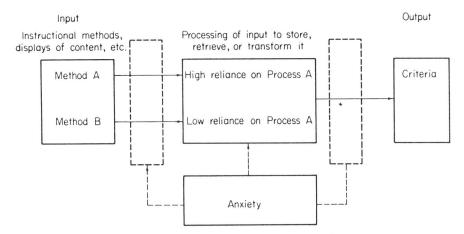

FIG. 3.1 A research model for the effects of anxiety on learning from instruction (From Tobias, 1977. Copyright 1977 by Lawrence Erlbaum Associates. Reprinted by permission.)

Preprocessing

Sarason (1972) and Wine (1971) suggested that those high in anxiety divide their attention between task demands and ruminations stimulated by high anxiety. Conversely, those lower in anxiety learn more since they devote more of their attention to task demands and less to anxiety related preoccupations. Preprocessing interference suggests that while anxious students are occupied with off-task concerns such as worry, they may miss some proportion of instructional input. The diversion of attention to off-task concerns, then, interferes in learning by reducing the proportion of nominal input that becomes effective for high anxiety learners. Preprocessing interference is especially debilitating since any proportion of input not encoded cannot subsequently be processed.

The model hypothesizes that any procedure which permits students to reinstitute input will reduce the potential interference of anxiety at this stage. Procedures such as being able to review segments of text, or having the option to rewind audio or video tapes are predicted to reduce preprocessing interference and, therefore, should be especially beneficial for the performance of high anxiety students. The performance of low anxious students is expected to be unaffected by these procedures.

Deutsch and Tobias (1980) tested this part of the model in a study in which students were assigned to view four video modules either individually, permitting review of the video tape, or in group form where such review was not possible. A significant interaction between test anxiety and the opportunity to review was obtained and is depicted in Figure 3.2. As expected, highly anxious students who viewed the modules independently and had the opportunity to review learned more than anxious students who viewed the modules in groups without the review option. Furthermore, the differences in posttest scores between high and low anxiety students in the independent, review-possible condition were smaller than those in the group administered condition.

Further support for preprocessing interference came from a study by Tobias and Sacks (1983). Three groups read a text passage; of special interest was one group ($n = 35$) which received adjunct questions concerning previously read text segments. Students in this group were informed that they could review preceding text whenever they wished. Correlations between the number of reviews and the Worry-Emotionality scale (Liebert & Morris, 1967), administered with instructions for subjects to respond in terms of the way they felt while reading the passage, were .54 with worry, and .41 with emotionality ($p = <.01$). Correlations between Worry-Emotionality scales administered after the posttest and number of reviews were comparable: .54 with Worry and .40 with Emotionality. These results suggest that as anxiety increased students tended to review prior content more frequently, as predicted by the preprocessing formulation. Presumably, highly anxious students tried to make up for inattentiveness by reviewing preceding text more frequently than their less anxious counterparts.

Processing Interference

At this stage the model assumes that external instructional input has been encoded and subjected to cognitive processing. A limited capacity information processing formulation intended to clarify the manner by which anxiety affects learning during processing will be advanced below. It was expected that three types of factors were likely to have important effects on cognitive processing of instruction: difficulty, reliance on memory, and task organization.

Difficulty.   Research has shown repeatedly (Covington, 1983; Heinrich & Spielberger, 1982; Sieber, O'Neil, & Tobias, 1977) that anxiety is more debilitating to learning on difficult content than on easy material. Reducing the difficulty of material, then, can be expected to be differentially beneficial for anxious students. The interaction between anxiety and task difficulty will be reviewed below.

Reliance on Memory.   There is evidence suggesting that performance of highly anxious students is especially debilitated on tasks calling for short and intermediate term memory (Mueller, 1980). It is reasoned that for highly anx-

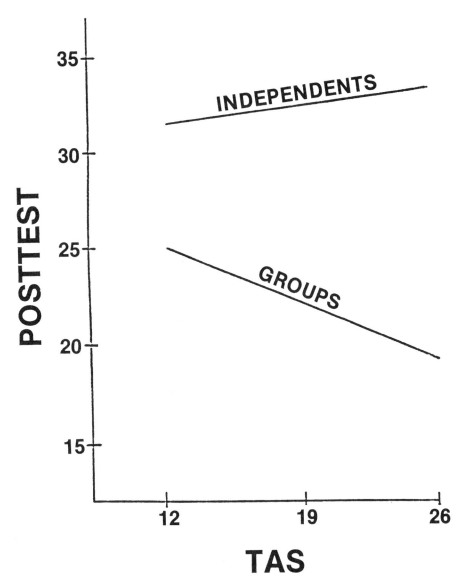

FIG. 3.2   The interaction of test anxiety with opportunity to review. (From Deutsch & Tobias, 1980).

ious students cognitive interference in processing reduces recall. Kreitzberg and Tobias (1979) provided evidence that anxiety interferes with the rehearsal required to maintain stimuli in short term memory. Sieber (1977) reported a number of investigations in which anxious students who had to rely on intermediate term memory performed less capably than their less anxious counterparts.

Organization. The model predicts that the presentation of well organized content will result in superior achievement for anxious students compared to those lower in anxiety. It is assumed that any manipulation which organizes instruction more effectively is expected to be differentially beneficial for highly anxious students.

Post Processing Interference

This effect is meant to represent interference in the retrieval of previous learning, such as during a test. When the model was first proposed (Tobias, 1977) it was indicated that there were no empirical studies in support of this type of interference, though students often "claimed to have studied diligently yet 'freeze up' on tests" (Tobias, 1979, p. 576). In the last few years a number of studies have questioned the occurrence of post processing interference, and these will be discussed next.

TEST ANXIETY: INTERFERENCE OR SKILLS DEFICIT?

A number of studies have been critical of the traditional *interference* model in which worry and other anxiety related ruminations are hypothesized to interfere with student performance during testing. The interference model implies that high and low anxiety students may have mastered the content on which they are to be examined to a comparable degree, but that retrieval of this previously acquired information by high anxiety students is debilitated by the cognitive interference experienced as a result of the evaluative threat posed by examinations (Sarason, in press; 1972; Wine, 1971, 1980). Recent research has proposed a *deficit* model in which the reduction in test performance is attributed to either a study skills or test strategy deficit.

Study Skills Deficit. This interpretation suggests that high test-anxious students may have poorer study skills than those lower in anxiety leading to less thorough initial learning. Poor posttest performance is a function of this deficit and the observed elevation in anxiety is attributable to student's metacognitive (Flavell, 1979) awareness of their incomplete learning. In terms of the research model (Tobias, 1979), the study skills deficit formulation questions the existence of the post processing effect.

Test Taking Deficit. This formulation suggests that high test-anxious students may have poorer test taking skills than those lower in anxiety, leading to reduced test performance. Again, elevations in test anxiety may be a reflection of student's knowledge of their less effective test taking behavior.

Review of Research on the Deficit Model

A number of studies examined the relationship between test anxiety and study skills. The impetus for this research probably came from frequent findings, summarized by Allen, Elias, and Zlotlow (1980), by Denney (1980), and by Tobias (1979), that "a very large percentage of [test anxiety reduction] programs succeed in reducing student's anxiety as determined by a variety of self-reported measures. A decidedly smaller percentage of outcome studies has found that the symptomatic reductions are accompanied by an improvement in scholastic or cognitive performance indices" (Tobias, 1979, p. 580).

Desiderato and Koskinen (1968) and Wittmaier (1972), using Alpert and Haber's (1960) Achievement Anxiety Test, found that anxious students had less effective study skills than those lower in anxiety. After a similar study Mitchell and Ng (1972) concluded that "a reduction in test anxiety is no guarantee of subsequent improvement in academic performance when the level of study habit competence is ignored" (p. 496). Allen (1972) reached similar conclusions.

Culler and Holahan (1980) found that high, compared to low test-anxious subjects had significantly poorer study habits and spent more time studying. They also found that "high test-anxious students who had developed and exercised better study skills did better academically than those with poor study habits. . . . The findings . . . tend to contradict the common stereotype of the high test-anxious student who knows the subject matter but 'freezes up' at test time" (p. 18). Student's study time per week was significantly correlated with the grade point average (GPA) for the high test-anxious group but not the low, suggesting that anxious students may compensate for poor skills by studying more hours. The superior study skills of low-anxious subjects may reduce the importance of study time.

Kirkland and Hollandsworth (1979) found that test anxiety scores correlated significantly with the total score of Brown's (1975) Effective Study Test. Three of five subtests had significant correlations with test anxiety. The Achievement Anxiety Test also correlated significantly with total study skills score. When GPA was a criterion in a stepwise multiple linear regression analysis only the difference score between facilitating and debilitating anxiety and the Examination Behavior Scale added significant variance above that accounted for by scholastic aptitude. These writers "raise the question whether anxiety interferes with effective test-taking behavior or whether the lack of effective skills results in anxiety" (p. 435).

Benjamin, McKeachie, Lin, and Holinger (1981) found that high test-anxious subjects had significantly poorer multiple choice (considered a storage index) and fill-in (considered a retrieval index) test scores than those lower in anxiety. Highly anxious students had lower scores on the fill-in than on the mulitple choice test. In an analysis of covariance, with fill-in scores as the covariate and multiple choice scores as the dependent variable, performance difference between high and low anxiety students disappeared. These results were interpreted to suggest that retrieval, as measured by short answer fill-in exams, appeared to be more of a problem for test-anxious students than storage and encoding of the information. High anxiety students reported significantly more problems both in learning and in reviewing, and spent more study time the week before, and the last 24 hours before an exam, supporting the findings of Culler and Hollahan (1980).

In a second study Benjamin et al. (1981) found differences between high and low anxiety students on essay, short answer, and take home exams, but not on multiple choice tests. On a study habits questionnaire high test anxiety students did not differ from those lower in anxiety on delay avoidance items, but reported more difficulty picking out important information. In general, the higher the test anxiety the greater the problems reported in initial learning, in reviewing, and in remembering on examinations. Furthermore, high test anxiety students reported spending more time studying during the last week before a final exam. The authors propose a causal sequence in which lower ability may lead to achievement anxiety which, in turn, leads to less effective study habits, less effective processing of input, and poorer test performance.

Wendell and Tobias (1983) administered tests shortly after learning and again before an exam approximately 3½ weeks later to differentiate between acquisition and retrieval mechanisms. A total of 84 students in educational psychology classes watched six televised modules dealing with course relevant content. A pretest was given immediately before each module and readministered after its completion. A summative posttest, containing all the items of the six module tests, was presented later. As expected, significant negative correlations between test anxiety and both immediate module posttests and the delayed summative test were found.

Wendell and Tobias computed several derived scores. One of these, abbreviated as "Fail-Pass-Fail," consisted of items which the students failed on pretest, passed on posttest immediately after the module, and failed on the summative posttest administered later. A second derived score, "Pass-Pass-Fail," consisted of items passed on both pre- and immediate posttest, and failed on summative posttest. These two scores were expected to serve as a retrieval index of previous learning since they were composed of items passed immediately after the module, and failed three weeks later when that information had to be retrieved from long-term memory. Positive correlations between Sarason's (1972) Test Anxiety Scale (TAS) and these indices were expected since high anxiety was expected to be related to the greater incidence of retrieval difficulties.

The results, presented in Table 3.1, yielded conflicting evidence. The correlation between the TAS and one retrieval index. Pass-Pass-Fail score was .22. (p. = <.05). The other retrieval index yielded nonsignificant results. The positive correlation between TAS and the third derived score Fail-Fail-Pass, was unexpected. One might speculate that anxious students may have been more aware of missed items and spent more time studying prior to the summative post test, accounting for this unexpected result.

There are a number of difficulties with the Wendell and Tobias investigation. First the indices used were change scores and subject to the well known reliability problems of such measures (Thorndike, 1963). A second problem was the fact that the module posttests included items dealing with content from the beginning, middle, and end of the modules. Since an average of about 35 minutes was required to view the modules and the test was administered at their conclusion, students may have been responding to material covered more than half an hour ago on some items. Module posttests were considered to tap working memory, while the delayed posttest was expected to measure recall from long-term memory. However, since some proportion of the content tapped by test items may have been acquired over half an hour earlier, many items can be conceived of as tapping long-term memory at two different points in time.

In a study of test-taking skills deficit Kirkland and Hollandsworth (1980) compared a skills acquisition approach which placed *no* emphasis on anxiety reduction, to several anxiety reduction techniques. The skills acquisition treatment resulted in improvements in academic performance, while the two anxiety reduction techniques did not. On an anagram test, the skills acquisi-

TABLE 3.1
Means, SDs, Number of Cases and Correlation with TAS for Selected Variables

	Modules 1–6 Combined		Delayed Posttest	Fail Pass Fail	Pass Pass Fail	Fail Fail Pass
	Pretest	Posttest				
N	78	78	73	73	73	73
Mean	2.93	5.95	6.68	4.30	.98	9.37
SD	.78	1.64	1.59	2.78	1.05	4.05
r	−.35*	−.40*	−.28*	.13	.22*	.33*

(From Wendell & Tobias, Note 4)
*p < .05.

tion group solved more problems under stress-inducing conditions than other groups, and students from this group reported more knowledge of effective test taking behavior. These results led the authors to speculate that "perhaps it is time to give the phrase *test anxiety* a respectful burial and talk about inadequate test performance in terms that more accurately describe what it is, namely ineffective test taking" (p. 438).

A recent study (Tobias, in preparation) examined whether test anxiety affected acquisition, retrieval, or the employment of learning strategies. Students (N = 69) studied two lists of words for 30 seconds per trial. Each list was composed of three equal categories. Subjects studied the first list to a criterion of one perfect repetition, but the second list was exposed only three times. It was reasoned that these formed an analog to situations in which students learned various content in different courses which then competed with one another in recall. When both lists were completed, four scales of Weinstein's (1983) Learning and Study Skills Inventory were administered, and students were then asked to recall the preceding lists. Sarason's (1972) TAS had been administered previously, and the Worry-Emotionality (Liebert & Morris, 1967) scales were administered at three points: at the beginning, after List 2, and again after delayed recall.

The results indicated that both the anxiety and study skills measures had little effect on acquisition of List 1, though Worry significantly affected retrieval of words from long-term memory. On the second list, both anxiety and the study skills scales exerted a significant effect on retrieval of the second list. Stepwise regression analysis indicated that once worry entered the regression equation none of the other variables contributed significant variance to the retrieval indices. The results provide clearcut confirmation for the post processing effect in Tobias' model (1977, 1979), that is, worry significantly affected retrieval from long-term memory. The findings also confirmed predictions from the interference model. It should be noted, however, that study skills also contributed significantly to number of the dependent variables.

MACROPROCESSES AND INSTRUCTION

It has been hypothesized that "the most important variable accounting for learning from instruction (is) *macroprocesses,* or the frequency and intensity with which students cognitively process instructional input" (Tobias, 1982, pp. 4–5). A number of studies dealing with macroprocesses relevant to test anxiety have been conducted in classroom contexts and will be discussed below. Other studies utilizing computers to keep track of student's processing of instruction (Tobias, 1983) are presently underway.

Peterson, Swing, Stark, and Waas (1983) examined the macroprocesses of minority students from two fifth-grade classes. Mathematics lessons were videotaped, and students then interviewed regarding their cognitive processes during the lesson. Of special relevance to anxiety was a category called "Students' Affective Thought", which was divided into subsidiary categories. A number of affective categories were discarded for lack of relationship with dependent measures, including both anxious thoughts and task oriented thoughts aimed at getting the correct answers.

The most frequently reported category of affective thoughts in Peterson et al.'s (1983) study represented students' concern with getting the problems right. This category included statements like the following: "(I was thinking) how to get them right and how to count 'em right" (p. 18). In contrast, the least frequently reported affective thoughts consisted of expressions of worry and anxiety which included statements like the following: "I was kinda nervous and felt kinda funny" (p. 18). Despite their infrequency, the category "negative evaluation of self" had significant correlations with achievement raw score $(r = -.24)$, and with percent correct of total attempted $(r = -.26)$. Some examples of negative self thought were: "I thought I was going to get them wrong." "I was having trouble understanding: I wasn't too quick on the answers, so other people beat me to 'em before I could get my hand up" (p. 41). Because negative self thoughts were unrelated to scores on standardized achievement tests, their negative relationship with achievement was independent of student's mathematics ability.

Rohrkemper, McCauley, and Slavin (1983) interviewed a total of 66 third-to-sixth-grade students from an inner city school system about their cognitive activities while participating in mathematics instruction. They found efficacy statements to be the second most frequently occurring type of self report. These statements dealt with the difficulty of the task and expected success or failure. Most efficacy statements occurred early in students' task engagement, and 21 of 29 statements were negative in tone; for example, "If I don't get this right I will maybe fail. Then I start to scribble on my paper" (p. 7). Another category, affective reactions, was the least characteristic of student's speech, but all reported statements were negative; for example, "I say I hate myself." While Rohrkemper et al. did not conceptualize their study with respect to anxiety, two of their categories, negatively toned efficacy statements and affective reactions, appeared to have strong resemblance to the negative preoccupations reported as characteristic of high test anxiety students (Sarason, 1972, in press; Wine, 1971).

Peterson et al. (1983) reported that verbalizations of worry and anxiety were infrequent, though significantly related to outcome measures. Their most frequently reported category had a strong resemblance to the efficacy statements reported in the Rohrkemper et al. (1983) study. On the basis of the examples given, it would appear that some of the cognitions reported in both studies were similar to cognitive interference reported by high test anxiety students. If, in fact, Peterson's category of "student's concern with getting the problems right" does include anxiety related cognitions, then, when these are combined with the overtly anxious verbalizations, concerns with getting the answer right and fears of failure appear to occur relatively frequently during classroom instruction. Rohrkemper et al.'s data also suggest that when two frequently occurring categories (negative efficacy statements and infrequent affective reactions) are combined, cognitive thoughts similar to those of test-anxious students take up a large percentage of student's cognitive activity during instruction. As indicated above, the fact that these cognitions were unrelated to mathematics ability (Peterson et al., 1983) suggests that arithmetic skill deficits are not prominent components of these verbalizations.

TEST ANXIETY: INTERFERENCE, RETRIEVAL AND INFORMATION PROCESSING CAPACITY

Several of the investigations reviewed above question the utility of the test anxiety construct and interpret these phenomena in terms of deficits in test taking or acquisition skills. In terms of Tobias' model (1979), these studies question the occurrence of post processing interference and suggest that the interference occurs during either preprocessing or processing. The researchers are, apparently, divided regarding whether they accept anxiety as a cause of interference at these prior stages, or simply attribute the acquisition deficit to a failure in learning. Benjamin et al. (1981) would apparently accept a role for anxiety in their model, the other writers probably not. In addition to the support of the post processing effect in Tobias' (in preparation) recent investigation there appear to be several other problems with the deficit formulation.

The deficit hypothesis assumes that students who are poorly prepared for an examination have elevations in test anxiety caused by their metacognitive awareness of inadequate mastery. Recent findings (Tobias, in preparation) of no correlations between students' metacognition and either anxiety of study skills do not support this formulation. In addition, attributing anxiety to awareness of poor preparation makes it difficult to understand the research reports (Benjamin et al., 1981; Culler & Hollahan, 1980) of students with good study skills who are also highly test-anxious. If the deficit formulation is accurate, such students should have little to be anxious about since their test anxiety scores *cannot* be explained by either study or test taking skills deficits. Apparently, something other than skills deficit must be invoked to explain the anxiety scores of such students.

The deficit formulation also makes it difficult to understand why anxiety reduction programs succeed in reducing anxiety without increasing cognitive performance. If high test anxiety is caused by student's awareness of inadequate test preparation, the reduction in test anxiety is difficult to understand.

Since performance has *not* improved, anxious students should, according to the deficit rationale, continue to be anxious after these treatment programs since they are now as poorly prepared as before. While it is possible to maintain that such programs merely teach students to feel better, these more positive feelings cannot be attributed to perceived mastery. Presumably, then, reduced negative affect must be related to other sources.

The correlations between study skills and anxiety appear to account for a modest percentage of the variance. Kirkland and Hollandsworth (1979) reported a correlation of $-.26$ between test anxiety and total study skills score. Spielberger, Anton, Algaze, Ross, and Westberry (1980) reported correlations between test anxiety and study skills ranging from $-.14$ to $-.51$; generally, correlations for males were higher than for females. Since these results suggest that a substantial percentage of the common variance between test anxiety and study skills is *unaccounted* for it appears unwise to suggest at this stage that either of these variables can replace the other.

Finally, research results on the relationship between ego involving instructions (sometimes called stress instructions) and test anxiety are not easily explained by the deficit formulation. A frequent finding in the anxiety literature (Sarason, 1972; Wine, 1971) has been that test anxiety interferes with performance only in situations where students are led to believe that the research task has high relationships with measures of intelligence, or achievement in schools. Where such instructions are omitted, few differences between high and low test-anxious students are reported. If poor test performance is to be attributed only to study skills deficits, it is difficult to understand why stress induced when students are being tested should have affected the retrieval of *previously acquired learning*. While a test taking deficit interpretation could be invoked to explain these results, such a hypothesis would still have difficulty explaining why performance differences between high and low test-anxious students occur mainly in stress situations, and not in non-stress contexts. It would appear that some interference notion has to be invoked to account for these results.

The problems discussed above suggest that neither the interference nor the deficit formulation may be adequate to account for the research results. The most reasonable interpretation of the available evidence is that the lower test performance of test-anxious students may be attributed to both interference and skills deficit. It may be useful to reconceptualize these phenomena in terms of information processing capacity.

Information Processing Capacity

Broadbent's (1958, 1971) formulation that humans have a limited capacity information processing system provides a useful point of departure by which both the interference and deficit interpretations can be conceptualized.

Whether the negative affective preoccupations associated with test anxiety are seen as the result of poor test preparation, or as the result of a fear of failure, there is ample evidence (Sarason, 1972; Wine, 1971) that such students have elevations of affect characterized by unfavorable self-perceptions, fear of failure, and similar negative self-preoccupations. The cognitive representation of such preoccupation must absorb some portion of the person's information processing capacity leaving less capacity for coping with task demands. This conceptualization is similar to that proposed by Hamilton (1975).

The limited cognitive capacity formulation clarifies the source of interference by anxiety in the processing section of Tobias' model (1977, 1979) and also explains classical findings in the test anxiety literature whether attributable to interference or skills deficit. Thus, it has often been observed (Sarason, in press; Tobias, 1980; Wine, 1980) that the performance of students preoccupied with negative self-concerns is debilitated on learning tasks. When cognitive capacity is partially engaged by negative self-preoccupations less capacity is available for performance on cognitive tasks, thus reducing learning.

The present analysis suggests that two types of events would reduce interference in performance: (1) reducing the processing capacity absorbed by affective preoccupations, or (2) reducing the information processing demands of the task. The findings (Sarason, in press; Wine, 1980) that reassuring students improves their performance indicates that the cognitive capacity tied up by such rumination can be reduced when students are reassured regarding the threat posed by the task, or reassured about their abilities to succeed. Additionally, the findings that even relatively trivial manipulations, such as suggesting to students that they concentrate more on a task and less on extraneous matters, improves performance (Sarason, in press; Wine, 1980), can be similarly interpreted. Such instructions enable students to devote a greater proportion of processing capacity to the task, and less to anxious self-ruminations. The enhancement of performance is, of course, attributable to having more cognitive capacity available for task solution.

The second way to improve the performance of students with negative affective preoccupations is to reduce the information processing demanded by tasks. The type of manipulations suggested in the processing section of Tobias' (1977, 1979) model, such as increasing the organization of instructional content, reducing its difficulty, and decreasing reliance on memory are likely to reduce the processing capacity required by tasks. This reduction should result in improved performance especially by students whose processing capacity is partially allocated to off-task concerns.

Difficulty and Information Processing Capacity.   The cognitive capacity model easily explains findings in which anxious individuals perform more poorly than those lower in anxiety. Furthermore, findings of no difference between those high and low in anxiety on tasks requiring little information processing capacity can also be accommodated by the model, since the capacity absorbed by the task may be too small to interfere with task performance. The capacity model does have some difficulty accommodating to findings of superior performance by anxious individuals compared to those lower in anxiety. Such findings are hypothesized by Spence-Taylor drive theory (Spence, 1958; Taylor 1951) which predicts that performance on easy tasks will be facilitated by anxiety. There is little basis for expecting enhanced performance in the limited capacity processing model suggested above. Research and theory in this general area will be briefly examined below.

Drive theory hypothesizes that emotional responses like anxiety raise the drive level of all relevant responses to a stimulus, thus increasing their probability of occurrence. On an easy task it is assumed that the correct response is dominant, and competing responses are much lower in habit strength. Raising drive level is expected to facilitate learning by eliciting the correct dominant response more frequently than the weaker incorrect responses. In complex learning tasks, drive theory assumes that there is no one dominant response, hence anxiety may raise the drive level of both relevant and irrelevant responses above threshold. The occurrence of more incorrect responses leads to the interference of anxiety in performance.

The paradigm of analyzing tasks into discrete competing responses is not easily applied to instructional situations. In an examination of the research findings dealing with anxiety and task difficulty, Heinrich and Spielberger (1982) note that "it is generally not possible to accurately determine the correct and incorrect (competing) response tendencies on complex learning tasks. Rather the difficulty of a given task is generally established to be relatively easier or more difficult than another task" (p. 149). The relative ordering of task difficulty is not entirely satisfactory for relating drive theory even to performance on complex laboratory tasks, much less tasks in instructional situations. One issue raised in reviews of the anxiety-task difficulty literature, such as that by Heinrich and Spielberger, is whether a particular task was easy enough to warrant the expectation of performance facilitation predicted by drive theory. Such concerns are substantially increased in instructional situations.

The limited capacity cognitive processing model was advanced to account for findings in instructionally relevant situations. A review of this literature (Sieber, O'Neil, & Tobias, 1977; Tobias, 1980) revealed few findings indicating that anxious individuals performed at a higher level than those lower in anxiety. After reviewing five different studies designed to clarify the relationship between task difficulty and anxiety, O'Neil (a co-author of each of the studies), Judd, and Hedl (1977) concluded that drive theory predictions were "*not* confirmed. Thus, for meaningful computer-assisted instruction tasks of varying levels of difficulty, drive theory seems to have limited utility in predicting the relationships between state anxiety and performance" (p. 208).

Spence (1958), a principal proponent of drive theory, observed:

> In order to derive implications concerning the effects of drive variation in any type of complex learning task, it is necessary to have, in addition to the drive theory, a further theoretical framework concerning the variables and their interaction, that are involved in the particular learning activity. (p. 137)

There would appear to be consensus that relating drive theory to learning from instruction encounters major difficulties until a subject matter theory, such as that described by Spence, is available. Such a theory might also permit specification of an unambiguous task difficulty measure. Contemporary research in cognitive psychology and instruction (Resnick, 1981) is in the process of building just such a theory in different subject matter fields, permitting a more definitive test of this position in the future.

Study Skills and Cognitive Capacity.   It can be hypothesized that good study skills also have the effect of reducing the information processing demands of tasks. Students who relate new information to prior cognitive structures concentrate effectively on the task at hand, and maintain ongoing metacognitive awareness of task performance probably require less information processing capacity for instructional tasks, than those who are less effective in the utilization of these study skills. The latter probably rely more on actively rehearsing information in short term memory and similar strategies which absorb a greater proportion of cognitive capacity.

This formulation clarifies the relationship between test anxiety and study skills. Interference by anxiety and employing poor study skills both reduce performance, though for somewhat different reasons. High test anxiety may reduce performance by absorbing a large proportion of information processing capacity, leaving a reduced amount for task solution. Poor study skills, on the other hand, are hypothesized to interfere with performance by increasing the proportion of cognitive capacity required for task solution. Obviously, students with high anxiety and poor study skills would be the least effective learners since a large proportion of processing capacity is tied up with anxious ruminations, and task solution makes high demands on processing capacity. Conversely, students low in test anxiety with strong study skills will perform most effectively since little capacity is absorbed by off-task concerns, and the good study skills reduce the amounts of processing required for learning. The performance of students with high test anxiety and good study skills or low test anxiety and poor study skills obviously is expected to be in the middle of the two extreme groups.

GENERAL DISCUSSION

The research results and the limited capacity model suggest that at present it is most prudent to view test anxiety from the joint perspective of both interference and skills deficit. It is possible to interpret the research supporting the deficit interpretation as an attempt to identify the cognitive processes mediating the effect of anxiety on performance. As suggested in Tobias' model (1977, 1979) affective states can impact on cognitive performance only indirectly by engaging the cognitive processes controlling that performance. It seems altogether reasonable that deficits in study and test taking skills may be one important component accounting for the observed reduction in learning as a result of anxiety. The cause and effect chain regarding whether affect is a consequence of cognitive deficit, or causes cognitive deficit, is of some theoretical interest, and certainly warrants further investigation. The research on study skills has enlarged our understanding of the variables affecting learning from instruction.

It is interesting to note that the attempt to identify the cognitive processes accounting for the test anxiety effect is similar to research paradigms in other areas. Thus, there has been a great deal of research activity in the last decade to identify the cognitive processes accounting for intelligence. Researchers in various laboratories (Hunt, 1978; Snow, 1980; Pellegrino, & Glaser, 1980; Sternberg, 1981) have tried to clarify the cognitive processes of which intelligence is composed. Similar attention has been devoted to the clarification of other cognitive constructs, and some affective ones, such as motivation (Graham & Weiner, in press). It is, therefore, not surprising to see the beginnings of similar research devoted to the cognitive processes by which anxiety affects human performance.

Identifying study and test taking skills as cognitive components of test anxiety is, of course, only a beginning. An important question to be answered by such research deals with the possibility of training subjects to overcome the deficits, and to determine the degree to which this training is generalizable. Some preliminary results (Wine, 1982) have indicated that training students in particular cognitive strategies so that they can maximize their learning from instruction may well be effective for a particular task, but have limited generalizability. These concerns are likely to lead to a clearer identification of the variables, associated with the reduction in performance observed in relationship to test anxiety, in addition to clarifying the cognitive constructs by which humans learn from instruction.

REFERENCES

Allen, G. J. The behavioral treatment of test anxiety: Recent research and future trends. *Behavior Therapy,* 1972, *3,* 252–262.

Allen, G. J., Elias, M. J., & Zlotlow, S. F. Behavioral interventions for alleviating test anxiety: A methodological overview of current therapeutic practices. In I. G. Sarason (Ed.), *Test anxiety: Theory, research and applications*. Hillsdale, NJ: Lawrence Erlbaum Associates, 1980.

Alpert, R., & Haber, R. Anxiety in academic achievement situations. *Journal of Abnormal and Social Psychology*, 1960, *61*, 207–215.

Benjamin, M., McKeachie, W., Lin, Y., & Holinger, D. Test anxiety: Deficits in information processing. *Journal of Educational Psychology*, 1981, *73*, 816–824.

Broadbent, D. E. *Perception and communication*. London: Pergamon Press, 1958.

Broadbent, D. E. *Decision and stress*. London: Academic Press, 1971.

Brown, W. F. *Effective study test: Manual of directionss*. San Marcos, TX: Effective Study Materials, 1975.

Clark, M. S., & Fiske, S. T. *Affect and cognition:* The Seventeenth Annual Carnegie Symposium on Cognition. Hillsdale, NJ: Lawrence Erlbaum Associates, 1982.

Covington, M. V. Anxiety, task difficulty and childhood problem-solving: A self-worth interpretation. In H. M. van der Ploeg, R. Schwarzer, & C. D. Spielberger (Eds.), *Test anxiety research* (Vol. 2). Hillsdale, NJ: Lawrence Erlbaum Associates, 1983.

Culler, R. E., & Holahan, C. Test taking and academic performance: The effects of study-related behaviors. *Journal of Educational Psychology*, 1980, *72*, 16–20.

Denney, D. R. Self-control approaches to the treatment of test anxiety. In I. G. Sarason (Ed.), *Test anxiety: Theory, research and applications*. Hillsdale, NJ: Erlbaum, 1980.

Desiderato, O., & Koskinen, P. Anxiety, study habits, and academic achievement. *Journal of Counseling Psychology*, 1969, *16*, 162–165.

Deutsch, T., & Tobias, S. *Prior achievement, anxiety, and instructional method*. Paper presented at the annual convention at the American Psychological Association, Montreal, September 1980.

Flavell, J. Metacognition and cognitive monitoring: A new area of cognitive developmental inquiry. *American Psychologist*, 1979, *34*, 906–911.

Graham, S., & Weiner, B. Thinking-feeling-action sequences in instruction. In R. E. Snow & M. J. Farr (Eds.), *Aptitude, learning, and instruction: Cognitive and affective process analyses*. Hillsdale, NJ: Erlbaum, in press.

Hamilton, V. Socialization anxiety and information processing: A capacity model of anxiety-induced performance deficits. In I. G. Sarason & C. D. Spielberger (Eds.), *Stress and anxiety* (Vol. 2). NY: Halstead Press, 1975.

Heinrich, D. L., & Spielberger, C. D. Anxiety and coping in achievement situations. In H. W. Krohne & L. Laux (Eds.), *Achievement, stress and anxiety*. Washington, DC: Hemisphere, 1982.

Hunt, E. B. Mechanics of verbal ability. *Psychological Review*, 1978, *85*, 109–130.

Kirkland, K., & Hollandsworth, J. Test anxiety, study skills, and academic performance. *Journal of College Personnel*, 1979, *20*, 431–435.

Kirkland, K., & Hollandsworth, J. Effective test taking: Skills-acquisition versus anxiety-reduction techniques. *Journal of Counseling and Clinical Psychology*, 1980, *48*, 431–439.

Kreitzberg, C., & Tobias, S. *Test anxiety, attention, and short term memory*. Paper presented at the annual meeting of the American Psychological Association, NY, September, 1979.

Liebert, R. M., & Morris, L. W. Cognitive and emotional components of test anxiety: A distinction and some initial data. *Psychological Reports*, 1967, *20*, 975–978.

Mitchell, K., & Ng, K. Effects of group counseling and behavior therapy on the academic achievement of test-anxious students. *Journal Counseling Psychology*, 1972, *19*, 491–497.

Mueller, J. H. Test anxiety and the encoding and retrieval of information. In I. G. Sarason (Ed.), *Test anxiety: Theory, research and applications*. Hillsdale, NJ: Lawrence Erlbaum Associates, 1980.

O'Neil, H. F., Jr., Judd, W. A., & Hedl, J. J., Jr. State anxiety and performance in computer-based learning environments. In J. E. Sieber, H. F. O'Neil, Jr., & S. Tobias (Eds.), *Anxiety, learning, and instruction*. Hillsdale, NJ: Lawrence Erlbaum Associates, 1977.

Pellegrino, J. W., & Glaser, R. Components of inductive reasoning. In R. E. Snow, P. A. Federico, & W. Montague (Eds.), *Aptitude, learning and instruction: Cognitive processes analysis* (Vol. 1). Hillsdale, NJ: Lawrence Erlbaum Associates, 1980.

Peterson, P. L., Swing, S. R., Stark, K. D., & Waas, G. A. *Students' reports of their cognitive processes and affective thoughts during classroom instruction*. Paper presented at the annual meeting of the American Educational Research Association, Montreal, April 1983.

Resnick, L. B. Instructional psychology. *Annual Review of Psychology,* 1981, *32,* 659–704.

Rohrkemper, M., McCauley, K., & Slavin, R. E. *Student cognition study: Investigating students' perceptions of cognitive strategies as learning tools*. Paper presented at the annual meeting of the American Educational Research Association, Montreal, April 1983.

Sarason, I. G. Test anxiety, cognitive interference and performance. In R. E. Snow & M. J. Farr (Eds.), *Aptitude, learning, and instruction: Conative and affective process analyses*. Hillsdale, NJ: Lawrence Erlbaum Associates, in press.

Sarason, I. G. Experimental approaches to test anxiety: Attention and the uses of information. In C. D. Spielberger (Ed.), *Anxiety: Current trends in theory and research* (Vol. 2). New York: Academic Press, 1972.

Schwarzer, R., van der Ploeg, H. M., Spielberger, C. D., *Advances in test anxiety research* (Vol. 1). Hillsdale, NJ: Lawrence Erlbaum Associates, 1982.

Sieber, J. E. A paradigm for research on treatments designed to modify anxiety or its effects. In Sieber, J. E., O'Neil, H. F. Jr., & Tobias, S. *Anxiety, learning, and instruction*. Hillsdale, NJ: Lawrence Erlbaum Associates, 1977.

Sieber, J. E., Kameya, L. I., & Paulson, F. L. Effects of memory support on the problem solving abilities of test anxious children. *Journal of Educational Psychology,* 1970, *61,* 159–168.

Sieber, J. E., O'Neil, H. F., & Tobias, S. *Anxiety, learning and instruction*. Hillsdale, NJ: Lawrence Erlbaum Associates, 1977.

Snow, R. E. Aptitude processes. In R. E. Snow, P. A. Federico, & W. E. Montague (Eds.), *Aptitude, learning and instruction: Cognitive processes analysis*. Hillsdale, NJ: Lawrence Erlbaum Associates, 1980.

Snow, R. E., & Farr, M. J. *Aptitude, learning, and affective process analyses*. Hillsdale, NJ: Lawrence Erlbaum Associates, in press.

Spence, K. W. A theory of emotionally based drive (D) and its relation to performance in simple learning situations. *American Psychologist,* 1958, *13,* 131–141.

Spielberger, C. D., Gonzalez, H. P., Taylor, C. J., Anton, W. D., Algaze, B., Ross, G. R., & Westberry, L. G. *Test anxiety inventory*. Palo Alto, CA: Consulting Psychologists Press, 1980.

Sternberg, R. Nothing fails like success: The search for an intelligent paradigm for studying intelligence. *Journal of Educational Psychology,* 1981, *73,* 142–155.

Taylor, J. A. The relationship of anxiety to the conditioned eyelid response. *Journal of Experimental Psychology,* 1951, *41,* 81;92.

Tobias, S. *Test anxiety and post processing interference*. In preparation.

Tobias, S. *Macroprocesses and adaptive instruction*. Paper presented at the annual convention of the American Educational Research Association, Montreal, April, 1983.

Tobias, S. When do instructional methods make a difference? *Educational Researcher,* 1982, *11,* (4), 4–9.

Tobias, S. Anxiety and instruction. In I. G. Sarason (Ed.), *Test anxiety, theory, research, applications*. Hillsdale, NJ: Lawrence Erlbaum Associates, 1980.

Tobias, S. Anxiety research in educational psychology. *Journal of Educational Psychology,* 1979, *71,* 573–582.

Tobias, S. A model for research on the effect of anxiety on instruction. In J. E. Sieber, H. F.

O'Neil, Jr., & S. Tobias (Eds.), *Anxiety, learning, and instruction.* Hillsdale, NJ: Lawrence Erlbaum Associates, 1977.

Tobias, S., & Sacks, J. *Aptitude treatment interactions, adjunct questions, review and macroprocesses.* Paper presented at the annual convention of the Northeastern Educational Research Association, Ellenville, NY, October, 1983.

Thorndike, R. L. *The concept of overachievement.* New York: Teachers College Press, Columbia University, 1963.

van der Ploeg, H. M., Schwarzer, R., & Spielberger, C. D. *Advances in test anxiety research* (Vol. 2.) Hillsdale, NJ: Lawrence Erlbaum Associates, 1983.

Weinstein, C. E. *Learning and study strategies inventory.* (Mimeo). Austin, TX: University of Texas, 1983.

Wendell, A., & Tobias, S. *Anxiety and the retrieval of information from long term memory.* Paper presented at the annual convention of the Northeastern Educational Research Association, Ellenville, NY, October, 1983.

Wine, J. D. Test anxiety and direction of attention. *Psychological Bulletin,* 1971, *71,* 92–104.

Wine, J. D. Cognitive-attentional theory of test anxiety. In I. G. Sarason (Ed.), *Test anxiety: Theory, research, applications.* Hillsdale, N.J.: Erlbaum, 1980.

Winne, P. H. *Matching students' processing to text with instructional objectives or adjunct questions.* Burnaby, BC: Simon Fraser University, Instructional Psychological Research Group, 1982.

Wittmaier, B. Test anxiety and study habits. *Journal of Educational Research,* 1972, 352–354.

4 Differences in Anxiety Among Androgynous Women: Relation to Achievement Motivation Variables

Larry W. Morris
Paula M. Ponath
Middle Tennessee State University

Recent research indicates clearly that women who attribute more masculine characteristics to themselves in completing sex role inventories have higher levels of personal adjustment in general and lower levels of trait anxiety in particular (Bander & Betz, 1981). Specifically, masculine males and females as well as androgynous males and females have been shown to be less anxious than feminine and undifferentiated males and females, demonstrating the importance of the inverse masculinity-anxiety relationship for women and men alike.

In contrast, a body of achievement motivation research suggests that achievement oriented females have considerably more anxiety problems than other groups because of the role conflict and strain inherent in their achievement striving (e.g., Bremer & Wittig, 1980). Combining insights from these two research areas leads to the conclusion that androgynous and masculine career oriented females are generally successful in coping with these conflicts and thus derive the personal and social benefits of a successful and productive lifestyle, but that a minority of achievement oriented women have marked difficulty with anxiety, perhaps as a result of uncertainty about one's adequacy as a woman or as a result of conflicting priorities in scheduling day-to-day activities concerning home and career.

The purpose of the present study was to subdivide a group of androgynous/masculine females into groups differing on two adjustment variables, trait anxiety and locus of control. Trait anxiety refers to a proneness to become anxious in situations involving threat to a person's self-esteem or a tendency to be sensitive to and threatened by the possibility of personal evaluation. Locus of control refers to differences in expectancies of being able to control the events (reinforements) in one's life. An external locus of control is related to various anxiety dimensions, including trait anxiety, and refers to feelings of helplessness and lack of control. Identifying variables related to differences in trait anxiety and locus of control among the individuals in this group should be informative.

METHOD

The A-trait scale of the State-Trait Anxiety Inventory (Spielberger, Gorsuch, & Lushene, 1970), Rotter's (1966) Locus of Control scale, and the Bem (1974) Sex Role Inventory (BSRI) were administered to 187 undergraduate psychology students, 111 females and 76 males. For purposes of comparing sex role groups of both sexes on locus of control and trait anxiety, students were classified as either androgynous, masculine, feminine, or undifferentiated depending on whether they scored above 4.90 on the masculine and feminine scales of the BSRI. Females classified as either androgynous or masculine were asked to complete an additional battery of tests consisting of Helmreich and Spence's (1978) Work and Family Orientation Questionnaire (WOFO) designed to measure aspects of achievement motivation, the Jenkins Activity Survey (JAS; Krantz, Glass, & Snyder, 1974) designed to assess the Type A behavior pattern associated with proneness to coronary problems, and Zuckerman and Allison's (1976) Fear of Success scale designed to assess the individual's concern with the possible negative consequences of achieving success. Thirty-seven volunteers completed the battery.

With masculinity restricted to average and above among these androgynous/masculine females, the first hypothesis was that elevations in trait anxiety and external locus of control would be associated with femininity scores on the BSRI, with fear of success scores, and (inversely) with the WOFO Personal Unconcern scale, on which low scores indicate fear of success. Support for this hypothesis would indicate that increased anxiety results from aspects of femininity being too strong to integrate well with masculinity and achievement strivings.

The second hypothesis was that elevations in trait anxiety and external locus of control would be associated with lower scores or deficits on two of the WOFO scales, Work Orientation and Mastery, both of which reflect positive aspects of achievement motivation which, though traditionally masculine, should be easily integrated with a feminine lifestyle. The Work Orientation scale reflects a positive attitude toward working hard and toward producing high-quality work, and the Mastery scale reflects a preference for challenging and difficult tasks. One of the JAS scales, Hard-driving/Competitiveness, is defined as involving hard work and a conscientious, serious, responsible attitude toward work and probably has much in common with these WOFO scales. A deficiency in such masculine characteristics in the achievement oriented female lifestyle may create an actual or perceived deficit which results in poorer adjustment.

The third hypothesis was that elevations in trait anxiety and external locus of control would be associated with higher scores on the WOFO Competitiveness scale and the scales of the JAS measuring Type A behavior pattern. Findings supporting this hypothesis would indicate the existence of some types of masculine achievement striving which are particularly difficult to integrate into a female lifestyle. Olds and Shaver (1980) found evidence for this line of reasoning using the WOFO Competitiveness scale. Only indirect evidence concerning Type A behavior exists, based on DeGregorio and Carver's (1980) finding of the incompatibility of Type A and low masculinity.

The fourth hypothesis was that combining trait anxiety and locus of control would be fruitful in that low-trait-anxious internals and high-trait-anxious externals should be more clearly differentiated on the relevant variables than if subjects were grouped on the basis of each dimension separately. The question is whether these conceptually and empirically related variables are overlapping, complementary, or independent in their relationship to achievement motivation variables in this sample.

RESULTS

Data from the entire subject pool of 187 were subjected to $2 \times 2 \times 2$ (Sex $\times$ Masculinity $\times$ Femininity) analyses of variance. The only significant effects on either trait anxiety or locus of control scores were the Masculinity main effects, $F(1,179) = 8.89$ and 7.88, respectively, $p < .01$. The high masculinity group, consisting largely of 41 masculine males and 39 androgynous females, had significantly lower trait anxiety scores (35.73 ± 7.42 versus 40.57 ± 8.30) and significantly more internal locus of control scores (10.03 ± 3.51 versus 11.51 ± 3.81) than the low masculinity group, which consisted largely of 46 feminine females and 35 undifferentiated subjects of both sexes. Pearson product-moment correlation coefficients computed for all subjects combined and for female and male subjects separately confirmed an inverse relationship between masculinity and both trait anxiety, r's $= -.39$ to $-.46$, $p < .05$, and external locus of control, r's $= -.17$ to $-.26$ (nonsignificant only for the female group). Neither trait anxiety nor locus of control was correlated significantly with femininity, r's $= -.02$ to $-.13$ and $.06$ to $-.14$, respectively, or with androgyny, r's $= /.17$ to $-.09$ and $.05$ to $-.08$. Trait anxiety and external locus of control were significantly positively related for all three groupings of subjects, r's $= .34$ to $.36$, $p < .05$.

Table 4.1 presents the means and Pearson product-moment correlations among the ten achievement motivation variables for the 37 androgynous/ masculine females and the correlations between achievement motivation variables and sex role and adjustment variables. In comparison with the larger subject pool from which they were drawn, these subjects were similar to the high masculinity subjects described above in both trait anxiety (35.97 ± 8.66) and locus of control (9.97 ± 3.36), that is, relatively internal in orientation and low-trait-anxious. In comparison with published norms for trait anxiety (Spielberger, Gorsuch, & Lushene, 1970), these subjects scored, on the average, at the 45th percentile for undergraduate college females. As in the larger subject pool, trait anxiety was inversely related to masculinity, r (35) = $-.40$, $p < .05$, but not to femininity or androgyny, r (35) = $-.07$ and $-.03$, respectively. Unlike in the larger subject pool, locus of control was not significantly related to masculinity nor to trait anxiety, r (35) = $-.05$ and .30, respectively. Locus of control was also unrelated to femininity and androgyny, r (35) = $-.03$ and $-.02$, respectively.

Correlations involving the trait anxiety variable indicate that elevations in trait anxiety among these subjects were related to three factors. First, as noted above, elevations in trait anxiety were associated with deficits in masculinity per se. Second, elevations in trait anxiety were related to deficits in positive attitudes toward work as reflected on the WOFO Work Orientation scale and total WOFO scores, r (35) = $-.34$ and $-.40$, respectively. Work orientation and masculinity were unrelated and thus must be seen as independent deficits related to trait anxiety, though total WOFO scores were positively related to masculinity, r (35) = .34. There were a number of other achievement motivation variables whose inverse relationships with trait anxiety approached significance (WOFO Mastery, Personal Unconcern; JAS Hard-driving/Competitive), each of which was positively though not necessarily significantly correlated with both work orientation and masculinity; partialling out either work orientation or masculinity reduced the correlations of each of these variables with trait anxiety to nonsignificance. Thus, elevations in trait anxiety were related to deficits in masculinity, work orientation, and a cluster of related variables, which together appear to reflect a theme of independence, dominance, and risk-taking, high expenditure of effort and conscientious attitude toward the quality of one's work, preference for difficult and challenging tasks, and lack of concern with the negative reactions of others to one's personal achievement. The Work Orientation, Mastery, and Hard-driving/Competitive scales were especially strongly interrelated. This cluster of achievement motivation variables was clearly unrelated to femininity and androgyny.

Third, correlations involving the trait anxiety variable indicate that elevations in trait anxiety may also be related to an excess: a positive relationship between trait anxiety and JAS Speed/Impatience scores approached signifi-

TABLE 4.1

Means and Pearson Product-Moment Correlations: 37 Androgynous/Masculine Females

Variables	1	2	3	4	5	6	7	8	9	10
Mean	20.35	21.89	13.65	11.03	66.92	97.59	247.05	156.76	123.78	527.59
St. Dev.	4.76	2.02	3.12	3.03	7.86	12.92	68.24	60.94	27.35	129.28
Mastery (1)										
Work Orientation (2)	.42*									
Competitiveness (3)	.30**	.22								
Personal Unconcern (4)	.00	.20	−.33*							
Total WOFO (5)	.83*	.68*	.51*	.30**						
Fear of Success (6)	−.35*	−.13	−.13	−.34*	−.42*					
Type A (7)	−.28**	−.05	.37*	−.18	.23	−.22				
Speed/Impatience (8)	−.03	−.32**	.18	−.32**	−.15	−.04	.72*			
Hard-driving/Comp. (9)	.56*	.51*	.46*	.02	.66*	−.40*	.44*	.00		
Total JAS (10)	.25	−.07	.38*	−.24	.19	−.22	.96*	.85*	.44*	
Masculinity	.32**	−.05	.18	.22	.34*	−.33*	.27	.19	.20	.27
Femininity	.06	.13	−.23	.14	.03	.06	−.50*	−.61*	.03	−.54*
Androgyny	.09	.04	.04	−.04	.07	.20	.09	.34*	−.07	.19
Trait Anxiety	−.30**	−.34*	−.06	−.28**	−.40*	.13	.04	.29**	−.29**	.09
Locus of Control	.08	.07	.10	−.22	.02	.08	.31**	.33*	.19	.36*

*p < .05
**p < .10

59

cance, r (35) = .29. This positive relationship was independent of the anxiety-masculinity relationship, but partialling out work orientation reduced the correlation to nonsignificance. Thus, the excessive Speed/ Impatience of the more anxious subjects is to be considered in connection with the deficient work orientation cluster, adding the element of time urgency. Note that only this specific element of the general Type A behavior pattern was involved, and that Speed/Impatience is the only variable in the work orientation cluster related (inversely) to femininity and androgyny, r (35) = −.61 and .34, respectively.

However, the generality of these correlational results is called into question by the finding of nonsignificant differences between groups differing in trait anxiety, whether based on a median split or on upper and lower thirds. Table 4.2 presents the mean scores of 18 high-trait-anxious and 19 low-trait-anxious subjects, who differed significantly only in masculinity, F (1,33) = 5.58, p = .02. The significant negative correlations, in the absence of significant group differences, apparently resulted from the presence of a few high-trait-anxious subjects (scores greater than 47) who had low scores on the achievement motivation variables in question and a few low-trait-anxious subjects (scores less than 25) who had high scores on those variables.

Correlations involving the locus of control variable (see Table 4.1) and analyses of group differences between internals and externals (see Table 4.2) consistently indicate that externality among these androgynous/masculine females was related solely to excesses in Type A behavior patterns, excluding the Hard-driving/Competitive factor. The positive correlations of locus of control with Speed/Impatience and with total JAS scores were significant, r (35) = .33 and .36, respectively, and with the Type A subscale approached significance, r (35) = .31. Likewise, the 18 externally oriented subjects tended to score higher than the 19 internally oriented subjects on Type A, Speed/Impatience, and total JAS, F (1,33) = 3.85, 3.74, and 4.01, respectively, $p < .06$. These three scores were strongly interrelated, reflecting tendencies toward rapidity of action, time urgency, irritability, and impatience, as well as more general Type A tendencies toward perceiving everyday life and work as filled with struggles and challenges to be met and overcome. These scores were positively but nonsignificantly related to masculinity, r's (35) = .18 to .27, and were strongly inversely related to femininity, r's (35) = −.50 to −.61, neither of which accounts statistically for their relationship to locus of control, which was totally unrelated to both.

Theoretically, individuals with both low trait anxiety and internal locus of control should be the most well-adjusted of the group, in contrast with externals high in trait anxiety. Two-way analyses of variance were thus computed on the data presented in Table 4.2, resulting in only one significant interaction effect, on the WOFO Work Orientation scale, F (1,33) = 4.23, $p < .05$. Though the small number of subjects in the off-diagonal cells makes interpretation tenuous, it was the low-trait-anxious externals who scored highest

TABLE 4.2
Mean Scores: Trait Anxiety × Locus of Control Groupings

	Low Anxiety				High Anxiety			
	Internal n = 12		External n = 6		Internal n = 6		External n = 12	
	Mean	SD	Mean	SD	Mean	SD	Mean	SD
Masculinity	545.00	35.10	545.00	54.86	521.29	25.43	512.08	25.89
Femininity	530.42	62.14	519.17	45.32	553.00	45.44	547.92	43.82
Androgyny	59.58	46.19	59.17	63.44	46.00	22.33	55.00	29.31
Mastery	20.75	6.20	21.17	4.96	20.86	3.29	20.35	4.09
Work Orientation	21.67	2.23	23.33	0.82	22.29	2.36	21.17	1.80
Competitiveness	13.50	2.97	15.50	2.59	12.57	4.20	13.50	2.78
Personal Unconcern	11.50	2.50	10.83	2.32	12.57	2.44	9.75	3.82
Total WOFO	67.42	10.16	70.83	5.42	68.29	5.50	63.67	6.91
Fear of Success	93.67	10.41	105.17	12.51	95.00	8.98	99.25	16.36
Type A	240.17	68.13	290.50	67.17	212.43	57.39	252.42	69.82
Speed/Impatience	145.50	65.46	171.17	84.37	125.14	29.22	179.25	52.24
Hard-driving/Comp.	125.08	35.01	127.50	28.15	119.86	25.90	122.92	21.80
Total JAS	510.75	124.33	589.17	169.34	457.43	108.04	554.08	116.33

on this positive aspect of achievement motivation, while high-trait-anxious externals scored lowest as would be expected. To test the fourth hypothesis more directly, the 12 subjects scoring above the median on both the trait anxiety and locus of control scales were compared with those (n = 12) scoring below the median on both. The high-trait-anxious externals scored lowest of the four groups on masculinity, total WOFO scores, Mastery, Work Orientation, and Personal Unconcern, and highest on the JAS Speed/Impatience scale; however, the low-trait-anxious internal group did not score at the opposite extreme of the four groups on these variables, and the two groups did not differ significantly on any of the variables except masculinity, t (22) = 2.62, p = .02.

Fear of Success.   According to the pattern of correlations presented in Table 4.1, Zuckerman and Allison's fear of success scale belongs to the cluster of variables characterized by low masculinity, low WOFO total scores, specifically Mastery and Personal Unconcern, and low JAS Hard-driving/ Competitiveness. Unlike the other variables in the cluster, fear of success showed no tendency to relate to differences in trait anxiety.

DISCUSSION

The most clearcut finding reflected in these data is the relationship between masculinity per se and trait anxiety. Neither degree of femininity nor amount of balance between masculinity and femininity (androgyny) appears to be very relevant, but deficits in masculinity were consistently associated with elevations in trait anxiety. Furthermore, the magnitude of the inverse relationship was essentially invariant across samples of males, females, males and females combined, and even in the sample of females who all had average-or-above masculinity scores. Masculinity was also inversely related to external locus of control, but the relationship was of somewhat lower magnitude and less general, not holding at all for the sample of females with average-or-above masculinity scores.

The inverse relationship between masculinity and adjustment in general populations of both males and females is well-documented. That the same relationship holds for androgynous/masculine females has not been reported previously. These findings support the second hypothesis in contrast to the first hypothesis, arguing against the positions which hold that achievement oriented women have problems with anxiety to the degree that they develop excessive masculinity per se, or to the degree that their masculinity becomes too dominant over their femininity, or to the degree that the femininity accompanying their masculinity is excessive. These findings rather support a deficit position regarding anxiety in achievement oriented females, that is, that anxiety is more of a problem to those who have a relative deficit in traditionally masculine achievement characteristics. Whether anxiety results from the deficit or the deficit is an effect of anxiety, is a cause and effect question on which these data can shed no light.

Findings supporting the third hypothesis concerning possible excesses related to trait anxiety and external locus of control must be interpreted in light of the deficit position outlined above, that is, must not be interpreted as a result of excessive masculinity per se. The Speed/Impatience factor of the Type A behavior pattern, involving a hurried, time urgent, impatient, irritable approach to one's work, is a somewhat masculine characteristic (correlated positively but nonsignificantly with masculinity), but is more notably an unfeminine characteristic. This is the primary variable bearing a relationship to the feelings of helplessness and lack of control exhibited by these female subjects. It is possible that this finding is unique to achievement oriented females, that the hurried lifestyle and impatient attitudes which often are inevitable consequences of an achievement orientation are particularly inconsistent with female self-perceptions of adequacy and acceptability.

Otherwise, the findings concerning deficits related to trait anxiety do not appear to reveal anything unique to achievement oriented females, but rather a general principle which is useful in understanding anxiety. In other words, it seems unlikely that one would expect any different pattern of results regarding these deficits in a sample of achievement oriented males. The principle that emerges is that if one lacks or perceives oneself to lack the attitudes, temperament, or behavioral characteristics conducive to the accomplishment of one's goals, in this case career goals, then one will have problems with anxiety and evaluative threat. Any male or female choosing to enter traditionally masculine domains needs to develop the traditionally masculine characteristics which have proven successful there; it is only in this sense that they are "masculine." Whether this masculinity is accompanied by a high degree or low degree of femininity, at least among these female subjects, appears to be irrelevant.

Since not all the variables associated with masculinity in this study were related to trait anxiety, it is possible to further specify the nature of the masculinity deficit. Masculinity as assessed by the BSRI consists essentially of dominance and independence, which are perceived to be socially desirable for males. The specific variables inversely related to trait anxiety suggest that the deficits lie particularly in the areas of positive attitudes toward hard work and high-quality work, positive attitudes toward difficult challenges, and positive attitudes toward the attainment of success.

REFERENCES

Bander, R. S., & Betz, N. E. The relationship of sex and sex-role to trait and situationally specific anxiety types. *Journal of Research in Personality,* 1981, *15,* 312–322.

Bem, S. L. The measurement of psychological androgyny. *Journal of Consulting and Clinical Psychology,* 1974, *42,* 155–162.

Bremer, T. H., & Wittig, M. A. Fear of success: A personality trait or a response to occupational deviance and role overload? *Sex Roles,* 1980, *6,* 27–45.

DeGregorio, E., & Carver, C. S. Type A behavior pattern, sex role orientation, and psychological adjustment. *Journal of Personality and Social Psychology,* 1980, *39,* 286–293.

Helmreich, R. L., & Spence, J. T. The work and family orientation questionnaire: An objective instrument to assess components of achievement motivation and attitudes toward family and career. *JSAS Catalog of Selected Documents in Psychology,* 1978, *8,* 35 (Ms. No. 1677).

Krantz, D. C., Glass, D. C., & Snyder, M. R. Helplessness, stress level and the coronary-prone behavior pattern. *Journal of Experimental Social Psychology,* 1974, *10,* 284–300.

Olds, D. E., & Shaver, P. Masculinity, femininity, academic performance, and health: Further evidence concerning the androgyny controversy. *Journal of Personality,* 1980, *48,* 323–341.

Rotter, J. B. Generalized expectancies for internal versus external control of reinforcement. *Psychological Monographs,* 1966, *80,* No. 1 (Whole No. 609).

Spielberger, C. D., Gorsuch, R. L., & Lushene, R. E. *Manual for the State-Trait Anxiety Inventory.* Palo Alto, CA: Consulting Psychologists Press, 1970.

Zuckerman, M., & Allison, S. N. An objective measure of fear of success: Construction and validation. *Journal of Personality Assessment,* 1976, *40,* 422–430.

5 Two Kinds of Shyness

Arnold H. Buss
University of Texas

We are most familiar with shyness in adults and especially in adolescents. Occurring mainly with people who are strangers or casual acquaintances, shyness may be defined as discomfort, inhibition, or awkwardness in the presence of others. Differing from speech anxiety, which involves the same kind of reaction but only when one is in front of an audience, shyness occurs only in dyadic or other social *interactions* in which there is a back-and-forth responsivity.

The reactions that occur in shyness may be divided into two components, one being more observable than the other. The *instrumental* or action component is more observable. Actually, this component consists mainly of the relative absence of instrumental activity: withdrawal, reticence, and inhibition of speech and gestures. When we are shy, we tend to remain on the fringe of a conversational group, do not speak up, mumble minimal replies if addressed, and generally fail to hold up our end of the social interaction. When the shyness is especially acute, social behavior can become disorganized: clumsy gestures, stuttering, or even tremors.

The *emotional* component, which is less observable, consists of distress that may be accompanied by arousal of the autonomic nervous system. The person experiences feelings of fear, vulnerability, and a transient drop in self-esteem. These feelings and emotions can be so aversive as to motivate an immediate attempt to escape from the social interaction.

The distinction between the instrumental and emotional components of shyness is not the dichotomy referred to in the title of this paper. The title refers to a different assumption, specifically, that the shyness we observe in adults consists of an early-developing kind and a late developing kind. The dichotomy, first suggested in my book on self-consciousness (Buss, 1980, pp. 224–228), will be elaborated, modified, and specified in greater detail.

LATE DEVELOPING SHYNESS

This kind of shyness begins at roughly the fourth or fifth year of life, although it may occur in a few precocious children as early as the third year. It is marked by acute self-consciousness, but only the kind of self-consciousness that ordinarily occurs in social situations. Such public self-awareness involves a focus on those aspects of the self that can be observed by anyone: body, face, clothes, speech, gestures, and manners (Buss, 1980). *Private* self-consciousness, in contrast, involves a focus on those aspects of the self that are not observable by others: sensations, feelings, daydreams about oneself, and self-reflections. When public self-awareness is acute, there is typically a feeling of nakedness and complete exposure to the scrutiny of others, as if there were no barriers to being observed and no place to hide. The intense scrutiny of others, especially when one is engaging in what is ordinarily a private act, may lead to embarrassment, which I construe as the extreme end point of shyness (a conceptual change from my earlier position).

Why do we blush? Why do we experience public self-awareness? I assume that embarrassment and public self-awareness can occur only in those who have a *social self,* which originates in parents and other caretakers telling young children about their impact on others. An important part of socialization is the learning about onself as a social object; when in the presence of others, children gradually become aware of those aspects of themselves that are open to observation and are likely to be noticed. Such awareness is analogous to being the object of others' attention. The difference is that in public self-awareness, both the perceiver and the person being perceived are the same one. This ability to focus on the public aspects of oneself is not present in infants, who lack the necessary advanced cognitions.

The advanced cognitions at issue are part of what I call an advanced, *cognitive self,* which is present only in older children and adults. What about the higher apes, who are capable of mirror-image recognition (Gallup, 1977)? I regard such self-recognition, along with awareness of the boundaries of the body, as aspects of a primitive, *sensory* self. Animals and human infants who have a primitive, sensory self are assumed to lack the advanced cognitions required for a cognitive self. This advanced self may be recognized by attributes present only in older children and adults: self-esteem, understanding the difference between shared and unshared feelings (feelings I have that you cannot observe versus my laughter or anger that you can observe), and knowing that others have a different perspective, which occurs during the fourth or fifth year of life. For an elaboration of these issues, see Buss (1980, pp. 2–5 and 237–240).

In brief, late developing shyness requires an advanced cognitive self that, when combined with appropriate socialization, leads to an awareness of oneself as a social object. Now the person possesses sufficient consciousness to have something to be embarrassed about; now shyness can occur because of an awareness of precisely those aspects of oneself that others may be observing. This is *self-conscious shyness*.

Immediate Causes

An important cause of late developing shyness is either extreme of *attention from others*. It is normal to receive a modicum of social attention, for unless others look at us and listen to us, we cannot engage in social behavior with them. No normal person wishes to be ignored, but the reaction of an infant to being ignored is different from that of older children or adults. Infants demand attention and cry, if necessary. Older children and adults, in contrast, are likely to feel awkward and uncomfortable, and wonder if they have done something wrong (Fenigstein, 1979). The more common problem arises from an excess of social attention, when a person is being stared at or examined closely by others. The discomfort caused by such scrutiny would seem to arise from an association between parental scrutiny and negative comments about the child's public self. It is rare for a parent to point out how good the child's manners are, how neat the child is, or how well the child is behaving. Most of the time, when a parent examines a child, the parent comments about the child's sloppiness, bad manners, inappropriate dress, and generally, about the poor impression the child is likely to make on others. This link between scrutiny and a negative public image tends to make older children and adults uncomfortable whenever they are subjected to the stares of others. Somehow our defenses seem to be stripped away in the same way that earlier in our lives, parents saw immediately what was wrong with our appearance or social behavior. Such discomfort tends to be intensified by the teasing of siblings and peers. It is not so much criticism per se, but exposure of oneself to the cruel spotlight of others' examination.

A closely related cause is the *conspicuousness* that arises from being confronted with the difference between oneself and others in the immediate group. Consider the plight of a girl who walks into a classroom of boys, a jockey surrounded by basketball players, or a white man who enters an elevator filled with Black nuns. In each of these situations, the person is made acutely aware of his or her public self by its distinctiveness, and the almost inevitable reaction is self-conscious shyness.

The more *formal* the situation is, the more likely self-conscious shyness will occur. In formal situations the social script is spelled out in more detail, and adherence to the implicit rules of behavior is more expected and rigidly enforced. The clearest examples are ceremonial, public events, such as funerals, weddings, graduations, religious ceremonies, initiations, and also parties and dinners that are designated as formal. Formality also includes situations in which status is important, especially when there are differences in status. In banks, many businesses, the military, and the clergy, those lower in status are expected to act with a demeanor appropriate to their inferior position, and those of higher status are likely to enforce the "rules." Virtually all formal situations occur in highly public contexts, so that the participants are likely to be observed. In brief, formal situations tend to cause self-conscious shyness because: (1) in the face of more regulations and more specific regulations about behavior, mistakes are more likely, and one solution is to be cautious and inhibited; (2) status tends to be emphasized, which is likely to inhibit the behavior of those of lesser status; and (3) formal situations tend to be so public that the participants feel exposed and vulnerable.

Breaches of privacy tend to cause the most acute form of self-conscious shyness, which is embarrassment. Infants are taught about bodily modesty as soon as they can benefit from such learning. Throughout childhood, an important aspect of socialization is the learning of which acts are permitted in public and which are allowed only in private. Privacy involves not only bodily functions but also social acts that are intimate, as well as daydreams and romantic fantasies that might make a person feel ridiculous if they were disclosed. When a private act is made public or a private sentiment is inadvertently revealed, the reaction is inevitably one of embarrassment, often accompanied by blushing. The only difference between embarrassment and other shyness reactions is the parasympathetic response (blushing) or a feeling of foolishness that exceeds the usual discomfort of acute public self-awareness.

EARLY DEVELOPING SHYNESS

This kind of shyness starts during the first year of life. During the latter half of the first year of life, infants begin to act shy, though this label is ordinarily not used. Earlier investigations used the term *stranger anxiety,* and more recently the term *wariness* has enjoyed wide acceptance. Typical facial expressions are a wary brow and a cry face, and sometimes the infant will start to cry. The child may attempt to hide behind the mother or seek her comfort. Heart rate is typically accelerated. The large literature on wariness has been reviewed by Sroufe (1977). These reactions of the first year of life gradually wane for most children, as both their social and nonsocial fear reactions diminish and they become habituated to a variety of social contexts. For a minority, however, anxiety in the face of novel social situations persists.

In older children, this early developing shyness is characterized less by crying and outright avoidance, and more by those features seen in adults: inhibition or disorganization of speech, shaking voice or limbs, and a worry about future interactions that sometimes borders on phobia. What they are experiencing is a fear that is no different in its reaction from any other fear. The difference lies in the cause of the fear: It is other people, which is why early developing shyness is regarded as a *social anxiety*.

Immediate Causes

One cause of fearful shyness, already suggested, is *social novelty*. Fear of strangers is not limited to infants; it occurs in older children, in adults, and also in animals. Such prudence may be adaptive in that the consequences of being too friendly with a stranger may be catastrophic, whereas the consequences of failing to become friends with a stranger are only mildly negative.

Closely related as a cause is *intrusiveness*. Infants may become frightened if a stranger approaches too quickly, and adults tend to become edgy when even an acquaintance comes too close. Hall (1966) has suggested that there are spatial zones surrounding each of us, which we prefer not to be penetrated by most people. Outside of a few intimates, we tend to react with discomfort or even fear when others approach too closely.

As children mature, they start to evaluate others and *are evaluated* in turn. The usual criteria are attractiveness, modesty, friendliness, and whether the object of the evaluation meets various standards of comportment and conformity to social rules. As we like or dislike others, so others are reacting to us in similar ways. To discover that one might not be liked or that one might be disliked is sufficient to cause concern, reticence, and social caution — all hallmarks of shyness. Children must of course possess sufficient maturity to be aware of such evaluation, and therefore fear of rejection is a cause of shyness only later in childhood and never in infancy.

SELF-CONSCIOUS VERSUS FEARFUL SHYNESS

The two kinds of shyness are compared in Table 5.1 The early kind appears in the first year of life; the late kind appears during the fourth or fifth year of life, although an occasional precocious child might show it a year earlier. Early developing shyness requires no special sense of self, but there is a primitive self in the social animals (including humans) who manifest fearful shyness: It is a sensory self, which is inferred on the basis of the distinction between self and other that such animals are capable of making. Later developing shyness cannot occur until there is a sense of oneself as a social object. Neither animals nor human infants possess such self-awareness, presumably because they lack the advanced cognitive ability that underlies such a social self. This advanced self is inferred not only from the occurrence of embarrassment but also from the presence of self-esteem and the ability to understand that others' perspectives are different.

TABLE 5.1
Two Kinds of Shyness

	Early Developing	Later Developing
first appearance	first year	fourth-fifth year
kind of self	sensory	cognitive
affective response	fear, wariness	acute self-awareness, embarrassment
autonomic reaction (if any)	sympathetic	parasympathetic

immediate causes	novelty
	intrusion
	evaluation:
	    fear of
	      rejection*
		extremes of social attention
		being (feeling) conspicuous
		formality: rules, status*
		breach of privacy

*These causes do not start until late childhood and have peak impact at adolescence.

Note: Early developing shyness occurs in animals, too; late developing shyness occurs only in humans.

The affective response in early developing shyness is fear or its milder form, wariness. The autonomic aspects of fear involves a dominance of the sympathetic division of the autonomic nervous system. The affective response in later developing shyness is acute public self-awareness, the extreme of which is embarrassment. This kind of shyness is usually accompanied by no autonomic arousal, but if the self-consciousness is extreme and blushing occurs, it is obviously a parasympathetic phenomenon.

The immediate causes of early developing shyness are social novelty, intrusion of one's personal space by another, and (later in development) evaluation by others and its consequent fear of rejection.[1] The immediate causes of late developing shyness are being ignored or closely observed by others, being conspicuously different from others, formal situations involving rules, status, and public contexts, and breaches of privacy, which usually cause embarrassment. There is a sense in which novelty is also a cause of late developing shyness. When we first meet others, we tend to focus on the observable aspects of ourselves, just as we also focus on the observable aspects of those whom we are meeting. Thus novelty immediately leads to a feeling of conspicuousness, a feeling that those we are meeting are observing us. As such, any shyness must be attributed to conspicuousness per se and not to the fact of

---

[1]It may appear paradoxical to list a cause of early developing shyness—in this case, fear of rejection—which occurs later in childhood. The shyness ordinarily begins during the first year of life, but events that occur later in childhood can either maintain this shyness or intensify it.

novelty, hence the absence of novelty as an immediate cause of late developing shyness in Table 5.1

SHYNESS AS A PERSONALITY TRAIT

We know from causal observations of everyday life that there are marked individual differences in shyness. Some people are so inhibited that they avoid job interviews, and at the opposite end of the dimension, others display considerable social initiative and interact without inhibition. Shyness is rarely measured as an isolated trait. It is more often found as part of a personality questionnaire or extraversion or sociability. Perhaps shyness has rarely been measured by itself because most psychologists implicitly regard it as nothing more than low sociability. If that were true and we assessed sociability and shyness separately, the correlation between the two should be strongly negative.

There is now empirical evidence on this issue (Cheek & Buss, 1981). It was necessary first to define sociability and shyness independently, for otherwise they would be related merely by definition. Therefore, sociability was defined as the tendency to affiliate with others and to prefer being with them. Shyness was defined as being tense, inhibited, and uncomfortable in the presence of strangers or casual acquaintances. Items were constructed to assess either sociability or shyness, and the resulting 14-item questionnaire was administered to over 912 college students. A factor analysis yielded two factors, one for sociability and one for shyness, as follows:

Shyness

I am socially somewhat awkward.
I don't find it hard to talk to strangers.
I feel tense when I'm with people I don't know well.
When conversing I worry about saying something dumb.
I feel nervous when speaking to someone in authority.
I am often uncomfortable at parties and other social functions.
I feel inhibited in social situations.
I have trouble looking someone right in the eye.
I am more shy with members of the opposite sex.

Sociability

I like to be with people.
I welcome the opportunity to mix socially with people.
I prefer working with others rather than alone.
I find people more stimulating than anything else.
I'd be unhappy if I were prevented from making many social contacts.

The shyness and sociability scales correlated $-.30$, a significant relationship suggesting that to some extent shyness represents low sociability. The size of the correlation, however, denies that shyness is nothing more than low sociability. Though related, the two traits are sufficiently independent for there to be sizable minorities who are both sociable and shy, and both unsociable and unshy. Furthermore, in a study of social behavior at first acquaintance, both the sociability and shyness traits were significant determiners of how people acted (Cheek & Buss, 1981).

Given the theoretical perspective of this paper, the trait of shyness must consist of both public self-consciousness (late developing shyness) and fearfulness (early developing shyness). The trait of public self-consciousness can be assessed by the following scale, which emerged from a factor analysis of self-consciousness items (Fenigstein, Scheier, & Buss, 1975; see also Buss, 1980):

> I'm concerned about my style of doing things.
> I'm concerned about the way I present myself.
> I'm self-conscious about the way I look.
> One of the last things I do before I leave my house is look in the mirror.
> I'm concerned about what other people think of me.
> I'm usually aware of my appearance.
> I usually worry about making a good impression.

When this scale and the shyness scale mentioned earlier were given to 912 college students, the correlation was .26. The shyness scale was also correlated with a self-report measure of fearfulness (Buss & Plomin, 1975). The fearfulness items are:

> I am often insecure.
> I am easily frightened.
> I have fewer fears than most people my age. (reversed)
> When I get scared, I panic.
> I tend to be nervous in new situations.

This fearfulness scale, which contains no items that refer to fear in specifically social situations, correlated .50 with the shyness scale. The difference between these two correlations with shyness, .50 for fearfulness and .26 for public self-consciousness, suggests that in adults, the trait of shyness tilts more toward the early developing kind (fear) than toward the later developing kind (self-consciousness). Part of the reason for the higher correlation with fearfulness may be the content of three of the shyness items:

I feel *tense* when I'm with people I don't know well.
When conversing, I *worry* about saying something dumb.
I feel *nervous* when speaking to someone in authority.

Each of these items contains a term (italicized) associated with fear: tense, worry, and nervous. The presence of these items may have resulted in the higher correlation between fear and shyness.

Aside from this possible artifact, there may be a logical reason for the higher correlation between shyness and fear. Fear is a more intense emotion than public self-consciousness; we are certainly more upset and disturbed when afraid than when embarrassed. If this assumption is correct, people with the most intense shyness are likely to be fearful, and people who are only a little shy are likely to be self-conscious. Though logical, this hypothesis needs to be tested, preferably in a laboratory where social behavior might be observed.

Personality Determinants

The task here is to specify the personality traits underlying individual differences in both kinds of shyness. Let us start with early developing shyness, which must originate, at least in part, from the trait of fearfulness. We cannot infer causation merely from the correlation of .50 between fearfulness and shyness. Fearfulness, however, has been shown to have a genetic component (Buss & Plomin, 1975), which seems to be a reasonable basis for inferring that it causes shyness rather than that shyness causes fearfulness.

Once the tendency to be shy is established through fearfulness, it may be maintained by low sociability. The unsociable child, by definition, has a weaker motivation to be with others and is less rewarded by their company. Such a child is more likely to avoid making new friends and meeting strangers, and he or she is less likely to remain in a social interaction because the rewards are insufficient. As a consequence, there is less opportunity for habituation to novelty to occur, and novel social situations are likely to continue to elicit fear and a tendency to avoid or escape them.

Late developing shyness would seem to originate in two different personality traits. Public self-consciousness must be involved, almost by definition. Some parents and caretakers oversocialize children, telling them early and often that they are constantly being observed and that their impact on others is of crucial importance. Such children tend to be corrected frequently for defects in appearance, manners, and social behavior generally. As a result, they develop acute public self-consciousness and are likely to feel tense and awkward in public social situations and also inhibit spontaneous social behavior.

Low self-esteem can also cause people to feel as though others are watching them and are likely to notice the inferiority they prefer to hide (people low in self-esteem may not be inferior, but they feel inferior, by definition). The correlation between shyness and self-esteem is $-.51$, which again raises the issue of the direction of causation. This time the issue is more difficult to resolve because shyness might cause low self-esteem, just as low self-esteem might cause shyness. Self-esteem, however, is a broader concept, encompassing evaluation of oneself in a variety of nonsocial as well as social arenas of life. This suggests that shyness is more likely to be part of and therefore derivative from low self-esteem rather than the opposite. This conclusion, however, must be regarded as highly tentative. Suffice it to say that low self-esteem must be considered a *potential* cause of shyness, one that is more speculative than the others.

It may not have escaped notice that the four personality traits just described differ not only in their connection with one or the other kind of shyness but also in their own origins. Both fearfulness and sociability have been shown in behavioral genetics research to have an inherited component (Buss & Plomin, 1975). These two traits contribute to early developing shyness but not to late developing shyness. Public self-consciousness originates in the way children are socialized, as has already been discussed. Self-esteem is believed by most psychologists to originate in the way children are treated by parents and other important figures and also by the children's individual experiences. Self-esteem and public self-consciousness, both of environmental origin, contribute to late developing shyness but not to early developing shyness. Thus in terms of personality trait determinants of shyness, early developing shyness originates in inherited traits, and late developing shyness originates in environmental traits.

The formulation has several implications. Even the current measures of the trait of shyness that are uncontaminated by sociability do not differentiate between fearful and self-conscious shyness. This distinction would seem to be important in any attempt at remediation of shyness. For fearful shyness, the treatment of choice might be systematic desensitization, in which the client learns to relax to increasingly feared stimuli. For self-conscious shyness, treatment might focus on ways for the person to divert attention from himself or herself.

The distinction between the two kinds of shyness also has implications for who is at risk for shyness. The young child who is high in the temperament of emotionality, from which fearfulness differentiates, is likely to develop fearful shyness, which tends to be maintained by low sociability. The child who undergoes stricter and more intense socialization by parents and other caretakers is likely to develop self-conscious shyness, as is the child who is low in self-esteem. These various implications, which are testable hypotheses, will ultimately reveal whether this formulation is worthwhile beyond any advantage in integrating the diverse phenomena and determinants of shyness.

REFERENCES

Buss, A. H. *Self-consciousness and social anxiety.* San Francisco: Freeman, 1980.

Buss, A. H., & Plomin, R. *A temperament theory of personality development.* New York: Wisely-Interscience, 1975.

Cheek, J. H., & Buss, A. H. Shyness and sociability. *Journal of Personality and Social Psychology,* 1981, *41,* 330–339.

Fenigstein, A. Self-consciousness, self-attention, and social interaction. *Journal of Personality and Social Psychology,* 1979, *37,* 75–86.

Fenigstein, A., Scheier, M. F., & Buss, A. H. Public and private self-consciousness: Assessment and theory. *Journal of Consulting and Clinical Psychology,* 1975, *43,* 522–527.

Gallup, G. G., Jr. Self-recognition in primates: A comparative approach to the bidirectional properties of consciousness. *American Psychologist,* 1977, *32,* 329–338.

Hall, E. T. *The hidden dimension.* Garden City, NY: Doubleday, 1966.

Sroufe, L. A. Wariness of strangers and the study of infant development. *Child Psychology,* 1977, *48,* 731–746.

6 Social Support, Social Behavior, and Cognitive Processes

Barbara R. Sarason
University of Washington

Until recently most of the literature on social support has been clinical, impressionistic, and speculative. This literature has been valuable in directing attention to the relevance of social ties to personal adjustment. However, there has been sufficient research that employs the careful controls and manipulations characteristic of experiments. This paper describes a series of laboratory studies dealing with behavioral and cognitive dimensions of social support. It is hoped that this approach will contribute to the specification of mediational processes that may be involved in the clinical phenomena that have been extensively described.

Studies of social support have proliferated dramatically in recent years for a variety of reasons. Observations in a variety of settings have highlighted the positive roles played by social attachments and psychological adjustment in health. Health professionals daily note the salutary effects of their attention and expressed concern on patient's well-being in recovery from illness. Psychotherapists try to provide their clients with the acceptance needed to pursue self-examination. Soldiers develop strong, mutually reinforcing ties with each other that contribute to their success in survival. In addition to this generally informal observational data, United States military experience in Vietnam produced evidence of the importance of social support under stress to later well being. The readjustment problems among Vietnam veterans are unusually high; recent estimates place these problems affecting anywhere from 20% to 60% of veterans (Friedman, 1981). Several causes for this high rate of post-stress syndrome have been suggested. The war was a controversial one and many members of the military did not feel that the public displayed sympathy and backing for their efforts and sacrifices. Perhaps even more important was a change in military procedure in which, unlike the practice in previous wars, soldiers entered and left the Vietnam combat area as individuals, not as cohesive groups.

Theorists have also stimulated work on social support. Perhaps one of the most influential of these is John Bowlby, whose theory of attachment has generated research into the supportive role of social relationships for both adults and children (Bowlby, 1969, 1980). Spurred on by both formal and informal theories, researchers have begun to investigate in a systematic fashion a variety of aspects of social support including how it contributes to positive adjustment and personal development and also the way it provides a buffer against the effects of stress. Several hundred articles have been published in the past few years that deal with social support, particularly with regard to the health consequences of its presence or absence.

Despite the growth in interest in the topic of social support, the task of empirically demonstrating its effects and especially of specifying the mechanisms involved in these effects has barely begun. One of the barriers to objective research has been the lack of a reliable, general, and convenient index of social support. Some researchers have simply gathered information about subjects' confidants and acquaintances; others have focused their attention on the availability of helpful others in coping with certain work, family, and financial problems; and still others have devised questionnaires and other techniques to assess social support. These devices range from simple paper and pencil scales to detailed interview schedules.

The diversity of measures of social support is matched by the diversity of conceptualizations concerning its ingredients. However, regardless of how it is conceptualized, social support would seem to have two basic elements: (1) number of available others to whom one can turn in time of need and (2) degree of satisfaction with the available support. Sarason, Levine, Basham, and Sarason (1983) have recently constructed an instrument, the Social Support Questionnaire, that reliably assesses these dimensions of social support. The Social Support Questionnaire (SSQ) seems to be a reliable, psychometrically satisfactory instrument. Scores on the SSQ seem more strongly related to positive than negative life changes, and have an inverse relationship to psychological discomfort, although this last relationship is stronger among women than men. Social support as measured by the SSQ also seems to be an asset in enabling a person to persist in a task under frustrating conditions.

As mentioned above, most of the research carried out on social support has been conducted in clinical and applied settings. There are several reasons for suggesting a need for experimental studies of social support. One of these is the greater degree of control in a laboratory setting, and another is the possibility of deriving more objective and reliable dependent measures. Laboratory studies hold the promise of specifying some of the behavioral and cognitive mechanisms that may be involved in social support. In particular, the time now seems ripe for studies that investigate social support simultaneously from assessment and experimental standpoints.

SELF DESCRIBED SOCIAL SUPPORT, SOCIAL BEHAVIOR, AND SELF RELATED COGNITIONS

One of the most important questions about social support concerns the relationship between social support and social skills. Do people have many or few social supports because of their levels of social skill? Conversely, to what degree can social skills be regarded as outcomes of socially supportive experiences in one's life? Social support and social skills may be related in complex ways. Clinical, developmental, and experimental studies are needed to provide information about these relationships.

Probably the first question to be answered is whether social skills and a high level of perceived social support are related. Only then should questions of causality be addressed. In a study designed to look at this relationship, pairs of subjects differing in social support scores were videotaped first while they spent 5 minutes getting acquainted and then another 5 minutes discussing how to solve a hypothetical problem about a troublesome roommate (Sarason, Sarason, Hacker, & Basham, in press). Each subject's social skills were then rated by the experimenter on the basis of his initial contact with the subject, by both the subject and the subject's partner after the role plays, and finally by raters who viewed the videotape. Raters also assessed subject's physical attractiveness from color snapshots. In addition, the subjects completed a social competence questionnaire and several problem solving tasks designed to measure social skills. These were modeled after the Means-Ends-Problem-Solving (MEPS) story format developed by Platt and Spivack (1975). Subjects were given the beginnings and endings of situations and the task of the subject was to link the beginnings and the endings: "Your job is to make up a story which connects the beginning that is given you with the ending given you. In other words, you make up the middle of the story." An example of the stories is as follows:

> (Beginning) I am eating my lunch. Another person is sitting across the table from me eating lunch, and also reading a magazine. The person seems pleasant, and I think I would enjoy talking with the person . . .
> (Middle) (Fill-in. Please be as complete as possible)
> (Outcome) . . . We have a nice talk and decide to meet again.

Subjects high in self-described social support scored higher than those low in social support on all of these social skill measures. Those low in social support were described on all measures as less likeable and less effective. Of special interest was the high correlations among the subject's appraisal of his or her own social competence, the appraisals of others, and the subject's competence as measured by knowledge of appropriate behavior in problem situations.

Not only did both those high and low in social support elicit different responses from others, they also seemed to have different cognitions in social situations. Those low in social support described themselves as feeling uncomfortable when looking at others directly, having problems in getting people to notice them, and lacking confidence in their ability to make friends. An interesting sex difference was also observed. Men's self-ratings were higher than those of women although men tended to be rated lower than women by both the experimenter and by those rating their performance from the videotapes.

Although this study does not directly address causal factors in the social skills-social support relationship, it is interesting that those high in social support were rated as more physically attractive than low social support individuals by raters who saw only a color photograph of each subject. This suggests that if people respond more positively to physically attractive persons, the high social support individual has a kind of built in advantage.

ADMINISTERED SOCIAL SUPPORT AND PROBLEM SOLVING

The main focus of the Sarason, Sarason, Hacker, and Basham study just described was the relationship of social support to skillful social behavior and to adaptive cognitions regarding such behavior. The study also demonstrated that people high in self-described support are able to set forth more effective solutions to hypothetical problems than can those low in social support.

Another study (Lindner, 1982) investigated the relationship of problem solving skills and social support levels as well as the role of experimentally administered social support on this type of problem solving. Some of the stories used by Lindner were of the type described earlier, others related to more emotionally loaded situations:

H. loved his girlfriend very much, but they had many arguments. One day she left him. H. wanted things to be better. The story ends with everything fine between him and his girlfriend. You begin the story with his girlfriend leaving him after an argument.

One group of subjects was provided with experimental social support. This was in the form of the following communication:

Some of you will feel uneasy about writing stories. Remember that you are not the only person who feels this way. Just relax and do your best. Do you have any questions? I'll be available to you throughout your work to answer any more questions you have. After you are done, please take your stories next door and there will be someone to debrief you and give you any more information that you should want or need.

The relevant ingredient in this communication was telling the subject that he or she could obtain help if needed (in fact, no subjects sought the help of the experimenter). Other groups of subjects were told either that no questions were allowed or perfunctorily asked for questions at the end of the instruction without including either the statement on debriefing or the empathetic sentence recognizing possible subject discomfort with the task.

Lindner, like Sarason, Sarason, Hacker, and Basham found that high assessed social support subjects told stories that were rated as being more effective than the low assessed social support subjects. She also found important interactions between levels of assessed social support and experimentally provided social support. In general, when people with less assessed social support were offered support during the problem solving process, the quality of their solutions was better than the solutions of the low SSQ scorers who were not offered support. In fact, the quality of solutions given by people with low SSQ scores who were also given experimental support improved to within the range of the quality of those with high SSQ scores. Whereas experimenter-provided social support was a definite asset to performance for low social support subjects, the performance of high SSQ subjects was not improved by the experimental conditions. The low assessed support subjects were also much more likely to emphasize cognitive activity in their stories than the high SSQ subjects. They stressed thinking about the problem more than the high SSQ subjects, although this thinking about the problem was not followed by a high quality solution. People with high-assessed social support tended to describe problem solving behavior as occurring without a great deal of prior cognitive activity of thinking about what to do in the situation. It is possible that those low in social support think so much about what to do that their effective action is compromised. This interpretation of becoming "bogged down" in thinking is also suggested by the earlier finding of a negative relationship between SSQ scores and the Neuroticism scale of the Eysenck Personality Inventory (Eysenck & Eysenck, 1975) and by Sarason and his coworkers (Sarason, Levine, Basham, & Sarason, 1983).

Lindner also found that subjects with high- and low-assessed social support reported different types of cognitions during the experiment as measured by the Cognitive Interference Questionnaire (CIQ) (Sarason & Stoops, 1978). Somewhat surprisingly, those with low assessed social support reported less cognitive interference than high assessed support. Lindner interpreted the cognitive interference reported by high SSQ individuals not as worry, but as a greater receptivity to cues in the environment which in turn provide guidance for the best solution to certain kinds of interpersonal situations. It may also be that those high in social support were more confident about their social abilities and felt they could afford to let their minds wander. People with low assessed social support seem to have difficulty making decisions in problem solving situations and feel less confident about their solutions even if the solutions are judged to be good ones by others. Lindner further found that experimental interventions in terms of an offer of support can counteract the difference in performance between high and low social support subjects but not the difference in the reported cognitive activity or feelings of confidence (or lack of it) that differ in the two groups.

ADMINISTERED SOCIAL SUPPORT AND TEST ANXIETY

Lindner's study strongly suggests the value of experimentally manipulating social support. In an earlier study, Sarason (1981) employed a social support manipulation in an experiment with subjects who differed in test anxiety. Social support was provided by a group discussion focused on sharing concerns and solutions concerning students' problems of stress and anxiety in testing situations. Several confederates worked to heighten social association by suggesting a meeting after the experimental session. The group discussion was followed by an anagrams task which was presented as a separate, unrelated experiment run by another experimenter that was combined into the same session for the sake of efficiency.

The results showed that performance and self-preoccupation as measured by the CIQ were affected by this specially created opportunity for social association and acceptance by others. Performance on the anagrams task increased and self-preoccupation decreased as a function of the social support manipulation. However, this change was pronounced only in subjects who were high in anxiety as measured by the Test Anxiety Scale (TAS) (Sarason, 1978). The performance of those low in test anxiety was essentially unchanged by the support manipulation. This finding parallels Lindner's result using assessed social support rather than anxiety as the independent variable.

In a recent study dealing with the same general problem, the measure of test anxiety was the total score on the Reactions to Tests (RTT), a new multidimensional measure of test anxiety (Sarason, 1984). In this study, Sarason and Türk (1983) investigated various ways of teaching strategies that might be useful in coping with testing situations. One group received a written summary of five coping strategies. These were: (1) approach the test with a clear mind and a positive attitude, (2) don't start the test pitying yourself, (3) don't let your mind wander, (4) pay no attention to what others are doing, and (5) don't panic if your mind goes blank on specific items. In a second condition, these same five coping strategies were presented in a group discussion situation in which subjects were asked to talk about these topics for 5 minutes. In a third condition, the subjects also spent 5 minutes in a free-wheeling discussion about testing situations. Another experimental group was a distraction condition in which subjects wrote an essay about problems related to school (but not dealing with test taking problems). In addition, there was an untreated control condition.

Following these initial treatments all subjects were given the task of solving moderately difficult anagrams. While Sarason and Türk made a number of comparisons between subjects differing in test anxiety, only the findings pertaining to the experimentally created conditions are described here, since these are the ones most clearly linked to the social support construct. When the coping strategies were presented in written format, there was no significant influence over either subjects' performance or their perceptions of their performance. However, when the coping strategies were presented in a group setting, that is, where the strategies were discussed among the college students who were the subjects, performance reached relatively high levels. The group setting in which a free-wheeling discussion took place was not nearly as effective as the coping skill discussion, but was comparable in performance to the group that read about coping strategies. Therefore, helpful strategies per se or interaction alone were not sufficient to have any effects on the performance of subjects. The combination of information and support appeared to be the relevant factors. A further interesting result was the improved performance of high-anxious subjects under the distraction condition in which subjects wrote essays. Although not quite as effective as the group coping strategies condition, writing an essay apparently served to distract high test-anxious subjects from their self-preoccupations and thus improved their performance.

The most interesting aspect of the Sarason and Türk study from the present focus was the effects of the treatments on cognitive interference. Paralleling the performance differences discussed above were differences in self-preoccupation as assessed by the CIQ. In the group engaged in discussion of coping strategies, decreases in CIQ scores accompanied increases in performance. This result may provide a clue that cognitive mechanisms may play an important role in the relationship between social support and at least some types of performance.

REACTIONS TO SOCIAL SITUATIONS

The studies described thus far have dealt specifically with both assessed and manipulated social support and their relationship to performance and to an individual's cognitive behavior. Because the perception of social support can be viewed as an outgrowth of people's cognitive responses in social situations, Sarason and Sarason have recently developed an instrument, Reactions to Social Situations (RSS), which parallels the Reactions to Tests instrument in format and content. While the Reactions to Social Situations will be described in more detail in a later report, it is relevant to report here that anxiety experienced in social situations, and particularly worry over one's performance in social situations, is very significantly related to cognitive interference as measured by a special version of the CIQ. While much more research is needed to map the constructs involved in the RSS, data we have gathered thus far suggests that cognitive interference, especially self-preoccupation, is related to worry over social performance just as worry over test taking performance is also linked to cognitive interference.

DISCUSSION

I have tried in this paper to characterize briefly recent experimental work on the social support construct, particularly as it applies to characteristics of individuals who describe themselves as high or low in social support and to the interaction between assessed social support characteristics and experimentally provided social support. The results of these studies support the idea that concepts like social support and social anxiety are amenable to objective study and, in particular, to experimental investigations. In general, the results are consistent with the idea that when people are placed in social situations that arouse worries and preoccupations about self-adequacy, self-reported cognitive interference increases and performance is affected.

An interesting observation arising from this review of some recent experiments is that a supportive intervention is helpful in improving the performance of both highly test-anxious individuals and those low in self-described social support, but that such interventions do not alter performance level for those low in anxiety or high in self-described social support. Previous evidence has shown that the TAS and the SSQ are not significantly correlated (Sarason, 1980). This improved performance was not related to a change in reported level of cognitive interference for the social support variable, but was accompanied by a decrease in cognitive interference for highly anxious individuals.

The question of the relationship of cognitive interference to performance, to personality factors and to skills level, is a complex one. Teasing out these intricate relationships has important theoretical and practical implications.

REFERENCES

Bowlby, J. *Attachment and loss* (Vol. 1). *Attachment*. New York. Basic Books, 1969.

Bowlby, J. *Attachment and loss* (Vol. 3). *Loss: Sadness and Depression.* New York: Basic Books, 1980.

Eysenck, H. J., & Eysenck, S. B. G. *Manual of the Eysenck personality questionnaire.* London: University of London Press, 1975.

Friedman, M. J. Post-Vietnam syndrome: Recognition and management. *Psychosomatics,* 1981, *22,* 931–943.

Lindner, K. C. *Life change, social support and cognitive problem-solving skills.* Unpublished doctoral dissertation. University of Washington, 1982.

Platt, J. J., & Spivack, G. *Manual for the means-ends problem-solving procedure.* Philadelphia: Department of Mental Health Sciences, Hahnemann Community Mental Health/Mental Retardation Center, 1975.

Sarason, B. R., Sarason, I. G., Hacker, T. A., & Basham, R. B. Concomitants of social support: Social skills, gender, and physical attractiveness. *Journal of Personality and Social Psychology* (in press).

Sarason, I. G. The test anxiety scale: Concept and research. In C. D. Spielberger & I. G. Sarason (Eds.), *Stress and anxiety* (Vol. 5). Washington, DC: Hemisphere, 1978.

Sarason, I. G. Unpublished data. 1980.

Sarason, I. G. Test anxiety, stress, and social support. *Journal of Personality,* 1981, *49,* 101–114.

Sarason, I. G. Stress, anxiety and cognitive interference: Reactions to tests. *Journal of Personality and Social Psychology,* 1984, *46,* 929–932.

Sarason, I. G., Levine, H. M., Basham, R. B., & Sarason, B. R. Assessing social support: The social support questionnaire. *Journal of Personality and Social Psychology,* 1983, *44,* 127–139.

Sarason, I. G., & Stoops, R. Test anxiety and the passage of time. *Journal of Consulting and Clinical Psychology,* 1978, *46,* 102–109.

Sarason, I. G., & Türk, S. *Coping strategies and group interaction: Their function in improving performance of anxious individuals.* Unpublished paper, 1983.

7 Coping With Life Events: When the Self Comes Into Play

Sigrun-Heide Filipp
Peter Aymanns
Walter Braukmann
University of Trier

SELF-ATTENTION AND COPING: TWO DOMAINS OF RESEARCH IN NEED OF INTEGRATION

The present chapter represents one of the few attempts to interrelate two areas of research, which to date have not taken much notice of each other, although simultaneous consideration of both seems to be highly valuable. It is argued here that coping with life-events can be far more precisely predicted and explained with regard to the selection of certain modes of coping as well as their referential outcomes, if theorizing on self-focused attention is related to the issue of coping.

Of course, it has been stated quite frequently that processes of attentive regulation play an important role when individuals cope with critical life-events or with any other stressful situation. Sometimes these processes have even been equated with special modes of coping itself. However, the self-focus in attention has not gained much interest in coping research as a distinct phenomenon, although many assumptions proposed by self-attention theory almost call for verification in the field of coping behavior as well.

We briefly summarize in this section the main issues of self-attention theory and its empirical realization as well as some of the basic questions addressed in coping research. The next section is directed to bridging the gap between both areas of research.

Self-Attention Theory: A Brief Overview

The interest in self-reflective processes and self-referent thought has a long tradition within psychology; even scientific paradigms (e.g., psychoanalysis) are routed from here and are based almost completely on knowledge about human behavior that stems from individuals' self-reflections and introspections. Accordingly, within the last decade various therapeutic approaches have postulated the importance of a person to directing his or her attention to internal processes and private events as a main condition for behavioral change; for example Meichenbaum's (1975) self-instruction training, Kanfer's (1975) self-management technique, and Gendlin's (1974) "focusing approach." Also, Bandura's (1977) highly popular concept of "self-efficacy" points to the fact that "the self" is well and alive in today's psychology.

Within social psychology the concept of "objective self-awareness," proposed by Duval and Wicklund (1972), has become very prominent in hundreds of studies aimed at demonstrating the effects of self-awareness on human behavior in diverse domains. We briefly summarize here how self-attention was originally conceptualized, how the concept has meanwhile been modified, and what still seems to be in need of clarification. In doing this, we refer to the conditions that direct an individual's attention to his or her self and to the consequences of self-attention that have been repeatedly observed by various authors.

One basic, though hardly controversial, assumption in self-attention is that attentional focus determines to a large extent how reality is perceived and construed, and how the individual responds to it. It is proposed that attentional focus can be seen as dichotomized simply in terms of whether it is directed to objects outside the person (environmental focus) or to the self. Being in the state of self-focused attention, the individual is seen to generate self-relevant information, to seek out knowledge about his or her attitudes, aspirations, motives, feelings, and so on. The individual is considered to be the object of his own epistemic activities.

According to the theory of self-focused attention, this condition is created by all situational cues, which remind the person of his or her status as an object, for example being reflected in a mirror, hearing one's voice, or being observed by others. Recently it has been proposed by Hormuth (1983) that — in analogy to the figure-ground shift in perception — self-directed attention also comes about when an individual finds himself as a stranger in a highly unfamiliar environment. Furthermore, it is assumed that the individual will not dwell on those cues that created the self-focus, but will selectively attend to some self-aspect salient within that particular situation, whatever aspect that might be. The theory originally was not very precise in predicting what self-aspect would really be salient in a given situation (unless it had been manipulated experimentally), and this issue still remains unclear (cf. Carver, 1979 and Carver & Scheier, 1981).

By referring to general assumptions formulated in information processing theories (see also Hull & Levy, 1979, for that theoretical framework in their self-attention concept), it is suggested that sensoric input (stemming from either internal or external stimulation) will be compared to recognitory schemes or prototypes stored in memory:

> If the prototypes to which the environmental inputs correspond have cue implications for some specific self-information, the self-information is probably accessed (in a preliminary pre-attentive fashion) by the very process of classifying the environmental input. The aspect of self that is represented by that self-information presumably will be more salient than other self-aspects when attention is subsequently directed inward (Carver, 1979, p. 1260).

It therefore becomes clear why some self-aspects should become salient in a particular experimental situation, for example sexual attitudes (Gibbons, 1978), yet still leave the question open whether or not the subject indeed is focusing upon exactly that self-aspect.

Another basic theoretical assumption is related to the consequences of self-awareness. Self-awareness is supposed to lead to awareness of behavioral standards and aspirations, and, hence, to a comparison between "is" and "ought." In general, the individual will recognize some negative discrepancy between aspirations and actual behavioral outcomes, which is supposed to induce a negative affective state. This is one core assumption in Duval and Wicklund's (1972) formulation, and it is predicted that this negative state has powerful motivational effects on behavior in order to terminate the state of self-awareness. If this cannot be accomplished because self-focused attention is further maintained by external cues and because the situation cannot be escaped from, the individual will try to modify his or her behavior in accordance with his or her aspirations and standards. In short, the recognition of some discrepancy and the resulting negative affect motivates a change in behavior, thus creating a higher consistency between behavioral standards (norms, attitudes) and actual behavior.

The assumption that attending to the self is, in general, an aversive experience which has drive-like motivational consequences, is highly controversial within self-attention theory. Carver and Scheier (1981), by proposing a cybernetic model of self-regulatory processes, suggest that behavior is controlled by a system of hierarchically organized feedback-loops. This implies that behavioral standards can be formulated at different levels within that hierarchy and that a comparison between reference value and behavior is made continuously at a preattentive level. It is important here to note that these comparison processes are conceived of as affectively neutral, and therefore the reduction of discrepancies is not motivated by ending a negative state. Only when the efforts to reduce the discrepancy are interrupted by some event and when the individual additionally has low expectancies to overcome that hindrance, a negative affective state is likely to result. One central thesis in this formulation is that to correct or control one's course of action self-attention is required, which can be concentrated at different levels of control, such as the *sequence*-level for the control of motoric activities, or the level of logical or moral *principles*. Whatever level within the hierarchy is focused upon attentionally, it will provide the individual with a reference value or standard by which behavior can be corrected.

Self-attention theory has stimulated a host of experimental studies aimed at demonstrating the effects of self-focused attention in various behavioral domains. Some general conclusions from these studies can be drawn: Self-aware individuals have more accurate knowledge about their actual desires, inner states, and attitudes; they exhibit more non-ambiguous, highly differentiated self-descriptions; their self-reports have higher predictive validity for future behavior, and they behave in closer correspondence with their attitudes and beliefs. These phenomena have been interpreted, in general, as a result of the "matching-to-standard" process and as a result of a greater knowledge of and deeper insight into the self (Buss, 1980).

For example, if subjects are given false feedback on their physiological arousal, their suggestibility to that feedback is clearly reduced under conditions of self-awareness (cf. Gibbons, Carver, Scheier, & Hormuth, 1979). Self-attention causes the individual to examine proprioceptive information in a much more precise manner. At the same time, self-aware individuals are very sensitive to variations in their internal states and feelings. If the individual is emotionally aroused, self-awareness will intensify that affective state, as has been demonstrated for various affective states and reactions (e.g., aggression, Scheier, 1976; elation and depression, Scheier & Carver, 1977; fear, Scheier, Carver, & Gibbons, 1981). Using an analogy from optics, one could say that self-attention functions like a glass that concentrates incoming light rays: whatever is in focus will be exaggerated, intensified, and become overwhelming.

From this line of reasoning, it does not seem surprising that a high degree of self-awareness does not always exert a beneficial effect on behavior in terms of being more civilized and consistent (Wicklund & Frey, 1980). This can be demonstrated in situations where, because of self-attention, a course of action is interrupted, which results in failure to complete the action or task. Carver, Blaney, and Scheier (1979) report that self-aware subjects persist significantly less on a second task after experiencing failure than subjects lacking self-awareness. In this case, giving up too early and not accomplishing one's standard is the consequence of self-awareness. Similarly, expectancy of success induced by the first task will result in increased persistence in the second task only in the self-aware group. The results of this study clearly demonstrate that self-attention exaggerates the influence that other variables such as expectancies exert on behavior. This general effect can be considered especially dysfunctional in those situations, where persons hold low outcome expectancies, and in which higher self-focus will create a drop in motivation (Scheier & Carver, 1982).

Self-attention theory has also offered an explanation for the frequently described "bystander phenomenon", i.e. the tendency of individuals not to exhibit helping behavior when they are anonymous members of a group of people (Wegner & Schaefer, 1978). Finally, it has been demonstrated that causal attributions of success and failure do differ dependent on whether the individual is high or low in self-awareness (Duval & Wicklund, 1972). Thus, the heterogenity of behavioral domains that seem to be affected by self-focus of attention as well as the fact that numerous results have been replicated, represents an impressive amount of empirical validation.

So far, no distinction has been made as to which domain of the self is primarily focused upon. As has been suggested by Fenigstein, Scheier, and Buss (1975), at least two domains within the multi-facetted self can be differentiated in a global way, namely private and public aspects of the self. Private self-awareness, according to these authors, centers around aspects not directly observable by others (e.g. motives, feelings, attitudes), whereas public self-awareness focuses on those aspects that can be directly observed by the individual's social environment. Being self-aware in the latter sense should heighten concerns about one's impression on others, one's physical appearance, and the like. This state should be created, in particular, by feelings of being observed, by the expectation of getting social feedback, as well as by the seemingly dissimilar experience of being ignored in a group (see Wicklund & Frey, 1980).

Fenigstein et al. (1975) not only proposed a distinction between private and public self-awareness, but also formulated the novel assumption of self-consciousness as a rather stable disposition. According to this assumption, individuals differ both in the tendency and frequency with which they become self-aware. Thus, self-awareness as a *state* is now distinguished from self-consciousness as a *trait*.

As has been typical in the tradition of trait-oriented personality assessment, these authors developed a scale to measure private and public self-consciousness as well as social anxiety. This scale has been used in many studies, probably as often as some experimental manipulation of self-awareness. Several attempts have been made to design experiments in such a way that the effects of experimentally induced self-awareness and of interindividual differences in dispositional self-consciousness could be proved simultaneously. It has been further documented by various results that the psychological consequences of self-awareness as a state do parallel those of self-consciousness as a trait almost perfectly and, hence, both can be considered functionally equivalent.

As far as the above-mentioned distinction between private and public self-consciousness is concerned, it has been argued that both have somewhat opposite effects. This can be demonstrated most clearly by observing behavior in small group situations, in which attempts at changing group members' attitudes have been made. While individuals high in *private* self-consciousness prove to be highly resistant towards persuasion and conformity pressure, individuals high in *public* self-consciousness are much more ready to conform and give up formerly held opinions (Froming & Carver, 1981; Scheier, 1980).

Yet, aside from some conceptual similarities one could think of (such as Riesman's inner- versus outer-directed orientation), the differentiation between public and private self-consciousness has been criticized not only for methodological, but also for theoretical reasons. The distinction has not been empirically verified in all studies that used Fenigstein et al.'s Self-Consciousness Scale. The private and the public subscale do not seem to be uncorrelated, yielding coefficients that range from .23 (reported originally by Fenigstein et al., 1975) to .39 (for a German version by Heinemann, 1979) to .56 (Turner, 1978) up to .73 (for a German version including more items in each subscale by Filipp, 1978).

Furthermore, no attempts have been made to operationalize the construct differently than by using the original scale or some slight modification, and to look for other empirical referents of the construct. It would appear that a systematic application of the multitrait-multimethod approach would be highly valuable, if one takes into consideration the popularity of the concept itself.

It has been doubted recently by Wicklund and Gollwitzer (1983), whether there is any necessity at all to divide self-attention into two components. According to these authors, those experimental conditions, which have been used to induce public self-awareness are, by and large, identical with conditions of high conformity pressure. Since individuals with high scores in the public self-consciousness scale also have high scores in measures of social dependence, conformity, and anxiousness, the differential effects on behavior, which so far are attributed to differences in public self-awareness, could be explained by these variables in the same manner. Therefore, to think of "public self-awareness" in terms of a distinct concept, is regarded as superfluous.

The authors further argue that public self-awareness, almost by definition, does not mean attending to the *self,* but rather to *others* (e.g., expectations about one's behavior, other's impressions of oneself, etc.). Thus, in the state of public self-awareness, the person is regarded as not being affected by any preexisting personal aspect, as these authors suggest.

This critique obviously reflects a rather fundamental issue which so far has not been taken very seriously in self-attention theory. It has to do with the somewhat philosophical question about "the boundaries of the self." Any sort of theorizing on that question will come across issues that repeatedly have been stressed as crucially important by researchers in self-concept theory (e.g., Filipp, 1979). These issues are centered around the following questions: How do individuals cognitively construe their experiences and what do they learn from these about themselves? What is the information like that is encoded as self-referent (versus not), thus entering the system of self-knowledge? How is the continuous flow of self-referent information organized and stored in memory (that part of the memory usually referred to as "the self-concept")? Therefore, what it really means when individuals are thought of as attending to their selves can never be fully understood without looking at how their self-knowledge was generated and organized. Self-concept theory and self-attention theory obviously are in need of integration, too.

Coping Theory: Some Issues and Problems

"Coping" appears to be one of the widely used concepts within psychology, especially during the last two or three decades when the "stress of life" (Selye, 1956) became a topic of profound scientific as well as of practical interest. As is true for many other concepts, the popularity of the concept of coping and the degree of its theoretical and empirical precision, seem to be interrelated in a somewhat inverse manner. Moreover, it often seems as if the various attempts to conceptualize coping do not have much in common, thus giving the impression that coping is nothing more than a summary label for a host of heterogeneous and, in many aspects, differing behaviors. We will not go into greater detail here, but it is important to briefly comment on those basic conceptual differences within coping theory that cause quite a bit of confusion.

First, conceptualizations and empirical measures of coping differ in terms of what level of analysis is focused upon. Coping refers to behavioral strategies in terms of planned and highly reflective courses of action as well as to single behavioral responses (e.g., escape from a shock experience). In correspondence to that heterogenity, the question whether or not coping behaviors are highly conscious acts is discussed controversially (cf. Vaillant, 1977).

Second, the situations within which coping behaviors have been investigated often do not share any common element; accordingly, what is then referred to as coping behavior does not have very much in common except for the same categorical label. Without a clear-cut description of the specific features of a situation which evoke coping responses in contrast to other responses, the distinction of a special class of behaviors named coping does not make much sense.

Third, many authors have reserved coping only for those behaviors that serve some protective function, that is, help the individual to not be overwhelmed by the situation's demands and/or prevent serious impairment in the individual's functioning (e.g., Pearlin & Schooler, 1978). In contrast, other authors make judgments about the quality of coping only after its effects in various domains have been empirically assessed. Thus, whether or not coping was successful is not answered by a priori definition but by referring to its consequences.

Finally, somewhat related to the aforementioned distinction, many authors contrast coping with denial or defense in terms of the degree to which the individual has a veridical perception of the situation to be coped with (cf.

Haan, 1977). Other authors subsume all divergent behaviors to the coping concept that seem to reflect an individual's attempt to handle a stressful situation, including behaviors indicative of "denial" as well as highly instrumental acts to change the situation (cf. Lazarus & Launier, 1978).

Within life-event research the idea has become widely accepted that coping behaviors do contribute to a higher predictability of the outcomes observed after the occurence of critical life-events; the coping concept has, therefore, been introduced into that research domain. In this special case, coping is observed not only in its natural context, but also in light of an individual's life situation which may involve long or everlasting changes and bears considerable affective dynamics. Therefore, there is a tremendous extension of the "situation" to be coped with in time and space and it seems quite unclear, whether our efforts to describe various modes of coping, mostly based on short-term observations in either experimental or clearly circumscribed natural situations such as surgery, are still appropriate. Can these conceptualizations be equally applied to describe how individuals try to handle the loss of a spouse, the loss of a job, the confrontation with serious illness like cancer, or other instances of life-events that are more than "one-shot-experiences."

It is proposed here that many behaviors can be called coping, as well as not, at the same time. What makes the crucial difference is their underlying instrumentality in overcoming an actual non-fit between the individual and his or her environment. Since an actual non-fit calls for other than usual ways of acting, the individual's need for exerting control over a changed situation is highly threatened. Thus, behaviors conceived of as coping represent nothing more than efforts to (re)construct the fit between person and environment. Whatever single behavioral act may serve, according to the individual's instrumental beliefs, that fundamental purpose is representative of what can be called coping (for a further discussion see Braukmann & Filipp, 1983).

As will be argued in the next section, shifts in attentional focus during long-term processes of coping with critical life-events are seen as one basic principle, according to which coping behaviors can be classified: Whatever the focus of attention will be at a given point in time will have important implications for the type of behaviors that are activated. What outcomes from coping with a critical life-event will be observed and whether or not coping can be called "effective," is primarily a question to be answered empirically, and not by reserving the concept of coping behavior for "adaptive" behaviors by a priori definition. The "effectiveness" of coping will be dependent on two conditions: First, the outcome variable considered to be crucial in the person-environment-system (e.g., health status); and, second, the point in time at which it is considered. What might prove to be helpful in a short-term perspective may be quite maladaptive and highly dysfunctional under a long-term perspective, as has been concluded by Mullen and Suls (1982b) from the results of their metaanalysis of various studies.

To summarize, coping research has been preoccupied for too long a period of time with the search for coping *styles* or the identification of different *types* of individuals according to their coping behaviors, rather than looking for variations and fluctuations in coping behaviors across time within the same individual(s). Yet, a process-oriented approach is especially warranted, when investigating the way in which individuals cope with critical life-events. These events often call for temporally extended periods of coping, because they often create dramatically changed demands and affective states of high intensity that make it difficult to quickly reorganize a balanced state with one's environment; in addition, they ask for a much greater plasticity in coping behaviors than has been acknowledged so far.

Nevertheless, coping behavior should not only be seen as determined by external demands of a stressful situation and/or by the transient affective states of the individual, but should also be investigated in relation to rather stable characteristics of the individual. Only by doing this, we will come closer to precise predictions of coping behaviors in light of various life-events and stressful situations. It is suggested here that self-consciousness among other personality variables should be taken into consideration.

In the following section, we try to bridge the gap that has existed up till now between self-attention theory and research on coping processes, and it is demonstrated that the bridge can be accessed from either side rather easily.

BRIDGING THE GAP BETWEEN SELF-ATTENTION THEORY AND COPING RESEARCH

Coping Theory's Contribution

From its very beginning, research on coping processes has been concerned with the concept of "attention," despite numerous attempts to conceptualize coping processes in other terms or shifts in emphasis on the concept of attention or related ideas. In general, almost all attempts to differentiate various modes of coping have taken into consideration the extent to which stressful aspects of an individual's situation ("stressors") are within, versus outside, the individual's focus of attention.

This type of theorizing started as early as the work of Janis and his colleagues (see Janis, 1958), and since then various other conceptualizations, although more or less within the same domain, have been proposed. Recently, it has been emphasized by Cohen (1980) that modes of handling a stressful (medical) situation can be grouped into two distinct classes of coping behaviors, namely "vigilance" and "avoidance." In a similar manner, Miller (1980) tried to differentiate coping responses by referring to them as "monitoring" versus "blunting" strategies. And finally, there is the popular concept of "repression" versus "sensitization," which has the longest tradition and which was recently reformulated by Krohne and Rogner (1982) as well as extended and refined by Asendorpf (1981). Whatever terms and theoretical assumptions have been favored by various authors, it appears that focus of attention or degree of stress-related attention is one basic principle proposed to account for differences in coping behaviors and allow for their distinction.

Yet, as is argued in the following section, neither conceptualization has taken into consideration that focusing one's attention upon the stressful encounter (i.e., exhibiting a "vigilant," "monitoring," "sensitizing" coping strategy) may have two different meanings. In the first case, the individual's attention may center on his or her inner states and reactions to the stressful event, thus being in the state of self-directed attention, whereas in the second case the stressful event itself may be primarily focused upon attentionally, that is, attending to external demands, nature of environmental change, aspects of the stress experience, and so forth. Whether attention centers mainly on "inner" or "outer" aspects of a stressful person-environment-transaction seems to be highly valuable for differential description of coping processes and also for more precise predictions about what individuals will really do in a stressful situation and which coping responses are more likely to occur.

Self-attention Theory's Contribution

Research on self-attention and self-consciousness has so far evolved around two basic questions: Under what conditions will an individual's attention become directed inwardly, and what causes natural variations in his or her focus of attention? What follows from the state of self-focused attention and how does it influence behavior?

It has been well documented that self-directed attention does have a powerful effect on behavior in various domains, for example, prosocial behavior, resistance towards persuasion, and attribution of behavioral outcomes. Matching one's behavior to personal or social standards salient in a particular situation seems to be one common effect of self-directed attention, as originally proposed by Duval and Wicklund (1972) and recently reformulated by Carver and Scheier (1981) within a broader conceptualization of self-regulatory processes in human action. But despite the host of studies within that theoretical field, we have little evidence about the impact of self-attention on coping responses as one special class of behavior. Why should self-attention make a difference in coping, and why should the self come into play in situations that have to be coped with?

It is proposed here that critical life-events, stressful encounters, or any other situation in which an individual cannot merely "behave" but which have to be coped with, are almost prototypical for situations in which a natural occurring shift from outward-directed towards inner-directed attention should be observed — not considering interindividual differences in the tendency to become more or less self-aware. This line of reasoning is proposed because of three distinct reasons. First, by definition and their psychological meaning, these situations do not allow for responding in a "mindless" way (Langer & Imber, 1979) or exhibiting rather automatic behaviors. The appropriateness of routine behavior to meet the demands of an often dramatically changed situation, as in the case of loss events, is highly questioned. Affective reactions and high arousal may create states of "affective noise," which in turn might even hinder the installation of so-called "routines"; the situation is highly resistant and full of barriers against usual adaptive functioning. Moreover, in many cases critical life-events expose individuals to highly unfamiliar life-situations, for which new modes of action have to be developed and proved. Using relocation as a paradigm, Hormuth (1983) was able to find support for a similar assumption, that is, self-focus is aroused in new environments. Since the course of action lacks its usual smoothness, the individual not only *tends* to, but will even be *forced* to, direct his or her attention to the self, for example, in terms of self-reflective examination about what one can or should do and about one's resources to help cope with the situation.

Second, when looking at stressful or critical life-situations we often are dealing with situations that have important implications for the individual's self-system, in general. Many situations are "critical" in the sense that they carry self-referent information that either attacks feelings of self-worth (Fairbank & Hough, 1979) and/or calls for changes in self-conceptions, thus threatening the individual's sense of personal continuity (Horowitz, 1980). From here, almost automatically, the self comes into play and elicits self-focused attention.

Third, since critical life-events are by definition accompanied by intensive affective reactions, the chance for the self to become prominent within the perceptual field is very high. As has been demonstrated experimentally by Wegner and Giuliano (1980), the experience of heightened emotional arousal creates the state of self-awareness and selective attention to self-referent cues within the situation. Therefore, naturally occurring alterations in affective arousal, as are common in the confrontation with critical life-events, should direct the individual's attention to the self.

To summarize, it seems highly plausible from various grounds that a general tendency exists to attend selectively to the self after critical life-events or stressful situations have come upon the scene. With regard to the question of what causes natural variations in attentional focus asked by self-attention theory, we now offer an additional answer. After having tried to convince the reader that coping individuals are highly self-attending individuals as well, let us now speculate what the effects of self-attention on modes of coping might be like. Again, we neglect here interindividual differences and look for some general assumptions that might help to explore the effect on coping responses.

According to self-attention theory in general, it can be predicted that heightened self-attention leads to a closer fit between observed behavior and some underlying salient standard. But this, although being the predominant effect of self-attention, seems to be less likely when *coping* responses are elicited. Behavioral standards in coping situations often are either less obvious or they do not even exist: stressful situations are frequently stressful because of the absence of behavioral guidelines, a lack of behavioral goals, and a general loss of behavioral orientation (see Kommer & Röhrle, 1981). It can be assumed that the most salient self-aspect in this situation is not some personal or internalized social standard of behavioral conduct, but the individual's emotional pain and arousal. If the premise can be accepted that self-directed attention in coping situations initially makes individuals' *emotions* the salient dimension to focus on, then we might parallel self-attention in coping situations with attention to one's affective state. Yet, as repeatedly demonstrated, self-attention does intensify affective states, hence making the emotional consequences of critical life-situations even more severe and salient. One could expect that coping responses are then primarily aimed at reducing the effect of being emotionally overwhelmed by the situation — a class of coping responses that has been introduced as "emotion-centered coping" by Lazarus and Launier (1978). The assumption that self-awareness leads to higher emotional intensity is also supported by those theories that postulate proprioceptive information about one's arousal as well as one's facial expressions as powerful determinants in the experience of emotion (for an overview see Kuhl, 1983). By introducing the concept of "affective vigilance", Asendorpf (1981) similarly argued that affective vigilance, as one mode of dealing with emotions, cannot occur without high self-attention. Yet, the question whether these phenomena share the same empirical referents, needs further investigation. Coming from the general assumption that self-attention heightens the experience of emotional arousal, it can be further argued that critical life-events are "critical" because they not only alter emotional states, but because they have an inherent tendency to make individuals self-aware, thus intensifying whatever emotion (e.g., sadness, depression, and the like) is predominant.

Self-attention as a (situationally) induced state has been our primary concern, so far. Let us now turn to the second conceptualization of self-attention as a personal disposition or trait referred to as "dispositional self-consciousness." Individuals high in that trait should direct their attention inwardly more often and more quickly, and should in light of stressful encounters be more self-attending than individuals low in that trait. If we are interested whether self-attention has some effect on coping with naturally occurring stressful events, we are forced to look at the dispositional conceptualization because any form of experimental manipulation either seems inappropriate or does stand out against a chance for empirical realization.

EMPIRICAL ILLUSTRATIONS OF THE LINK BETWEEN
SELF-ATTENTION AND COPING WITH LIFE-EVENTS

The Moderating Effect of Self-Attention on
Event-Consequences

Recently, two studies were published that demonstrate how focus of attention and long-term effects of life-events may be interrelated. The special interest of the first study by Mullen and Suls (1982a) was the moderating effect of self-consciousness on illness onset after the occurrence of undesirable and uncontrollable life-events. Self-attention theory would predict that persons high in private self-consciousness are more sensitive to changes in internal bodily states than those low in private self-consciousness. Extending this to individuals who are coping with stressful life-events, the authors formulated the assumption that high private self-consciousness may ameliorate the effects of uncontrollable and undesirable life-events on illness. Since individuals high in self-consciousness are considered to have easier access to their psychological and somatic reactions to event-induced stress, they should exhibit highly instrumental coping behaviors that prevent any impairment in their functioning. Mullen and Suls tested this assumption in a prospective study: Eighty-eight students completed the Self-Consciousness Scale (Fenigstein et al., 1975), a life-event schedule, and an illness scale in which all illnesses experienced during the last 3 weeks had to be reported. At the second time of measurement, subjects reported life-events and illnesses, again for the past 3 weeks. Using cross-lagged panel correlation analyses, one significant relationship was revealed. Only when subjects experienced uncontrollable and undesirable events, and were *low* in private self-consciousness, did life-events, measured at t_1, raise the illness frequency, measured at t_2 ($r = .43$). The health of persons *high* in self-consciousness was completely unaffected by the incidence of life-events. It has to be noted that both groups did not differ in the amount of uncontrollable events or illness rate at t_1.

Without a doubt, this study proves some consequences of private self-consciousness on behavior surrounding life-events, which have been observed over a longer time-span than in many experimental studies on the effects of self-awareness. However, it is not clear from these results whether individuals with different degrees of self-consciousness also differed in how they coped with critical life-events, because coping strategies themselves were not assessed in this study. Therefore, it is still speculative to assume that persons high in private self-consciousness have different coping strategies and are more prone to act instrumentally in order to prevent negative consequences of life-stress.

The second study by Hull, Young, and Swank (1982) investigated the conditions of relapse following alcohol detoxification, based on a self-awareness model of alcohol consumption. It was predicted from the model that detoxified alcoholics are more likely to relapse when they experience life-events indicative of personal failure ("self-referent event"), and are at the same time high in self-consciousness. High self-consciousness should raise negative self-evaluations following failure, and alcohol use is considered to be one way to reduce self-awareness and the negative implications of failure events for the self. Thus, relapse should be highly probable for that group. Accordingly, the experience of *success* should *protect* persons high in self-consciousness from relapse. For the group of alcoholics low in self-consciousness, no predictions were made about differential effects of self-referent life-events on relapse. The results of the study with 35 alcoholics confirmed these assumptions: Probability of relapse 3 months after detoxification was significantly higher after the experience of personal failure for alcoholics high in self-conciousness than for those low in self-consciousness.

What can be concluded from these studies? The present state of research does not allow for formulation of a clear-cut principle about the way in which self-consciousness influences coping behaviors and how it moderates the effects of life-events. Obviously, high or low private self-consciousness has different effects, depending on the type of life-events an individual is exposed to and his or her present state. High degrees of self-consciousness have been proven to have beneficial effects (as in the Mullen and Suls study) as well as being dysfunctional (as in the Hull et al. study) in coping with life-events. In addition, further research has to demonstrate to what degree self-consciousness influences other variables than those studied so far, and which are considered consequences of critical life-events. The EPE study, to be reported in the following section, did relate the degree of self-attention, primarily to *modes of coping* with life-events, without focusing on the health-related consequences of life-events or other potential outcomes. This study, therefore, tries to relate self-attention and life-events by looking more closely at the ways in which individuals try to handle event-induced stress and life-change.

Coping with Life-Events and Self-Attention in a Developmental Perspective — the EPE Study[1]

Conceptual Background and Main Purpose. Developmental psychologists have started to look more closely at the issue of intraindividual change versus stability within the years of middle age and old age. In addition to the

---

[1]The EPE study is run under collaboration of Alois Angleitner, Inge Ahammer, Walter Braukmann, Sigrun-Heide Filipp, and Erhard Olbrich, with a male sample of the city of Trier. It is supported by a grant from Volkswagenwerk Foundation, and the initials refer to "*E*ntwicklungs*p*sychologie des *E*rwachsenenalters" (Developmental psychology of adulthood).

necessity of assessing change or stability in various domains in a descriptive manner, it has always been a dominant concern to reveal those factors that contribute to change as well as to stability within the second half of life.

Only recently has the concept of "significant life-events" been introduced into developmental psychology as one organizing principle, which might allow for the explanation of intraindividual change across the life-span (see Baltes, 1979; Filipp, 1981; Hultsch & Plemons, 1979). Following this line of reasoning, the general objective of the EPE study was to look at the relationship between life-events and personality change in adulthood (Filipp, Ahammer, Angleitner, & Olbrich, 1980). Data were collected using a longitudinal design across a time-span of almost 4 years with 218 males from five birth cohorts (year of birth: 1905, 1912, 1925, 1935, 1945). For the purpose of this chapter, we will only focus upon modes of coping with critical life-events that had been assessed concurrently to the events' occurrences, and upon the relation of coping modes to individual differences in self-consciousness.

Assessment of Life-Events.   Two general strategies of collecting information about exposure to actual life-events during that time period were applied. From the beginning of the study, subjects were asked to report immediately whatever "noteworthy event" occurred to them. Each individual was then sent a set of structured questionnaires that should assess his subjective perception of the event, associated feelings, and coping behaviors. This strategy of data collection is highly individualized in the sense that many subjects either do not experience "noteworthy events," or are less likely to report them spontaneously, therefore creating "missing values" in the data.

In addition, we asked at eight different points in time (approximately every four months) for some "unpleasant experience," during the preceding weeks leaving it up to the respondent what kind of major or minor event he chose to report. Consequently, we have data on eight events for each subject which reflect a wide range of human experience: daily hassles ("I missed an appointment"), milder events ("I ran out of money"), as well as major life-events such as serious illness or death of a spouse. To classify the events, we asked the subjects to rate each event on four dimensions, namely desirability, controllability, perceived importance, and perceived challenge. In addition, each event was grouped according to the life domain in which it was primarily located (family, health, work, and so forth) as well as to the subject's centrality in the events' occurrence (e.g., subject became ill versus his spouse became ill). Thus, instead of assessing the "stressfulness" or life-events by standardized weights, we relied on subjective event-parameters and the distribution of events across various life domains (see also Filipp & Braukmann, 1983). Amount of exposure to different types of events can then be related not only to cohort membership but also to personality measures from different points in time.

Assessment of Coping Behaviors.   For each event that had been reported, either spontaneously or in the fixed-interval data collection, our subjects had to fill in a German version of the "Ways of Coping Checklist" by
Lazarus and his colleagues (see Braukmann, Filipp, Angleitner, & Olbrich,
1981). This instrument is aimed at the assessment of coping behaviors in light
of actually occurring events, each of which had to be briefly described at the
top of the list. Coping behaviors are conceptually subdivided into "problem-
centered" and "emotion-centered" modes indicating that coping behavior is
either primarily aimed at the regulation of event-induced affective states or at
the solution of event-related problems in one's situation (see Lazarus &
Launier, 1978).

The checklist consists of 68 items that describe various activities, overt as
well as mental ones, and the subject has to respond in terms of whether or not
he or she exhibited each behavior after the event in question had occurred.
Results from various factor analyses of these items suggested the construction of two separate subscales, each consisting of 18 items, that yielded one
score for emotion-focused (E-Scale) and one score for problem-focused
(P-Scale) coping. Internal consistency and reliability of these subscales can
be considered as satisfactory (Cronbach Alpha varied from .71 to .82 for the
P-Scale and from .64 to .76 for the E-Scale across the different points of
measurement), and differences in scores dependent on type of event can be
interpreted as an initial indication of their validity. Yet, further analyses are
necessary before more can be said about the psychometric properties of this
coping scale.

Assessment of Self-Attention.   A German translation and modified version of the Fenigstein et al. scale (Filipp, 1978) was administered to our subjects. From this version, the social anxiety subscale was excluded and items of
equal content were added to the two other subscales (private subscale now
consisting of 17 items; public subscale consisting of 12 items). Contrary to
other results the scores from both subscales are highly intercorrelated
($r = .73$), and 79% of the common variance in all items can be explained by
only one factor. Although our results to be reported here are based on the
separate computation of a score for private self-consciousness, a further distinction of both components of self-consciousness does not make very much
sense from our data. However, conceiving of self-consciousness in terms of a
rather stable personality disposition is highly supported by our data. Various
measures of change did not yield significant results, although t_1 and t_4 were
almost 3 years apart. In addition, differences between cohorts could not be
proved to be significant, although the oldest cohort had been 78 years of age
at t_4 and the youngest cohort 38 years of age. Results from factor analyses,
which included many other personality measures, regularly yielded one distinct factor with loadings exclusively in the self-consciousness items. Only

when *factor scores* entered the analyses, was a second-order factor revealed which pointed to interrelations between self-consciousness scores and two or three motivational variables measured by Jackson's Personality Research Form (Angleitner, Filipp, & Braukmann, 1982).

Relationship Between Self-Attention and Coping.   Our general question had been whether or not coping modes (emotion-focused and problem-focused coping scores) differ across individuals with varying degrees of private self-consciousness. In particular, it was assumed that individuals high in private self-consciousness would experience event-induced affective states much more intensely, hence using emotion-focused coping modes more often than individuals low in self-consciousness. Low private self-consciousness was considered to be indicated by a preference for problem-focused coping responses, because external demands are predominant in the individual's attentional focus. For that purpose we correlated the private subscale scores assessed in t_1 with both coping scores, assessed at the same point of measurement. Coefficients from a product-moment correlation are only $r = -.09$ for emotion-focused, and $r = .11$ for problem-focused coping score.

To be noted here is the fact that coping behaviors were assessed on a wide variety of different life-events. Therefore, variance in coping behaviors might be explained much better by variations in event-parameters than by variations in any personality measure. This led us to "control" for type of event by tabulating all life-events measured at one point in time according to their parameters (desirability, controllability, perceived importance, perceived challenge) on the basis of configuration frequency analysis (Krauth & Lienert, 1973). Results from this analysis revealed one highly significant type of life-event, namely low in desirability, low in controllability, high in importance, and low in challenge. This configuration of event-parameters showed up in more than one third of all cases of events, although 15 other configurations were theoretically existent. We repeated our correlation analysis based on that special type of event in a subsample of $N = 62$. Again, even when the type of event is controlled for in terms of subjective event-parameters, no significant relationship between private self-consciousness and coping could be found!

Of course, it is still possible to see whether other types of events (in terms of life-domain or defined by more objectively assessed properties) are more sensitive to the moderating effects of dispositional self-consciousness on coping. We do not believe that present theory allows for precise predictions about the types of life-events which lead to differences in coping behaviors between individuals low or high in self-consciousness. Thus, our next data analyses will be addressed to a more systematic exploration of this issue. We will also try to prove whether subjective perceptions of life-events themselves, as they have been used here to describe and classify events, can be considered more powerful determinants of coping behaviors than the degree of self-consciousness. In addition, further investigation of whether moderator effects may be responsible for the result of coping behaviors independent of self-focused attention seems necessary. Because the few studies referred to in this section served primarily for illustration purposes, we will not go into a deeper discussion of the results of the EPE study, particularly since the study has not yet been completed and data analyses are still going on. The following last section will serve to summarize and comment briefly on the question why the effects of self-attention on coping and on the outcomes of coping behaviors may not always be observed in natural situations.

COPING WITHOUT SELF-AWARENESS? SOME CONCLUDING REMARKS

It has been argued repeatedly throughout this paper that coping responses to naturally occurring stressful situations should be highly determined by dispositional self-consciousness. Coping theory as well as self-attention theory seem to touch upon each other in certain domains and to share more common elements than has been realized by researchers, so far. Yet, this general assumption could not be proved to apply unequivocally to the phenomena that have been empirically studied in a few investigations. We briefly comment on this and add a few remarks.

First, one has to be aware of the fact that the concept of "critical life-events" represents a highly vague term for the description of what individuals are exposed to and have to cope with throughout their lives. This term covers a wide range of human experiences, the high diversity and heterogenity of which is not to be overlooked. Yet, it points to one common element shared by all events, namely that *coping* behaviors are called for when the person-environment fit has to be rearranged and the affective dynamics inherent in each event have to be managed. Many successful attempts have been made to differentiate life-events according to various dimensions and properties (e.g., Brim & Ryff, 1980; Reese & Smyer, 1983). But the question remains unanswered as to what degree these classifications reflect differences in the probability of the self coming into play within the coping process and for self-attention to determine coping behaviors. By introducing "self-referent events" as one special class of events, a first step in that direction has now been made by Hull et al. (1982). Further attempts should be made to differentiate life-events according to whether they call for self-focused attention or lead to heightened self-awareness. Simultaneously, one has to take into consideration that critical life-events, whatever their nature and source may be, possibly do heighten self-attention rather universally, thus creating a ceiling effect and minimizing the effect of differences in dispositional self-consciousness.

Second, critical life-events have not been investigated thoroughly enough in terms of how they relate to different motivational dispositions. One could think of types of events in terms of the motives they primarily arouse. For example, if the need for maintaining personal control is challenged more than any other motive, individual differences in control motivation should be more powerful in determining modes of coping than differences in self-consciousness. In general, it can be argued that not only do life-events need to be differentiated, but one has to consider the dynamic interplay between various properties of events on the one hand and individuals' motives and present states on the other. A closer look should enable us to predict more precisely when self-attention will be important and when this will not be the case in determining coping behaviors.

Our third remark concerns the conceptualization and assessment of coping itself. It has been stated quite often that one has to think of coping as a *process* rather than as a single act or a "one-shot-phenomenon." Yet, these statements have not been applied to the assessment of coping responses. When individuals describe how they cope with a life-event that has recently occurred by indicating "yes" or "no" on a checklist of behavior items (as in the EPE study reported above), how should these descriptions be treated? Either these reports are conceived of as referring to certain coping *episodes* within the coping process (e.g., "I tried not to think of the situation"), or they are conceived of as being representative of what happens throughout the whole process. Variations on coping behaviors across time have not been observed systematically and a process-oriented measurement strategy has not been applied, so far. Therefore, it is open to debate whether the coping episodes, addressed by our measures, offer valid descriptions of the coping process as a whole. From this line of reasoning it can be concluded that differences in dispositional self-consciousness do make a difference in coping behaviors, not in general, but possibly in the interaction with the actual coping episode observed. Whether or not this might be a useful differentiation of the proposed relationship between self-attention and coping, can only be answered after we have gained a better understanding of the coping process itself.

Our last comment refers to the fact that the studies mentioned in the preceding section differ in one aspect, which might be important in understanding the differing results. These studies were aimed at either relating self-consciousness to coping behavior directly or to the presumably existing outcomes of coping behaviors, for example health status. While behavioral *outcomes* proved to be predictable from differences in self-consciousness in the first two studies, the mere onset of certain coping modes, as described in the third study, appeared to be unrelated to the degree of self-consciousness. Although these few empirical examples are far from being sufficient to draw any general conclusions, we would like to point to one possible explanation for the different results.

We would like to speculate for a moment on the idea that diverse coping behaviors, although phenomenally different and heterogeneous, might be highly equifunctional in obtaining those behavioral outcomes under investigation (e.g., the prevention of an impairment in health status). The observation that dispositional self-consciousness might be related to *outcomes* of coping responses rather than to coping behavior itself can be referred to that general assumption. It does underline that whatever coping behaviors are present in an individual's repertoire, and whatever his or her predominant behavioral tendencies are, they will become extremely important in bringing about an observed outcome particularly in individuals of high self-consciousness. In the case of "positive" outcomes (e.g., Mullen & Suls, 1982a), high self-consciousness seems to facilitate the effective search for appropriate coping responses in one's repertoire as well as highly valid judgments concerning their appropriateness. However, in the case of "negative" outcomes (e.g., relapse in a group of alcoholics, Hull et al., 1982), high self-consciousness seems to make individuals aware of their dominant *affect,* in light of failure experiences, rather than of ways to handle the situation. Negative affective states that are preexistent in highly self-conscious individuals may thus hinder the onset of appropriate coping behaviors. One can easily think of the distinction suggested by Kuhl (1981) in terms of state versus action orientation and assume that in the case of state orientation, high self-conciousness might be considered dysfunctional, whereas in the case of action orientation it might prove to be a facilitating condition for exhibiting effective coping behaviors.

In general, it can be concluded that dispositional self-consciousness may exert a highly indirect influence on coping behaviors that can only be revealed if the individual's present affective state and motivations are taken into consideration. Together with these conditions, high self-consciousness may be helpful in bringing about positive or negative outcomes in coping with life-events, yet allows for a great variation in the coping behaviors to be observed.

REFERENCES

Angleitner, A., Filipp, S. -H., & Braukmann, W. Testtheoretische Prüfung der Fragebogen-verfahren zur Erfassung ausgewählter Personmerkmale. (Handlungsleitende Kognitionen, Bedürfnisstrukturen und Wertsysteme) Trier: *Forschungsberichte aus dem E.P.E.-Projekt* Nr. 20, 1982.

Asendorpf, J. *Affektive Vigilanz.* Gießen: Universität Gießen, Dissertation, 1981.

Baltes, P. B. Life-span developmental psychology: Some converging observations on history and theory. In P. B. Baltes & O. G. Brim, Jr. (Eds.), *Life-span development and behavior* (Vol. 2, pp. 256–279). New York: Academic Press, 1979.

Bandura, A. Self-efficacy: Toward a unifying theory of behavioral change. *Psychological Review,* 1977, *84,* 191–215.

Braukmann, W., & Filipp, S. -H. Strategien und Techniken der Lebensbewältigung. In U. Baumann, H. Berbalk, & G. Seidenstücker (Eds.), *Klinische Psychologie. Trends in Forschung und Praxis.* (Band 6, pp. 52–87). Bern: Huber, 1983.

Braukmann, W., Filipp, S. -H., Angleitner, A., & Olbrich, E. *Problem-solving and coping with critical life-events — A life-span developmental study.* Trier: Forschungsberichte aus dem E.P.E.-Projekt Nr. 15, 1981.

Brim, O. G., J., & Ryff, C. B. On the properties of life-events. In P. B. Baltes & O. G. Brim, Jr. (Eds.), *Life-span development and behavior* (Vol. 3, pp. 368–389). New York: Academic Press, 1980.

Buss, A. H. *Self-consciousness and social anxiety.* San Francisco: Freeman, 1980.

Carver, C. S. A cybernetic model of self-attention processes. *Journal of Personality and Social Psychology,* 1979, *37,* 1251–1281.

Carver, C. S., Blaney, P. H., & Scheier, M. F. Reassertion and giving up: The interactive role of self-directed attention and outcome expectancy. *Journal of Personality and Social Psychology,* 1979, *37,* 1859–1870.

Carver, C. S., & Scheier, M. F. *Attention and self-regulation: A control-theory approach to human behavior.* New York: Springer, 1981.

Cohen, F. Coping with surgery: Information, psychological preparation, and recovery. In L. W. Poon (Ed.), *Aging in the 1980s. Psychological issues* (pp. 375–382). Washington, DC: American Psychological Association, 1980.

Duval, S., & Wicklund, R. A. *A theory of objective self-awareness.* New York: Academic Press, 1972.

Fairbank, D. T., & Hough, R. L. Life-event classifications and the event-illness relationship. *Journal of Human Stress,* 1979, *5,* 41–47.

Fenigstein, A., Scheier, M. F., & Buss, A. H. Public and private self-consciousness: Assessment and theory. *Journal of Consulting and Clinical Psychology,* 1975, *43,* 522–527.

Filipp, S. -H. *Fragebogen zur Erfassung dispositionaler Selbstaufmerksamkeit (SAM).* University of Trier: Unpublished manuscript, 1978.

Filipp, S. -H. Entwurf eines heuristischen Bezugsrahmens für Selbstkonzept-Forschung: Menschliche Informationsverarbeitung und naive Handlungstheorie. In S. -H. Filipp (Ed.), *Selbstkonzept-Forschung* (pp. 129–152). Stuttgart: Klett-Cotta, 1979.

Filipp, S. -H. Ein allgemeines Modell für die Analyse kritischer Lebensereignisse. In S. -H. Filipp (Ed.), *Kritische Lebensereignisse* (pp. 1–52). München: Urban & Schwarzenberg, 1981.

Filipp, S. -H., & Braukmann, W. Methoden der Erfassung bedeutsamer Lebensereignisse. *Zeitschrift für Entwiklungspsychologie und Pädagogische Psychologie,* 1983, *15,* 234–263.

Filipp, S. -H., Ahammer, J., Angleitner, A., & Olbrich, E. Eine Untersuchung zu inter- und intraindividuellen Differenzen in der Wahrnehmung und Verarbeitung subjektiv erlebter Persönlichkeitsveränderungen. Trier: Forschungsberichte aus dem E.P.E. – Projekt, Nr. 11, 1980.

Froming, W. S., & Carver, C. S. Divergent influences of private and public self-consciousness in a compliance paradigm. *Journal of Research in Personality,* 1981, *15,* 159–172.

Gendlin, E. T. Client-centered and experiental psychotherapy. In D. A. Wexler & L. N. Rice (Eds.), *Innovations in client-centered therapy* (pp. 211–246). New York: Wiley, 1974.

Gibbons, F. X. Sexual standards and reactions to pornography: Enhancing behavioral consistency through self-focused attention. *Journal of Personality and Social Psychology,* 1978, *36,* 976–987.

Gibbons, F. X., Carver, C. S., Scheier, M. F., & Hormuth, S. Self-focused attention and the placebo effect: Fooling some of the people some of the time. *Journal of Experimental Social Psychology,* 1979, *15,* 263-274.

Haan, N. *Coping and defending: Processes of self-environment organization.* New York: Academic Press, 1977.

Heinemann, W. The assessment of private and public self-consciousness: A German replication. *European Journal of Social Psychology,* 1979, *9,* 331-337.

Hormuth, S. E. Transitions in commitments to roles and self-concept-change: Relocation as a paradigm. In V. Allen & van der Vliet (Eds.), *Role transitions.* New York: Plenum, 1983.

Horowitz, M. J. Psychological responses to serious life-events. In V. Hamilton & D. M. Warburton (Eds.), *Human stress and cognition* (pp. 235-264). Chichester: Wiley, 1980.

Hull, J. G., & Levy, A. S. The organizational functions of the self: An alternative to the Duval and Wicklund model of self-awareness. *Journal of Personality and Social Behavior,* 1979, *37,* 756-768.

Hull, J. G., Young, R. D., & Swank, L. E. *Self-consciousness, self-relevant life-events, and relapse following alcoholic detoxification.* Indiana University, Indianapolis: Unpublished paper, 1982.

Hultsch, D. F., & Plemons, J. K. Life-events and life-span development. In P. B. Baltes & O. G. Brim Jr. (Eds.), *Life-span development and behavior* (Vol. 2, pp. 1-36). New York: Academic Press, 1979.

Janis, J. L. *Psychological stress: Psychoanalytic and behavioral studies of surgical patients.* New York: Wiley, 1958.

Kanfer, F. H. Self-management methods. In F. H. Kanfer & A. P. Goldstein (Eds.), *Helping people change* (pp. 309-355). New York: Pergamon, 1975.

Kommer, D., & Röhrle, B. Handlungstheoretische Perspektiven Primärer Prävention. In W. R. Minsel & R. Scheller (Eds.), *Prävention* (= Brennpunkte der Klinischen Psychologie. Band 2, pp. 89-151). München: Kösel, 1981.

Krauth, J., & Lienert, G. A. *KFA – Die Konfigurationsfrequenzanalyse.* Freiburg: Alber, 1973.

Krohne, H. W., & Rogner, J. Repression-sensitization as a central construct in coping research. In H. W. Krohne & L. Laux (Eds.), *Achievement, stress, and anxiety* (pp. 167-193). Washington, DC: Hemisphere, 1982.

Kuhl, J. Motivational and functional helplessness: The moderating effect of state versus action orientation. *Journal of Personality and Social Psychology,* 1981, *40,* 144-170.

Kuhl, J. Emotion, Kognition und Motivation: I. Auf dem Wege zu einer systemtheoretischen Betrachtung der Emotionsgenese. *Sprache & Kognition,* 1983, *2,* 1-27.

Langer, E., & Imber, L. Mindlessness and susceptibility to the illusion of incompetence. *Journal of Personality and Social Psychology,* 1979, *37,* 2014-2025.

Lazarus, R. S., & Launier, R. Stress-related transactions between person and environment. In L. A. Pervin & M. Lewis (Eds.), *Perspectives in interactional psychology* (pp. 287-327). New York: Plenum, 1978.

Meichenbaum, D. Self-instructional methods. In F. H. Kanfer & A. P. Goldstein (Eds.), *Helping people change* (pp. 357-391). New York: Pergamon, 1975.

Miller, S. M. When is a little information a dangerous thing? Coping with stressful events by monitoring versus blunting. In S. Levine & H. Ursin (Eds.), *Coping and health: Proceedings of NATO conference* (pp. 145-169). New York: Plenum, 1980.

Mullen, B., & Suls, J. "Know thyself": Stressful life changes and the ameliorative effect of private self-consciousness. *Journal of Experimental Social Psychology,* 1982a, *18,* 43-55.

Mullen, B., & Suls, J. The effectiveness of attention and rejection as coping styles: A meta-analysis of temporal differences. *Journal of Psychosomatic Research,* 1982b, *26,* 43-49.

Pearlin, L. I., & Schooler, C. The structure of coping. *Journal of Health and Social Behavior,* 1978, *19,* 2–21.

Reese, H. W., & Smyer, M. A. Dimensionalization of life-events. In E. J. Callahan & K. A. McCluskey (Eds.), *Life-span developmental psychology. Non-normative life-crises.* New York: Academic Press, 1983.

Scheier, M. F. Self-awareness, self-consciousness, and angry aggression. *Journal of Personality,* 1976, *44,* 627–644.

Scheier, M. F. Effects of public and private self-consciousness on the public expression of personal beliefs. *Journal of Personality and Social Psychology,* 1980, *39,* 514–521.

Scheier, M. F., & Carver, C. S. Self-focused attention and the experience of emotion: Attraction, repulsion, elation, and depression. *Journal of Personality and Social Psychology,* 1977, *35,* 625–636.

Scheier, M. F., & Carver, C. S. Self-consciousness, outcome expectancy, and persistence. *Journal of Research in Personality,* 1982, *16,* 409–418.

Scheier, M. F., Carver, C. S., & Gibbons, F. X. Self-focused attention and reactions to fear. *Journal of Research in Personality,* 1981, *15,* 1–15.

Selye, H. *The stress of life.* New York: McGraw-Hill, 1956.

Turner, R. G. Consistency, self-consciousness, and the predictive validity of typical and maximal personality measures. *Journal of Research in Personality,* 1978, *12,* 117–132.

Vaillant, G. E. *Adaptation to life.* Boston, MA: Little Brown, 1977.

Wegner, D. M., & Giuliano, T. Arousal-induced attention to self. *Journal of Personality and Social Psycholoogy,* 1980, *38,* 719–726.

Wegner, D. M., & Schaefer, D. The concentration of responsibility: An objective self-awareness analysis of group size effects in helping situations. *Journal of Personality and Social Psychology,* 1978, *36,* 147–155.

Wicklund, R. A., & Frey, D. Self-awareness theory: When the self makes a difference. In D. M. Wegner & R. R. Vallacher (Eds.), *The self in social psychology* (Vol. 1, pp. 31–54). New York: Oxford Univesity Press, 1980.

Wicklund, R. A., & Gollwitzer, P. M. *The fallacy of the private-public self-focus distinction.* University of Texas at Austin: Unpublished manuscript, 1983.

Functional and Dysfunctional Responses to Anxiety: The Interaction Between Expectancies and Self-Focused Attention

8

Charles S. Carver
University of Miami

Michael F. Scheier
Carnegie-Mellon University

Many of the authors who are represented in this volume are interested primarily in the experimental and behavioral phenomena that come together under the label "anxiety." In their explorations of that topic area, they have found that there are important associations between the experience of anxiety and various kinds of self-related cognitions. We, in contrast, come to the subject matter of this volume from the opposite direction. We have been interested for some time in a specific set of cognitive and behavioral processes that are related to the self. In our explorations of these processes, we have come to find that they have some interesting implications for the understanding of anxiety and other unpleasant feelings that are created in stressful circumstances, feelings such as frustration and depression.

We have been interested in this particular set of self-processes since our exposure as graduate students to Duval and Wicklund's (1972) initial studies of their properties. To be more specific, the self-processes that have absorbed our professional attention for the past dozen years are those that are associated with the self's marvelous capacity to be reflexive, to turn its focus inward upon itself (James, 1890). This capacity has been a touchstone for generations of self theorists (e.g., Cooley, 1902; Mead, 1934). But in recent years it has re-emerged in a different light. As has been true of most subjects of psychological inquiry, contemporary investigations of the reflective consciousness of the self have been marked by a rigorous empiricism that was simply not present in earlier analyses. No longer must this concept be restricted to serving as a subject of philosophical debate. Its workings are beginning to open to the scrutiny of scientific research.

What, then, has this scrutiny revealed? What happens when people focus back or inward upon the self? There are several answers to this question, some of which even the most naive reader of this chapter will be able to anticipate. Sometimes the result of self-focus is simply a more pronounced awareness of the physical sensations that help to make up the self's present experience, for instance, the experience of emotion (see, e.g., Carver, Blaney, & Scheier, 1979a; Scheier, 1976; Scheier & Carver, 1977). In the same vein, but with a very different sort of twist, sometimes focusing inward creates a more pronounced awareness of the *absence* of physical sensations that the person has been led to anticipate feeling (Gibbons, Carver, Scheier, & Hormuth, 1979; Scheier, Carver, & Gibbons, 1979; see also Brockner & Swap, 1982). In other situations, focusing inward gives a broader view on the self, allowing one to make more accurate summary statements about what one is like, what one's typical behavioral characteristics are (e.g, Pryor, Gibbons, Wicklund, Fazio, & Hood, 1977; Scheier, Buss, & Buss, 1978; Turner, 1978; Underwood & Moore, 1981).

There are cases, however, in which focusing inward has consequences that are even more elaborate than this. From considering the complexities of these latter effects of self-focus, and borrowing from other work in social psychology, cognitive psychology, and elsewhere, we have extrapolated a rather general theoretical orientation to the self-regulation of behavior. In the first portion of this chapter we outline this orientation, and describe some of the research evidence of the important involvement of self-awareness in the self-regulatory dynamics we have postulated. We then turn to the concept of anxiety, and indicate places where the approach we have offered has some specific things to say about the relationship between anxiety and self-related cognitions.

CONTROL PROCESSES AND BEHAVIOR

We have come to assume that behavioral self-regulation is guided by the operation of feedback systems, which comprise essentially the same functions as take place in thermostats, guided missiles, and other automated self-regulatory devices (see also MacKay, 1966; Powers, 1973; Wiener, 1948). The guidance of human behavior is distinguished from self-regulation in these other systems primarily by virtue of its greater complexity, the fact that the system in which it is taking place is biological rather than electromechanical, and the fact that we are able to introspect upon its occurrence throughout our waking lives. The component functions implied by this view of human behavior include the following. People monitor or check on their present activities, qualities, or states, a function that is labelled in Figure 8.1 as "input function." These perceptions are then compared against salient reference values or standards (at the point in Figure 8.1 marked "comparator"). If the two are discrepant, the person attempts to bring the one into line with the other by making a change — changing what he or she is doing, or attempting to change the personal qualities that he or she is manifesting. This attempt to change is represented in Figure 8.1 by what is labelled "output function."

This approach to understanding behavior assumes a continuous (or a repeated) self-reflective monitoring of the effects of one's actions. More specifically, it assumes that this monitoring focuses on how closely the action outcomes match the reference values to which the actions are intended to

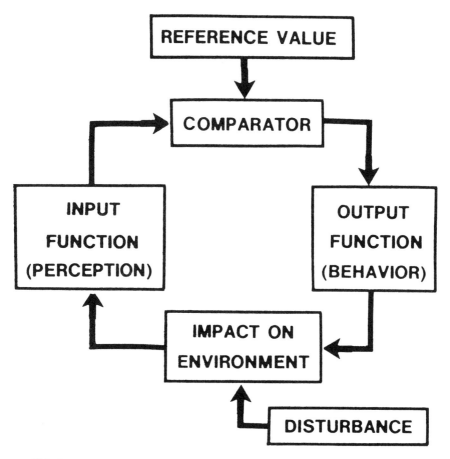

FIG. 8.1.   Representation of a negative feedback loop, the basic unit of analysis of cybernetic control.

conform. The function of a feedback system — taken as a whole — is to minimize any sensed discrepancies between the two.

There are two facets of what we just said that are important, though for different reasons. The first, perhaps the more obvious of the two, is the argument that human action displays the characteristics of feedback control. The second concerns what is happening at what is labelled the comparator of the feedback system (Figure 8.1). "Comparator" is a generic name for a component processor whose function it is to make comparisons. In terms that are intuitive or psychologically meaningful, the function that is taking place at the comparator is what occurs when people self-reflectively check on the correspondence between what they are doing and what they are trying to do. The key word here is "self-reflectively."

This notion returns us, of course, to the more elaborate function of the self's capacity of reflexivity, to which we alluded earlier. We have argued (e.g., Carver & Scheier, 1981a, 1982a, 1983) that focusing attention inward to the self when some behavioral reference value has been made salient promotes the action of the comparator of the feedback system that is being used to self-regulate the person's action. As the comparator is engaged, behavior is altered so as to more closely approximate the reference value. In this fashion, we believe, self-awareness serves as the moderator of consciously controlled behavior.

Self-Attention and the Comparator Function

There are two lines of evidence that support this reasoning. The more basic, if also the more recent, concerns the function that presumably takes place at the comparator. Recent research has found that high levels of self-focus are associated with efforts to seek out concrete information that would allow one to make a mental comparison at a more abstract level between actual performance and the situationally salient performance standard (Scheier & Carver, 1983a). As one illustration of the kind of information to which we are referring, consider test norms. Norms provide people with information that allows them to assess the adequacy of their performance on the test in question (cf. Trope, 1975, 1979). Seeking out norms thus may be seen as an active attempt to engage in a comparison between one's own test behavior and some meaningful reference value. Persons who are highly self-attentive (either via an experimental manipulation or by disposition) seek out normative information to a greater degree than do less self-attentive persons (Scheier & Carver, 1983a). The findings of this research thus appear to indicate that self-directed attention (in this sort of situation) does promote a function very much like that of the comparator in Figure 8.1.

The second line of evidence bears on the overall function of the feedback system — that is, reducing discrepancies. This line of evidence consists of a large accumulation of research findings indicating that self-directed attention promotes closer behavioral correspondence to salient reference values. One illustration of this sort of finding (Carver, 1975) comes from research in which people were preselected as having one of two specific attitudes on the use of punishment as a technique — some favored it, others opposed it. Subjects then attempted to teach another person in what was portrayed as a concept formation procedure. The procedure required the administration of punishment for incorrect responding, but the subjects were free to choose from a wide range of punishment intensities. The instructions told all subjects to choose intensities according to what they thought would be best, thereby making each person's attitude salient as a reference value.

For some subjects, self-attention was increased experimentally while they were engaged in the teaching task. Subjects in this conditon chose shock intensities for administration that were in line with their attitudes. That is, pro-punishment subjects administered relatively intense shocks, anti-punishment subjects administered shocks of relatively low intensities. When self-focus was lower, however, subjects' behavior was much less in line with their attitudes, with both attitudinal groups administering intermediate levels of punishment.

This study illustrates the basic principle that self-focus facilitates discrepancy reduction in behavior. But describing this single study does not begin to do justice to the wide range of behavioral contexts in which conceptually similar effects have been demonstrated. The behaviors in question have been as diverse as speed of letter copying (Carver & Scheier, 1981b; Wicklund & Duval, 1971), the taking of candies from a Halloween bowl (Beaman, Klentz, Diener, & Svanum, 1979), and the use of the equity norm in resource allocation (Greenberg, 1980). In each of these cases, the result of higher levels of self-focused attention was enhanced conformity to the salient behavioral standard.

Before we continue, let us interject a word about how self-attention is varied in the studies we are describing. Both experimental and correlational techniques are available for use in research. People can be made more aware of themselves at given points in the experimental session by the presence of such devices as mirrors facing the subject. There are also chronic individual differences in the tendency to be aware of oneself, which are measured by an instrument called the Self-Consciousness Scale (Fenigstein, Scheier, & Buss, 1975). Both techniques — experimental manipulation and personality disposition — have been subjected to a good deal of validity testing, with both standing up quite well in that regard (see Carver & Scheier, 1981a, Chapter 3, for a detailed discussion of this evidence, as well as a treatment of the issue of ecological validity). In our own research we have attempted to use a converging approach, in which we conduct conceptual replications with experimental manipulations in some studies, and individual differences in other studies.

This approach gives us greater confidence that we know what is mediating a given behavioral effect, and has provided a continued flow of information concerning the overall validity of the self-attention construct.[1]

CONCEPTUAL ELABORATIONS

Directing attention to oneself, briefly or for longer periods, once or perhaps repeatedly, appears on the basis of the evidence just reviewed to promote conformity to salient reference values. But there are two additional qualifications or elaborations that need to be mentioned. One of them carries us into complexities that are somewhat peripheral to the focus of this chapter, though not entirely unrelated to it. The other we see as being critically important for an adequate examination of anxiety and its effects on behavior.

Hierarchical Organization

One elaboration follows from this question: When people monitor their actions, they seem to monitor just one quality of it. How is it that the behavior is done correctly — physically — on the basis of such a circumscribed check? In addressing this question, we have tentatively adopted the argument of William Powers, who has pointed out that feedback systems can be organized hierarchically (Powers, 1973). Recall the single loop from Figure 8.1. Powers' argument is that the reference value of a basic, primitive, low-level feedback loop is provided as the behavioral output of an overriding or superordinate loop (see Figure 8.2). Each system monitors feedback input at the level of abstraction that is appropriate to its own functioning.

In principle, this kind of organization can be multi-leveled (cf. Shavelson & Marsh, this volume). Powers (1973) has argued for the utility of postulating nine different levels of control. These were intended to account for self-regulation from what might be thought of as the superordinate reference value of one's idealized self (at the highest level) on downward through concrete action strategies (at a more intermediate level) on downward to the level of muscle tensions (at the very lowest level). If self-regulation is active at the very highest level of control — if, for example, something has caused you

---

[1] There is an additional issue that we should mention in passing here concerning the assessment and manipulation of self-directed attention. A useful distinction has been proposed between "private" self-aspects and "public" self-aspects (e.g., Fenigstein et al., 1975). Given this distinction, it seems obvious that attention can be directed to either self-aspect selectively. There are many circumstances where it matters a great deal which self-aspect is taken as the object of one's attention, and where it thus is important to keep this distinction in mind (see Carver & Scheier, 1985; Scheier & Carver, 1981, 1983b, for reviews of this literature). It is relatively easy to avoid this issue in the present context, however, and we have chosen to do so for the sake of simplicity.

to wonder whether you are currently living up to your idealized self-image—behavior is simultaneously regulated on downward through the hierarchy (relatively automatically, at lower levels) in the effort to ensure discrepancy reduction at that highest level (see Carver & Scheier, 1981a, for greater detail). Figure 8.2 is a partial portrayal of a momentary slice of the behavior of a person who is presently involved in such an attempt to minimize discrepancies concerning his self-image.

Only three or four of the levels of control postulated by Powers are of much direct interest to personality/social psychologists. These are the levels toward the top of the hierarchy.[2] But assuming the existence of the totality of such an organization (or an organization with similar functional characteristics—see, e.g., Dawkins, 1976; Gallistel, 1980) appears to have several virtues. It accounts for the actual physical creation of behavioral acts, in a fashion that seems quite compatible with current conceptualizations of the nature of motor control (e.g., Adams, 1971, 1976; Kelso, 1982; Marteniuk, 1976; Stelmach, 1976). It also provides a conceptual basis for accounting for two indisputable facts: that identical actions can have completely distinct purposes at different times, and that extraordinarily different actions can serve identical purposes (a pair of facts that behavioristic theorists have felt most comfortable in simply ignoring).

These two facts are usually addressed—when they are addressed at all—at a relatively low level of abstraction (e.g., the process by which a rat creates a bar press in a Skinner box). But these relationships among action qualities and the goals to which they are directed are obviously important in complex human behavior as well. In a hierarchical organization of action qualities, extremely diverse concrete behaviors—for example, doing well on an exam, solving a problem in the electrical system of your car, helping a little old lady across the street—can serve similar discrepancy reducing functions with regard to superordinate goals—for example, feeling a sense of self-worth.

Interruption and Disengagement

The ideas we have discussed thus far provide a basis for thinking about successful, effective behavior. But one thing we have not yet considered is the fact that behavior is not always successful. Sometimes people have trouble attaining the goals they have taken up. Sometimes the actions being produced do not reduce the discrepancies to which they are directed. Any viable analy-

---

[2]Interestingly enough, qualities of action that are very similar to those at the top of Powers' hierarchy also appear in other conceptualizations that have been developed independently by other theorists who are interested in the structure of the self-regulation of complex behavior (cf. Schank & Abelson, 1975; Vallacher & Wegner, in press).

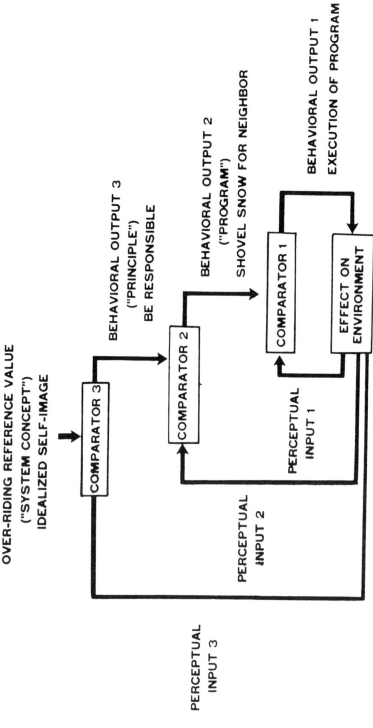

FIG. 8.2. A three-level hierarchy of feedback systems, in which the superordinate system "behaves" by specifying reference values to the system at the next lower level of abstraction (cf. Powers, 1973). At the very lowest level of abstraction the behavioral output is literally behavior (changes in muscle tensions, in the case of human behavior). This figure displays only the uppermost three levels of control postulated by Powers in his discussion of the human nervous system as an elaborate set of control devices (see Carver & Scheier, 1981, 1982a, 1983, for more complete treatments). This illustration portrays a person who is attempting to live up to his self-image, by following the principle of responsibility, which is being realized in terms of the programmatic activity of shoveling snow off the front walk of the elderly woman next door.

sis of behavior (including this one) needs a way of talking about how people respond to blockages in discrepancy reduction attempts.

We assume that the self-regulation mediated by self-focus is ordinarily quite straightforward and proceeds uninterrupted until and unless cues begin to appear that discrepancy reduction is not taking place.[3] Impeded efforts, or rising anxiety, may induce the person to stop for a moment — to interrupt the attempt — and to consider, if only for a moment, what the chances are of the desired outcome occurring (cf. Simon, 1967). Presumably this assessment process (which is discussed in greater detail elsewhere, Carver & Scheier, 1981a, Chapter 10) makes use of several different sources of information concerning the present situation, one's preceding activities, and the relative effectiveness with which those activities have moved one toward the behavioral goal.

Though in previous statements we have not emphasized this point, the expectancy-assessment process can be conceptualized fairly straightforwardly as involving a distinct and separate feedback system. The expectancy-assessment system, however, perceives and regulates an informational quality that differs in at least one very important respect from the information monitored by the system that is guiding overt action. The simplest way to put it is that the assessment loop is checking on the *progress* of the action loop. "Progress" is a quality that must be integrated across time and effort expended, in much the same way as "acceleration" must be integrated from successive instances of "velocity." The assessment loop takes as its reference value some *rate of progress* toward discrepancy reduction (as opposed to the goal of the discrepancy reduction attempt per se — which, even if abstract, is more fundamental).[4]

The perception of positive progress constitutes discrepancy reduction for this expectancy-assessment system. It is experienced subjectively as a favorable expectancy, or hope, with regard to the behavioral activities monitored by the action loop (cf. Stotland, 1969). The perception of an absence of progress

---

[3]Roy Baumeister (personal communication, June 1983) has pointed out to us quite correctly that there are also activities, particularly those that take place over relatively longer periods of time, in which periodic interruptions are built in, as a function of the structure of the activity itself.

[4]We should distinguish explicitly between what we are discussing here and an emerging literature concerning various parameters of goal setting (see, e.g., Bandura & Schunk, 1981; Kirschenbaum, Humphrey, & Malett, 1981; Kirschenbaum, Tomarken, & Ordman, 1982), one of which is how close or far away in time the goal is. The level of abstraction of the variables manipulated in the goal-setting research is invariably the level of the overt action loop. Subjects in that research can (and presumably do) make expectancy assessments periodically based on their "progress" toward whatever goal has been set. "Progress," in each case, still must reflect an integration across some span of time and effort, regardless of how near or far the goal is (see also Carver & Scheier, 1981a, Chapter 10; 1982a).

or diminishing progress constitutes a discrepancy in this expectancy-assessment system, or may even constitute discrepancy enlargement. It is experienced subjectively as an unfavorable expectancy, or doubt, with regard to the behavioral activities being monitored by the action loop.

Note that the size of the discrepancy confronted by the action loop does not play an important role in expectancy assessment. Even a very large discrepancy perceived at the level of the action loop can be associated with perceptions of either positive or negative expectancies. If the expectancy-assessment system perceives a positive rate of progress (i.e., toward discrepancy reduction at the action loop), expectancies will be favorable.

It is most straightforward to imagine this expectancy-assessment system utilizing as its reference value the mere existence of "progress" (yes versus no). But this system (as is normally true of feedback systems in complex organizations) is fully capable of monitoring with respect to varying definitions of "progress." For certain kinds of action programs — for example, the training process in medical or law school — progress must keep pace with the demands of the program of training, which are themselves time-dependent (cf. Carver & Scheier, 1982a). Here, even continuous positive progress in an absolute sense (i.e., successful learning of required material) is inadequate if it does not occur at a rate equivalent to the pacing of the course. Thus, in this sort of circumstance the expectancy-assessment loop must evaluate progress with respect to a more stringent standard.

The preceding discussion was rather abstract. The consequences of the expectancy-assessment process, however, are much more concrete, and do not require control-process vocabulary to describe. We view expectancy assessment as constituting a sort of psychological "watershed," leading to one of two categories of behavioral response (see Figure 8.3). If expectancies are sufficiently favorable, the person thereupon engages in renewed efforts. If expectancies are sufficiently unfavorable (having thereby passed the watershed point), the result is a tendency to disengage from further efforts (cf. Klinger, 1975; Kukla, 1972). Sufficiently extreme doubts about discrepancy reduction produce abandonment of the goal or reference value altogether. (In effect, the person backs out of whatever corner he or she happens to be in, and eventually takes up a new goal.) The level of subjective probability at which efforts give way to disengagement presumably varies with the subjective importance of the behavioral dimension. Regardless of where the watershed occurs, both the renewed efforts and the disengagement are presumed to be exaggerated by subsequent self-focus.

Research Support.   Evidence supportive of the watershed aspect of this model also comes from a fairly wide range of sources. Perhaps the most explicit experimental test of these ideas was a study in which we looked at how task-directed efforts were influenced by self-focus and expectancies concern-

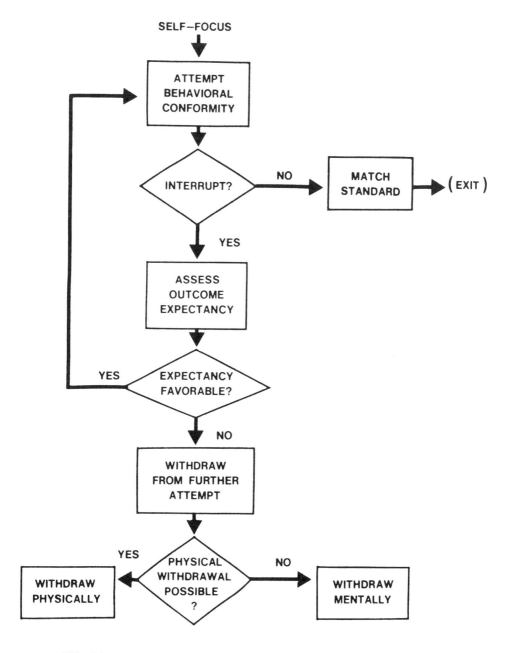

FIG. 8.3. Postulated sequence following from self-directed attention when a behavioral reference value is salient, including the possibilities of interruption (leading to expectancy assessment) and disengagement (if expectancies are sufficiently unfavorable), which may be either overt or covert (adapted from Carver, 1979).

ing discrepancy reduction (Carver, Blaney, & Scheier, 1979b). Large discrepancies on the salient behavioral dimension were created among all subjects in
this research by causing them to fail on an initial task. An experimental manipulation was then introduced in which we varied subjects' expectations of
being able to reduce this discrepancy by doing well at a second, ostensibly
closely related task.

The second task in this research was actually a measure of persistence — a
design problem that is to be traced with a continuous line, but which is insoluble according to the rules that have been given (Feather, 1961). The measure
of interest in this research was the degree to which subjects would display
continued efforts in the face of this frustration. Our prediction was that there
would be an interaction between these experimentally manipulated expectancies and level of experimentally manipulated self-directed attention. The results were exactly as predicted (Figure 8.4). High levels of self-directed atten-

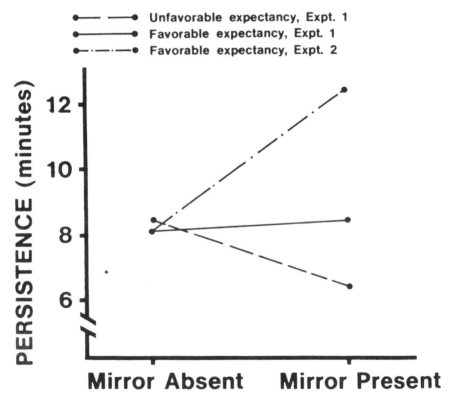

FIG. 8.4.   Persistence at an insoluble puzzle as a function of experimentally increased
self-attention (mirror presence) and favorable versus unfavorable expectancies (adapted
from Carver, Blaney, & Scheier, 1979b).

tion caused an increase in the persistence of the hopeful subjects. And high levels of self-attention caused a decrease in the persistence of the doubtful subjects.

Results conceptually similar to these have also been obtained in a variety of other studies. The studies have looked at the effects of several independent variables as antecedents of disengagement, for example, prolonged failure (Carver & Scheier, 1982b; Scheier & Carver, 1982), and have also used a range of different dependent variables, including maze performance (Carver & Scheier, 1982b) and anagram solution (Scheier & Carver, 1983c).

Very recent research (Carver, Antoni, & Scheier, 1985) has also extended this interactive principle to the information seeking that presumably mediates the action of the comparator. Recall that seeking out test norms can be construed as reflecting the attempt to compare one's behavior against salient reference values. Consistent with the interactive behavioral effect shown in Figure 8.4, this information seeking phenomenon appears very much dependent upon the holding of reasonably positive expectations of doing well on the test in question. After a pronounced and prolonged failure on an initial task, self-focus promoted instead a tendency toward active avoidance of normative information concerning what ostensibly was a closely related task. This is just what one would expect to see on the part of a person who is trying to disengage from active self-regulation on that behavioral dimension.

Disengagement: Additional Issues

There are several additional assumptions in this portion of the model, stemming from the fact that people cannot always withdraw easily from their discrepancy reduction attempts. One aspect of this problem is that there are many circumstances in which one would like to withdraw physically from the attempt to match behavior to a reference value, but the social context does not sanction it (or in some cases the physical setting does not permit it). We assume that under these conditions the disengagement impulse is likely to be expressed psychologically, rather than overtly (see Figure 8.3, earlier).

As what may be a rather trivial illustration of this point, imagine the plight of a "football widow," a woman whose husband spends every possible minute watching football games. The woman in question happens to hold the principle that people whom she holds dear should be catered to occasionally. Her husband has always wanted her to enjoy football, and today she has decided to go along with him to a game and do her best to really enjoy it.

Fifteen minutes later she is bored to tears, no longer feels she can tolerate the attempt to understand what is going on, and is ready to get up and go home. Given the social context, however, this is not what she does. Instead, her eyes glaze over and she begins to daydream. She thinks about things she would rather be doing, perhaps plans what she will do if the game ever ends, perhaps spends some time simply looking at the other faces in the crowd. All of these activities can be seen as reflecting psychological disengagement from the attempt to enjoy the game. Perhaps she even engages in small-scale (sanctioned) overt withdrawals, such as trips to the concession stand.

This example gives a sense of what we mean by mental disengagement. It does not, of course, give a very good sense of the kinds of situations we have studied in our research (we have not yet been able to obtain funding to study behavior at football games). In the kinds of situations to which we have given the greatest research attention, mental disengagement is most likely to mean disengagement of effort or attention in some task the person has been assigned. This in turn, is typically measured as a decrement in task performance (e.g., Carver & Scheier, 1982b; Scheier & Carver, 1983c), though in principle it can also be measured in other ways, such as through some index of off-task thinking (cf. Diener & Dweck, 1978).

Mental disengagement is sometimes a very useful strategy for people. (It would probably get our football widow successfully through the afternoon, for example.) But the strategy can not always be carried out completely, or for long periods of time. It is important for theoretical reasons to consider more fully what happens when people experience this impulse to disengage and cannot give it full expression.

Remember that the impetus to disengage comes from perceived failure to reduce discrepancies between one's behavior and some reference value, and more particularly from doubts about being able to reduce those discrepancies in the future. Unfortunately, it is often the case that the reference values in question — the values that are at the heart of all of this — are important, even central to one's life. It is possible to refuse to attend to those values — for a while. But without a rather drastic reorganization of one's value system (or of the pattern of one's life activities), it is impossible to avoid for very long reconfronting those psychological dimensions, and thereupon reconfronting the doubts that prompted the disengagement impulse in the first place (see Figure 8.5).

It is here that we re-encounter the notion of hierarchical organization, and the potential importance and usefulness of that notion. That is, given a hierarchical structure of values, a failure to reduce discrepancies at a low level (e.g., programmatic activity such as drafting a book chapter) often has serious implications regarding discrepancy reduction at a higher level (one's ideal self-image as a professional writer). Indeed, a disengagement from efforts at the lower level may be seen as creating discrepancy *enlargement* at that higher level. The logic of hierarchical organization thus suggests that programmatic activities acquire their importance in large part via this relation to higher order goals.

Let us now return to our example, which at this point becomes somewhat less trivial. Imagine that the reference value with respect to which the woman

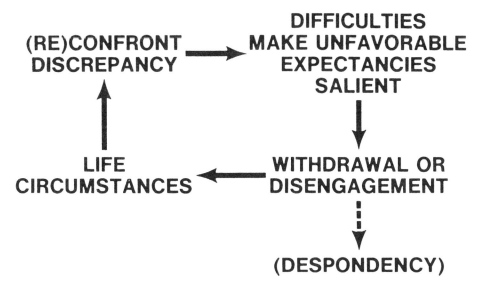

FIG. 8.5. Attempts to disengage (behaviorally or psychologically) from salient and personally important reference values are often prevented by the fact that life circumstances cause one to reconfront the behavioral dimension in question. This in turn often leads to reconfronting the doubts that prompted disengagement in the first place. The long term effect of this cycle is despondency and depression.

is attempting to self-regulate is not just the principle that her husband should be catered to now and again, or the programmatic goal of enjoying the game. Imagine instead that this woman's sense of self-respect (a very high-level reference value) is intimately bound up in enjoying the activities her husband likes. To do this, she feels compelled to go to those football games not just once, but every week. Now that there is even a springtime football league, she gets to look forward to going to a football game practically every weekend for the rest of her life.

This woman can hardly bear the thought of sitting through a single game. She simply cannot make herself "enjoy" the experience, and thereby share it with her husband. She knows, even as she begins the attempt, that it will not work. But leaving the game, or declining to go at all, means a great deal more than simply annoying her husband, or admitting defeat at this restricted activity. It means to her (given the structure of her reference values) that she is failing as a human being. She can avoid thinking about it for a while, but not for very long. Every time she looks out at the field, she wants to leave, and can't.

Add to this picture one final assumption, alluded to earlier but not made explicit: the watershed among behavioral responses to expectancy assessment is paralleled by the generation of affect of two sorts. Favorable expectancies (even if discrepancy reduction in the action loop has a very long way to go) give rise to positive affect — hope, even elation. Unfavorable expectancies give rise to negative affect — doubt, or when more extreme, depression or despair (see Carver & Scheier, 1982b; Weiner, 1982, for supporting evidence).

We assume a rough inverse relation between behavioral and affective responses, with affect being most intense when the person is simply focusing on the expectancy rather than engaging in whichever behavioral response the expectancy leads to (cf. Peters, 1970). The most salient implications of this assumption concern the negative side of the watershed, and particularly those cases in which behavioral or mental disengagement is somehow being prevented. In this set of circumstances, the result should in theory be a festering of aversive feelings.

The hypothetical example we have been discussing may appear to some to be so frivolous that it hardly has any relevance for a serious consideration of the nature of personal problems in self-management. We suggest, very much to the contrary, that the structure implicit in the situation we have described is extremely common, though the concrete elements obviously vary quite widely. This structure may represent in fact the most common source of anguish in human experience.

To reiterate, we would argue that the holding of severe doubts with regard to discrepancy reduction on a behavioral dimension that is personally valued as important leads to a predictable cycle (cf. Kanfer & Hagerman, 1981). People in this situation repeatedly reconfront the large discrepancies between their existing states and those reference values (Figure 8.5). They may engage in sporadic efforts at reducing the discrepancies, but eventually they are overtaken by their doubts, leading once again to disengagement. The diminished efforts that are engendered by awareness of the unfavorable outcome expectancies often contribute to additional failures (which thereby help to reconfirm and solidify the doubts). Because focusing on this inability is impossible to avoid for long, and because such a focus generates negative affect, the result is often depression and despondency.

ANXIETY AND COPING

This, then, is the theoretical model with which we approach the understanding of human behavior. We should re-emphasize that the elements of this model were not developed specifically to account for people's behavior or cognition in anxiety-inducing situations. Nor was the model even devised as a way of accounting for difficulties in self-management. Rather, it was developed to represent the structure of ordinary behavioral activity, ranging in scope from the successful execution of intentions, to giving up the attempt to play guitar because of perceived lack of personal efficacy, to being unable to buy dog food because it is a holiday and all the stores are closed.

Despite this more general path of derivation, however, we believe that the model also has some very important things to say about people's responses to anxiety.

Confronting a Feared Stimulus

The first explicit test of the "watershed" aspect of our theoretical approach to self-regulation was in fact a study of the behavioral and cognitive consequences of anxiety. Subjects in this research (Carver et al., 1979a) were persons who reported having moderate levels of fearfulness concerning nonpoisonous snakes. This self-rated level of chronic fearfulness was identical among all subjects. The subjects varied, however, in another important respect. When asked what they would do if requested to pick up a snake, some subjects said that they were unsure that they would be able to go through with it (doubtful). Others said they thought they could do it despite the clear discomfort they would experience (confident).

All subjects later came individually to sessions in which they were asked to put on gloves, enter a corridor, walk up to an aquarium, open the top, and pick up and hold a boa constrictor (approximately 1 m. in length). Self-focus was experimentally increased among half of the subjects during their attempt to do this. Dependent measures included how far in the approach sequence subjects went before removing themselves from the area of the aquarium and returning to their starting point; a post-experimental self-rating of how much anxiety subjects had experienced during the attempt; and self-reports of what subjects had been focusing on during the attempt.

Recall that self-focus during the experience of intense affect makes that affect particularly salient. Thus, consistent with our expectation, there was a main effect for self-awareness condition on subjects' anxiety ratings. Those who were more self-aware reported having experienced greater anxiety than did those who were less self-aware. The pattern of all other data was in marked contrast to this main affect — but completely in line with our predictions. That is, all other measures displayed interactions between self-focus and subjects' chronic coping expectancies.

Confident subjects reported having focused more on the comparison between their behavior and the goal (holding the snake) when self-focus was high than when it was lower. Doubtful subjects reported having focused *less* on that comparison when self-focus was higher than when it was lower, with a compensatory increase in focus on doubts and inadequacies. Behavioral responses paralleled these retrospective accounts. Confident subjects were undeterred by high levels of self-focus (despite the increased anxiety it engendered). Doubtful subjects responded to that increased anxiety by disengaging from the approach attempt at an earlier stage when self-focus was high than when it was low.

Thus, self-directed attention and expectancies concerning one's capacity to cope interacted to determine behavior (and the contents of consciousness) in an anxiety-provoking situation. Though both sets of subjects experienced anxiety (and did so to enhanced degrees under conditions of high self-focus), confident subjects responded with active striving, whereas doubtful subjects responded with physical withdrawal from active striving.

This study documents the relevance of our model of self-regulation to the analysis of responses in anxiety-inducing situations. However, the study is limited in important ways. It is not too often, for example, that people's lives are seriously hampered by the fear of nonpoisonous snakes. It might plausibly be argued that such a fear is sufficiently unimportant that it represents a poor proving ground for any theory.

There are, on the other hand, several other fears that are of greater consequence in people's lives. We have also spent some time examining one of these fears. The case in question is the anxiety, and concomitant performance impairment, that many people experience when confronted by tests.

Test Anxiety

Test taking is apparently a stressful experience for most people, and difficulty in coping with this stress is a serious problem for many. We say that test taking is stressful for "most people" for a very good reason. Two recent studies have documented that people experience increases in physiological arousal both prior to and during tests (Hollandsworth, Glazeski, Kirkland, Jones, & Van Norman, 1979; Holroyd, Westbrook, Wolf, & Badhorn, 1978). These effects were found not just among persons whose verbal reports classified them as being test anxious, but also among persons who gave no outward indication at all of being test anxious.

This pattern of data is particularly intriguing when viewed from the perspective of our theoretical model. Specifically, it would appear to be the case that what distinguishes persons high and low in test anxiety from each other is not how aroused they become in the testing situation. Instead, what seem to be most important are the cognitive and behavioral responses to the arousal, and to the test situation more generally (cf. Deffenbacher, 1980; Morris & Ponath, this volume; see also Mahoney's, 1979, analysis of similar processes in a different behavioral arena). Said differently, when examining test-taking behavior, we see two groups of persons under stress — one group engaged in active coping, the other group engaged in something else. The parallels between these two categories of persons and the "confident" versus "doubtful" subjects described just above seem to us to be quite striking.

We would characterize the experience of the test anxious person who is in the exam room in the following way. These people are doubtful about being able to cope with their fear, about being able to do well on the exam, and about thereby satisfying the desires or demands of significant others (Ellis, 1962; Nicholls, 1976; Wine, 1982). As the tension mounts, or as frustration regarding task solution is experienced, efforts directed toward the task are interrupted, leading to assessment of outcome expectancies.

Given chronic doubts (paralleled in most cases by situationally specific doubts), this assessment leads to an impetus to withdraw, to get away or disengage from the exam. But the test situation is one in which social sanctions prevent overt withdrawal. The impulse thus can only be expressed covertly, giving rise to off-task thinking, daydreaming, and the like (see, e.g., Nottelman & Hill, 1977). This has the further result of causing readily available task relevant cues to be neglected or misinterpreted (Geen, 1976; West, Lee, & Anderson, 1969; see also Tobias, this volume). Consistent with this picture, and with our theoretical position, is the recent finding (Galassi, Frierson, & Sharer, 1981) that the most frequently occurring thought during a test among test-anxious students (as reported retrospectively) concerned escaping from the situation.

Though covert disengagement may occur, it cannot be sustained. As we noted earlier, task goals are sometimes intimately bound up with higher-order goals. When this is true, it is very difficult for the person to disengage for long, before the situation is reconfronted. Though this may promote a return to efforts, such a return is temporary, with renewed interruption, and repeated reminders of the doubts and perceptions of inadequacy. The result is a phenomenology of self-deprecatory rumination (e.g., Deffenbacher, 1978; Mandler & Watson, 1966; Meichenbaum, 1972), evidence of which among the test anxious has been well catalogued by Wine (1971, 1982).

Among persons lower in test anxiety, a different sequence occurs. We assume that even these people occasionally interrupt their efforts, due to tension or task frustration, and assess their expectancies for coping with the demands of the test. Being more confident, however, these people thereupon renew their efforts at the task at hand. Though interruption may occur more than once, indeed may occur fairly often, persons on the positive side of the psychological watershed will not experience the disengagement impulse that we see as underlying the off-task thoughts, and (given a longer chain of processes) as underlying the self-deprecatory cognition. Thus neither of these types of cognition occurs very frequently. Nor is task performance impaired.

Though plausible, this reasoning would obviously be more compelling if supported by data. We have, in fact, recently reported two studies that appear to fit the analysis reasonably well (Carver, Peterson, Follansbee, & Scheier, 1983). Subjects in this research were students who were either high or low in test anxiety. They participated in individual sessions, in which they were told that they would be working on sets of items taken from an intelligence test that was currently in its last stages of development. An effort was made to create a situation that was moderately stressful for all participants.

Subjects in one study (Carver et al., 1983, Experiment 1) were then given a set of timed anagrams. They were told to call out item solutions to the experimenter (who faced away from the subject, and recorded solution times as well as item solutions). While engaged in this task, half the subjects sat before a self-focus inducing stimulus. The reasoning outlined above predicts that self-focus should be facilitative among subjects low in test anxiety, but should have the opposite effect among those high in test anxiety. As shown in Figure 8.6, this was exactly what occurred. Indeed, this effect was rather consistent across two levels of item difficulty.

Post-experimental self-reports of subjects' contents of consciousness also yielded a picture that was generally supportive of our reasoning. High levels of self-focus tended to be associated with self-reports of greater intrusion of task-irrelevant thoughts among the test anxious, and with less intrusion among those who were not test anxious (both compared to comparable low self-focus control groups). An interaction of the opposite form was found on an item asking subjects what percentage of the testing time they thought they

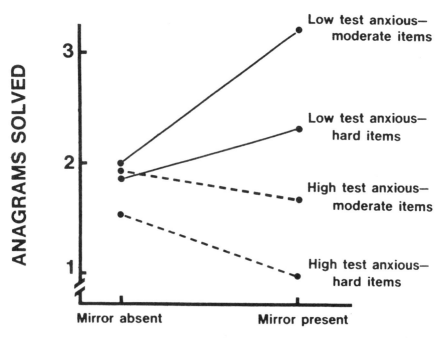

FIG. 8.6.   Anagram solutions as a function of experimentally increased self-attention (mirror presence) and premeasured level of test anxiety (from Carver, Peterson, Follansbee, & Scheier, 1983).

had devoted to focusing on the elements of the task. Self-focus was associated with an increase in this tendency among those who were not test anxious, and with a decrease in this tendency among those who were test anxious. These self-reports, as well as the behavioral effects, are conceptually quite similar to the data obtained in the earlier study of snake phobics (Carver et al., 1979a).

Recall that our analysis of the effects of test anxiety is based on the argument that performance impairments follow from a mental disengagement from task efforts. This argument follows, in turn, from the notion that there is an underlying impulse for overt, behavioral disengagement, but that the expression of that impulse ordinarily is stifled due to social constraints in the test situation (cf. Galassi et al., 1981). Because of those constraints, it is hard to obtain evidence of the existence of the behavioral impulse. On the other hand, such evidence would appear to be highly desirable as support for our reasoning.

In order to obtain overt disengagement, one must in some way create a situation in which disengagement is sanctioned. One way to do this involves reconstruing the test, and thus the test-taking behavior, in slightly different terms. Though we ordinarily think of subjects' response to the entire test as the behavior of interest, it is also possible to take the individual test item as the unit of analysis. This appears to provide a means of dealing with the problem that we confronted. If an opportunity were provided for subjects to return to any given item later on, disengagement from active attempts to solve the item should entail little or no concern about potential social sanctions.

This reasoning provided the basis for another study (Carver et al., 1983, Experiment 2). Subjects in this research were given the same general orientation as was used in Experiment 1, but the task procedures differed in several important ways. First, no mention was made of any time limit. Second, rather than call out item solutions, subjects were to record solutions themselves on an answer sheet. Finally, subjects were told that they could attempt a given anagram as often as they wished, but that they must attempt them in a specific order. If the subject wished to defer an item, it should be placed on the bottom of the deck.

This rationale was used in order to allow easy monitoring of the dependent variable. The first item of the set was insoluble, and all subjects eventually placed it at the bottom of the deck. The dependent measure of interest was persistence at that item, with lack of persistence indicating behavioral disengagement. As in the other study, self-focus interacted with level of test anxiety, leading to greater persistence among persons low in test anxiety, and to reduced persistence among persons high in test anxiety.

We close this discussion of test anxiety by making two brief points concerning our theoretical analysis. First, readers who are familiar with the recent history of theory in test anxiety will note some similarities between our ideas and what is commonly referred to as the "cognitive-attentional" theory of test anxiety (e.g., Sarason, 1975, 1978; Wine, 1971, 1982). There are, in fact, certain similarities. But there are very important differences, as well. These differences appear to allow our analysis to account for a broader range of observed phenomena—both within and outside the literature of test anxiety—than does the alternative framework. Though a complete treatment of this issue is beyond the scope of this chapter, readers who are interested in the differences between theories will find more extensive discussions elsewhere (Carver et al., 1983; Carver & Scheier, 1981a, 1984).

Finally, we wish to hark back to the fanciful example that we used earlier in the chapter to illustrate our assumptions—the woman who hates football, but finds herself attending a football game with her husband. We remind you of that example in order to point out that the situation confronting the person high in test anxiety—and the responses that occur in that situation—are structurally quite similar to that earlier description. In both cases there is an impulse to withdraw, the execution of which is prevented by social constraints. In both cases, the result is a tendency toward mental disengagement, and intrusion of off-task thinking. In both cases, if small-scale socially sanctioned opportunities for disengagement exist, they are taken advantage of. Though there are obvious differences between the situations (the earlier illustration, for example, did not involve an anxiety inducing task), these structural similarities highlight the generality of the functional elements for which we have argued.

Social Anxiety

Test anxiety is one specific category of instances in which people give evidence of being unable to cope effectively with anxiety or stress, encountered while attempting some instrumental activity. But this is certainly not the only domain of ineffective coping that has studied thoroughly enough to have received a label. Another class of phenomena to which it is easy to point is given the name social anxiety.

We have not ourselves thus far undertaken research on social anxiety. But others have already begun to utilize much the same reasoning as has been outlined in this chapter as a vehicle for understanding the dynamics underlying social anxiety. Most notably, Schlenker and Leary (1982) have proposed that social interaction involves attempts to realize certain self-presentational goals — usually the creation of a positive impression in the eyes of some other person. Social anxiety arises when people have doubts about being able to create the desired impression, or when events occur that appear to interfere with or repudiate the image that was intended to be conveyed (see also Haemmerlie & Montgomery, 1982, 1984).

Once again, the discussion revolves around chronic (or situation-specific) doubts about matching one's behavior to salient reference values, or perceived failures to have matched those values. And once again, the consequences are structurally similar to those discussed above: avoidance of social interaction when possible; a tendency to spend time wondering and worrying about what kind of impression is being created (i.e., expectancy assessment) when interaction is actually taking place; and mental disengagement from the interaction process, which in turn is manifest in awkwardness, intrusion of stray thoughts, and the like. Because these various processes typically interfere with effective interaction, the result is often that outcomes are less than successful, and the expectations of poor future outcomes become more solidified.

As noted above, we have not yet undertaken research designed to examine the involvement of self-awareness processes in the phenomena of social anxiety. But at least one other set of investigators has recently begun to do so. Their study (Burgio, Merluzzi, & Pryor, 1982) yielded effects that were quite similar to the interaction discussed throughout this chapter: self-focus facilitating persons low in social anxiety, but impairing those high in social anxiety.

ADDITIONAL ISSUES

In the preceding sections we have described the applicability of our general approach to behavioral self-regulation to three specific settings in which appreciable anxiety is generated among at least a substantial minority of persons. In each case, the conceptual analysis appears to fit well with available research evidence. There are, however, at least three issues that deserve our further attention.

Expectancies and Skills

The first issue stems from the fact that expectancies rarely exist in a psychological vacuum. They are usually based heavily upon the person's history of prior experiences and outcomes in whatever behavioral domain is associated with the anxiety (see Carver & Scheier, 1981a, Chapter 10, for a broader discussion). More specifically, if one has coped successfully before, one will expect to cope successfully again. If one has failed to cope before, one may expect to fail to cope again.

This derivation of expectancies is, of course, subject to many kinds of influence, including attributions concerning the causes of prior outcomes (see, e.g., Bernstein, Stephan, & Davis, 1979; Covington & Omelich, 1979; Diener & Dweck, 1978; Dweck, 1975; Weiner, Nierenberg, & Goldstein, 1976). One important adverse influence on expectancies is the perception that one has in-adequate mastery of whatever skills are needed for coping (see, e.g., Bandura, 1977; Kanfer & Hagerman, 1981). Said more plainly, sometimes people have unfavorable expectancies because they believe themselves to be incapable of doing the things they need to do.

This perception is often well founded. Many students who are test anxious, for example, are people who have deficiencies in study skills, people who are in reality ill-prepared for the test they are about to take. On the other hand, although these skills may be necessary for successful coping, they appear not to be *sufficient* to ensure active coping (cf. Daly, 1978). If a person has the needed skills but lacks confidence of favorable outcomes, those skills are not likely to be deployed effectively, due to the disengagement of serious effort that follows from focusing on the unfavorable expectancies.

This argument has rather straightforward implications for the attempt to produce more effective coping. Indeed, it suggests two possible approaches (see also I. Sarason, this volume). The first would be to take both outcome expectancies and skills as targets of the behavior-change process. This line of reasoning seems consistent with the cognitive therapy procedures suggested by Beck (e.g., 1972, 1976). The second approach would be to induce people who have this sort of problem not to engage in expectancy assessment at all. This seems to be the tack taken by Meichenbaum (1977; see also Blaney, Strack, Ganellen, & Coyne, 1982; Brockner & Hulton, 1978; Kuhl, 1981).

Self-Related Cognitions as Epiphenomena

A second issue concerns how best to conceptualize the role of the phenome-nology of persons who are attempting to cope in anxiety-provoking circum-stances. The subject matter of this volume is "self-related cognitions in anxi-ety" (and motivation). This label conveys the implicit assumption that self-relevant cognitions play an important part in the phenomena associated with anxiety. Certainly this point of view has been expressed many times be-fore (see, e.g., Sarason, 1975, 1978; Wine, 1971, 1982). And there is a sense in which we obviously agree with that sentiment.

We wish, however, to draw attention to a difference between the role that we have assumed for certain of these cognitions and the role that appears to have been asssumed by other theorists. We are speaking here specifically of self-deprecatory rumination—what is to many people the most important category of self-related cognition in anxiety inducing situations. As outlined earlier, we see this set of cognitions as being a *consequence* of a series of pro-cesses, one consequence among several. Whereas other theorists emphasize the possibility that such cognition may be a cause of performance problems, we emphasize instead that it is an effect of other dynamics—just as are the performance problems themselves.

What this means is that the self-deprecatory rumination is, in an important sense, epiphenomenal. It is not, in our view, the heart of the matter. The mere process of self-reflection is surely not debilitating per se — even when anxiety is fairly high (Carver et al., 1979a; Carver et al., 1983). Behavioral impairment occurs as a function of self-reflection only when the content of that self-reflection is unfavorable outcome expectancies.

We make this point here because we believe that others have overemphasized the role of self-related rumination in instances of ineffective coping, due to its phenomenological prominence. We regard this overemphasis as somewhat ill-advised, because it can be misleading. It has apparently led many to be satisfied with a description of a phenomenology in which very little attention is paid to the processes that generate the phenomenology.[5]

We do not mean to suggest that these self-deprecatory cognitions are trivial. The circumstances in which they occur involve the generation of negative affect — thus they are impactful phenomenologically for the person who is experiencing them. Furthermore, these cognitions may play an important role in the solidifying of unfavorable expectancies for the future, via redundant encoding of this expectancy-related information. But we would stop short of according them causal primacy in the concomitant impairment of behavior.

The Creation of Anxiety

A final issue to be addressed concerns the anxiety arousal itself. The issue is where the anxiety comes from. How is it generated? Simon (1967) has suggested that emotions such as anxiety constitute "interruptors" of focal processing, serving to indicate the possible need for rearranging the priorities of the goals to which behavior is directed. That is, goals are often ordered in terms of their priorities, and efforts are directed first at the attainment of the highest priority goal, with other goals left waiting in line (cf. Shallice's, 1978, discussion of the "dominant action system"). Anxiety represents a signal that some goal or activity not presently being worked at should be accorded a higher priority than is now the case, perhaps even a higher priority than the goal that is presently focal.

---

[5]There is a second sense in which the prominence of this phenomenology can be misleading, as well. Specifically, the fact that this rumination is so obviously self-related has led many writers to equate this phenomenology with the term "self-focus," and thereupon to contrast it with "task focus" (see, e.g., Blaney et al., 1982; Brockner & Hulton, 1978; Csikszentmihalyi & Figurski, 1982; Wine, 1971, 1982). Taking this position, however, completely ignores the large number of findings (discussed throughout the chapter) which indicate that in the proper circumstances self-focus induces task focus. Thus the difference in salient phenomenology has obscured in some minds the important role of self-focus in active coping efforts.

In some respects we have taken a similar position here concerning the interrupting function of anxiety. We have not, on the other hand, emphasized the notion of re-prioritization. Let us now consider the nature of anxiety more closely in that regard.

Anxiety arises when people have some reason for being concerned about their well-being, in a present or pending situation. This concern may be based on perceptions of the possibility of physical harm, the possibility of psychological harm, the possibility of harming the self-image that one holds or the image of oneself that is held by people around one. The danger may be real or imaginary. It appears reasonable, however, to suggest that increasing expectations of harm (of any of these sorts) lead to increasing anxiety.

Anxiety often (though not always) arises in the context of some task-directed behavior. In many cases the attempt to execute this specific behavior, in and of itself, poses no threat. What is threatening are the consequences, with regard to some *other* reference value, of failing to execute the behavior adequately. More concretely, it is not physically difficult to pick up and hold a snake. But carrying out this task involves (in the minds of at least some people) the risk of physical harm from the snake. The failure to answer test questions correctly poses no intrinsic threat. But failure on a test may threaten a self-image, and may eliminate behavioral alternatives that one desires to pursue (e.g., going on to a higher level of education, or getting a better job). Even the task of parachuting from an airplane is not difficult or threatening per se. What is threatening is the possibility of rather extreme consequences should the behavior not be carried out to the intended conclusion.

Anxiety, then, appears (in many cases, at least) to require the parallel processing of information concerning present states with regard to two goals. One goal is focal, whereas processing regarding the other goal may occur largely outside awareness (cf. Shallice, 1978). Anxiety appears to occur when there is being generated, in this secondary monitoring system, some sign of discrepancy enlargement with respect to the reference value being used by that system.

This assertion is, of course, speculative. But it would appear to be conceptually consistent with arguments made earlier in the chapter about the difficulties that are created when behavior concerning one reference value results in discrepancy enlargement regarding another (superordinate, in the previous discussion) reference value.

CONCLUDING STATEMENT

In this chapter we have reviewed our general orientation to the self-regulation of behavior and described several points at which that orientation has implications for understanding the cognitive and behavioral concomitants of anxiety. Though our emphasis here has been on anxiety, consistent with the theme of the volume, it should be obvious that the processes under discussion have implications for other emotional phenomena as well. The concept of depression has cropped up at several points in the discussion, and ideas similar to those detailed here are being investigated by other researchers who are interested in depression (Blaney et al., 1982). The same sort of reasoning has also been applied to the effects of having a low level of self-esteem (Brockner, 1979). Finally, these concepts appear similar in many respects (though providing unique contributions, in other respects) to the concepts that are typically invoked in discussions of human helplessness (see Carver et al., 1979b; Carver & Scheier, 1981a, Chapter 13; Scheier & Carver, 1983c).

Throughout this research, the view of human behavior that guides our thinking is one in which the person takes up — or synthesizes — goals, and monitors progress toward those goals. We close by restating one last time two themes that characterize this viewpoint: First, the monitoring of the goal of the dominant action system is a self-reflective process, involving conscious attention. Without this involvement of consciousness, overt action loses its purposive character. Second, it seems to us that the resemblance between this picture of active coping and the functional elements of the feedback loop is inescapable.

ACKNOWLEDGMENTS

Portions of the research reported in this chapter, and preparation of the chapter itself, were facilitated by grants BNS 81-07236 and BNS 80-21859 from the National Science Foundation. The chapter was written while the first author was Guest Professor at the Max-Planck-Institut für Psychologische Forschung, München, Federal Republic of Germany.

REFERENCES

Adams, J. A. A closed-loop theory of motor learning. *Journal of Motor Behavior,* 1971, *3,* 111–149.

Adams, J. A. Issues for a closed-loop theory of motor learning. In G. E. Stelmach (Ed.), *Motor control: Issues and trends.* New York: Academic Press, 1976.

Bandura, A. Self-efficacy: Toward a unifying theory of behavioral change. *Psychological Review,* 1977, *84,* 191–215.

Bandura, A., & Schunk, D. H. Cultivating competence, self-efficacy, and intrinsic interest through proximal self-motivation. *Journal of Personality and Social Psychology,* 1981, *41,* 586–598.

Beaman, A. L., Klentz, B., Diener, E., & Svanum, S. Self-awareness and transgression in children: Two field studies. *Journal of Personality and Social Psychology,* 1979, *37,* 1835–1846.

Beck, A. T. *Depression: Causes and treatment.* Philadelphia: University of Pennsylvania Press, 1972.

Beck, A. T. *Cognitive therapy and the emotional disorders.* New York: International Universities Press, 1976.

Bernstein, W. M., Stephan, W. G., & Davis, M. H. Explaining attributions for achievement: A path analytic approach. *Journal of Personality and Social Psychology,* 1979, *37,* 1810–1821.

Blaney, P. H., Strack, S., Ganellen, R. J., & Coyne, J. Attentional style and response deficits. Paper presented at the meeting of the American Psychological Association, Washington, DC, 1982.

Brockner, J. The effects of self-esteem, success-failure, and self-consciousness on task performance. *Journal of Personality and Social Psychology,* 1979, *37,* 1732–1741.

Brockner, J., & Hulton, A. J. B. How to reverse the vicious cycle of low self-esteem: The importance of attentional focus. *Journal of Experimental Social Psychology,* 1978, *14,* 564–578.

Brockner, J., & Swap, W. C. Resolving the relationships between placebos, misattributions, and insomnia: An individual-differences perspective. *Journal of Personality and Social Psychology,* 1983, *45,* 32–42.

Burgio, K. L., Merluzzi, T. V., & Pryor, J. B. The effects of self-focused attention and performance expectancies on social interaction. Paper presented at the meeting of the Eastern Psychological Association, Baltimore, 1982.

Carver, C. S. Physical aggression as a function of objective self-awareness and attitudes toward punishment. *Journal of Experimental Social Psychology,* 1975, *11,* 510–519.

Carver, C. S. A cybernetic model of self-attention processes. *Journal of Personality and Social Psychology,* 1979, *37,* 1251–1281.

Carver, C. S., Antoni, M., & Scheier, M. F. Self-consciousness and self-assessment. *Journal of Personality and Social Psychology,* 1985, *48,* 117–124.

Carver, C. S., Blaney, P. H., & Scheier, M. F. Focus of attention, chronic expectancy, and responses to a feared stimulus. *Journal of Personality and Social Psychology,* 1979, *37,* 1186–1195. (a)

Carver, C. S., Blaney, P. H., & Scheier, M. F. Reassertion and giving up: The interactive role of self-directed attention and outcome expectancy. *Journal of Personality and Social Psychology,* 1979, *37,* 1859–1870. (b)

Carver, C. S., Peterson, L. M., Follansbee, D. J., & Scheier, M. F. Effects of self-directed attention on performance and persistence among persons high and low in test anxiety. *Cognitive Therapy and Research,* 1983, *7,* 333–354.

Carver, C. S., & Scheier, M. F. *Attention and self-regulation: A control-theory approach to human behavior.* New York: Springer-Verlag, 1981. (a)

Carver, C. S., & Scheier, M. F. The self-attention-induced feedback loop and social facilitation. *Journal of Experimental Social Psychology,* 1981, *17,* 545–568. (b)

Carver, C. S., & Scheier, M. F. Control theory: A useful conceptual framework for personality-social, clinical, and health psychology. *Psychological Bulletin,* 1982, *92,* 111–135. (a)

Carver, C. S., & Scheier, M. F. Outcome expectancy, locus of attributions for expectancy, and self-directed attention as determinants of evaluations and performance. *Journal of Experimental Social Psychology,* 1982, *18,* 184–200. (b)

Carver, C. S., & Scheier, M. F. A control-theory model of normal behavior, and implications for problems in self-management. In P. C. Kendall (Ed.), *Advances in cognitive-behavioral research and therapy* (Vol. 2). New York: Academic Press, 1983.

Carver, C. S., & Scheier, M. F. Self-focused attention in test anxiety: A general theory applied to a specific phenomenon. In H. van der Ploeg, R. Schwarzer, & C. D. Spielberger (Eds.), *Advances in test anxiety research* (Vol. 3). Hillsdale, NJ: Lawrence Erlbaum Associates, 1984.

Carver, C. S., & Scheier, M. F. Aspects of self, and the control of behavior. In B. R. Schlenker (Ed.), *The self and social life.* New York: McGraw-Hill, 1985.

Cooley, C. H. *Human nature and the social order.* New York: Scribners, 1902.

Covington, M. V., & Omelich, C. L.   Are causal attributions causal? A path analysis of the cognitive model of achievement motivation. *Journal of Personality and Social Psychology,* 1979, *37,* 1487–1504.

Csikszentmihalyi, M., & Figurski, T. J.   Self-awareness and aversive experience in everyday life. *Journal of Personality,* 1982, *50,* 15–28.

Daly, S.   Behavioral correlates of social anxiety. *British Journal of Social and Clinical Psychology,* 1978, *17,* 117–120.

Dawkins, R.   Hierarchical organisation: A candidate principle for ethology. In P. P. G. Bateson & R. A. Hinde (Eds.), *Growing points in ethology.* Cambridge: Cambridge University Press, 1976.

Deffenbacher, J. L.   Worry, emotionality, and task-generated interference in test anxiety: An empirical test of attentional theory. *Journal of Educational Psychology,* 1978, *70,* 248–254.

Deffenbacher, J. L.   Worry and emotionality in test anxiety. In I. G. Sarason (Ed.), *Test anxiety: Theory, research, and application.* Hillsdale, NJ: Lawrence Erlbaum Associates, 1980.

Diener, C. I., & Dweck, C. S.   An analysis of learned helplessness: Continuous changes in performance, strategy, and achievement cognitions following failure. *Journal of Personality and Social Psychology,* 1978, *36,* 451–462.

Dweck, C. S.   The role of expectations and attributions in the alleviation of learned helplessness. *Journal of Personality and Social Psychology,* 1975, *31,* 674–685.

Duval, S., & Wicklund, R. A.   *A theory of objective self-awareness.* New York: Academic Press, 1972.

Ellis, A.   *Reason and emotion in psychotherapy.* New York: Lyle Stuart, 1962.

Feather, N. T.   The relationship of persistence at a task to expectations of success and achievement-related motives. *Journal of Abnormal and Social Psychology,* 1961, *63,* 552–561.

Fenigstein, A., Scheier, M. F., & Buss, A. H.   Public and private self-consciousness: Assessment and theory. *Journal of Consulting and Clinical Psychology,* 1975, *43,* 522–527.

Galassi, J. P., Frierson, H. T., Jr., & Sharer, R.   Behavior of high, moderate, and low test anxious students during an actual test situation. *Journal of Consulting and Clinical Psychology,* 1981, *49,* 51–62.

Gallistel, C. R.   *The organization of action: A new synthesis.* Hillsdale, NJ: Lawrence Erlbaum Associates, 1980.

Geen, R. G.   Test anxiety, observation, and range of cue utilization. *British Journal of Social and Clinical Psychology,* 1976, *15,* 253–259.

Gibbons, F. X., Carver, C. S., Scheier, M. F., & Hormuth, S. E.   Self-focused attention and the placebo effect: Fooling some of the people some of the time. *Journal of Experimental Social Psychology,* 1979, *15,* 263–274.

Greenberg, J.   Attentional focus and locus of performance causality as determinants of equity behavior. *Journal of Personality and Social Psychology,* 1980, *38,* 579–585.

Haemmerlie, F. M., & Montgomery, R. L.   Self-perception theory and unobtrusively biased interactions: A treatment for heterosexual anxiety. *Journal of Counseling Psychology,* 1982, *29,* 362–370.

Haemmerlie, F. M., & Montgomery, R. L.   Purposefully biased interactions: Reducing heterosocial anxiety through self-perception theory. *Journal of Personality and Social Psychology,* 1984, *47,* 900–908.

Hollandsworth, J. G., Jr., Glazeski, R. C., Kirkland, K., Jones, G. E., & Van Norman, L. R.   An analysis of the nature and effects of test anxiety: Cognitive, behavioral, and physiological components. *Cognitive Therapy and Research,* 1979, *3,* 165–180.

Holroyd, K. A., Westbrook, T., Wolf, M., & Badhorn, E.   Performance, cognition, and physiological responding in test anxiety. *Journal of Abnormal Psychology,* 1978, *87,* 442–451.

James, W.   *The principles of psychology.* New York: Holt, Rinehart, & Winston, 1890.

Kanfer, F. H., & Hagerman, S.   The role of self-regulation. In L. P. Rehm (Ed.), *Behavior ther-*

apy for depression: Present status and future directions. New York: Academic Press, 1981.

Kelso, J. A. S. (Ed.). *Human motor behavior: An introduction.* Hillsdale, NJ: Lawrence Erlbaum Associates, 1982.

Kirschenbaum, D. S., Humphrey, L. L., & Malett, S. D. Specificity of planning in adult self-control: An applied investigation. *Journal of Personality and Social Psychology,* 1981, *40,* 941–950.

Kirschenbaum, D. S., Tomarken, A. J., & Ordman, A. M. Specificity of planning and choice applied to adult self-control. *Journal of Personality and Social Psychology,* 1982, *42,* 576–585.

Klinger, E. Consequences of commitment to and disengagement from incentives. *Psychological Review,* 1975, *82,* 1–25.

Kuhl, J. Motivational and functional helplessnesss: The moderating effect of state versus action orientation. *Journal of Personality and Social Psychology,* 1981, *40,* 155–170.

Kukla, A. Foundations of an attributional theory of performance. *Psychological Review,* 1972, *79,* 454–470.

MacKay, D. M. Cerebral organization and the conscious control of action. In J. C. Eccles (Ed.), *Brain and conscious experience.* Berlin: Springer-Verlag, 1966.

Mahoney, M. J. Cognitive skills and athletic performance. In P. C. Kendall & S. D. Hollon (Eds.), *Cognitive-behavioral interventions: Theory, research, and procedures.* New York: Academic Press, 1979.

Mandler, G., & Watson, D. L. Anxiety and the interruption of behavior. In C. D. Spielberger (Ed.), *Anxiety and behavior.* New York: Academic Press, 1966.

Marteniuk, R. G. *Information processing in motor skills.* New York: Holt, Rinehart, & Winston, 1976.

Mead, G. H. *Mind, self, and society.* Chicago: University of Chicago Press, 1934.

Meichenbaum, D. Cognitive modification of test anxious college students. *Journal of Consulting and Clinical Psychology,* 1972, *39,* 370–379.

Meichenbaum, D. *Cognitive behavior modification: An integrative approach.* New York: Plenum, 1977.

Nicholls, J. G. When a scale measures more than its name denotes: The case of the test anxiety scale for children. *Journal of Consulting and Clinical Psychology,* 1976, *44,* 976–985.

Nottelman, E. D., & Hill, K. T. Test anxiety and off-task behavior in evaluative situations. *Child Development,* 1977, *48,* 225–231.

Peters, R. S. The education of emotions. In M. B. Arnold (Ed.), *Feelings and emotions: The Loyola Symposium.* New York: Academic Press, 1970.

Powers, W. T. *Behavior: The control of perception.* Chicago: Aldine, 1973.

Pryor, J. B., Gibbons, F. X., Wicklund, R. A., Fazio, R. H., & Hood, R. Self-focused attention and self-report validity. *Journal of Personality,* 1977, *45,* 514–527.

Sarason, I. G. Anxiety and self-preoccupation. In I. G. Sarason & C. D. Spielberger (Eds.), *Stress and anxiety* (Vol. 2). New York: Wiley, 1975.

Sarason, I. G. The test anxiety scale: Concept and research. In C. D. Spielberger & I. G. Sarason (Eds.), *Stress and anxiety* (Vol. 5). New York: Halsted-Wiley, 1978.

Schank, R. C., & Abelson, R. P. *Scripts, plans, goals, and understanding.* Hillsdale, NJ: Lawrence Erlbaum Associates, 1977.

Schlenker, B. R., & Leary, M. R. Social anxiety and self-presentation: A conceptualization and model. *Psychological Bulletin,* 1982, *92,* 641–669.

Scheier, M. F. Self-awareness, self-consciousness, and angry aggression. *Journal of Personality,* 1976, *44,* 627–644.

Scheier, M. F., Buss, A. H., & Buss, D. M. Self-consciousness, self-report of aggressiveness, and aggression. *Journal of Research in Personality,* 1978, *12,* 133–140.

Scheier, M. F., & Carver, C. S. Self-focused attention and the experience of emotion: Attraction, repulsion, elation, and depression. *Journal of Personality and Social Psychology,* 1977, *35,* 625–636.

Scheier, M. F., & Carver, C. S. Private and public aspects of the self. In L. Wheeler (Ed.), *Review of personality and social psychology* (Vol. 2). Beverly Hills, CA: Sage, 1981.

Scheier, M. F., & Carver, C. S. Self-consciousness, outcome expectancy, and persistence. *Journal of Research in Personality,* 1982, *16,* 409–418.

Scheier, M. F., & Carver, C. S. Self-directed attention and the comparison of self with standards. *Journal of Experimental Social Psychology,* 1983, *19,* 205–222.

Scheier, M. F., & Carver, C. S. Two sides of the self: One for you and one for me. In J. Suls & A. G. Greenwald (Eds.), *Psychological perspectives on the self* (Vol. 2). Hillsdale, NJ: Lawrence Erlbaum Associates, 1983. (b)

Scheier, M. F., & Carver, C. S. *Learned helpfulness or egotism: Do expectancies matter?* Unpublished manuscript, 1983. (c)

Scheier, M. F., Carver, C. S., & Gibbons, F. X. Self-directed attention, awareness of bodily states, and suggestibility. *Journal of Personality and Social Psychology,* 1979, *37,* 1576–1588.

Shallice, T. The dominant action system: An information-processing approach to consciousness. In K. S. Pope & J. L. Singer (Eds.), *The stream of consciousness: Scientific investigations into the flow of human experience.* New York: Wiley, 1978.

Simon, H. A. Motivational and emotional controls of cognition. *Psychological Review,* 1967, *74,* 29–39.

Stelmach, G. E. (Ed.). *Motor control: Issues and trends.* New York: Academic Press, 1976.

Stotland, E. *The psychology of hope.* San Francisco: Jossey Bass, 1969.

Trope, Y. Seeking information about one's own ability as a determinant of choice among tasks. *Journal of Personality and Social Psychology,* 1975, *32,* 1004–1013.

Trope, Y. Uncertainty-reducing properties of achievement tasks. *Journal of Personality and Social Psychology,* 1979, *37,* 1505–1518.

Turner, R. G. Consistency, self-consciousness, and the predictive validity of typical and maximal personality measures. *Journal of Research in Personality,* 1978, *12,* 117–132.

Underwood, B., & Moore, B. S. Sources of behavioral inconsistency. *Journal of Personality and Social Psychology,* 1981, *40,* 780–785.

Vallacher, R. R., & Wegner, D. M. *A theory of action identification.* Hillsdale, NJ: Lawrence Erlbaum Associates, in presss.

Weiner, B. The emotional consequences of causal ascriptions. In M. S. Clark & S. T. Fiske (Eds.), *Affect and cognition: The 17th annual Carnegie symposium on cognition.* Hillsdale, NJ: Lawrence Erlbaum Associates, 1982.

Weiner, B., Nierenberg, R., & Goldstein, M. Social learning (locus of control) versus attributional (causal stability) interpretations of expectancy of success. *Journal of Personality,* 1976, *44,* 52–68.

West, C. K., Lee, J. F., & Anderson, T. H. The influence of test anxiety in the selection of relevant from irrelevant information. *The Journal of Educational Research,* 1969, *63,* 51–52.

Wicklund, R. A., & Duval, S. Opinion change and performance facilitation as a result of objective self-awareness. *Journal of Experimental Social Psychology,* 1971, *7,* 319–342.

Wiener, N. *Cybernetics: Control and communication in the animal and the machine.* Cambridge: MA: MIT Press, 1948.

Wine, J. D. Test anxiety and direction of attention. *Psychological Bulletin,* 1971, *76,* 92–104.

Wine, J. D. Evaluation anxiety: A cognitive-attentional construct. In H. W. Krohne & L. C. Laux (Eds.), *Achievement, stress, and anxiety.* Washington, DC: Hemisphere, 1982.

9 Fitting to the Environment and the Use of Dispositions

Robert A. Wicklund
Universität Bielefeld

It is commonly thought in psychology that our concepts of ourselves are delivered to us on the basis of our relation to the environment. Self-conceptions are regarded as a kind of reflection of reality — as a repository of our past interactions with the physical and social world. In fact, there are at least two highly specific ways of talking about the development of self-conceptions, or personalities, or dispositions — one of these based in self perception theory, the other based in symbolic interactionism. They share the implicit premise that individuals are responsive to their own experiences and accomplishments, and especially to social feedback, in arriving at particular views of the self. To the degree that one has behaved competently in the past, one presumably concludes, "I am competent." Or, if the social milieu takes a look at someone and begins to react as though that person is performing as a capable and useful member of society, that person's cognizance of the social milieu's reactions will lead to the development of socially-mediated self-conceptions.

This chapter takes exception to such an orderly view of the origin of conceptions about oneself. It will be argued that self references, in particular self-conceptions about socially-valued characteristics, and the frequency of thinking about such characteristics, are not a simple function of prior contact with reality. Rather, it is proposed that the *absence* of a firm contact with certain kinds of realities is responsible for the individual's preoccupation with components of the self, that is, with abilities or traits. First, however, a brief description of the self-perception and symbolic interactionist views is necessary.

BEHAVIORAL REALITY AS A STARTING POINT

Origin of Dispositions in Self-Perception

Self-perception theory (Bem, 1965; 1972) makes the individual highly dependent on subjectively free, overt behaviors. The theory has generally been applied to the development of attitudes or values, but a liberalization of the concept in the direction of development of self is not outside the theoretical realm. Locksley & Lenauer (1981) have done exactly this. They give as an example people who come to know themselves as extraverts. It is assumed that, when it occurs to people to ask, "Am I an extravert?" a cognitive search of past relevant behaviors is undertaken. The more instances of extraverted behavior that are called up from past interactions, the more certain one can be of one's trait of "extraversion." Of course, within the framework of self perception theory, the relevant past behaviors must have been chosen freely.

It is no problem to translate the Locksley and Lenauer analysis to arenas outside social interaction. Should someone ask, "Am I a capable gardener," a search will be set off, whereby the would-be gardener will search back through past relevant experiences. If the person has had no pertinent experiences, then nothing can be said about "gardening" aspects of self. On the other hand, the more often that the person has produced a successful harvest in the backyard, the higher is the "probability" (Locksley & Lenauer) that the individual will lay claim to the possession of gardening skills, or capability as a farmer, or something similar.

The important element in this view is the following: One's self-conceptions, knowledge of own dispositions, capabilities, attitudes, and so forth are limited in a very strict manner by one's own behavioral relation to the environment. The development of the self-concept does not race ahead of the actual behaviors, experiences, or decisions.

Origin of Dispositions in Symbolic Interactionism

The source of information about the self in this case is not one's own behavior; at least the source is not one's own behavior directly. Self-conceptions are said to be mediated by a certain social feedback. According to Mead (1934), for instance, people can form self-views only when they have the capacity for placing themselves into the roles of others. Perspective-taking enables people to see themselves as others see them, and from this point, according to the Meadian argument, we develop a self-view that has its origin in the view of the other.

Although the person's own behaviors are not a central feature within the Meadian approach to socialization and development of self, we might suppose that the person must first *do something* before society can have any kind of perspective toward that person. Thus the person acts openly, in a friendly manner, and hospitably on several social occasions, and the immediate society comes to base its perspective on these behaviors. Once the individual comprehends the societal perspective, an internalization of the perspective follows. The self-conception "friendly" is, therefore, a socially-mediated product that has perspective-taking ability as a pre-requisite.

Exactly the same process would occur in the case of capability in planting a garden. First the society needs some raw material to which to react, that is, the individual's undertakings in the garden. And once society forms a perspective, having observed the person, that person's self-conception should then develop accordingly. The end result, then, will be a sense of one's own competence that is directly in line with the societal perspective.

The implicit assumption is that the eventual self-view has a basis in the person's relation to the environment. It would be hard to imagine that society would form its perspectives about individuals in a totally random manner, but rather, society waits until there is some basis for forming its perspective. Then, once the individual understands that perspective, the eventual self-view will correspond to his own accomplished, behavioral history. Should the system break down, that would be due to faulty perspective taking, or perhaps to the fact that a particular group would have come to the incorrect conclusion by faulty observations of the individual's behavior.

An unstated principle of the above two schools, as well as an assumption of psychology in general, is that one's objective "success" in the environment and one's self-conceptions are closely intertwined. If we focus just for a moment on characteristics that society values, such as diligence, creativity, intelligence, generosity, reliability, and others, the Bemian and Meadian conceptions lead one to suppose that a positive self-conception, in any given specific respect, represents a positive or successful relation to some facet of the environment.

It is the purpose of this paper to propose exactly the opposite thesis—that a failure to relate one's behavioral repertoire to the environment leads to a preoccupation with self-ascription of dispositions, and correspondingly, that a successful match to the environment is accompanied by a *lack* of interest in one's own dispositions. As an introduction to this thesis, a distinction must first be drawn, in the following section.

FITTING TO THE ENVIRONMENT: THE DYNAMIC FIT AND THE CATEGORY

Many of the terms included under "self-conception" or "self-observation" are short-cuts for describing a person's behavioral potential. Accordingly, these numerous terms (artistically gifted, intellectual, mechanical, generous, sly) are thought of as dispositions — as vague conditions of potential that imply classes of behaviors. However, these dispositions, or trait names, should not be treated as labels for an invariant mode of behavior. To say that someone is "fast" or "creative" is not to imply that corresponding behaviors will be run off independent of all surrounding conditions. Rather, the sense of these disposition names, and presumably the reason why they have come to be, is that people differ with respect to how they react to specific environments.

Suppose that a 2-year-old child is exposed to all varieties of music, and no matter what the music, the child rocks and kicks and chatters in perfect correspondence with the rhythm of the music. Somewhat later, as the child receives his first toy xylophone, he quickly demonstrates the capacity to play melodies that he has heard on the radio. What is the reaction of the immediate society?

Since that society is exposed to that same environment — that is, the same kinds of music — and since it is important for society that at least some people be able to cope directly and capably with that environment, it becomes functional to find labels, or categories, for those who can in fact fit to the environment. The "fit" in this instance is easy to describe; at least we would think so. The environment offers a certain rhythmical pattern, a definite melody, a tempo, and a degree of loudness. If the person can fit himself, via singing, playing an instrument, or rocking and kicking, into that environment, then a certain objective success has been attained. At least, this is objective success as viewed by the nearby society. The term *dynamic fit* will be used to characterize this relation between the environmental complexities and the complexity of reaction. It will be useful to view the relation of the person to environment as one of interlocking pieces. For instance, the more complex the music, the more complex must be the action.

Similarly, when the environment consists of a hypothetical garden, and the immediate society places great value on successful garden crops, we have a further instance in which the person is confronted with a certain degree of complexity. If the person manages to consider simultaneously the kinds of seeds, quality of soil, weather conditions, planting and harvesting time, and to react to all of these conditions appropriately, we would consider the relation between the person and environment to be a dynamic fit.

If every person in society could execute this same dynamic fit equally well, and if every member were in fact to execute this same dynamic fit regularly, how would society then react to the child? Perhaps this question is better posed in the context of performances that are in fact executed by all, such as walking. This is a class of behaviors for which there are practically no typologies, categories, or dispositional terms. To be sure, one can differentiate among people according to whether they like to walk, or one can place very young children in a category of not yet being able, but otherwise, it is the case that the relevant environment and the basic behavioral components are visible and accessible to virtually everyone. Thus there is no special reason, from societal grounds, to label or categorize people according to their having *a special potential* within the realm of walking. It is not as though some are "walkers" while others are "non-walkers."

In contrast are potential dynamic fitting relations to the environment that are not shared universally, such as a rhythmical reaction to music, or the capacity for a dynamic fit relation to the elements of a garden. The relevant environment is, of course, highly salient for many members of society, but they cannot all form a fit relation to these salient, culturally significant environments. In part, they do not completely see all of the environmental aspects involved, and in part, they do not have the behavioral repertoire necessary for a 100% match to the environmental complexities. Thus it becomes a crucial matter, for those who don't have direct access, to react to that environment in some other manner, as long as the environment remains salient and personally or culturally central. The only manner of reacting, then, given that one feels compelled to react, is through those who have a more immediate contact with the environment, and here is where the culturally-based categorization begins. By identifying those who can, or who do, deal directly in dynamic-fit fashion with the environment, society can make such environments more accessible. And at the same time, society gains a predictability over those who have a dynamic fit relation to the specified environment.

Accordingly, the child in the above example is placed by society into such categories as "musical," "innate sense of rhythm," "musically creative," and so forth. And the person who can produce a crop of potatoes or tomatoes with great efficiency is labeled variously "botanically-gifted," "green-thumb," "horticulturist," and so forth. These societally-given categories then make up for society's lack of relevant knowledge and skills: Because the pertinent elements of the environment are in part invisible or unknowable for many people, and because many of the corresponding behavioral elements are also invisible or unknowable for many, the category names can be brought to bear—as a method of having indirect contact with certain, specified environments.[1] Thus, since each member of society cannot have complete knowledge of every complexity of the environment, and since every member does not develop the requisite skills (or whatever modes of behavior) for dealing with the multiple environments, it becomes important to have a method of characterizing those who do see the relevant complexities of par-

---

[1]A clear example of this function of categories is in the realm of creativity. It is a common procedure in creativity research to examine the personality characteristics, habits, interests, motives, and attitudes of highly creative people, the idea being that it is much easier and quicker to spot creative people via these categories than by trying to recognize the actual creative act (Mehlhorn & Mehlhorn, 1977).

ticular environments, and who have developed modes of acting vis-à-vis those environments.

TRANSITION TO A SET OF POSTULATES: A DUAL PARADOX

The Performer

Suppose that someone is especially apt at landscape painting. The pertinent environment consists in part of the landscape itself, a societal need for quality paintings, and the necessary equipment. With great regularity and accuracy, this person can paint landscape after landscape. Under what circumstances, or why, would such a person attempt to place himself accurately within a societal category — a category that would be a shorthand description or label of his functioning regarding landscape painting? The answer in terms of our opening models — self perception theory and the school of symbolic interactionism — is straightforward. The person necessarily realizes that he is in the category once a category-relevant behavior has been enacted (self-perception theory) or once he receives feedback from society on the basis of such behaviors (symbolic interactionism). Thus it is assumed, by both of these schools of thought, that one's behaviors must precede the actual formation of a self-conception.

However, if one has successfully reached a stage of dynamic fit in the context of some given environment, perhaps in landscape painting or gardening, why would one then want to establish with certainty one's own category membership? Psychology (e.g., Wicker, 1969) already knows that such categories are not behaviorally specific; they are a haphazard but perhaps efficient way of designating those who have specific talents and other kinds of behavioral propensities. For the performer to become preoccupied with fitting himself into categories would literally be a regression in terms of the accuracy and specificity of his relation to the environment. The painter, gardener, sociable person, or Machiavellian would need thousands of words (plus graphics) to characterize adequately what goes on in the dynamic fit. One would also have to find words for feelings and kinesthetic feedback — and to be sure, there are no words. Thus to rework one's dynamic fit into an "economical" set of categories would, for the performer, in no sense capture the functioning of the dynamic fit. Yet, at the same time, much of psychology — and the rest of society — would like to assume that the performer's self-categorization efforts would follow a successful match with the environment, and that the better the fit, the more the person will show a readiness to perform the self-categorization. Herein lies the paradox.

The Observer of the Performer

The second part of the paradox belongs to the member of society who presumably would have use for the system of categories, in the sense of placing others appropriately into categories. The issue here is, "Who is in the position to place people appropriately into categories?" The answer would seem rather clear. If the elements of a complex dynamic fit to the environment are difficult to see, then obviously not everyone is in a position to judge whether another person is in fact in a dynamic fit relation to the environment. The manifold complexities of the environment in question, and the corresponding complexities of the behavioral repertoire, would be seen only by someone who also is capable of that same dynamic fit relation. If others were to attempt to fit performers into behaviorally specific categories, they would fall into error. Thus society must, by this reasoning, rely on those who already possess the capacity for a mosaic. And here is the paradox: If someone sees and feels the pertinent parts of the environment, and can also react to those complexities with correspondingly complex behaviors, the category would, for that person, not be necessary. For such a person the category is a regression — an inaccurate and insufficient means of labeling those who appear to have the potential. At the same time, if the function of categories is to bring to light, or make identifiable, those who can function particularly well in specified environments, then it would seem that those who have *no* capacity to function in those environments themselves would be the ones to concern themselves with categories. This is because the presumed function of the categories is to spot, or identify, or "understand" those who do possess the dynamic fit to certain environments.

SOME POSTULATES STEMMING FROM THE DUAL PARADOX

Environmental Perspective and Perspective Pressure

The term "environment," which we have used up until this point, is not sufficient to describe the processes central to this chapter. It will be useful to talk about the environment, no matter whether physical or social, as containing a variety of *perspectives*. For example, when an official writes us a letter and demands a reply, that can be called a perspective. Or when a child stands alone on the street and cries, that is also a perspective. If we are driving along a country road and a tree has fallen in front of the car, that is also an environmental perspective. The central defining characteristic of a perspective is that it has the potential to call up a reaction. Clearly, in an objective sense, one need not necessarily react to every social and non-social situation that offers the possibility of exercising some behavioral repertoire.

One of the elements associated with the human in the context of the perspective is whether one even sees (i.e., "knows") the perspective. Many people would look at a rock not as an occasion to behave in any particular way, but rather just as a part of the landscape. On the other hand, a rock could elicit a whole repertoire of stone-throwing behaviors from a child, and from someone trained in geology, the rock could set off an archeological inquiry. Or when background music is played in an airport, many people would treat the music simply as a background, as an inert part of the environment, while others would treat it as a perspective that could potentially instigate a set of behaviors—that is, attuning oneself to the rhythm, melodies, and other components of the perspective.

Thus the first conceptual element here is the extent to which a person perceives a certain part of the environment as a perspective, that is, as a possible basis from which one might react. One person would regard the airport music as just "there," and nothing more than that, while others would find in the music a *potential* basis for humming, singing along, or otherwise reacting to the components.

Perspective pressure is the next step. Given that someone sees an aspect of the environment as something that can be reacted to, that is, sees it as a perspective, then the next question is whether that person feels impelled to react to the perspective. The concept "perspective pressure" is identical to what Murray (1938) intended with "press"—the extent to which the environment pushes the person to react. A very simple example can be derived from the area of pro-social behavior. In the context of Milgram (1965), for instance, the perspective pressure emanating from the target person was made progressively stronger by bringing subjects closer to the target. Thus the pressure on the subject not to deliver shocks (i.e., to act charitably) was comparatively weak when the target was in the adjoining room, but was very strong when the target was within sight, and even stronger when the target was within touch. The extensive research by Darley & Latané (1968) also varied the pressure on individuals to help. The smaller the group of potential helpers, the greater is the pressure on any individual member to intervene in the emergency situation. Still another case may be found in research on psychological reactance (Brehm, 1966; 1972), in which varying amounts of force are exerted upon individuals to comply with a request. It is clear in the reactance context that the reaction is greater—whatever its form—the more pressure is placed on a person to react within a social influence setting.

The deeper issue here is why a person feels impelled to act, given that an environmental perspective is perceived. For the present it is impossible to review (or attempt to integrate) everything that would be relevant in terms of learning theory, habits, drives, stimulus incongruity, and so forth. Quite independent of the precise psychological source of any given perspective pressure, the only assumption here is that such pressure can be treated as a variable. It can be raised or lowered through manipulating the environment, and it can vary as a function of whatever needs and resources the individual brings to the situation. Quite aside from the ultimate psychological roots of particular perspective pressures, the central starting point here is just the individual's subjectively perceived pressure to act.

Perspective pressure would not invariably have to emanate from such social settings as in the foregoing examples. Suppose that someone decides to make a 1-month trek, alone, through the most rugged mountains of Alaska. After about 2 weeks, the hiker comes to a river that blocks his progress entirely. Without crossing the river he can go no further. The perspective in this case consists of multiple components: his existing need, or commitment, to continue the journey, the knowledge that he must continue in the same direction, the fact of the river, and the knowledge that it cannot be swum or waded. Thus the perspective is certainly comprehended. And the perspective pressure is at a high point — he is called upon by the several parts of the perspective to act.

It is also clear that we could arrange various components of the perspective so as to lessen the pressure. For instance, if in fact he had already reached the end of his planned journey, and could turn back, the perspective pressure is weakened considerably. If the river were shallow, or if it were only one meter wide, the perspective would create much less pressure. However, as in the example, the pressure would be an undeniable psychological fact. The hiker must *do something*. This is not to say that he will begin to construct a bridge or find an ingeneous way to swing across the river through the tree tops. All we want to say at this point is that the hiker experiences a considerable perspective pressure.

The Repertoire

The central question here is, how does the person react when confronted with the perspective pressure? The concept of a dynamic relation to the environment has already been discussed above. If the person possesses the behavioral repertoire necessary to fit to each aspect of the perspective, then the dynamic-fit relation can be undertaken. Either by training, by observation, or in part by maturation or genetic readiness, the person may or may not have the qualities that are necessary to fit to the perspective pressure at hand.

A theoretically important facet of the many possible repertoires is that it is impossible to describe them directly. We can characterize the training conditions in great detail. In just as much detail we can describe many of the individual behaviors that stem from each behavioral repertoire. But the essence of the human quality that underlies the performance is hardly to be seen. It is ultimately a set of neurons or synapses, or memory traces, or certain musculature, but other than by means of a reduction to neurology and physiology, there is no direct manner of talking about the quality itself. Accordingly, when someone can in fact execute a dynamic fit to a perspective, and then attempts to describe directly what is happening, the words will have to do with the character of the perspective, with the specific behaviors, and perhaps with the training. Interestingly, it is linguistically impossible for the individual to describe the "potential" or "quality" that resides within.[2]

The Static Orientation

Beginning at this point we will talk about two qualitatively distinguishable orientations. The one, the dynamic fit relation to a perspective, we have already described. It is perhaps best viewed as a direct 1:1 relation between one's own potentials, or repertoires, and the perspective. The static orientation is quite the opposite. If a dynamic relation is impossible, for reasons to be enumerated below, then the person will begin a static orientation with respect to the perspective, as long as the perspective pressure remains. That is, if one is subject to sufficient perspective pressure (one must act), then an alternative to a dynamic mode of functioning is the static orientation. It is assumed here that the static orientation is undertaken out of necessity, and begins because the dynamic mode of reaction is not possible.

The character of the static orientation is to be distinguished from the dynamic mode of reacting, both on a behavioral and on a cognitive level. All that they have in common is the initial realization of the perspective and the experience of perspective pressure. On the behavioral level, within the static orientation, there is in no sense a 1:1 fitting to the perspective. Rather, the elements of the perspective are pushed aside or denied, since one does not react

---

[2]The reader may note a certain parallel to the thesis of Jones and Nisbett (1971). Within their conceptual framework, in which the actor versus observer difference is central, it is proposed that actors (or "performers") seldom talk about themselves in terms of traits, but rather, in terms of the relevant environment to which they are reacting. The reason given is that the actor must focus on the environment in order to behave at all, and that the actor understands much more about his environment than does the observer.

The thesis here is different, in two basic respects: (1) It is assumed here that there is no sufficient way to characterize the quality that is basic to the behavior. That is, the dispositional language is necessarily inadequate. If we think about the quality that enables, or allows, someone to recite a memorized poem, we would eventually have to talk in terms of neural processes. (2) The core assumption here is that the dispositional terms are used by observers, as well as by performers, only when an adequate comprehension of the perspective and of the behavioral elements is lacking. Thus rather than a fundamental actor versus observer difference, the idea here is that dispositions are employed generally — by all — out of a lack of understanding of the perspective and out of a lack of behavioral repertoire. This central thesis will become clearer in the pages to follow.

to them in a dynamic-fit manner. On the cognitive level, the person does not think of appropriate behaviors, or of the various elements of the perspective toward which behaviors might be directed. Rather, assuming that the person has knowledge of categories pertinent to the perspective, the thinking process becomes taken up with categorization. Why is this?

It is important here to make a certain premise regarding the motivational consequences of a societal phenomenon: Society makes up categories which serve, at least in part, to designate individuals who have dynamic fit relations to certain perspectives. In a cocktail party the "extravert" and "introvert" categories become important, on the athletic field such categories as "quick," "agile," "dynamic" are central, in the business world we speak of "shrewd" or "calculating." The categories stand, presumably, for one's *potential* in fitting to a given perspective, thus society is highly dependent on the categories in order to know who will react successfully or regularly to which perspective. Since much of society cannot see the elements of the dynamic fit directly, the *category itself* comes to be a highly valued entity (Hass & Shaffir, 1977).

Because the category, or membership within the category, is valued in itself, the person who does not have a dynamic fit to a certain part of the perspective can respond to the perspective by building himself into the category. Another way of saying this is that the person will come to dwell on his own *potential,* with respect to the perspective. We need only assume that society values those who have the earmarks of potential, that is, those who belong to categories that signify some kind of meaningful relation to the environment.

The underlying premise here is that the perception of a perspective, and the felt pressure that can emanate from that perspective, call upon the person to act. To react to perspective pressure (no matter whether it is a call for help, an intellectual accomplishment, or a repair job) is something that is valued by society. However, since systems of categories exist that correspond in some vague manner to various dynamic-fit reactions, the person continues to be a valued entity as long as some category membership is evident. Accordingly, the arousal, or motivation, or impulse that is set off by the perspective pressure can steer itself in either of two directions — the dynamic fit to the perspective, or else to the static orientation. In both cases the individual continues to be a valued, functioning entity within society.

Two Ways of Reacting to Perspective Pressure

The "non-fit" to which we have referred can come about in a number of ways, and it should not be equated with simple incompetence. It is assumed that the person will readily take up the dynamic form of functioning as long as the complexity of his potential, or repertoire, fits almost exactly with the complexity of the perspective. In short, when the two parts — the perspective and the human — fit one another in an interlocking form, the person's readiness to react directly to the environment is maximized.

If the complexity of the perspective is too great for the current state of development of the person's quality, or if it is physically impossible to execute a mosaic at some given time or place, then the person will move toward the static mode of functioning. Alternatively, if the perspective is insufficient in complexity, there is once again a non-match, and the person will not readily take up the dynamic mode of functioning. In fact, in these instances in which the character of the perspective is too complex, or else too simple, or alternatively, not even accessible, there could be no dynamic fit even if the person were to try. Accordingly, the continued and invested dealing with the environment can be expected only when the possibility of a good fit is there. Otherwise the person will gravitate quickly toward the static orientation.

Figure 9.1 shows how the relation between the person's existing quality and the perspective produces varying degrees of dynamic orientation or static orientation. On the abscissa is the extent of "challenge" in the particular perspective. As the perspective becomes more demanding of the person's quality, up to approximately 100%, the tendency to execute the dynamic function climbs. Beyond that point the person abandons the dynamic mode.

An integral part of the figure is the variable *perspective pressure*. These two orientations — dynamic and static — should be in evidence only to the extent that the person is subject to a substantial pressure from the pertinent perspective. For instance, if we know that we have to write a composition, but that it is not due for 6 months, the pressure emanating from that perspective is minimal. Or take the case of someone who needs help: The further that person is removed from our visual or auditory senses, the weaker is the perspective pressure, hence the flattening of the curve in Figure 9.1.

Denial of Perspective

A cognitive aspect of the dynamic orientation is that the person stays closely attuned to the several parts of the perspective. If the person thinks and talks about what is going on during the process, the language is necessarily closely tied to the characteristics of the perspective. However, once the static orientation is taken up, the cognitive accompaniments consist of category names and fine distinctions regarding categories. The result is quite clearly a neglect, or apparent denial, of the perspective. Accordingly, one can make the general statement that the higher the static orientation, the greater will be the denial of the perspective (as diagrammed in Figure 9.2).

Specific Effects: What Is the Appearance of These Two Orientations?

The dynamic fit.   The dynamic mode of functioning is to some extent similar to what Csikszentmihalyi (1975) has termed the "flow experience." In this mode there is no consciousness of performing the task (or playing, or

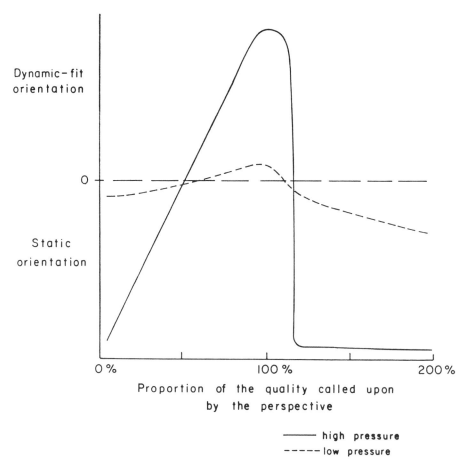

FIG. 9.1.   Perspective Pressure and Quality of Orientation.

whatever the activity) in order to gain some definite sense of "self." Rather, the person is, in a psychological sense, at one with the task. Similar to this characterization is one of the criteria that Heckhausen (1980) has set up as part of the definition of intrinsic motivation: The behavior and the goal of the behavior are "gleichthematisch," that is, one's behaviors in some psychological sense belong to the goal. Still, what can the psychologist measure? How is this fit between person and perspective to be assessed?

1. On a cognitive plane the most obvious feature is the person's orientation toward the complexities of the perspective. The dynamic-oriented person should think about such complexities more, remember them better, and more readily differentiate one part of the perspective from another part.

2. Also on a cognitive plane, the person should be attuned to behavioral nuances. By this is not meant an attunement to one's potential, or evaluation

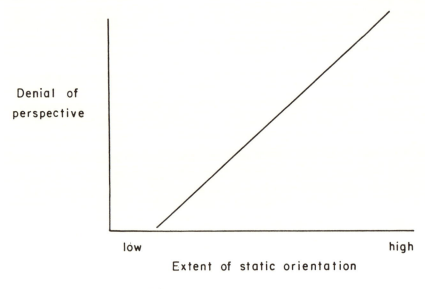

Denial of
perspective

low   high

Extent of static orientation

FIG. 9.2.   Denial of Perspective.

of pertinent abilities, but rather, simply an attentional focus on the detail of the movements, insofar as they are not automated.

3. There should be a disregard of potentially competing perspectives. Accordingly, the dynamic-dominated person should show little interest in alternative perspectives, and would not be oriented toward his potential vis-à-vis those other perspectives.

4. One would expect that the person would be content, or generally experiencing positive affect, relative to someone who is driven to the static mode of functioning. Perhaps this prediction goes without saying, in that the person who is driven to a static mode has necessarily experienced a kind of interruption, frustration, or boredom. Either the perspective has been too difficult, or else is so simple as to be boring or insulting.

5. On a behavioral level: There should be a constant readiness to explore the perspective and to learn more about the perspective at hand, thereby maximizing the possible fit between perspective and repertoire. This means two things on an empirical level:

a. The person should be open to finding out more about the intricacies of the perspective, and
b. The person should be open to finding out more about improving the behavioral repertoire so as to maximize the dynamic functioning.

6. Also on a behavioral level: There will be a literal sense in which the perspective pressure can be satisfied. As long as someone is functioning in the

dynamic mode, that person "belongs" to the perspective, and thus is carried along by it. Thus the perspective governs whether one should continue, and how long, and in what manner.[3]

The Static Function.   The processes associated with a static orientation can best be described in terms of postulates that parallel (and largely oppose) those just listed.

1. The person's attention will be away from the elements of the perspective. In place of thinking about the perspective, as something to which one can fit one's behaviors, the person will instead focus on the categories that are seen as relevant to the perspective. For example, instead of thinking (e.g., in the context of landscape painting) "roof with 30° angle, white and green, with moss," one devotes attention to the human *potential as artist,* thus to such matters as "confidence in being a decent artist" or "a bit weird" or "long hair" or "studied at X School of Art."

2. The process of building oneself into categories will manifest itself in the following ways. For one, there will be a general preoccupation with one's *potential,* thus the simple frequency of thoughts about one's own category membership will be high in the static condition. To the extent that the static orientation can be described as a condition of being goal-oriented, then the goal is to work oneself, as definitely as possible, into the categories that have to do with momentary potential.

A more specific consideration of these kinds of phenomena has been worked out in a theory of symbolic self-completion (Wicklund & Gollwitzer, 1982), such that building oneself into a category of potential has to do with self-descriptions, attempts to influence, and the use of relatively permanent (or material) symbols of one's own potential, such as a title, or association with prestige groups, or the ownership and display of the correct tools or implements. Building oneself into categories consists largely of what Wicklund and Gollwitzer have called "self-symbolizing," which amounts to employing self-relevant remarks and material entities so as to build up one's sense of having a specific potential.

3. Just as with the dynamic oriented function, other perspectives will be disregarded. However, there is a very important difference: The person in a

---

[3]For example, in the case of a perspective that consists of an emergency situation, the person who can fit to that perspective essentially "belongs" to the setting, and if the fit is perfect, the perspective will signal when, and how, the momentary dynamic orientation can come to an end. Or in the case of looking at a piece of art work: One's repertoire, in the sense of the capacity to find "meaning" in the art, together with the extent of the perspective, will determine the goodness of fit, and will also determine the extent of the search through the elements of the painting. Once the perspective has been explored, the momentary fit can come to an end.

static orientation will not have a direct interest in *any* perspective: there should be an absence of focusing in a detailed and curious way on the perspective at hand. Rather, attention will be on one's category membership per se, the perspective having been pushed aside.

4. The person should be discontent, since the static process will consist in part of a certain element of frustration, irritation, or boredom. One is driven to the static mode of functioning out of the failure of dynamic functioning, thus it is necessarily a less satisfactory state of affairs.

5. With respect to learning about either the perspective or about possible repertoires that would strengthen dynamic functioning, the person is closed. Mental energy is directed elsewhere—toward the categories. This means, among other implications, that the static oriented person will be singularly uncreative, given that creativity demands that one follow up leads and directions that are given in perspectives. To function within the static mode is to be trapped within a societally-given set of categories, thus the possibility of a creative response is impossible. In this sense a certain rigidity, or conservatism, will earmark the static mode of functioning.

6. The perspective pressure cannot be satisfied in the same manner as with dynamic functioning. All that one accomplishes with the static mode is that of "promising" society that one has a vague potential. However, the potential cannot be realized, since placing oneself into categories cannot improve dynamic functioning. The possibility of satisfying a given perspective pressure, in the sense of "completing" the task set forth by that pressure, is non-existent.[4]

THREE FURTHER ISSUES CENTRAL TO THE DYNAMIC-STATIC DIFFERENCE

1. Perceiving Other People

Thus far we have focused primarily on how one's own competencies and self-categorizations influence one another. But there is a further effect that has to do only with other people as targets of perception and evaluation. This other effect is really no different from the effects depicted in Figure 9.1, although the orientation—whether dynamic or static—in this case has its ef-

---

[4]Should someone experience the perspective pressure associated with an emergency situation, and be unable to react to perspective—thereby falling into the static mode—a fit between perspective and person will not bring the mode of funtioning to a natural conclusion. In fact, there is no fit. Rather, since the static mode of functioning is not dictated by the details of the perspective, but instead by the person's quest after category memberhip, the search for membership in the category can prolong itself, unconstrained by the character of the perspective.

fects on perception of others, rather than on one's self. It works in the following way:

Assume that someone is fully involved in a dynamic mode of functioning, and at the same time is asked to comment on other people who are subject to that same perspective pressure. They could be colleagues, fellow workers; they could also be relatively distant others. It is proposed that the others would be treated in exactly the same way as oneself, in the sense that the other would be "dealt with" by describing the perspective to which he is responding and by describing his specific, perspective-fitting behaviors. Thus the various processes associated with the dynamic function, detailed out above, would also apply when another person is the object of judgment.

Similarly, once the individual who is considering a second person falls out of the dynamic mode of functioning, and comes to deal with the perspective in a static manner, others are regarded in kind. In short, a certain quality of cognitive process belongs to the person who is in the static mode of functioning, and that cognitive process applies to the treatment of others just as to oneself.[5]

It will be useful to trace the postulated process from beginning to end. If a person is currently functioning in the dynamic mode, then thoughts will be directed toward the elements of the perspective at hand and in part toward the behaviors that fit to that perspective. At the moment of engagement in the dynamic fit, the person cannot be oriented toward a static mode of functioning, since the corresponding categories would be foreign to the ongoing, active endeavor. As noted above, it would be regressive, and counterproductive, for a dynamic-oriented person to try to think of what is going on in terms of categories. Therefore, by the same reasoning, it would be equally impossible for the dynamic-oriented person to think of *other people* in terms of categories.

The landscape artist, for example, will be thinking in terms of shapes of trees, shadows, the time of day, colors, and which brushes to use. If a novice

---

[5]A certain, highly reliable difference between the way people treat themselves (evaluatively) and the way they treat others needs to be discussed briefly. As summarized in Snyder, Stephan, & Rosenfield (1978), it is common that the attribution of traits to oneself follows a relatively defensive course: People are reluctant to cast themselves into unfavorable categories following a poor performance. In sharp contrast, there is a relative absence of such defensive attributing when dealing with someone else.

Viewed from the present standpoint, these are important differences that go on *within* the static orientation. It should go without saying that an aspect of building oneself into categories that signify potential is the simultaneous attempt to view others as having less claim to those same categories. Accordingly, even though one's current condition of static orientation leads to viewing others in a static manner, there is good reason to think that the specific, quantitative end result of the classification endeavor will vary depending on whether self-classification or other-classification.

were to stroll up and express interest in what is going on, the artist's thoughts (relative to the static mode) would not be "in what category does that person belong?" Rather, the ongoing absorption in parts of the task will transfer to the artist's view toward the second person; he will think of the second person as someone who is also interested (or potentially interested) in the features of the landscape, in the type of brushes, and perhaps in the kinds of brush strokes. All of this follows from the idea that the dynamic-oriented person excludes all other perspectives, including the perspectives that are associated with society's use of static categories for what he is doing.

Should the bystander happen to be in a static mode of functioning (which is entirely likely, given the fact of inexperience), then the artist and bystander will be thinking and speaking on two different levels. The artist's remarks will be concentrated on the features of the perspective and on the behaviors, while the bystander's remarks will be directed toward categories — his own membership in them as well as the functioning artist's membership in them.

It should be emphasized that the bystander does not have the equipment with which to talk about the elements of the perspective, and certainly could not begin to think about, or talk about, the corresponding actions. Thus the only manner in which the bystander can respond to the perspective pressure is by adopting a concern with categories, as a result of the failure to react directly to the elements of the perspective. The necessary result, then, is a static mode of thinking in regard to landscape painting, as long as the perspective pressure remains high. The bystander will treat himself in terms of relevant categories; he will also treat the other in terms of relevant categories.

2. Socialization as a Pre-requisite for the Static Mode

Early in this chapter it was stated that the categories are a societal abbreviation for being able to develop a dynamic mode of functioning within particular parts of the environment. All of the above considerations have assumed that everyone has uniform access to systems of categories for all possible perspectives. And it is here that we have to point to the centrality of a socialization variable.

If a person does not understand the systems of categories that are valuable for society, and if a person does not understand that one is valued by means of membership in the categories, then there is no possible categorization response to perspective pressure. A small child, for instance, can function only in terms of the dynamic mode. Not yet having been socialized into the system of *potentials* (i.e., categories), a failure to develop a dynamic mode of functioning will leave the child with a feeling of worthlessness, or of not being valued. At the same time, of course, the absence of a possible recourse to categories makes the child a stronger candidate for persistence and learning within the dynamic mode of functioning. Quite the opposite can be the case when the child comes to comprehend the subtleties of the categories. When the dynamic functioning fails, the child can then proceed to work himself into the corresponding categories — his *potential* will then be appreciated by society, and the failing of the dynamic fit will thereby be less of a psychological trauma for the child.

The further implication is that familiarity with a particular categorization system would vary, as a function of culture and as a function of kind of training, and that the readiness to fall into the static mode of functioning would be directly related to the person's familiarity with the system of categories. This relation is depicted in Figure 9.3.

In looking at the figure, one can see that a firm grounding in knowledge of the categories would actively interfere with a dynamic orientation. In essence, the possibility of belonging to a category, or thinking in terms of belonging to a category, affords the person the luxury of never having to master the dynamic relation between oneself and the perspective.[6]

Another way of stating this principle is that the readiness to learn, the readiness to be taught, the attempt to understand all aspects of the perspective, are propensities that hang together with a *lack* of access to the systems of categories. Once the person understands that society needs and respects those who belong to the categories, then the dynamic orientation stands to suffer. A young child, or someone just initiated into a culture, really has no choice but to continue to try to master the elements of the perspective — as long as the pressure is high.

3. Forcing a Reaction to an Unseen and Unknown Perspective

A characteristic research paradigm in psychology asks subjects to evaluate themselves on all possible kinds of competence dimensions, such as sociability, motor dexterity, or artistic potential. It is not infrequent that a respond-

---

[6]A tangentially relevant area of inquiry in psychology is called "overjustification" (de Charms, 1968; Deci, 1971, 1975; Lepper, Greene, & Nisbett, 1973). One may characterize their work (without really doing justice to the theoretical aspects) in terms of the thesis that active involvement in a task or game will be reduced, or interferred with psychologically, to the extent that oversufficient external rewards are provided for the work (or play). By way of comparison, the formulation outlined in the present chapter proposes, on a highly general level, that dynamic functioning and static functioning simply interfere with one another. To the extent that people work themselves into categories, their active involvement in the perspective will thereby be curtailed. And to the extent that they are actively involved in fitting to a perspective, their thinking in terms of the static condition will be curtailed. The static orientation, however, should not be thought of as a "justification" or "reward." Rather, the concept is qualitatively much different, in the sense that the static orientation revolves around one's belonging to a category that signifies potential.

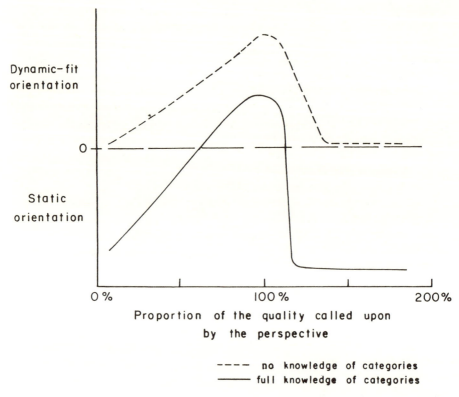

Dynamic-fit
orientation

O

Static
orientation

0 %   100 %   200%

Proportion of the quality called upon
by the perspective

- - - - no knowledge of categories
———— full knowledge of categories

FIG. 9.3.   Access to Categories and Quality of Orientation.

ent indicates "I can't do that kind of activity," "That doesn't make any sense to me," "I don't see it," "I would be the world's worst . . . ," "My ability is zero," and in comparing such respondents to others, who appear to have a higher appraisal of their own potentials, it often seems as though the various respondents are not responding to identical perspectives. For example, suppose we ask a young American, "How much ability do you think you have to play cricket?" The young person very likely has no idea about the context of the question. The game is a mystery, he doesn't know the rules, nor does he know the character of the playing field, nor how the teams are organized, nor the specific behaviors involved. Against this background he is asked to judge his ability on the characteristic Likert-scale, from "no ability at all" to "very high ability."

Obviously there can be no judgment on the basis of prior behaviors (cf. the self-perception approach to the formation of opinions about one's self), and similarly, there can be no basis for laying claim to membership in a category on the basis of what has been discussed here. The reason is simple: The person must first be able to *know* the perspective, and second, to experience the pressure of that perspective, before either the dynamic mode or the static mode will come into being. If the respondent has no idea of what the perspective is, then there will be no impetus to categorize the self, thus the actual form of his response will be determined by various other factors — quite independent of the processes discussed here.

The apparent admission of having "zero ability" can, then, have a very important hidden meaning. The psychological reality of such respondents would be better served by giving them a scale that asks whether they understand anything about the perspective, since the psychologically more real response in the situation is "I have no idea what cricket is."

The purpose of this example is to indicate that people do not invariably try to push themselves into categories that indicate potential. It is not as though the respondent hears the name of the category and then immediately tries to lay claim to category membership. Rather, sensing the perspective must come first, and experiencing the perspective pressure must then follow. Given these prerequisites, we are then in a position to talk about the relationship between the extent of non-fit to the perspective and working oneself into categories. Thus a given case of a person's ostensibly admitting to having "no" category membership leaves open the crucial question of whether that person even sees the perspective in question. As this question is seldom asked in psychology, there is correspondingly little pertinent research.

DEALING WITH DISPOSITIONAL TERMS: A CONTRAST WITH LOCKSLEY AND LENAUER AND WITH SYMBOLIC INTERACTIONISM

Psychology in general, not just Locksley and Lenauer (1981) and symbolic interactionism, generally assumes that one's sense of having dispositions is based on realistic feedback from the physical or social environment. However, when we consider the character of the person's possible relation to the environment, in the sense of reacting in dynamic form to perspectives, it appears as if an entirely different, sometimes opposing, process characterizes the relation between a human and thinking in terms of categories. Beginning with the dual paradox, and moving through several postulates, it looks as though people who *could,* with the most behavioral accuracy, place themselves and others into dispositional categories, are the very ones who would have little use for such classifying. The implication is straightforward: Someone who is highly competent and who exercises that competence will not be concerned about belonging to any particular category. Further, owing to the concentration on the perspective, that same person will not be engaged in the process of categorizing others.

Perhaps one of the difficulties in most conceptions about the origin and change of the self is that it has generally been assumed, albeit implicitly, that people automatically come to ask themselves whether they have particular dispositions. If the preceding postulates have any plausibility, then it would be the people who *cannot* respond to a perspective who, in that moment, would come to concern themselves with "who they are." Therefore, it is not as though a smooth-functioning performance results automatically in the performer's then looking back (cf. Locksley & Lenauer, 1981) and concluding something in detail about one's abilities. Rather, the person who cannot approach the perspective with matching behaviors would be the one who would be concerned with fitting oneself, and others, into a category.

Knowing oneself comes to have entirely different meanings, depending on which theoretical starting point one takes. If the reality-based view of knowledge-of-own-dispositions is assumed, then self-knowledge is a summary statement of what one would and could do, given specified situational constraints. "Knowing oneself to be artistic" would mean that, owing to earlier creative performances, the person can now conclude with accuracy that he can produce original literature or art, for instance. The idea of self-knowledge is something that is highly valued in society; those who lay claim to self-knowledge are valued as being in touch with the reality of their behavioral repertoires.

If we take a different theoretical starting point — namely the one represented here — we come to quite a different conclusion. Self-knowledge, as an entity that consists of the self-ascription of various traits or dispositions, consists by definition of the societally-grounded categories that have been discussed here. As such, the accumulation of, and the dwelling on, self-knowledge would stem out of a combination of strong perspective pressures and the absence of a dynamic relation to the various perspectives. A wealth of so-called self-knowledge would simply be a societally-acceptable accumulation of self-categorizations stemming from the failure of potential dynamic functioning. Such a statement should not appear as ironic or non-common sense, given the above discussions. Those who are in fact involved in a dynamic manner with a perspective would simply have no use for self-categorization within that realm.

TWO DIMENSIONS: GOODNESS-BADNESS AND FREQUENCY

Practically every piece of research and every conception that has to do with the self treats the human as a self-evaluator. The starting assumption, generally implicit, is that everyone is, at almost any time, ready to make some kind of evaluative or judgmental statement about the self. Thus the *frequency* or *intensity* of considering one's own nature is neglected. In the literature on attribution and on formation or change of self-concept, the common answer to the question "When does the person evaluate the self?" is treated in a nonsystematic manner. The starting point is characteristically, "When the person starts evaluating the self, then . . . ." And correspondingly, in the literature we see almost exclusively just good-bad dimensions, or perhaps a "has-the-trait versus does-not-have-the-trait" dimension.

Against such a background, the implications for frequency, or intensity, or concern with one's category membership are relatively clear from the preceding postulates. The further one is driven from the dynamic mode, the greater the frequency of the processes associated with the static mode. However, when we turn to a more usual methodology, which asks all respondents to place themselves along dimensions, what should we then expect? The general idea stemming from the above is that those in the static mode of functioning would be expected to place themselves into categories such that *potential* in the general domain of the perspective would be evident. This is to say, the less able they are to react directly to the perspective, the more potential they would claim in that particular domain.

At first glance this seems preposterous. But if we consider the motivating quality of the perspective pressure (one must do something), it becomes understandable. Given that the person must react immediately, there are two ways for a person to remain a valuable part of society. The one is to react directly to the perspective, and in this case there will be no special motivation to rate oneself as having extremely high potential. The category membership is superfluous. On the other hand, the static-oriented person has no other way to satisfy the pressures; it becomes crucial to fit oneself into a condition of having a definite potential to perform.

If the perspective pressure is not there, then all of these processes will become weaker, and other factors (including certainly the reality constraints implied by the self-perception or symbolic interactionism notions) will come into play. But when the pressure is intense, one can sometimes observe such interesting phenomena as that reported by Stephan, Fischer, and Stein (1983). Students at the University of Trier took a very important oral examination (hence the perspective pressure), and just after receiving feedback on their performance they were asked several questions regarding their confidence vis-à-vis the exam — for example:

> whether they were satisfied with their preparations,
> whether they would reach or excel their aspiration levels,
> whether they were confident that they would be successful.

Quite remarkably, confidence scores correlated with examination performance at the level of $r = -.43$. In terms of the present thinking, the result implies that the students who were, in fact, least able to fit to the perspective pressure were the very ones who fit themselves into a category of having potential, in this case into the highly simplistic category of "having confidence."

Also interesting is the correlation between the students' level of confidence and whether they felt that confidence would affect their examination grades. The r value was $+.71$, suggesting that society generally (and the students in particular) have a strong belief that category membership is a shorthand way of describing actual potential. That is, "confident" people *should* be able to perform. But in reality, the actual performers were relatively modest with respect to self-confidence ratings.

A parallel phenomenon is described by Gollwitzer and Wicklund (1985). Male university students, each of whom claimed to have a high interest in some athletic, artistic, or intellectual endeavor, were given differential feedback about their potential in their respective areas. In other words, they found that they did (or did not) have the potential to pursue their particular interests.

Shortly thereafter they had to rate their percentile standing, plus two highly-related self-evaluative items, within their interest areas. The correlation between strength of potential (as defined by the experimental feedback) and self-rating (including percentile standing) was $r = -.39$. Thus the less basis they had for thinking that they could respond successfully in the future, the more they built themselves into the category of someone with potential. When independent observer-subjects were shown these ratings, and then were asked to predict the subjects' actual potential, the correlation was $r = +.63$. Once again, it seems that society uses self-descriptions, among other categories, to infer that the person has some real potential. Yet, at the same time, the involved person, who is having trouble or potential trouble in reacting to the pertinent perspective, builds himself into the category in proportion to the *lack* of actual potential.

PSYCHOPATHY OR PRO-SOCIAL BEHAVIOR?

One is inclined to say that people who fit themselves into favorable-sounding categories, owing to a failing in the dynamic realm, are liars. But such a value judgment is not at all necessary, and to be sure, it is unlikely that such category-fitting is undertaken as a conscious or willful act of duplicity. Rather, society has created the problem for itself, by making two opposite reactions to perspective pressure feasible as well as desirable.

There is, of course, a societal constraint against placing oneself into categories, in the sense that society would like to think—along with self-perception theory—that good performance precedes prime placement into categories. On the other hand, no matter how a person arrives at an eventual category membership, society is prepared to react as if that person *could* enact something on a dynamic-fit level.

But society mistakes the appearance (the category) for the ostensible underlying dynamic function. The person who is presently encountering problems in fitting his repertoire to a perspective will not stop to contemplate the societal genesis, and function, of categories. Rather, the fact that they originally are *supposed* to signal performance will not be an issue, since the categories, as culturally-valued entities, have come to have a functional autonomy. They are a positive thing in themselves.

TRAINING FOR DYNAMIC FIT OR TRAINING FOR CATEGORIES?

It is a popular conception that humans can best deal with the environment "once they know who they are" or "once they know their abilities." By this conception, a very definite idea of who one is, in terms of traits or dispositions or propensities, will lead to a better level of performance in relation to the world. But on such a simple level the idea does not seem to work. For instance, Meyer (1983) has summarized a wealth of studies in which objective performance was correlated with self-rated ability. The modal outcome is one of no relationship between the two. Nonethelss, even in the face of such empirical facts, society (perhaps more particularly psychology) persists in the idea that self-knowledge — that is, knowing that one belongs to a valued category — leads to something objectively positive.

This being the case, it becomes interesting to consider the differential kinds of training that children (or others) receive. Starting at the dynamic-fit level, a teacher could train the child in a specific area by forcing attention onto the perspective, by dwelling on the behaviors, thus in a systematic way bringing about the possibility of a dynamic relation to the perspective.

On the other hand, a "teacher" — as a representative of society — need not necessarily think only about the child's dynamic connection to the environment. The child can be transformed into a valued entity by means of building up categories around the child, thereby signalling its "potential." One has only to think of certain segments of society, in which a grey suit, an air of self-confidence (cf. Stephan et al., 1983), and a set of jargon are prerequisites for admission into a high-paying position. A segment of society looks at these signs of category membership and accords the resident of the category a status. Value is bestowed upon the person. Very seldom is the question posed, "Exactly what peformances are signalled by the category membership?"

We might guess that the more automated a society, and the further one is from early childhood, the less urgent are dynamic connections to the physical or social environment. Thus "teaching" can have rather different meanings, dependent on whether we are speaking of a dynamic or static starting point.

However, the important notion here is that one's propensity to react in a dynamic form, given some particular perspective pressure, is largely a function of the kinds of training one has had in these two realms. To the degree that one's socialization has focused exclusively on category membership, then dynamic relations to perspectives are necessarily neglected and retarded. Those who "know themselves best," in the sense of having ready access to a wealth of self-ascriptions and self-characterizations, should be the same ones who were trained largely in terms of thinking in categories. To the degree that one's socialization has focused exclusively on dynamic functioning vis-à-vis a given perspective, the resulting tendency to pursue the elements of perspectives, and to refrain from adopting a static mode of functioning, should be relatively great.

ACKNOWLEDGMENTS

The writing of this chapter was facilitated by a stipend from the Alexander von Humboldt-Stiftung, and also by the Ruhr-Universität Bochum. The author is grateful to Prof. Heinz Heckhausen for providing an atmosphere that prompted what is written here. Several associates and students gave particularly good feedback on an earlier version of the manuscript: Silvia Binotsch, Edward L. Deci, Martina Eckert, Astrid Geisler, Peter M. Gollwitzer, Thomas Grözinger, Wolfgang Heinemann, Uwe Machleit, Clemens Moll, Angelika Pohl, Rudolph Schiffmann, and Ulrich Wagner.

REFERENCES

Bem, D. J. An experimental analysis of self-persuasion. *Journal of Experimental Social Psychology,* 1965, *1,* 199–218.

Bem, D. J. Self-perception theory. In L. Berkowitz (Ed.), *Advances in experimental social psychology,* Vol. 6. New York: Academic Press, 1972.

Brehm, J. W. *A theory of psychological reactance.* New York: Academic Press, 1966.

Brehm, J. W. *Responses to loss of freedom: A theory of psychological reactance.* Morristown, NJ: General Learning Press, 1972.

Csikszentmihalyi, M. *Beyond boredom and anxiety.* San Francisco: Jossey-Bass, 1975.

Darley, J. M., & Latané, B. Bystander intervention in emergencies: Diffusion of responsibility. *Journal of Personality and Social Psychology,* 1968, *8,* 377–383.

de Charms, R. *Personal causation: The internal affective determinants of behavior.* New York: Academic Press, 1968.

Deci, E. L. Effects of externally mediated rewards on intrinsic motivation. *Journal of Personality and Social Psychology,* 1971, *18,* 105–115.

Deci, E. L. *Intrinsic motivation.* New York: Plenum Press, 1975.

Gollwitzer, P. M. & Wicklund, R. A. Self-symbolizing and the neglect of others' perspectives. *Journal of Personality and Social Psychology,* 1985, *48,* 720–715.

Hass, J., & Shaffir, W. The professionalization of medical students: Developing competence and a cloak of competence. *Symbolic Interaction,* 1977, *1,* 71–88.

Heckhausen, H. *Motivation und Handeln.* Berlin: Springer-Verlag, 1980.

Jones, E. E., & Nisbett, R. E. *The actor and the observer: Divergent perceptions of the causes of behavior.* Morristown, NJ: General Learning Press, 1971.

Lepper, M. R., Greene, D., & Nisbett, R. E. Undermining children's intrinsic interest with extrinsic rewards: A test of the overjustification hypothesis. *Journal of Personality and Social Psychology,* 1973, *28,* 129–137.

Locksley, A., & Lenauer, M. Considerations for a theory of self-inference processes. In N. Cantor & J. F. Kihlstrom (Eds.), *Personality, cognition, and social interaction.* Hillsdale, NJ: Lawrence Erlbaum Associates, 1981.

Mead, G. H. *Mind, self, and society.* Chicago: University of Chicago Press, 1934.

Mehlhorn, G., & Mehlhorn, H.-G. *Zur Kritik der bürgerlichen Kreativitätsforschung.* Berlin: VEB Deutscher Verlag der Wissenschaften, 1977.

Meyer, W.-U. Das Konzept von der eigenen Begabung als ein sich selbst stabilisierendes System. *Zeitschrift für personenzentrierte Psychologie und Psychotherapie,* 1983, *2,* 21–30.

Milgram, S. Some conditions of obedience and disobedience to authority. *Human Relations,* 1965, *18,* 57–76.

Murray, H. A. *Explorations in personality.* New York: Oxford University Press, 1938.

Snyder, M. L., Stephan, W. G., & Rosenfield, D. Attributional egotism. In J. H. Harvey, W. Ickes, & R. F. Kidd (Eds.), *New directions in attribution research* (Vol. 2). Hillsdale, NJ: Lawrence Erlbaum Associates, 1978.

Stephan, E., Fischer, M., & Stein, F. Self-related cognitions in test anxiety research: An empirical study and critical conclusions. In H. M. van der Ploeg, R. Schwarzer, & C. D. Spielberger (Eds.), *Test anxiety research* (Vol. 2). Hillsdale, NJ: Lawrence Erlbaum Associates, 1983.

Wicker, A. W. Attitudes versus actions: The relationship of verbal and overt behavioral responses to attitude objects. *Journal of Social Issues,* 1969, *25,* 41–78.

Wicklund, R. A. & Gollwitzer, P. M. *Symbolic self completion.* Hillsdale, NJ: Lawrence Erlbaum Associates, 1982.

10 The Dynamics of Self-Determination in Personality and Development

Edward L. Deci
Richard M. Ryan
University of Rochester

Organic theories in psychology begin with the assumptions that the nature of a living organism is to act on the environment in accordance with its capacities, and through this activity to develop an increasingly elaborated and unified internal structure that represents the organism and its environment (Blasi, 1976). A motivational theory of the active organism, and in particular of a human being, requires a concept that allows for a description of both the energetic and structural aspects that underlie the dialectical interplay of the organism acting on its surroundings and being impinged upon by them. In our work (Deci & Ryan, 1985), this concept is *self-determination.*

Self-determination refers to a qualitative aspect of human behaviors and psychological processes. According to our approach, self-determination is in evidence when the source of initiation for an action is the awareness of one's needs and feelings and the behavioral sequence is accompanied by the experience of choice. Thus, for example, a behavior is not self-determined if it is controlled by an environmental event or initiated by a nonconscious process. Nor would it be considered self-determined if it were initiated by awareness of a need or feeling and experienced by the person as something he or she *had* to do. Self-determination requires the experience of freedom both with respect to forces in the environment and forces within the person.

The empirical study of self-determination has been an outgrowth of research on intrinsic motivation, which is a related though not equivalent concept. Intrinsically motivated action is that which occurs for its own sake, action for which the only rewards are the spontaneous affects and cognitions that accompany it. Intrinsically motivated behaviors require no external supports or reinforcements for their sustenance; they are a manifestation of one's interests, and they flourish under conditions of competence feedback and choice (Deci & Ryan, 1980). Intrinsic motivation is especially apparent in young children, supporting much of their initial engagement with and assimilation of their world. But intrinsic motivation also plays an important role in the lives of adults, especially in their effectance-related and leisure time activities.

Intrinsically motivated behaviors are, of course, self-determined; however, it has become increasingly clear that behaviors which are extrinsically motivated, or were acquired under conditions of extrinsic motivation, *can* also be self-determined. It is the more general case of self-determined activity that is the focus of this chapter. We will consider the dynamics of self-determination in personality and development by addressing not only intrinsically motivated and autonomous, extrinsically motivated actions, but also important psycholoical processes such as internalization and the integration of one's self. Recent theory and research on these points will be summarized in four sections. The first is a very brief review of the extensive body of studies which have detailed the conditions that enhance versus diminish self-determination. The second focuses on self-regulatory processes, some of which represent self-determination and some that do not; the third extends this reasoning to the level of personality orientations. The fourth section presents some preliminary work on the development of self-determination, and considers the problem of internalization.

THE ENVIRONMENT AND SELF-DETERMINATION

Most research on the effects of environmental events on self-determination has used intrinsic motivation as the dependent measure, although recently, various other dependent measures have been used and have yielded similar results. *Cognitive evaluation theory,* in its most recent formulation (Deci & Ryan, 1985), describes the effects of initiating events on intrinsic motivation and, more broadly, self-determination. It identifies three broad categories of environmental events that have markedly different effects on self-determination. The first category is *informational* events. These are environmental events which are perceived by recipients as providing effectance-enhancing information in the context of choice. The second category, labeled *controlling,* consists of events that are perceived as pressures to think, feel, or behave in specified ways. And the third, called *amotivating,* is composed of events for which the outcomes people receive are felt to be unattinable given their behavioral options. Therefore, they are neither predictable nor controllable. These three types of psychological circumstances represent the functional aspects of the environment that are relevant to motivated behavior.

Any interpersonal event such as the promise of a reward, the imposition of deadlines, or the delivery of verbal feedback can have more than one aspect. Most reward structures, for example, are somewhat informational and somewhat controlling. According to the theory, the relative salience of these aspects defines the nature of the event and is the basis for predicting its effects on the person's self-determination.

Informational events promote self-determination by enhancing intrinsic motivation and allowing choice with respect to extrinsic goals. They facilitate a perceived internal locus of causality — that is, they maximize the perception that the actions which follow are one's own. Controlling events tend to undermine self-determination by making behavior dependent on implicit or explicit contingencies and inducing the experience of pressure and tension. They promote a perceived external locus of causality — the sense that one is being coerced or seduced by forces external to one's *self*. Controlling events can result in either compliance or reactance. With compliance the person does what is demanded or expected, whereas with reactance the person tends to do the opposite. But in either case, whether the directional relationship of the demand and behavior is positive, as in compliance, or negative, as in reactance, the behavior is determined by the controlling event and is accompanied by some form of pressure and tension. With compliance this tends to involve shame and guilt, whereas with reactance it tends to involve hostility. Finally, amotivating events tend to undermine both intrinsic and extrinsic motivation. They promote amotivation and the experience of incompetence. Behaviors following from amotivating conditions are described as having a perceived impersonal locus of causality, meaning that the actor has no sense of personal causation with respect to his or her behavior or goal attainment (deCharms, 1968).

These are, of course, general conclusions for which there are various limiting conditions. However, these principles have been supported by the results of dozens of studies accumulated over the past decade by various researchers. For example, Deci and Ryan (1980; 1985) have reviewed numerous studies showing that externally administered prizes, rewards, deadlines, surveillance, or punishments, all of which presumably facilitated the perception of an external locus of causality, could undermine intrinsic motivation (Deci, 1971; Lepper & Greene, 1975), recall (Kruglanski, Friedman, & Zeevi, 1971), creativity (Amabile, 1982b), and psychological flexibility (McGraw, & McCullers, 1979).

However, none of these structures *necessarily* undermines intrinsic motivation and self-determination. The organismic position holds that it depends upon how they are experienced, and that the meanings of rewards, competition, observation, and so forth, can differ in their informational or controlling salience, primarily depending upon the interpersonal context in which they are (or were on past occasions) received. As a demonstration of this point, Ryan, Mims, and Koestner (1983), like Harackiewicz (1979), reported that performance-contingent rewards could either enhance or diminish intrinsic motivation relative to no rewards, depending on whether they were informationally or controllingly administered. When the administration conveyed that the rewards were merely a way of letting people know that they had done well, their intrinsic motivation increased, whereas when the administration conveyed the surplus meaning that the subjects *should* (according to the experimenter) do well and would be rewarded if they did, their intrinsic motivation decreased. The control implicit in the word "should" had a dramatically negative effect on people's self-determination and therefore their intrinsic motivation.

Positive, effectance-relevant feedback is inherent in performance-contingent rewards. Therefore, to understand the full effect of performance-contingent rewards it would be necessary to compare the two reward conditions to two other conditions in which there were no rewards but there was positive effectance-relevant feedback comparable to that inherent in the rewards. Ryan et al. (1983) did just that. They found that both informationally and controllingly administered performance-contingent reward conditions decreased intrinsic motivation relative to no-reward conditions in which positive feedback was given in an amount and style comparable to that given in the two types of reward conditions.

In sum, therefore, it appears that rewards are generally experienced as controlling and therefore decrease intrinsic motivation relative to a condition without rewards but with comparable feedback. Presumably, this is because rewards are so widely used, and therefore so widely experienced, as instruments of control. It does, however, appear to be possible to use rewards to enhance intrinsic motivation, relative to no rewards and no feedback, by providing performance-contingent rewards that are informationally administered—that is, administered in a way that conveys freedom and choice rather than expectations and pressure.

Actually, although a great deal of research has focused on rewards as sources of information or control, they are really just an instance of the more general case of interpersonal communications. Any interpersonal communication, whether or not it is accompanied by a tangible contingency, can be either informational or controlling and, like rewards, will have dramatically different effects depending on which way it is experienced. Ryan (1982) investigated this using performance feedback and found that when the feedback was made controlling by referring to how subjects should perform, the feedback decreased intrinsic motivation relative to when it was informationally administered. This underscores the point that to include positive feedback in a communication is not enough to make the communication informational; it must be experienced within the context of freedom or choice.

The concept of should, introduced into any communication, seems to remove felt choice and make the communication a controlling one, thus tending to undermine intrinsic motivation and self-determination.

Pittman, Davey, Alafat, Wetherill, and Kramer (1980) did a study in which informational versus controlling positive feedback yielded the same results as in the Ryan study. They made positive feedback controlling by emphasizing that they (the experimenters) needed the subjects to do well. Thus, positive feedback tended to imply that the subjects were doing well "for the experimenters" and hence that they were being controlled by the experimenters' expectations. The general point is that interpersonal communications can be made controlling in a wide variety of verbal and non-verbal ways. Anything in a communication that is experienced as a pressure to behave, think, or feel in specific ways will tend to undermine intrinsic motivation and self-determination.

Many people have suggested that the *self-administration* of feedback will make it more informational, because people can "freely" administer the feedback themselves. Ryan (1982) argued, however, that one can self-administer either informational or controlling feedback — the latter being self-administered feedback that one uses to control oneself. If the self-administered feedback is controlling, it is likely to undermine intrinsic motivation relative to informational feedback. Ryan reported empirical support for this hypothesis. It did not matter whether the feedback was self- or other-administered; when it was controlling (i.e., when it employed the concept of should) it undermined intrinsic motivation relative to when it was informational.

All of the studies reported thus far used intrinsic motivation as their primary dependent measure, although they also employed self-reports of interest and enjoyment and of pressure and tension. Informational events generally enhance feelings of interest and enjoyment while controlling events generally amplify feelings of pressure and tension. Thus, a consistent pattern of results on self-reports of these variables may also be used to draw inferences about self-determination. When a person is being more self-determining, he or she will tend to experience greater interest and enjoyment and less pressure and tension.

Haddad (1982) did a study in which she operationalized self-determination quite differently. In her study, fourth- and fifth-grade children, preselected as being either high or low on Harter's (1981) measure of intrinsic versus extrinsic orientation in the classsroom, worked on anagrams and were given either informational or controlling positive feedback. Subsequently, when they were about to begin their last four anagrams, she told them they could select their own or that she would select for them. She then asked how many of the four they would like to select for themselves. Their responses were used as a measure of their desire for self-determination. The results revealed an interesting interaction. On the one hand, controlling feedback did not affect the extrinsically oriented children. Presumably, they had accommodated to being externally controlled, so they wanted feedback to tell them whether they were right or wrong. In other words, the controlling feedback did not affect their self-determination because they were not oriented toward being self-determining. On the other hand, however, the intrinsically-oriented children were strikingly affected by the controlling feedback. As predicted, it generally decreased the number of choices the children wanted to make for themselves. However, there were marked differences according to the child's gender which were of interest. Intrinsically-oriented females wanted virtually no choice following controlling feedback, whereas intrinsically-oriented males wanted a great deal of choice. In other words, for intrinsically-oriented children, type of feedback interacted with sex of subject. Controlling feedback led females to give up self-determination and look outward for further controls—in short, they complied with the controls— whereas controlling feedback led males to demand more choices for themselves—in short, they reacted (Brehm, 1966) against the controls. As we said earlier, neither the compliance nor the reactance represents self-determination; they are merely divergent responses to being controlled. In the Haddad study, self-determination in the controlling feedback condition would have been represented by the same number of choices being requested by the children as in the informational feedback condition.

To summarize, the evidence points to the conclusion that *controlling* external events are antagonistic to self-determination. They decrease intrinsic motivation and interest, increase pressure and tension, create a dynamic such that people either comply with the controls or rebel against them, and have a generally negative effect on the quality of performance which requires autonomy and independence. For practical purposes, however, it is important to keep in mind that any of the events that are sometimes controlling can also be made to be informational, and in that case will not have the deleterious effect. A study by Koestner, Ryan, Bernieri, and Holt (1984), which will be described later in the chapter, even showed that limits can be set on children's behavior in either an informational or a controlling way and will negatively impact intrinsic motivation and self-determination only if they are imposed controllingly. One of the important points that was illustrated by that study relates to the meaning of autonomy. Often autonomy is confused with permissiveness or the complete absence of structure. For us, however, autonomy means functioning in informational environments, namely environments where structures exist to provide people with effectance-relevant information in the context of choice. Permissiveness, or the absence of structure, encourages the unmediated operation of drives or affects, whereas informational environments encourage self-determination. The use of limits in child-rearing can, according to the Koestner et al. study, be used as informational structures rather than controls, and as such can encourage rather than undermine self-determination.

In our tripartite characterization of environmental events, the third type of environment is amotivating. Here, not only is the locus of causality outside the person as it is with controlling events, but control of outcomes is unpredictable and felt to be unattainable by the person. Amotivating events promote the feeling that one's actions will not effect desired outcomes; if the outcomes are received it is due to chance or fate. These environmental events are, of course, most damaging to people's self-determination since they undermine extrinsic motivation as well as intrinsic motivation. People end up with a perceived impersonal locus of causality for the behavior. We have not studied amotivating external events extensively in our own laboratories since they have been so carefully and extensively studied in the context of helplessness (e.g., Garber & Seligman, 1980; Seligman, 1975). However, the studies do confirm that when people experience environments as amotivating, they tend to become nonintentional and helpless.

INFORMATION, CONTROL, AND SELF-REGULATION

Thus far we have considered only events outside the person that initiate and regulate behavior. Even the self-administered feedback in the Ryan (1982) study was selected by the subjects from a list of feedback statements provided by the experimenter. Surely, however, much of a person's behavior is initiated and regulated by events that are inside the person — events that take the form of thoughts or feelings. For many theorists, this fact alone is enough to make the behavior self-determined; however, for us it is not. We define self-determination in terms of the behavior's being initiated and regulated by awareness of one's needs or feelings and being accompanied by the experience of choice. Thus, if the initiating event is inside the person, but it is nonconscious or it is experienced as an internal but coercive demand that the person do something, we would say that the behavior is *not* self-determined.

Accordingly, Ryan (1982) suggested that initiating events inside the person can be either informational or controlling, just as interpersonal events can be either. He referred to these events as *internally informational* and *internally controlling,* suggesting that only regulation by internally informational events represents true self-determination, and internally controlling events, because they are experienced as not allowing choice, undermine intrinsic motivation relative to internally informational events.

The idea that there are intrapsychic contingencies which function to control or motivate behavior is certainly not new. Within psychoanalytic theory, for example, the superego is said to function in a way that inhibits or promotes action by rewarding or punishing the person with internal praise or criticism (Freud, 1923/1962; Lewis, 1971; Schafer, 1968). These internally controlling communications are distinguished from more integrated, internally informational forms of self-regulation in which the observing ego (as opposed to the critical component of the superego) assesses performance and provides effectance feedback (Meissner, 1981). In the context of our empirically oriented hypotheses, we would argue that critical superego functioning represents the relative absence of self-determination in the regulation of oneself and would be detrimental to intrinsic motivation.

The first empirical demonstration of this was provided by Ryan (1982). To induce internally controlling regulation, he employed the concept of ego-involvement (which in the language of psychoanalytic theory would be more properly termed super-ego involvement) that had been previously researched by Frank (1941), Sherif and Cantril (1947), and others. In these paradigms when someone is ego-involved in an outcome, self-esteem is on the line. In order to maintain self-esteem the person must achieve the specified outcome, so the ego-involvement serves as a control that pressures the person toward that outcome (deCharms, 1968). Task-involvement, on the other hand, is more informational in nature. The person is focused on the activity and is receiving immediate feedback from his or her interaction with it. Ryan operationalized ego-involvement by telling college student subjects that their performance on a hidden figures task was a reflection of their creative intelligence requiring various flexible perceptual capacities. In fact, he added, "hidden figures tasks are used in some I.Q. tests." Ryan found that subjects in this internally controlling condition evidenced less subsequent intrinsic motivation than subjects in the internally informational (i.e., task-involved) condition. Further, the internally controlling condition led to reports of greater pressure and tension, which was primarily intrapersonally generated. It appears, then, that regulation by internally controlling events, although "within the skin" of the actor, does not really represent self-determination, since it results in the experience of pressure and it undermines intrinsic motivation.

In another study, Plant and Ryan (in press) replicated the task versus ego results reported by Ryan (1982) and they also explored how various forms of self-consciousness differ on the internally informational to internally controlling dimension. In particular, they followed the lead of Fenigstein, Scheier, and Buss (1975) who distinguished between *private* self-consciousness and *public* self-consciousness as two independent styles of attentional focus that have significant behavioral, cognitive, and affective influences on self-regulatory processes. Private self-consciousness refers to the tendency to be aware of internal states: one's thoughts, motives, and emotions. Public self-consciousness is the tendency to be aware of and focused upon oneself as viewed from outside; the tendency to experience oneself as a social object. The Self-Consciousness Scale (Fenigstein et al., 1975) measures the personality disposition to be high or low in these attentional styles. Carver and Scheier (1981) have also reviewed evidence that public and private attentional focus can be situationally induced by the presence of an audience or mirror, respectively. The "state" forms are labeled public and private self-awareness, while dispositional styles are called public and private self-consciousness.

Plant and Ryan suggested that the relative strength of public self-focus in the regulation of behavior would have important motivational implications. Since, in the "public" state or disposition, the person's behavior is more likely to be influenced and organized on the basis of perceived or projected external conditions, then the resulting behavior is more likely to have an external locus of causality and less felt self-determination. That is, the behavior is more likely to be seen by the actor as caused or brought about by actual or imagined external expectations or needs, rather than one's own initiations. This led to the prediction that both high dispositional and situationally induced forms of public self-focus would be related to less intrinsic motivation for an experimental task. Since the style of self-attention is, particularly in its dispositional form, a self-generated phenomenon, public self-focus was argued to be an internally controlling phenomenon — that is, a way of being controlling with oneself.

Plant and Ryan thus employed three levels of self-awareness: a non-self-focused group, a mirror group, and a video-camera group. Results revealed that both the mirror group and the video-camera group were less intrinsically motivated than the non-self-focused group, thereby supporting their reasoning. Furthermore, they found that the higher the subjects' dispositional public self-consciousness, the lower their intrinsic motivation, *regardless of condition*. As expected, there was not a significant relationship between private self-consciousness and intrinsic motivation.

To summarize, research on ego-involvement, objective self-awareness using both a video-camera and a mirror (Duval & Wicklund, 1972), and the disposition of public self-consciousness all point to the conclusion that events inside a person that initiate and regulate behavior in a way that is experienced as controlling tend to induce pressure and undermine intrinsic motivation relative to events inside the person that are experienced as informational.

Our research has concentrated on internally informational and internally controlling events; however, just as an event outside the person can be amotivating, so can an event inside the person. As an example, consider a man who thinks of an interesting idea for a paper, and then goes immediately into the thought that he could never carry through on it to the point of publication. The man has created an amotivating world in his mind; and he behaves in response to this internally amotivating event by giving up before he begins. There is no research that we know of that has focused on this issue, although the work on vicarious acquisition of learned helplessness by DeVellis, DeVellis, and McCauley (1978) and others is directly germane. To become helpless merely by observing a noncontingency in someone else's situation suggests that the helplessness has more to do with the person's internal processes than with the situation. In other words, the internally amotivating regulatory processes can be initiated with minimal prompting.

All of the research on internally informational versus internally controlling initiation of behavior is directly relevant to the general issue of the self-regulation of behavior. The main point to be derived from it is that there are quite different styles of self-regulation. We would describe one as self-determined; it corresponds to initiation and regulation of behavior by internally informational events. Here, people regulate themselves through choices. They are aware of their own needs and feelings and they act on the environment to achieve satisfaction of their needs or expression of their feelings. The cornerstone of self-determination is psychological flexibility and the experience of choice that accompanies it. A second style of self-regulation could be referred to as self-controlling, and is characterized by internally controlling initiation and regulation. One responds to inner demands and does as one *should* (or in some cases rebels against what one should do). Here, we find psychological rigidity (rather than flexibility), pressure, tension, and the absence of experienced choice.

Self-control has become a popular concept in recent psychological theories, resulting largely from the shift from an operant-behavioral to a cognitive-behavioral perspective. In self-control theories, such as that of Bandura (1977), many of the principles of operant theory have simply been moved inside the person. Thus, the theorists speak of structuring internally generated reinforcement contingencies dependent upon specific behavioral outcomes. The failure to break from the reinforcement perspective and to recognize the existence of intrinsic motivation, with all its ramifications for self-determination, perpetuates the focus on controlling people's behavior and producing performance changes (whether one's own or someone else's) rather than promoting choice. The research evidence that is now being amassed shows increasingly how *controlling* regulation, whether by oneself or by others, not only does not represent self-determination but can even be detrimental to self-determination.

This does not, of course, mean that internally controlling self-regulation does not have its place. Certainly, it is preferable to regulation by external controls and to no regulation. And in some clinical populations it may represent the most that can be hoped for. The problem is that the theories, being derivative of reinforcement theories, have portrayed self-control as the paradigmatic case of self-regulation and have, therefore, failed to map out the real possibilities and dynamics of self-determination.

SELF-DETERMINATION IN PERSONALITY

Thus far we have described the relation to self-determination and intrinsic motivation of various initiating and regulating events both outside and inside the person. We move now to the level of personality orientations. Our theory of personality orientations was derived from the concept of locus of causality as formulated by Heider (1958) and deCharms (1968). Heider distinguished between personal and impersonal causality on the basis of whether the behavior was mediated by intentionality. When people act with the intention of attaining an outcome there is personal causation, whereas impersonal causation refers to instances where behavior and outcomes are independent. deCharms elaborated this in his discussion of internal and external causation, both of which involve intentionality but for which the sources of initiation are different. According to deCharms, the source of initiation for internal causality is inside the person, whereas with external causality it is in some external demand or contingency.

Deci (1980) first used the concepts of internal, external, and impersonal causality to describe personality orientations. More recently, we (Deci & Ryan, in press) have refined the concepts and changed the names to capture the relevant phenomena more precisely. The *autonomy orientation* is based in the belief that behaviors and outcomes are related, and it involves behavior for which the source of initiation is the awareness of one's needs and feelings. When operating with an autonomy orientation, one experiences initiating events as informational (whether they are in the environment or inside oneself) and makes choices about how to behave to attain desired outcomes (whether the outcomes are intrinsic satisfaction or extrinsic rewards). The *control orientation* is also based in the belief in behavior-outcome dependence; however, here, the source of initiation is in demands and contingencies. One does what one should; one looks to controls, whether inside or outside oneself, to know what to do; the sources of initiation and regulation are implicit and explicit reinforcement (often self-esteem and social-approval related) contingencies. The *impersonally orientation* is based in the belief that outcomes cannot be predictably or reliably attained, so people tend to be passive. When operating with an impersonal-causality orientation, people tend to be amotivated and to feel helpless. They are neither intrinsically nor extrinsically motivated for, they believe, there is no reason to act.

In our work on the development of constructs to assess causality orientations we begin with the assumption that everyone is to some extent autonomy oriented, to some extent control oriented, and to some extent impersonally oriented. Therefore, we suggest, the best characterization of a person's orientation is stated in terms of the level of each.

Locus of causality is, of course, a different concept from locus of control (Rotter, 1966). In part this stems from the fact that the literature on locus of control and perceived control is focused on control of reinforcement-related outcomes, whereas the literature on motivation and self-determination is focused on the source of initiation and regulation of both reinforced and spontaneous behaviors. Yet there are points of convergence. Thus, in the terms of locus of control, *both* the autonomy and the control orientations would represent an internal locus of control since they both involve behavior-outcome dependence. In other words, the concept of "internal" locus of control does not distinguish between self-determined and control-determined causality. But there is a clear parallel between Rotter's external locus of control and our impersonal orientation since both lack personal causation and perceived behavior-outcome contingency.

As a further theoretical caveat, we would add that an internal locus of causality that is central to self-determination and an external locus of causality that is central to control-determination do *not* refer to whether or not the locus of causality is inside versus outside the physical being of the actor. As we saw, internally controlling events are inside the actor, but they constitute external causality. The key is whether the locus of causality is inside or outside the *Self* of the actor. When the locus of causality is internal to the self, initiating events will be experienced as informational, and there will be choice. When the locus of causality is external to the self, initiating events will be experienced as controlling, and there will be no choice. This point will become clearer in the discussion of development when we distinguish between introjection and integration.

Our initial efforts to explore the causality orientations construct involved the development of a general causality-orientations scale (Deci & Ryan, in press). We reasoned that, although one's pattern of causality orientations might be different for different domains, the validity of the construct depends in part upon whether it accounts for sufficient variance to be meaningfully associated with variables across domains. We established internal consistency and temporal stability for the general measure, and then we moved on to consider the relationship between each subscale and other variables that are theoretically linked to it. The autonomy subscale was found to be correlated with the adults' orientation toward supporting children's autonomy (Deci, Schwartz, Sheinman, & Ryan, 1981); the control subscale, with the Type-A coronary-prone behavior pattern (Jenkins, Rosenman, & Friedman, 1967) and public self-consciousness (Fenigstein et al. 1975); and the impersonal subscale, with external locus of control (Rotter, 1966), self-derogation (Kaplan & Pokorny, 1969), and both public self-consciousness and social anxiety (Fenigstein et al., 1975).

Causality orientations were originally formulated as a way of studying self-determination in personality. Therefore, we tested that relationship empirically. First, we correlated each subscale with the Janis-Field (1959) self-esteem scale and with Loevinger's (1976) ego-development measure. We reasoned that internal causality (the autonomy orientation) should be positively related to both since self-determination is theorized to involve and underlie self-esteem and the unified, autonomous self that is characterized by greater ego development. External causality (the control orientation) should be less positively or somewhat negatively related to each since it involves less self-determination, and impersonal causality (the impersonal orientation) should be most strongly negatively related to each since it is the antithesis of self-determination. These predicted relationships were found to exist in the data (Deci & Ryan, in press), indicating that a dimension of self-determination does underlie the three causality orientations.

The private self-consciousness subscale (Fenigstein et al., 1975) was positively related to all three causality orientations at the same modest magnitude of about $r = .25$. In other words, the more strongly oriented one is toward any understanding of causality, the more one is aware of the internal states that accompany it. When self-determined, presumably, one would be aware of relaxed interest and self-competence; when control-determined, of pressure, tension, and evaluation apprehension; and when impersonally-determined, of anxiety and helplessness. Once again, this points up the fact that focusing inside one's skin does not guarantee internal causality (i.e., self-determination). For example, if a person were motivated to withdraw from a group, feeling afraid and anxious, the causality would not be internal even though one might say that the source of initiation was the fear and anxiety, both of which are inside the person. Instead, the causality is impersonal since the behavior is organized by the belief that one cannot be effective in that situation and by the experience of incompetence and anxiety. The person is *impelled* to withdraw; he or she is helpless with relation to these forces. It is the qualitative aspects of behavior and psychological functioning that determine the locus of causality, and the central qualities of internal causality are psychological flexibility and the experience of choice.

Our discussion of the concept of self-determination, using the metaphor of locus of causality, has been a general one that has included several levels of analysis, ranging from the instigation of a single behavior by an event either inside or outside the person, to styles of self-regulation and personality orientations. The conclusions have also been general ones, based on a distillation of empirical investigations, so any of the levels of analysis could be elaborated with respect to specific cases, limiting conditions, and the like. For example, although controlling external events tend to undermine self-determination and promote either externally oriented compliance or reactance, a single presentation of a controlling event to a person who is strongly self-determined in orientation may have no effect on the person; he or she might easily take it as information and be unaffected by the control. Similarly, a noncontingency could be easily justified — that is, attributed to an unstable environment — and not cause amotivation and helplessness.

SELF-DETERMINATION AND INTERNALIZATION

The term *internalization* has enjoyed currency in psychology for over 50 years and has been a central issue within developmental and personality theories. It refers to the processes by which persons acquire attitudes, belief systems, or behavioral standards and regulations from outside sources, and progressively transform and absorb them into their own values and personality structures. In Hartmann and Loewenstein's (1962) classic definition, internalization represents the process through which organisms transform regulation by external events into regulation by internal events. In true internalization one takes on the values of socializing agents and assimilates them into the structure of one's *self*. This process is by nature an active one — it cannot be programmed by the environment or trained into the person. Rather, internalization represents a gradual integration of and identification with the social world, eventuating in a change in the personality structure of the subject. In stressing an active relationship between the person and the regulations presented by the environment, we suggest that internalization represents a pole in the ongoing dialectic between the person and the social context, a dialectic in which the emergent sense of self and autonomous functioning is the synthetic product.

In our work, we use the term internalization to describe the movement along a *continuum* from heteronomy or control by external forces to autonomy or self-determination in the regulation of action. The degree to which a given form of regulation is perceived as having an external locus of causality versus an internal locus of causality (that is, brought about by one's *self*) has been one of the organizing metaphors for our research. The change from external to internal locus of causality for certain regulations appears to us to be both a developmental process, and a matter of individual differences.

It is clear that there are many motivated actions for which the issue of internalization is not applicable. For example, intrinsically motivated actions occur spontaneously and do not require the initial presence of outside controls or incentives. Thus, we do not need to teach or program children to engage in or value exploration; they do so naturally (White, 1959; Deci & Ryan, 1985). Indeed, caretakers more often are compelled to train children where *not* to explore, whether for reasons of physical safety, convenience, or cultural taboo. The problem of setting such limits is pertinent to the issue of internalization, because we want children to "take on" the limits, safety concerns, and taboos *as their own*. But internalization concerns more than just what not to do. It is also involved in the countless behaviors, values, and beliefs which we want children to perform or identify with, but which they do easily or naturally. Thus, while children love to explore, make messes, play with and manipulate all shapes and forms of objects, they seem to display little spontaneous interest in washing their hands, picking up their toys, taking responsibility for chores, or being polite in public settings, to cite just a few examples. Initially, at least, the child's caretakers need to promote such actions, and this is often accomplished through the provision of consequences, such as tangible or social rewards or the opportunity to avoid negative outcomes or punishments. In other words, the process of internalization begins as the circumstances of *extrinsic motivation:* the behavior or regulation is accomplished by the child *in order to* get or avoid something from powerful or important others.

The domain of internalization is then defined as all those regulatios whose occurrence originally depends upon extrinsic incentives. The origins of internalization lie in the contingencies established in the social environment for behaviors that must be induced or fostered using available controls and incentives if they are to emerge.

Extrinsic controls are usually tangible for the very young child, for example, avoidance of punishment or administration of concrete rewards such as food or physical contact. Over time the focus of interest for the child becomes progressively more social. Increasingly, what matters, and therefore what motivates the child, are rewards and outcomes of a social nature. Thus, as the child grows into the social matrix, praise, approval, and the esteem of others become progressively more potent regulators in the promotion of otherwise non-spontaneous behaviors. Along with the child's concern for social acceptance comes an understanding of contingencies and an anticipation of consequences. Thus, the child is able to engage in rudimentary self-regulation. The regulations will, however, have been internalized in a rather unstable fashion, requiring the continual presence of external supports for their maintenance. But they are internalizations by virtue of the fact that one anticipates the consequences of action, and self-regulates with respect to what is anticipated. What has been internalized is the formerly external regulatory forces (or one's fantasy of them) in a structure akin to their original form.

To consider further developments along the internalization continuum we use the concepts of introjected regulation, regulation through identification, and integrated regulation, along with the developmental processes of introjection, identification, and integration through which these forms of regulation are established.

We, like Schafer (1968), use the term *introjection* to refer to the process whereby a regulation becomes internally represented in a form or nature that is modeled after an originally external regulatory function or agent, and the person then acts in accord with the demands of that now internalized representation. For instance, one might apply approval and disapproval to oneself in a manner that is isomorphic to a relationship that was formerly external. Thus, for example, a boy hears his mother tell him not to throw the ball in the house, "Good boys don't throw balls in the house." Through introjection, he establishes an internal version of his mother's admonition and regulates his ball throwing by complying with that internal command. The regulation is introjected and may involve the person's generating feelings of self-disparagement, negative self-evaluations, or alternatively self-aggrandizement or approval, contingent upon certain thoughts, feelings, or behaviors. Internally controlling states are introjects as portrayed in psychoanalytic theory (Schafer, 1968; Meissner, 1981), and as Ryan's evidence (1982) has suggested, there can be considerable pressure and conflict experienced in such regulation since one part of the person is controlling the rest (Perls, Hefferline, & Goodman, 1951). That is, there are conflicting impulses (to do or not to do, to refrain or not to refrain) which in the real sense of the term are not integrated, and thus require the superordinate support of cognitive-affective consequences in order for regulation to occur.

Introjected regulation is more stable than external regulation for it does not require the continual presence of external contingencies. The contingencies and rules have become wholly internal, and the regulation is often very persistent and can be quite inflexible and unyielding. Although it is different from externally mediated, extrinsic regulation and does not require direct external contingencies, it does share many qualitative characteristics with external regulation. The most notable is the conflictful, controller-controlled relationship and all that it entails. Whereas with external regulation, the controller and the controlled are separate people, with introjected regulation both are contained within the same skin, so the conflict is intrapersonal. Yet, in both cases there is the pressure, tension, and other feelings that are inherent in being controlled. Therefore, although introjected regulation occurs inside the person, it is not considered self-determined, for it lacks the integrated organization and unity of action that characterizes the autonomous, flexible functioning that we label self-determined. For regulation to be self-determined, it must be integrated into one's self and function as an internally informational event.

Regulation through identification is achieved through identification with the introjected controls. This means digesting and transforming them such that they will eventually fit into the psychological structure called self. When fully integrated, they represent a transformation of the self insofar as the differentiation that precedes and is inherent in the integration extends and modifies the identity that was previously there. Once the integration has occurred, the regulation that was formerly controlling will have moved into the realm of self-determination. The regulation is one's own and is effected for one's own reasons. This form of regulation is the hallmark of adjustment and is the organismic outcome of internalization that is not impeded. It represents the true meaning of socialization; it is not simply that one behaves according to the social standards, but rather that one behaves, feels, and thinks in a way that is congruent with the self *and* matches the extant social values.

With the increasing integration of self-regulation, the support of cognitive and affective consequences such as self-aggrandizement, self-disparagement, and other self-esteem related affects and contingencies becomes progressively less essential. The person experiences less pressure and greater flexibility, the two being inversely related. We do not mean to imply that integrated internalizations will never be in conflict with other aspects of oneself. Rather, there is no conflict over the existence of the regulation itself, and any conflict that does exist between that regulation and some other need or regulation is recognized and accepted so that real choices can be made flexibly in light of the alternatives available.

At the behavioral, or even the cognitive-behavioral level of analysis, introjected regulation may be indistinguishable from integrated regulation, in that the regulation occurs inside the person and there is an internal locus of control (not to be confused with locus of causality) for both. However, motivational and emotional analyses lead to a quite different alignment. Here we see that external regulation and introjected regulation both represent external causality, for the regulation in both cases is outside one's *self*, and the quality of functioning is similar for both. On the other hand, identified and integrated regulation are more comparable to intrinsic regulation since both represent internal causality and involve self-determination. This does not mean that the behavior governed by integrated regulations is instrinsically motivated. It is by definition extrinsically motivated, though self-determined, insofar as it is instrumental for reaching one's personal goals rather than being action which is rewarding in its own right.

To summarize, we have identified several points along a continuum, each of which represents a different form of self-regulation. External regulation depends upon external contingencies; introjected regulation depends upon introjected controls; regulation through identification means the regulations have become one's own; and self-determined regulation results from the identifications' becoming fully integrated. Self-determined behaviors, therefore, can be seen to be those that are either intrinsically motivated or are regulated by integrated internalizations.

Using this model we have begun exploring the development across childhood of self-regulation for those behaviors which initially required extrinsic motivation for their occurrence. Chandler and Connell (1984) did the first empirical exploration of this problem. They identified a variety of such behaviors after extensive pilot interviews with parents and children. The behaviors included items like cleaning up one's room, going to bed on time, doing homework, and others. These were behaviors that were initially disliked by children and were in need of extrinsic, parentally provided supports for their occurrence. They asked children between the ages of 5 and 13 to describe the reasons *why* they did these target behaviors, and the responses were recorded verbatim. A pretested coding system with high reliability was then used to classify these reasons. *Extrinsic* responses indicated that the behavior could be elicited only by extrinsic supports, for example, a reward or punishment contingency. In addition to tangible rewards, this category also included social contigencies, such that doing an activity in order to maintain peer or adult approval was classed as extrinsic. *Transitional* reasons were defined as verbalizations of general social rules or maxims that children knew should be followed but that did not specify either the person enforcing the rule or the consequences that would ensue for following or not following the maxim. Finally, *internalized* reasons represented those responses wherein the reasons for self-regulation were the achievement of a self-determined goal or decision. In sum, these global categories of children's reasons for behaving were constructed to represent a dimension with three points—done for external reasons, done for internalized but unintegrated reasons, and done for more integrated reasons. Thus, they represent a continuum of less to more internalized. Chandler and Connell (1984) hypothesized a positive correlation between age and children's report of more internalized reasons for performing these activities. They described this as a change in motivational orientation, and their results supported their predictions. Children's use of transitional and internalized responses increased with age, while emphasis on social controls and consequences decreased with age.

There was an important attitude which corresponded to the change in motivational orientations across these ages. Older children rated the extrinsic or chore behaviors as more *important* than younger children, and the attitude of importance was significantly related to children's use of transitional and internalized responses. The more important children felt it was to do chores (or follow parental rules) the more likely they were to give internalized reasons for performing them, and the less likely they were to give extrinsic reasons. These dual findings suggest that children's understanding of and attribution about importance of chores is linked to the proposed developmental process of internalization taking place in that domain.

Other research from our group (Ryan, Chandler, Connell, & Deci, 1983) indicates that the internalization process is intertwined with other motivational and self-related variables. These researchers found, in a large sample of third- through sixth-grade children, that greater internalization was associated with less anxiety, more mastery motivation (Harter, 1981) and greater self-esteem (Harter, 1982).

We believe that the concept of an intrinsic need for self-determination and competence gives intelligibility to these various findings. It helps predict and explain the direction of development away from simple responsiveness, toward integrated values; away from heteronomy and toward autonomy with respect to those behaviors not originally intrinsically motivated.

From the preliminary research we have gleaned that children seem to have a readiness to take on regulations as their own, that this becomes increasingly evident with age, and that more integrated regulation is accompanied by greater self-esteem and less anxiety. Our interpretation of all this is that the *process* of internalization is an aspect of the more general synthetic function of the self to develop an increasingly elaborated and integrated structure. This process we assert is a natural part of being effective in the environment (both the external and internal environment) and is motivated by the intrinsic need for competent, self-determined functioning. Stated differently, we are suggesting that the process of internalization is itself intrinsically motivated; the human organism, in its attempts to be effective, works to bring into harmony with the self those regulations that are necessary in its social world.

It is worth noting, parenthetically, that the process of integrating regulations into oneself requires some congruence between the nature of the organism and the regulation being integrated. Although keeping one's room clean is not intrinsically interesting, neither is it inherently antithetical to human nature. Therefore, it can be integrated. On the other hand, since the nature of the human organism is to explore, proscriptions on exploration can never be integrated; they can only be introjected.

Our belief is that persons are neither empty at birth nor infinitely malleable; the human organism has a *nature*. We do not presume to speculate about the nature, except for a few obvious points such as the fact that activity and curiosity are inherent; however, we suggest that the issue is researchable. Through the empirical exploration of internalization, through studying what does not and cannot be integrated, by using such indicators as the degree of pressure, tension, and anxiety that accompany self-regulation, we may have a means for studying what is naturally human.

INFORMATION, CONTROL, AND DEVELOPMENT

There remains one issue to be addressed in order to come full circle, and that is the antecedents of individual differences in causality orientations and internalization. Our analysis of this begins with two assumptions: first, the autonomy orientation involves regulation by intrinsic motivation and integrated internalizations, while the control orientation involves regulation by introjected controls and extrinsic contingencies; and second, the internalization process is itself an intrinsically motivated, natural process. This leads us to the following speculations: conditions which promote intrinsically motivated behaviors, and also promote the intrinsically motivated process of internalization, will be the antecedents of a strong autonomy orientation; conditions which arrest the internalization process and undermine intrinsic motivation will be the antecedents of a strong control orientation; and conditions which do not allow the internalization process to begin and that undermine both intrinsic and extrinsic motivation will be the antecedents of a strong impersonal orientation.

From the various empirical investigations on environmental conditions and motivation we can speculate still further. Informational environments during one's early years are, we propose, the antecedents of a an autonomy orientation, since they maintain intrinsic motivation and allow integration. Controlling environments are the antecedents of a control orientation, since they promote a dependence on controls whether outside or inside the person. And amotivating environments are the antecedents of an impersonal orientation, since they fail to provide the consistency of consequences that allow internalization to begin.

In our initial efforts to explore the effects of interpersonal (environmental) events on the development of self-determination, Koestner et al. (1984) investigated the practical problem of how to set limits on children's activity in a way that allows and maintains self-determination. They compared the effects of three limit-setting conditions upon children's intrinsic motivation and performance. Subjects were first- and second-grade children who were engaged in a watercolor painting activity in which limits concerning the use of the materials and neatness were administered. Koestner et al. constructed both controlling and informational limits and compared these to a third, no-limits condition. The controlling condition consisted of verbal limits which conveyed external control through the use of common imperatives and directive phrases. In this condition, the reasons for the limits were explained, yet the tone was one in which the limits conveyed how the children should or must behave. The informational group received verbal limits conveying the same constraints, but there was an absence of the imperative locutions.

The issue of informational limits is a somewhat more complex one than that of informational rewards or feedback. With rewards and feedback, people are doing things they want to do, indeed, things that often are intrinsically interesting. Therefore, interpersonal conditions that are informational need only allow choice and provide feedback. With limit setting, as an antecedent of internalization, the fact of setting limits implies that the behavior being elicited (whether it involves doing something or refraining from doing something) is likely to be in conflict with some need, feeling or impulse of the child's. Otherwise, there would be no need for the limits. Therefore, informational limits must acknowledge this potential conflict so the child will be able to work through the conflict and move toward integration. This allows the child to learn that there are certain situations in which it would be advantageous for him or her to behave in certain ways, rather than getting caught in a conflict about whether it is right or wrong to behave in certain ways. Further, it allows for a coexistence of feeling like doing one thing but deciding to do another.

In the Koestner et al. study, the informational limits included the acknowledgment of the potential conflict about being neat. Their dependent measures included intrinsic motivation, represented by the amount of painting in a free-choice period, self-reports of enjoyment, and the quality and creativity of the products as assessed by Amabile's (1982a) method. The intrinsic motivation, enjoyment, and quality of artisitc production were expected to be decreased by controlling limits relative to both no limits and informational limits, which were not expected to differ. The results provided substantial support for these predictions, suggesting that limits *can* be set without having a detrimental psychological impact, provided that they are informational — that is, provided that they are constructed with sensitivity toward the need for self-determination in the recipient.

From this study, we infer that informational limits are antecedents of self-determined functioning in situations where accommodation is necessary. The obvious next step is to explore the actual extent and nature of the internalization that results from informational versus controlling limits, and then to move toward an understanding of parenting orientations and behavior that affect the internalization process.

SUMMARY

In conclusion, we have outlined various elements of our general motivational approach to the study of human functioning. Our central concern is self-determination, a concern which developed out of our early empirical work on intrinsic motivation. From that work, several things became clear. First, although competence and self-determination are both involved in intrinsic motivation, self-determination is the more fundamental component. Thus, part of the importance of studying intrinsically motivated behavior so intensively is that it represents the paradigmatic case of self-determined functioning. Further, although extrinsic rewards and controls are often antagonistic to intrinsic motivation and self-determination, they need not be; in fact, it is possible for extrinsically motivated action to be self-determined. Therefore, since extrinsic incentives are so pervasive in society, the issue of promoting self-determination in the presence of extrinsic structures is really the critical applied issue for areas such as parenting, education, work, sports, and psychotherapy.

Our general organismic theory has several components, the first of which deals with environments. On the basis of dozens of research studies exploring the effects of environmental events on intrinsic motivation and self-determination, we have been able to characterize these events as being one of three types: informational (those that provide effectance-relevant information in the context of choice); controlling (those that pressure people to think, feel, or behave in specific ways); and amotivating (those that signify people's ineffectance at attaining desired outcomes). Informational events promote self-determination and enhance intrinsic motivation; controlling events promote external compliance or reactance and undermine intrinsic motivation; and amotivating events promote amotivation and undermine both intrinsic and extrinsic motivation.

Since many behaviors are initiated and regulated by events inside the person, rather than events in the environment, the theory also addresses these events. We have found that events inside the person can also be characterized in a way that parallels the classification of environmental events. Thus, internally-informational, internally-controlling, and internally-amotivating events have been studied and have been found to have effects on self-determination and motivation that directly parallel those of the three types of environmental events. According to the theory, only regulation by internally-informational events or by intrinsic motivation represent true self-determination. Self-control, in other words regulation by internally-controlling events such as self-reinforcements, does not represent self-determination; in fact, it is detrimental to it and also tends to undermine intrinsic motivation.

Our organismic theory has also addressed enduring characteristics of people. We have identified three causality orientations that we call autonomy, control, and impersonal, and we have developed a general instrument that assesses the strength of each orientation within a person. The autonomy orientation is characterized by interpreting events in the environment as informational and regulating oneself in an internally-informational fashion. The control orientation is characterized by interpreting events in the environment as controlling and regulating oneself in an internally controlling fashion. And the impersonal orientation is characterized by interpreting events in the environment and in oneself as amotivating.

Finally, our theory deals with the developmental process of internalization and with the roles that the environment plays in internalization and that the effects of the environment on internalization play in the development of the causality orientations. We suggest that the natural progression in internalization moves from external regulation to introjected regulation through the process of introjection and from introjected regulation to self-determined regulation through the processes of identifying with and then integrating the regulation into one's self.

The theory suggests that informational environments are necessary for integrated internalization to occur. Controlling environments foster introjection, but they exacerbate conflict and forestall integration. And amotivating environments fail to allow the internalization process to progress meaningfully.

A rapidly expanding body of literature, a small part of which was mentioned in this chapter, has supported the validity of various aspects of the motivational theory and of the general organismic approach to analyzing human functioning.

REFERENCES

Amabile, T. M. The social psychology of creativity: A consensual assessment technique. *Journal of Personality and Social Psychology,* 1982, *43,* 997–1013. (a)

Amabile, T. M. Children's artistic creativity: The detrimental effects of competition in a field setting. *Personality and Social Psychology Bulletin,* 1982, *8,* 573–578. (b)

Bandura, A. *Social learning theory.* Englewood Cliffs, NJ: Prentice-Hall, 1977.

Blasi, A. The concept of development in personality theory. In J. Loevinger *Ego development.* San Francisco: Jossey-Bass, 1976.

Brehm, J. W. *A theory of psychological reactance.* New York: Academic Press, 1966.

Carver, C. S., & Scheier, M. F. *Attention and self-regulation: A control theory approach to human behavior.* New York: Springer-Verlag, 1981.

Chandler, C. L., & Connell, J. P. *Children's intrinsic, extrinsic, and internalized motivation: A developmental study of behavioral regulation.* Unpublished manuscript, University of Rochester, 1984.

deCharms, R. *Personal causation: The internal affective determinants of behavior.* New York: Academic Press, 1968.

Deci, E. L. The effects of externally-mediated rewards on intrinsic motivation. *Journal of Personality and Social Psychology,* 1971, *18,* 105–115.

Deci, E. L. *The psychology of self-determination.* Lexington, MA: D.C. Heath (Lexington Books), 1980.

Deci, E. L., & Ryan, R. M. The empirical exploration of intrinsically motivated processes. In L. Berkowitz (Ed.)., *Advances in experimental social psychology* (Vol. 13). New York: Academic Press, 1980.

Deci, E. L., & Ryan, R. M. The general causality orientations scale: Self-determination in personality. *Journal of Research in Personality,* in press.

Deci, E. L., & Ryan, R. M. *Intrinsic motivation and self-determination in human behavior.* New York: Plenum, 1985.

Deci, E. L., Schwartz, A. J., Sheinman, L., & Ryan, R. M. An instrument to assess adults' orientations toward control versus autonomy with children: Reflections on intrinsic motivation and perceived competence. *Journal of Educational Psychology,* 1981, *73,* 642–650.

DeVellis, R. F., DeVellis, B. M., & McCauley, C. Vicarious acquisition of learned helplessness. *Journal of Personality and Social Psychology,* 1978, *36,* 894–899.

Duval, S., & Wicklund, R. A. *A theory of objective self-awareness.* New York: Academic Press, 1972.

Fenigstein, A., Scheier, M. F., & Buss, A. H. Public and private self-consciousness: Assessment and theory. *Journal of Consulting and Clinical Psychology,* 1975, *43,* 522–527.

Frank, J. D. Recent studies of the level of aspiration. *Psychological Bulletin,* 1941, *38,* 216–226.

Freud, S. *The ego and the id.* (Originally published, 1923). New York: Norton, 1962.

Garber, J., & Seligman, M. E. P. (Eds.), *Human helplessness.* New York: Academic Press, 1980.

Haddad, Y. S. *The effect of informational versus controlling verbal feedback on self-determination and preference for challenge.* Unpublished Doctoral Dissertation, University of Rochester, 1982.

Harackiewicz, J. M. The effects of reward contingency and performance feedback on intrinsic motivation. *Journal of Personality and Social Psychology,* 1979, *37,* 1352–1363.

Harter, S. A new self-report scale of intrinsic versus extrinsic orientation in the classroom: Motivational and informational components. *Developmental Psychology,* 1981, *17,* 300–312.

Harter, S. The perceived competence scale for children. *Child Development,* 1982, *53,* 87–97.

Hartmann, H., & Loewenstein, R. M. Notes on the superego. *The Psychoanalytic Study of the Child,* 1962, *17,* 300–312.

Heider, F. *The psychology of interpersonal relations.* New York: Wiley, 1958.

Janis, I. L., & Field, P. B. The Janis and Field Personality Questionnaire. In C. I. Hovland & I. L. Janis (Eds.), *Personality and persuasability.* New Haven: Yale Univ. Press, 1959.

Jenkins, C. D., Rosenman, R. H., & Friedman, M. Development of an objective psychological test for the determination of the coronary prone behavior pattern in employed men. *Journal of Chronic Diseases,* 1967, *20,* 371–379.

Kaplan, H. B., & Pokorny, A. D. Self-derogation and psychosocial adjustment. *Journal of Nervous and Mental Disease,* 1969, *149,* 421–434.

Koestner, R., Ryan, R. M., Bernieri, F., & Holt, K. Setting limits on children's behavior: The differential effects of controlling versus informational styles on intrinsic motivation and creativity. *Journal of Personality,* 1984, *52,* 233–248.

Kruglanski, A. W., Friedman, I., & Zeevi, G. The effects of extrinsic incentive on some qualitative aspects of task performance. *Journal of Personality,* 1971, *39,* 606–617.

Lepper, M. R., & Greene, D. Turning play into work: Effects of adult surveillance and extrinsic rewards on children's intrinsic motivation. *Journal of Personality and Social Psychology,* 1975, *31,* 479–486.

Lewis, H. B. *Shame and guilt in neurosis.* New York: International Universities Press, 1971.

Loevinger, J. *Ego development.* San Francisco: Jossey-Bass, 1976.

McGraw, K. O., & McCullers, J. C. Evidence of a detrimental effect of extrinsic incentive on breaking a mental set. *Journal of Experimental Social Psychology,* 1979, *15,* 285–294.

Meissner, W. W. *Internalization in psychoanalysis.* New York: International Universities Press, 1981.

Perls, F. S., Hefferline, R., & Goodman, P. *Gestalt therapy.* New York: Dell, 1951.

Pittman, T. S., Davey, M. E., Alafat, K. A., Wetherill, K. V., & Kramer, N. A. Informational versus controlling verbal rewards. *Personality and Social Psychology Bulletin,* 1980, *6,* 228–233.

Plant, R., & Ryan, R. M. Self-consciousness, self-awareness, ego-involvement, and intrinsic motivation: An investigation of internally-controlling styles. *Journal of Personality,* in press.

Rotter, J. B. Generalized expectancies for internal versus external control of reinforcement. *Psychological Monographs,* 1966, *80*(1), Whole No. 609, pp. 1–28.

Ryan, R. M. Control and information in the intrapersonal sphere: An extension of cognitive evaluation theory. *Journal of Personality and Social Psychology,* 1982, *43,* 450–461.

Ryan, R. M., Chandler, C. L., Connell, J. P., & Deci, E. L. Internalization and motivation: Some preliminary research and theoretical speculations. Paper presented at the meeting of the Society for Research in Child Development, Detroit, MI, April, 1983.

Ryan, R. M., Mims, V., & Koestner, R. The relationship of reward contingency and interpersonal context to intrinsic motivation: A review and test using cognitive evaluation theory. *Journal of Personality and Social Psychology,* 1983, *45,* 736–750.

Schafer, R. *Aspects of internalization.* New York: International Universities Press, 1968.

Seligman, M. E. P. *Helplessness: On depression, development, and death.* San Francisco: Freeman, 1975.

Sherif, M., & Cantril, H. *The psychology of ego involvement.* New York: Wiley, 1947.

White, R. W. Motivation reconsidered: The concept of competence. *Psychological Review,* 1959, *66,* 297–333.

11 Children's Responses to Evaluative Feedback

Ann K. Boggiano
University of Colorado

Diane N. Ruble
New York University

Concern or anxiety over evaluation is a central theme of a number of theories of achievement motivation. The tendency to react with anxiety about fear of failure, for example, is viewed as reducing the motivation to engage in achievement activities (Atkinson, 1964). There have been numerous studies examining the relationship between anxiety in students and subsequent achievement level, as well as conditions under which anxiety can be minimized (Dweck & Elliot, in press; Ruble & Boggiano, 1980). In contrast, there has been little research directed at understanding potential causes of the anxiety children feel about evaluation. In this chapter, we present a model that addresses a number of antecedents and consequences of evaluative concern in elementary school children, and present research that bears on the relationship between variables included in the model proposed (see Figure 11.1).

Based on this model, we describe research in our first section which points to negative consequences of evaluative concerns in children in achievement settings, such as performance deterioration, decreased motivation, and avoidance of feedback about ability level. We also suggest that two interrelated self-conceptions in school-age children (i.e., perceptions of competence and control over outcome) may mediate these achievement-related behaviors. In our second section, we present evidence that points to the motivational orientation of the child (i.e., extrinsic versus intrinsic) as a major determinant of both perceptions of competence and control in children. We also discuss findings that implicate use of controlling strategies as an important mediator of a child's motivational orientation in an achievement setting.

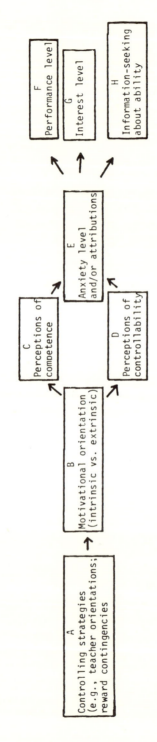

FIG. 11.1. Model of Antecedents and Reactions to Evaluative Feedback.

F
Performance level

G
Interest level

H
Information-seeking about ability

E
Anxiety level and/or attributions

C
Perceptions of competence

D
Perceptions of controllability

B
Motivational orientation (intrinsic vs. extrinsic)

A
Controlling strategies (e.g., teacher orientations; reward contingencies)

CONSEQUENCES OF CHILDREN'S SELF-CONCEPTIONS ABOUT COMPETENCE AND CONTROL ON ACHIEVEMENT-RELATED BEHAVIORS

The constructs of competence and control assume a major role in our conceptualization of determinants of achievement related behaviors. The placement of these constructs in the model is based on a long history of research suggesting their centrality to many theories about human behavior spanning a variety of perspectives and interests. For example, outside of the achievement domain, these constructs have recently come to take on significance in theoretical approaches concerned with modifying maladaptive behaviors. In the clinical literature, for instance, differences in clients' perceptions about control over therapy outcome and/or perceptions of competence are assumed to account for the effectiveness of therapy (Bandura, 1977) as well as maintenance of behavioral change after therapy is terminated (Deci & Ryan, in press). Moreover, investigators concerned with the physiological concomitants of perceptions of control have argued that low perceptions of control affect a number of significant human conditions, including the coronary-prone personality, ulcers, and susceptibility to cancer (Seligman, 1973, 1974, 1975; Glass & Carver, 1980).

In the area of achievement motivation, even early theorists underscored the importance of self-conceptions of competence and control as determinants of achievement-related behaviors. In an early paper, White (1959), for instance, assumed that such behaviors as exploration and play in infants are motivated by the desire for effectance or competence, and theorists have argued that even young infants seek out and prefer activities that maximize feelings of competence (Hunt, 1965; White, 1959). More recent theoretical approaches to achievement have expanded upon these seminal ideas by viewing an individual's perceptions about competence and/or control as an important mediator of a number of achievement behaviors, including expectancies about achievement level, and persistence at activities (Crandall, 1967; Dweck & Elliot, in press; Ryan, Chandler, Connell, & Deci, 1983; Weiner, Frieze, Kukla, Rest, Reed, & Rosenbaum 1971). However, as Dweck has noted (Dweck & Elliott, in press; Dweck & Bempechat, 1983), some have pointed to the attainment of approval of competence (i.e., an extrinsic factor) as the major purpose of achievement activities (e.g., Crandall, Katkovsky, & Preston, 1960), whereas others have seen the intrinsic pleasure of positive affect derived from success (i.e., an intrinsic factor) as the primary reason for achievement (e.g., Atkinson & Feather, 1966; Kukla, 1978).

In this section, we will utilize a developmental perspective to gain additional insight into the relationship between these self-conceptions and achievement responses. From this perspective, we review research that points to the importance of these developing self-conceptions as mediating variables in three possible reactions to evaluative feedback at a task: (1) subsequent *performance*; (2) subsequent *interest* in that activity; and (3) subsequent self-evaluative *information seeking*. In addition, we explore ways in which socializing agents influence children's emerging perceptions of competence and control in achievement settings.

Performance

One important index of an individual's reactions to evaluative feedback at a task is how he or she performs subsequently on the same task or on other achievement-related activities. A number of studies have been concerned with why maladaptive responses frequently follow negative evaluative feedback, and a wide variety of explanations (e.g., test anxiety, misattribution processes) have been proposed (Hill, 1977; Weiner, 1974). One theoretical perspective that integrates several of these explanations is that based on a phenomenon termed learned helplessness (i.e., the belief that failure is insurmountable).

Initial investigations of learned helplessness used a triadic design in demonstrating helplessness (Seligman & Maier, 1967). To illustrate, in one study, individuals were exposed to loud controllable noises that they terminated by pressing certain buttons, whereas others were exposed to the same loud noises that were terminated independent of their responses. In addition, a control group was included that did not receive exposure to these noises. On a second task involving different skills (i.e., solving anagrams), only those individuals receiving the prior uncontrollable noises showed the performance deficits of helplessness. In fact, the group confronted with the uncontrollable noises failed to solve *any* anagrams during the second session. The authors interpreted this finding as suggesting that the debilitating consequences of helplessness result from the perception that one's responses or efforts are independent of outcome (i.e., low perceptions of control).

The effects of helplessness may not stem only from the *uncontrollability* of an aversive event. Other analyses have suggested instead that the perception that an outcome is beyond one's personal control is necessary but not sufficient to produce helplessness deficits (e.g. low self-esteem). Of critical importance are the attributions of causality made by a person when exposed to failure (Abramson, Seligman, & Teasdale, 1978; Weiner, 1974). For example, when confronted with an insolvable math problem, individuals perceiving themselves to have low competence may attribute their failure to internal factors (e.g., "I'm dumb at math"); these internally stable attributions should produce negative affect, low motivation, and performance impairment in subsequent situations, even when these sessions include solvable problems. Conversely, attributions of failure to factors independent of subject's competence (e.g., "No one could do these impossible problems") would not be expected to produce these effects. Moreover, the reformulated model of help-lessness proposes that, as opposed to ascribing failure to stable factors such as ability, attributions of the same failure made to unstable factors (e.g., effort or luck) should not produce subsequent helpless behaviors. Finally, attributions to more global factors (e.g., "I'm just dumb at school stuff") should produce helplessness effects in a greater number of situations than attributions to more specific factors (e.g., "I just don't do well at tasks involving multiplication"). Thus, children who have low perceptions of their ability level should attribute events such as failure to internal, stable, and global factors and should exhibit more intense and debilitating effects of helplessness than those students who attribute the same failure to external, unstable, and more specific factors.

As applied to children's responses to evaluative feedback in an achievement situation, this analysis suggests that children's responses to negative feedback should depend on perceptions of ability level, as well as on perceptions of control. Based on this line of reasoning, one might expect children to exhibit two quite distinct patterns of reactions to negative evaluative feedback, depending on whether they perceive their ability level as high or low. Research conducted by Dweck and her colleagues provides support for the role of attributions about competence as a mediator of performance differences following failure feedback (Diener & Dweck, 1978, 1980; Dweck & Reppucci, 1973). The data indicate that some children exert more effort after a failure experience and will re-approach the task with renewed vigor as if eager to meet the challenge. In fact, they often perform better after failure. In contrast, other children appear frustrated and anxious after failure feedback. Their effort wanes markedly, and subsequent performance deteriorates. These different responses to failure are apparent in spite of the fact that performance level between the apparently "helpless" children and "mastery-oriented" children are virtually identical before the negative feedback.

What causes "helpless" children to respond to negative evaluative feedback or even confusing material (Licht & Dweck, 1983) in such a maladaptive manner? Clearly, the helpless children are not less capable than their mastery-oriented counterparts, since there have been no reported performance differences before the negative evaluation is presented. Instead, the helpless children, as they encounter the negative feedback, begin to think about their *incompetence* as the primary reason for being unable to comprehend the information or for experiencing failure (e.g., Diener & Dweck, 1978). They think self-deprecatory thoughts about their skills at the task, undoubtedly experience anxiety, eventually appear to regress in the type of strategy employed to problem-solve, and finally express a desire to withdraw from the task at hand. Mastery-oriented children, on the other hand, appear not to even consider low ability as the reason underlying their failure; and when prompted, ascribe their failure to insufficient effort expended. It appears, then, that one's perceptions about competence is a powerful mediator of the effect that aversive, uncontrollable events have on subsequent problem-solving ability and performance.

The importance of self-concept of ability in determining the effect of evaluative feedback is also demonstrated in the only published developmental study relevant to helplessness (Rholes, Blackwell, Jordan, & Walters, 1980). The pattern of data obtained in this study indicates that young children who have not yet developed stable concepts of their ability (cf. Ruble & Rholes, 1981) are less prone to performance impairment following failure than middle elementary school age children. Only by fifth grade did children evidence decreased persistence and performance at the task in which they had previously been given failure information. Since young children who have not formed stable estimates of their ability appear almost immune to helplessness deficits following failure feedback, attributions about competence appear to be a critical determinant of helplessness deficits shown in children in achievement settings (cf., Abramson et al., 1978). In terms of the model, then, it appears that one's perceptions about ability level (C) influence the attributions made (E) for uncontrollable events which, in turn, affect subsequent problem-solving ability and performance (F).

Differences in Interest

Another possible response to evaluative concerns is change in subsequent interest in an activity (G in Figure 11.1). In contrast to performance differences, however, changes in interest in achievement-related activities is apparently a less obvious reaction to evaluative feedback and has received less direct attention. Nevertheless, there is indirect evidence suggesting that achievement situations which appear to induce low perceptions of control have marked effects on interest in pursuing academic tasks.

There are a number of conditions that may create low feelings of self-determination or control when engaging in an achievement-related activity. Some of these conditions are particularly relevant to evaluative concerns, such as setting up standards of appropriate performance or the use of incentives to manipulate desired performance level (e.g., threat of punishment for failure). While negative effects on interest in pursuing activities as a consequence of concern over punishment after failure may not be surprising, it would appear less obvious that positive incentives such as rewards may reduce interest as well. For example, the concepts of functional autonomy of motives (Allport, 1961) and of secondary reinforcement (Cofer & Appley, 1964) suggest that offering a tangible inducement to perform an activity may serve to increase, if not evoke, later interest in performing that activity. Yet, recent documentations of the negative effects of such techniques on subsequent intrinsic motivation are striking. This body of research indicates that for activities of initial high interest, the addition of unnecessary controlling strategies such as evaluation or even tangible rewards leads to a reduction in interest in these activities after the incentives to perform are withdrawn (see Deci & Ryan, 1980, and Lepper & Greene, 1978, for reviews of this literature). Since interest in pursuing achievement-related activities, both inside and outside of the classroom, would appear to have far-reaching implications for overall achievement level, this line of research on the effect of controlling techniques on intrinsic interest has important practical as well as theoretical significance.

The basic paradigm developed to demonstrate the effect of controlling techniques on interest generally involves two comparison conditions. In one condition, subjects are asked to perform an interesting activity in the absence of reward. In a second condition, subjects are offered a tangible reward for performing the identical activity. Subjects are then given the opportunity either to engage in the activity for which they were initially rewarded, or to perform alternative interesting activities during a free choice session in which they are observed unobtrusively. In addition, subjects are made aware that reward is no longer available in this session. The typical finding is that rewarded subjects show less intrinsic interest in the target activity than subjects who are not rewarded, as indexed by the amount of time spent with the activity during the subsequent free choice session (see Deci & Ryan, 1980; Lepper & Greene, 1978, for reviews of this literature). Studies using attitudinal rather than behavioral measures of intrinsic interest have shown similar findings (e.g., Boggiano & Hertel, 1983; Boggiano & Ruble, 1981; Calder & Staw, 1975; Enzle & Ross, 1978).

One of the most widely cited explanations for the negative effect of incentives on subsequent motivation is that based on Cognitive-Evaluation Theory (Deci, 1975; Deci & Ryan, 1980). According to this theoretical perspective, techniques such as rewards and other extrinsic incentives have two major functions: to control, and to provide information. To the extent that the controlling function of reward or other incentives is operative, feelings of self-determination will decrease and intrinsic interest as the primary reason for enjoying any given task will be causally discounted. In other words, the person will assume that the behavior in question is being performed primarily to obtain the reward offered and, consequently, in the absence of reward, there is little motivation to perform that activity.

The second aspect of rewards is that they may provide an informational function. Under conditions in which obtaining a reward is not perceived as controlling behavior and represents positive evaluative feedback, this function of reward should augment components of intrinsic motivation (i.e., feelings of competence and self-determination) and intrinsic interest should be enhanced.

The distinction between the effects of the controlling versus informational function of reward has received support in several recent studies. Pittman, Davey, Alafat, Wetherill, & Kramer (1980), for example, provided informational feedback to one group of subjects by means of positive verbal feedback about performance level. In the controlling feedback condition, the subjects were also provided with positive verbal feedback; however, they were told as well that if they kept the performance level up, their data would be "useful" to the researchers. The data obtained in this study indicated a significant decrease in intrinsic motivation only for the groups exposed to the controlling feedback (see also Kast, 1983; Ryan, 1982).

Not only do controlling verbal statements and tangible rewards produce decreased motivation, but simple surveillance, a technique commonly used in achievement setting, appears to have the same effect. In an ingenious study conducted by Lepper and Greene (1975), it was found that having preschool children perform an activity while believing they were being observed through a TV camera reduced their later interest in performing this activity in comparison to children in a low surveillance or non-surveillance condition. Moreover, even providing a deadline to students leads to a decrease in subsequent motivation (Amabile, Dejong, & Lepper, 1976).

While this body of research suggests that there may be "hidden costs" associated with the use of rewards to motivate students, this need not always be the case if rewards are used in a manner which conveys information about competence, a strategy that will be described in some detail in our next section. An additional strategy involving rewards that could be employed to increase motivation might be to use the target activity in question as the "reward" rather than the "means" to obtain a reward.

In a recent study (Main, & Boggiano, 1984), we asked kindergarten and first-grade boys to play with a Lego game by themselves *and* a "follow me" game in which they would be playing Legos with another child, (the alleged "Ryan" and his activities were programmed onto a videotape). In one condition, we made the Legos the "means" and playing along with "Ryan" the "end" (i.e., "If you play with the Legos, then you get the chance to play with Ryan"). In a second condition, children engaged in the same activities and in the same order, but one activity was not made contingent on the other, ("First you can play with the Legos, and next you can play with Ryan"). The order of the two activities was counterbalanced.

The results suggested that the children lost interest in the activity presented as a means to an end, as can be seen in Figure 11.2. In contrast, presenting an activity as a reward for performing the first activity (the "mean" activity) reliably enhanced interest (however, see Lepper, Sagotsky, Dafoe, & Greene, 1982). It would appear, then, that even very young children, are well aware of the "means-end" contingency employed by adults to control behavior, and respond positively to the "bonus" part of the contingency. Of course, these

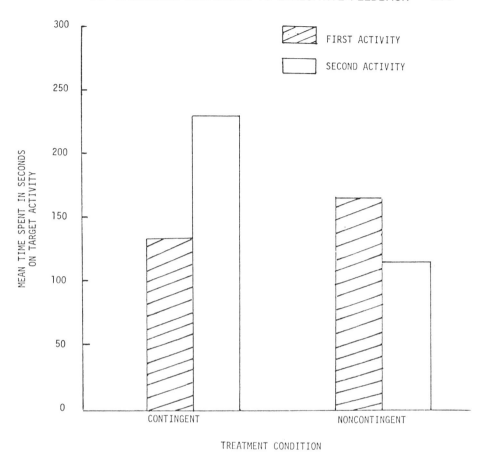

FIG. 11.2.   Mean intrinsic interest in the two target activities during 10-minute free play period, by condition.

findings suggest the futility of motivating children by having the activity in question used as the "means" (e.g., "If you complete your math, then you can have a long recess").

The results of the present study would appear to have practical as well as theoretical significance in that they point to the ways in which teachers may utilize contingencies with young children in classroom settings to increase motivation. While the present enhancement finding enables us to extend previous research by pointing to the positive outcomes of using such contingencies, a caveat is in order. Although the means-end contingency produced increased interest in the present study with young children, the use of the same contingency may not be beneficial with older children. As children get older they receive continued exposure to controlling strategies of teachers (Deci, Nezlek, & Sheinman, 1981) and, consequently, become more extrinsically oriented with age (Harter, 1981). Thus, accompanying this shift in motivational orientations may be an increased sensitivity to controlling techniques (see Kast, 1983). The "bonus" as part of a means-end contingency, as in the present study, may well have been seen as a manipulation by older children and, therefore, their interest in the end activity would not be expected to increase. For instance, while younger children may complete math assignments to obtain the bonus of cleaning a teacher's blackboard, such cleaning may be recognized by older children as a ploy to get them more involved in their math. Thus, it may be that the age of the child is a critical factor affecting the interpretation of means-end contingencies. The presence of such developmental differences remains an interesting issue to be studied.

In summary, to the extent that positive and negative incentives are seen as controlling behavior, and provide little information about competence, these incentives generally appear to produce a "boomerang" effect and decrease later interest. While the mechanism assumed to account for the decrement in intrinsic motivation is low perceptions of control, which in other contexts has produced anxiety (eg., Miller & Seligman, 1975), the causal relationship among these variables has not been tested directly and awaits future research.

Information-Seeking

A third possible response to evaluative feedback is the relative desire to approach or avoid information relevant to self-evaluation (H in Figure 11.1). Such information-seeking usually includes examining the relative outcomes of others (social comparison) or comparing one's current performance with previous performances or with an absolute standard (autonomous evaluation) (Levine, 1983; Rheinberg, 1983; Ruble, 1983; Veroff, 1969), though there are also a variety of other ways to assess one's competence (Bandura, 1982; Trope, 1983). The study of information-seeking is quite important from a developmental perspective because the nature and frequency of evaluative information sought can affect the emergence and maintenance of conclusions drawn about the self. We have been examining information-seeking reactions to evaluative feedback in children who vary in the likelihood of having evaluative concerns — namely, those experiencing classroom failure as opposed to success. We have also been investigating the emergence of evaluative concern in order to determine, for example, at what point during development relatively successful versus unsuccessful children exhibit differential information-seeking.

There is little direct evidence relevant to the relationship between evaluative concern and information-seeking. Intuitively it would seem that anxiety about and/or anticipation of negative feedback would lead to a relative avoidance of evaluation-relative information. There are some data with adults that support this hypothesis. Low achievement-oriented individuals are more likely than high achievers to avoid intermediate difficulty tasks and ability-diagnostic information (cf., Trope, 1983). Of more direct relevance are findings that self-perceptions of high ability lead to a relatively greater interest in diagnostic information (Trope, 1979). Thus, at least in adults, conclusions regarding low abilities are likely to be maintained because individuals tend to avoid evaluation-relevant information, thereby closing off the possibility of receiving discrepant information.

Although there are no comparable developmental data, there is indirect evidence that evaluative concern emerges during the early years of school. In general, children's conceptualization of performance factors becomes increasingly differentiated; and the concept of ability, in particular, becomes invested with a sense of stability, with implications for future behavior, at around 7-8 years of age (Nicholls & Miller, in press; Ruble & Rholes, 1981). Thus the nature and importance of evaluative processes are likely to show changes at this age. Indeed children do seem to show an increased interest in and use of comparative standards at around this age (Nicholls & Miller, in press; Ruble, 1983; Ruble, Feldman, & Boggiano, 1976).

Taken together, previous literature suggests two hypotheses regarding developmental trends in information-seeking. First, changes in the meaning of performance and ability should lead to increased interest in self-assessment during the early years of school. For children receiving relatively negative feedback, however, an approach-avoidance conflict is likely to emerge. Thus, the second predicted trend is an Age × Ability Level interaction with low ability children beginning to show less interest in evaluative feedback than high ability children.

We have examined the development of evaluation-relevant information-seeking in two studies. In one (Flett & Ruble, 1983), subjects were children aged 7, 9, and 11 years, who were classified as high, medium, and low in mathematics ability. They performed a series of arithmetic tasks, on which they were given ambiguous outcome information. During "rest" periods they had a chance to look at information relevant to evaluating their performance: (a) folders containing the outcomes on the same tasks of other children their age (social comparison information), and (b) folders containing information about their own outcome on previous tests at the same level of difficulty, and answer keys (autonomous evaluation information). The room also contained a set of age-appropriate toys. There were two measures of information-seeking: (1) the number of different folders the children looked at, and (2) the duration of time they spent with the folders. These behaviors were recorded from behind a one-way mirror.

Consistent with predictions, there were main effects of Ability Level and Age on both measures of information-seeking. Children low in ability showed the least interest in obtaining information relevant to evaluating their performance. Overall, interest in obtaining self-evaluative information increased with age, but the relative "avoidance" behavior of the low-ability children was generally consistent across ages. These data suggest that evaluation concern was present even in children as young as 7 years of age. Low ability children at this age were less interested in obtaining information they presumably expected to have negative implications for self-esteem. Moreover, even though information-seeking increased with age, differences in the overall interest level of children at the three ability levels did not vary significantly with age.

There was an Ability Level × Age interaction, however, in the relative duration spent viewing autonomous-evaluation versus social-comparison information, as shown in Figure 11.3. For high ability children, interest in social-comparison information decreased with age, while interest in autonomous evaluation increased dramatically. Medium-ability children preferred social to self-comparison folders at all age levels, with only slight increases in evaluation interest with age. Low ability children preferred social- to self-comparison information at the youngest two age levels. At 11 years, however, they showed equal interest (disinterest?) in both (see Figure 11.3).

Although we can only speculate about the meaning of these trends, they are consistent with our prediction that information-seeking would increase with age and that high and low ability children would show differential interest. The shift of high ability children toward autonomous evaluation is quite striking. One interpretation is that reaching a conclusion that one possesses high ability renders further self-assessment unnecessary. Thus, it becomes possible to turn attention toward mastering the task, and information available in the answer keys (autonomous folders) would be more relevant than social comparison.

Interestingly, findings from other research suggest that the shift toward preference for autonomous evaluation may represent a more general developmental trend between fifth and twelfth grade, separate from ability level (Rheinberg, Lührmann, & Wagner, 1977). The reason for this shift in preference for autonomous- versus social-based information may differ across ability levels. However, Rheinberg (1983) has suggested that the older children's preference for individual-based reference norms represents a kind of "meta-motivational strategy" to maintain the possibility of positive evaluation.

Our second study examined the development of evaluative concern over an age span including younger children (5–9 years) and involving measures collected in a more naturalistic context (Frey & Ruble, 1983). Kindergarten, first, second, and fourth graders were observed during independent work times in their classrooms, and their verbalizations and focus of attention were coded. Subsequently, the subjects were interviewed individually in order to assess their knowledge about performance and ability and their self-perceptions of ability level.

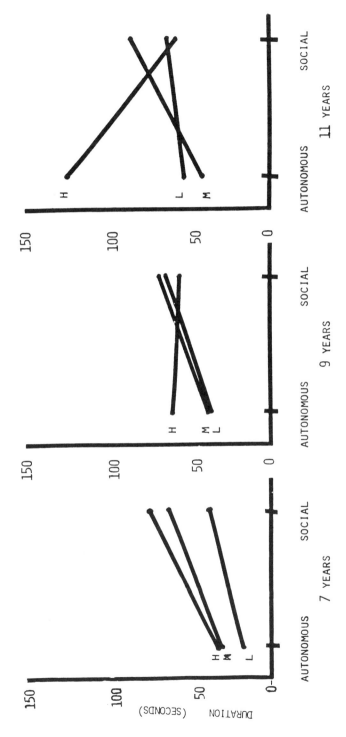

FIG. 11.3. MEAN duration information-seeking as a function of ability level, age, and type of information.

There were many measures in this study relevant to the development of evaluative concern. One set of measures consisted of the frequency of making performance-related statements, such as commenting on the ease or difficulty of the task. In general, these measures showed a curvilinear trend over age, with a peak at first grade, suggesting an initial increase then decrease in evaluation concern during the early years of school. A second set of measures consisted of performance-related information exchange, such as requests for information about peer progress (e.g., "What page are you on?"). These measures showed inconsistent trends over age. Requests for peer progress information showed a linear increase with age, consistent with previous research on the development of social comparison (Ruble, 1983) and with the information-seeking trends shown in the previous study (Flett & Ruble, 1983). In contrast, overt comparisons (e.g., "I got 20 and you only got 15.") and visual attention to peer's work showed an increase between kindergarten and first grade and then decreases after that, consistent with the trends shown in the first set of measures.

These different trends probably represent two converging processes. The first is based on the cognitive-developmental view that as children's beliefs about themselves are undergoing change, they are likely to seek information necessary to interpret those changes (Kohlberg, 1966). Thus, the heightened interest in performance and comparison shown by first graders may reflect the changing conceptualizations of performance and ability observed at this age. The second process concerns a growing recognition that such information is potentially sensitive both for self-esteem and for social harmony (Brickman & Bulman, 1977). Thus, overt and blatant forms of performance concern may decrease even if interest in information-seeking remains steady or increases. That is, the growing interest children exhibit in performance information at first grade may, by second grade, turn into anxiety or concern. The continued increase with age in a form of comparison that gathers information without self-disclosure both in the present study (i.e., peer progress information) and in the previous study (Flett & Ruble, 1983) supports this interpretation.

In order to examine the development of possible differential responses of children with self-perceived high versus low ability, canonical correlations were performed between three measures of self-perception and the three measures of social comparison. As expected, a significant relationship was found only for children at least 7 years of age. Higher levels of information-seeking, primarily in the form of peer progress requests, were associated with lower self-perceptions, as measured by the self-ranking of reading ability and frequency of spontaneous positive self-evaluative comments in the classroom.

These findings appear to be in direct contradiction with those of Flett and Ruble (1983). In the present study, low ability was associated with higher evaluation-relevant information-seeking, while the reverse occurred in the previous study. There are parallels for these divergent reactions in the social psychological literature. On the one hand, concern over evaluation may be reflected in *avoiding* information that may indicate incompetence. In this case, individuals anxious about self-evaluation would show less information-seeking than individuals without this concern. Both defensive attribution or the tendency to ignore information indicating failure (e.g., Stevens & Jones, 1976) and avoidance of tasks that have resulted in feedback of incompetence (Boggiano & Ruble, 1979) may be interpreted this way. On the other hand, evaluation concern may lead to heightened interest in information seeking in a quest to assess competence and/or in order to dispel doubts about adequacy. Findings of heightened effort after failure and heightened seeking of diagnostic information under conditions of uncertainty, (cf., Ruble & Boggiano, 1980; Trope, 1983) may be interpreted in this way.

Although no definitive resolution of the apparent conflict shown in our data is possible at this time, some differences between the two studies may provide insight into determinants of variations in information-seeking. First, the discrepancy between the studies was most pronounced for different kinds of evaluative information. High ability children in the Flett and Ruble study (1983) were much more likely to seek autonomous evaluation information, but there was less difference shown between high and low ability children's interest in social comparison information. Frey and Ruble (1983) examined only social comparison information.

Second, and perhaps more important, the studies examined information-seeking at different stages of evaluation. The children in the Flett and Ruble study had their final scores and could assess whether they had done well or poorly. It is not surprising that children who have reason to anticipate negative feedback would show less interest in information-seeking than their more skilled counterparts. In contrast, children in the Frey and Ruble study could solicit information at several different stages of evaluation. Thus, information-seeking may have a pragmatic component in that, prior to completing a task, children may use the information to identify ways of improvement. Trope (in press) also has suggested that information-seeking may vary at different phases of an achievement sequence.

ANTECEDENTS OF CHILDREN'S PERCEPTIONS OF CONTROL AND COMPETENCE: THE ROLE OF MOTIVATIONAL ORIENTATIONS

In the previous section we discussed the relationship between children's self-conceptions about competence or control and their reaction to evaluative feedback in terms of subsequent performance, interest, and information-seeking. We focus here on an issue that, to date, has been relatively neglected in the literature: potential antecedents of children's self-conceptions about control and competence. In this section we present research suggesting that the motivational orientation of a child (i.e., extrinsic versus intrinsic) may have a major impact on the development of children's self-conceptions. In addition, we discuss how various controlling strategies influence a child's motivational orientation.

The construct of motivational orientation refers to the motivational stance which a child may adopt toward achievement in the classroom. In an elegant set of studies designed to tap components of these different motivational orientations, Harter and colleagues (Harter, 1978; Harter & Connell, 1981) have identified five factors that differentiate between these two motivational orientations of children toward classroom learning. These are (1) a preference for challenge versus a preference for easy work assigned, (2) an incentive to work to satisfy one's own interest and curiosity versus working to please the teacher and obtain good grades, (3) independent mastery versus dependence on the teacher, (4) independent judgement versus reliance on teacher's judgement, and (5) internal criteria for success/failure.

In a comprehensive model of mastery orientation, Harter (1978, 1981) proposes that an extrinsic motivational orientation produces perceived lack of competence and control which, in turn, produces anxiety in mastery situations and overall reduced effectance motivation. The opposite set of predictions are held for children adopting an intrinsic motivational orientation. One of the most intriguing findings to emerge from this line of research is a documentation of age changes in the different components of children's motivational orientations. Children in grades three through nine showed a linear decrease in the competence-related components of motivational orientations (preference for challenge, curiosity, and independent mastery attempts), but an increase in the control-related components over age (independent judgement, internal criteria for success/failure).

We will discuss one line of research here which suggests a number of conditions that appear to produce avoidance of challenge, low curiosity, and lack of independence in mastery attempts in children which, according to the analysis described above, produced lack of perceived competence and subsequent low overall effectance motivation. It may well be that continued exposure in the classroom to conditions that induce an extrinsic motivational orientation may, in part, account for the developmental changes described above.

Motivational Orientations and Perceptions of Competence

Nature of Teacher Orientations.   One likely source of the different motivational orientations adopted by children is their teacher's orientation toward control versus autonomy. The results of an intriguing study conducted in the classroom by Edward Deci and his colleagues (Deci et al., 1981) suggest that a teacher's orientation strongly affects students' orientations toward classroom learning. Specifically, teachers in fourth- to sixth-grade elementary school classrooms oriented toward controlling their students through extrinsically motivating strategies (e.g., use of sanctions such as threat of punishment, surveillance, tangible reinforcers) were shown to have students who were less intrinsically motivated to learn. That is, students of teachers with a controlling orientation reported a lack of interest in schoolwork, a preference for easy rather than challenging tasks, a desire to please the teacher as opposed to working to satisfy their own interest and curiosity, and reported dependence on the teacher. As would be suggested by this negative attitude toward schoolwork, students of teachers using extrinsically motivating strategies also reported low perceptions of their own competence. In contrast, teachers who encouraged autonomy and used motivating strategies in a less controlling manner promoted an intrinsic orientation in students, as indexed by their student's strong curiosity, interest in challenging assignments, independent mastery attempts, and reported low dependence on teacher approval in evaluating performance. Furthermore, these students had positive perceptions of their competence level. Interestingly, such effects were evident after only 6 weeks of exposure to these different classroom teachers.

The results of other recent research support, at least indirectly, these "schooling" effects. In both field and laboratory studies, indices of children's motivation and self-perceptions were affected by teachers' evaluative orientations. Children evaluated in terms of *individual reference norms* (previous own performance) showed less fear of failure, more realistic goal setting, and fewer attributions to low ability than children evaluated in terms of *social reference norms* (the performance of others) (Rheinberg, 1983). Thus, teacher orientations that encourage greater student control appear to have positive effects on motivation and perceptions of competence.

Nature of Reward Contingency. A second factor which should theoretically determine the motivational orientation of children is the contingency of reward to performance level. Under conditions in which the controlling but not informational function of reward is operative, reward should produce an extrinsic motivational orientation detrimental to later mastery and interest. From this perspective, making reward contingent on simply performing an activity, without regard to performance quality, should make the controlling function of reward salient and subsequent interest should decrease. In contrast, to the extent that reward provides cue value about competence at an activity, the informational rather than controlling function of reward should predominate, and, consequently, later mastery and interest should be augmented. Thus, reward made contingent on meeting a standard of excellence should serve to enhance rather than undermine interest since this type of contingency should provide information about competence.

To test the competence hypothesis, Boggiano and Ruble (1979) conducted a study in which children at two age levels engaged in a task of high initial interest (an embedded figures task). Children were either assigned to a condition where reward was made contingent on meeting an absolute standard of success (performance contingent reward) or on simply performing the activity (task contingent reward). Children in both conditions were provided with identical information about performance on an embedded figures task (i.e., 3 out of 8 correct). In addition, we provided social comparison information indicating that either the children had performed better than peers, worse than peers, or they received no information about performance relative to peers. We predicted that, although later interest should be enhanced when reward attainment was made contingent on an absolute performance standard, if more direct information about competence or incompetence is additionally provided (in this case, performance level relative to others), subsequent motivation should vary directly with the type of competence information that is presented.

In this study, the competency hypothesis was also assessed by means of a developmental analysis of the effect of different kinds of competency information on intrinsic interest. According to Veroff's (1969) developmental theory of achievement motivation, it is not until 7-8 years of age that children derive feelings of competence from *comparative* standards of excellence; however, even very young children (e.g., preschoolers) are assumed to make evaluative judgments regarding their level of competence based on *absolute* performance standards (Ruble, Boggiano, Feldman, & Loebl, 1980; Ruble, Feldman, & Boggiano, 1976; Ruble, Parsons, & Ross, 1976). Thus, we expected the competence information conveyed in relative terms to affect subsequent motivation for older but not younger children.

Our data indicated that, as expected, the effect of the different types of competence information were found to depend on the age of the child. For the young children, performance contingent reward maintained but did not enhance interest, and task contingent reward decreased subsequent motivation. Moreover, comparative information had virtually no effect on later interest. For the older children, on the other hand, social comparison information appeared to supercede the effect of performance contingent reward on interest. Information about comparative excellence produced greater interest than information regarding inferior performance or no information about performance level relative to peers. Task contingent reward decreased interest, replicating the standard undermining effect of reward on interest, only when no information about relative competence was provided.

Thus, our results provided support for our developmental predictions about the effect of different types of competence information on later interest as well as for the influence of reward contingencies on motivational orientations. However, our predictions about the enhancing effect of performance contingent reward were not confirmed. Similar findings have been reported in other studies (i.e., Arkes, 1979; Harackiewicz, 1979). The finding that performance contingent reward sustains rather than undermines interest and often produces more interest than task contingent reward (Boggiano & Ruble, 1979; Enzle & Ross, 1978; Karniol & Ross, 1977) suggests that making reward contingent on performance quality counteracts the controlling function of reward to some extent (however, see Harackiewicz, 1979). Yet, the information conveyed by this reward contingency may not override completely its controlling function, since comparable information about competence in the absence of a reward contingency clearly enhances interest (Arkes, 1979; Boggiano & Ruble, 1979; Fisher, 1978; Weiner & Mander, 1978). Thus, it is possible that, regardless of the type of contingency employed, reward offered for task performance may be seen as controlling behavior, although making reward contingent on success may mitigate the controlling function of reward to some extent.

An alternative explanation for the finding that performance contingent reward does not enhance interest is that reward contingency may not have been presented to provide maximal cue value regarding competence, thereby reducing the informational function of reward. Since the magnitude of the negative effects of reward depends on the salience of the reward (Ross, 1975), it seems likely that the relative salience of the informational features of performance-contingent reward may be an important determinant of enhancement effects. Thus, presenting reward made contingent upon performance quality in a context which maximizes its informational function may well produce the elusive enhancement effect.

We recently conducted a study to examine this salience hypothesis (Boggiano, Harackiewicz, Main, & Bessette, in press). Reward was made contingent on either simply completing an activity (task contingent reward) or on performance quality (performance contingent reward). Additionally, rewards were manipulated so that the informational or controlling features were relatively more or less salient. Over a five-trial puzzle session, reward features were made more salient by emphasizing the relevant contingency of each trial. If task-contingent rewards are initially more controlling, and if performance-contingent rewards are initially more informational, continued emphasis on the contingency itself should highlight the more salient cue. We thus assumed that making the reward contingencies highly salient would maximize the difference in the effects of task and performance contingent reward.

To test this hypothesis, kindergarten age children worked on five maze puzzles in which objective feedback concerning success was available from the task itself. In fact, all children were able to complete the puzzles successfully. In the task contingent reward conditions, children were told that if they simply worked on the maze puzzles they would receive five colorful stickers. In contrast, children in the performance contingent reward conditions were told that they would be awarded up to five stickers for successfully completing the maze puzzles. In the *more salient* conditions, subjects were told that they would be awarded one sticker after completing (or successfully completing) each of the five mazes. A bowl was placed in front of the experimenter, in view of the subject, and a sticker was dropped into the bowl upon simple completion or successful completion of each maze, depending on contingency condition. Subjects in the *less salient* conditions were also told that they could receive up to five stickers for either completing the mazes or successfully completing the mazes. However, all five stickers were placed in the bowl before they began and were dispersed at the end of the puzzle series. Control subjects also completed the maze puzzles, but of course, reward was not mentioned. When subjects finished the puzzle series, and those in the reward conditions collected their stickers, the experimenter then unobtrusively observed through a one-way mirror the amount of time during a 5-minute period that the children spent working on the maze puzzles and alternative interesting activities.

Our predictions about the enhancing effect of performance contingent reward were confirmed for boys but not for girls. For boys, performance/more salient rewards reliably enhanced later interest, while performance/less salient rewards did not. In addition, task/more salient, but not task/less salient reward decreased interest in the target activity, as expected. Similarly, later interest was undermined for girls in the task/more salient but not the task/less salient reward condition. In contrast to boys, however, performance/more salient undermined rather than enhanced later interest in girls, while performance/less salient did not.

Our data, then, confirmed our predictions about the differential effects of making salient the informational and controlling aspects of reward. In this study, our subjects received identical performance feedback from the task itself. The experimenter provided no additional feedback or praise in any of the experimental conditions. Thus, children in performance contingent conditions did not receive competence information that was unavailable to task contingent or control subjects. In other studies (Enzle & Ross, 1978; Luyten & Lens, 1981), performance contingent reward has been compared with control conditions with no feedback provided, making it difficult to disentangle contingency and information effects. The enhancement effects observed in this study for performance contingent reward relative to equally informed task contingent reward and control groups indicate that an informational reward contingency can raise intrinsic motivation.

Interestingly, the enhancing effect of performance contingent reward was demonstrated for boys but not for girls. Previous research indicates that information about competence provided by means of verbal reward has an *undermining* effect on later interest for females but a positive effect on males' intrinsic interest (Deci, Cascio, & Krusell, 1975). Perhaps indiscriminate use of praise about performance by teachers for girls but not for boys (Dweck, Davidson, Nelson, & Enna, 1978) loses its intended effect in increasing perceptions of competence in girls. Alternatively, it may be that young girls are more likely than boys to have an external locus of control, which may lead them to respond negatively to positive information about competence (see Danner & Lonky, 1981). If perceptions of competence are not induced in girls by providing information about competence, as previous research suggests, then performance contingent reward may serve to decrease rather than increase their interest, since the reward in this case should be perceived as controlling.

In summary, results of these studies are consistent with our view that reward contingencies set up to control versus to provide information about outcome have an important bearing on a child's motivational orientation toward an activity (links A & B). Because the dependent measure employed in this line of research was interest in a specific task rather than a more stable, motivational orientation toward achievement, however, the data should be interpreted as providing indirect rather than direct support for this link in the model.

Nature of the task.   The research discussed so far points to factors such as incentives which, depending on which function of reward is operative, appear to have marked effects on later interest and/or independent mastery attempts, as indexed by continued motivation to perform activities in the absence of those incentives or feedback from an adult. In our next set of studies (Boggiano, Pittman, & Ruble, 1982; Pittman, Emery, & Boggiano, 1982) we asked whether these same factors affect an additional component of a child's more general motivational orientation toward achievement — that is, preference for challenge.

Evidence for differences in preference for challenge has been provided by Harter (1981). She found that children preferred more challenging items when an anagram task was described as a game than when the identical task was presented as a means to obtain a grade (Harter, 1978). Other research has shown similar effects of a "test" context on children's subsequent preference for forms of an activity varying in complexity level. In one study, for example, the easier tasks were preferred in the controlling as opposed to the nonevaluative context (Maehr & Stallings, 1972). Research with adults has shown similar findings (Condry & Chambers, 1978; Shapira, 1976).

The data obtained in these studies may not be particularly surprising. If an important incentive such as a grade is made contingent on successful performance, it is to be expected that an easy way of obtaining the incentive would be chosen if available. What may be less intuitive is that such preferences for challenge may carry over to new settings where controlling strategies or incentives are no longer present. Based on the assumption that a controlling strategy produces an orientation toward an achievement activity that reduces interest in mastery over challenge, we hypothesized that even if an activity is chosen in a context in which incentives are no longer available, the activity should be approached in a manner that suggests reduced mastery strivings. Specifically, we hypothesized that under conditions in which an extrinsic motivational orientation is adopted, and when forms of an activity varying in complexity or difficulty level are available, the least difficult or challenging form of the activity will be preferred, even when incentives are no longer present.

To test the mastery hypothesis, Pittman, Emery, & Boggiano (1982) conducted a study in which fourth-grade children were offered a Spalding rubber ball or not offered an incentive to perform a "find the hidden picture" game. Each child was presented with two sets of two hidden figures pictures. One stack contained two simple versions of the task and the other stack contained two intermediate versions of the task (see Boggiano et al., 1982, for normative data on these two versions of the task). Both order and picture type were randomized across subjects. Subjects were told that the object of the game was to circle as many of the four hidden pictures on each page as they could in the time allotted.

Following completion of the games, all subjects were told that they had found 7 out of 8 figures in one stack (the simple version) and 4 out of 8 in the other stack (the intermediate version). These levels of feedback were used to reinforce the two difficulty levels. Control of the feedback was made possible by including a few ambiguous cases on each page.

Subjects in the reward condition were then given their prize. For all subjects, the experimenter then explained that she had another task but needed some time to prepare it. She then produced several new games (marbles, crayons for a connect-the-dot picture game, and two mazes), as well as eight new hidden picture pages for *both* the simple and the intermediate difficulty stacks. The experimenter then left the room, and observed the subject's behavior through a one-way mirror concealed in a wall.

Our data provided clear support for the mastery hypothesis. We found that, as predicted, children who had been offered the incentive to perform the activity spent more time on the simple as opposed to the challenging activity, whereas nonrewarded subjects preferred the more challenging to the less challenging game. The negative effect of incentives on preference for challenge was evidenced even after the controlling strategy was removed. More recent research suggests that even a controlling *statement* (e.g., "You *should* do your best") has similar effects on both subsequent mastery strivings and interest (Boggiano, Main and Katz, 1983; Ryan, 1982).

Taken together, then, these studies suggest that use of controlling strategies can produce reduced mastery strivings, avoidance of challenge, and overall decreased interest in pursuing achievement-related activities. The continued exposure to controlling strategies over the elementary school years may well explain the developmental decrease in interest in learning and preference for challenge reported by Harter (1981). Moreover, it would not be surprising if developmental changes in these components of motivational orientations (e.g., reduced mastery strivings) account for the well-documented finding that older children have lower perceptions of competence than younger children (Crandall, 1960; Eccles, Midgley, & Adler, in press; Macey & Boggiano, 1983; Ruble et al., 1980). While highly speculative, it may also be the case that the developmental changes in components of motivational orientations such as avoidance of challenge is a factor contributing to increased test anxiety shown in older children (Hill & Sarason, 1966). Since older children who are more likely to adopt an extrinsic motivational orientation (see Harter, 1981; Kast, 1983) prefer tasks devoid of challenge, it would not be surprising to find that they are more anxious than younger children when presented with complex or difficult tasks. Since level of test anxiety as well as perceptions of competence have been shown to have dramatic effects on subsequent achievement level (Ruble & Boggiano, 1980; Wine, 1971), additional research is clearly needed to test this hypothesis about the causal relationship between age changes in motivational orientations, perceptions of competence and level of test anxiety.

Motivational Orientations and Perceptions of Controllability

The data reviewed here on the relationship between controlling strategies (e.g., teacher orientation) and perceptions of competence suggest that these strategies have a marked effect on perceptions of competence in school age children (Deci et al., 1981). Moreover, the findings suggest that use of controlling strategies reduces subsequent interest and preference for challenge. Other investigators suggest that adopting an extrinsic motivational orientation may even have additional negative effects. The evidence suggests that controlling strategies often produce low creativity (Amabile, 1979; Kruglanski, Friedman, & Zeevi, 1971), impairment in performance on tasks that require insight (McGraw, 1978; McGraw & McCullers, 1979), and an overall lower quality of performance (Greene & Lepper, 1974; Lepper, Greene, & Nisbett, 1973).

Interestingly, these effects on performance caused by adopting an extrinsic motivational orientation bear a striking resemblance to the deficits associated with learned helplessness described in our first section. These findings raise the intriguing question of whether these negative effects are mediated by perceptions of uncontrollability. More specifically, since an extrinsic orientation appears to result in greater helplessness behavior, and because perceptions of uncontrollability are theoretically assumed to mediate the same behavior, a relationship between an extrinsic motivational orientation and perceptions of uncontrollability is strongly suggested.

How might an extrinsic motivational orientation affect perceptions of controllability in a classroom setting? It may well be that children performing schoolwork for extrinsic reasons (e.g., to gain approval and/or to avoid the criticism of their teacher) come to see achieving these goals as less controlled by their own responses than other students who have adopted an intrinsic orientation. That is, attaining extrinsic goals such as teacher approval is often contingent on factors that lie outside of one's control, such as the mood state of the teacher, or one's performance relative to others. Furthermore, praise or criticism received may at times be unrelated to the relevant work at hand, and be based more on extraneous variables such as neatness or time taken to complete the assignment. These experiences may well produce a perception of effort-outcome independence. In addition, children who are extrinsically motivated often expend *more* effort to achieve the desired outcome than children who are intrinsically motivated. Yet, at the same time, the product is of lower quality than that of their intrinsically motivated counterparts (Greene & Lepper, 1974; Lepper et al., 1973). Thus, it is not unlikely that extrinsically motivated children would be apt to develop the perception of effort-outcome independence and, consequently, feel defeated and retreat in the face of failure.

Intrinsically motivated children, on the other hand, should not show deficits in problem-solving effectiveness and perseverance when confronted with a failure experience. Since intrinsically motivated children pursue activities for the pleasure inherent in the activity, the desired outcome is in large part tied to the effort expended in performing the activity and in the satisfaction gained from mastery over task components. Moreover, because intrinsically motivated children rely only partly on external evaluation of their performance and have internal criteria for success and failure (Harter, 1981), the role of their own effort in producing outcome should be highly salient. Thus, children adopting this orientation may ascribe failure to insufficient effort expended and may even show a "facilitation" effect when performance is less than adequate.

In a recent study, Boggiano & Barrett (in press) attempted to address the question of whether extrinsically motivated in comparison to intrinsically motivated children are more susceptible to the phenomenon of learned helplessness. A considerable amount of research indicates that failure feedback often produces helplessness deficits, including subsequent performance decrement and lowered motivation (Abramson et al., 1978). Since extrinsically oriented children are assumed to differ with regard to perceptions of controllability over outcome (Harter, 1981), it was predicted that extrinsic but not intrinsic children should show performance decrement following failure feedback. Similarly, only extrinsic children were expected to evidence lowered motivation when provided with a subsequent opportunity to perform the "failure" task. Moreover, the motivational deficit of helplessness was expected to generalize to tasks similar to the target task.

A second major question addressed in this study was the manner in which success feedback affects subsequent performance and generalization of interest. According to Cognitive Evaluation Theory (Deci & Ryan, 1980; Deci et al., 1981; Fisher, 1978), the effect of success feedback on later performance and interest should depend on the motivational orientation of the child. Thus, providing information regarding competence at an activity should enhance subsequent performance only for intrinsically motivated children. Moreover, when degree of similarity to the target task is varied, intrinsically motivated children provided with success feedback should approach the task similar to the target task, whereas extrinsically motivated children should tend to avoid tasks similar to this task.

An examination of the effect of success and failure information on subsequent performance and continued motivation would appear to have implications not only for learned helplessness theory (Seligman, 1975) but for cognitive evaluation theory as well. First, with regard to learned helplessness theory, if the data obtained support predictions that a child's motivational orientation moderates the effect of a failure experience on subsequent performance, then a better understanding of determinants of the debilitating versus facilitating effect of failure on performance would be provided (Wortman & Dinzer, 1978). Second, an explanation of generalization of helplessness across activities appears important since a number of investigators have argued that the relative significance of the phenomenon of learned helplessness depends on the degree of generalization of helplessness deficits shown across situations (Miller & Norman, 1979). Finally, the impact of success feedback on subsequent generalization of interest in pursuing activities for children of different motivations would provide additional support for assumptions of cognitive evaluation theory.

To test these hypotheses, fourth- and fifth-grade children were selected on the basis of their scores on the Scale of Intrinsic versus Extrinsic Orientation (Harter, 1981). Subjects were exposed either to failure information, success information, or were given no evaluative information about their performance on an incomplete picture task. Success and failure were manipulated by informing children that they were correct on 9 of the 10 pictures, or only 1 of the 10 pictures, respectively. In addition, children in these conditions were given social comparison information indicating the performance level of hypothetical peers, that is, others performing poorly or very well to ensure manipulation of success versus failure.

To test the effect of these different orientations and manipulations in producing helplessness, the children were subsequently asked by a second experimenter to complete an activity involving skills different from the incomplete picture task (i.e., a set of anagrams). The number of anagrams completed correctly served as the measure of the performance deficit associated with helplessness. To measure subsequent motivational differences, children were then given the opportunity to play with the target task (i.e., the incomplete picture task), a similar task (i.e., a hidden picture task) or a dissimilar task (i.e., a dots-to-dots game) during a 5-minute free-choice period in which they were observed unobtrusively.

The results obtained provided clear support with regard to our predictions about differential susceptibility to helplessness deficits as a function of motivational orientations. Contrasts revealed that while there were no differences in performance on the anagram task between children who had extrinsic versus intrinsic orientations given no evaluative feedback (control), performance of children with different motivational orientations showed clear differences on the anagram task as a function of success or failure feedback on the previous incomplete picture task. Specifically, children with an extrinsic motivational orientation showed performance impairment following failure, while children with an intrinsic orientation showed facilitation following the same negative information. In addition, intrinsic children's performance after success increased, whereas extrinsic childrens' performance did not (see Figure 11.4).

Finally, on the motivational measure, contrasts revealed that, as expected, failure decreased subsequent motivation on the target and generalization task for the extrinsic in comparison to the intrinsic children while only intrinsics showed enhanced motivation on the target and generalization task following success.

The differences shown in subsequent performance and motivation between intrinsically and extrinsically motivated children following failure feedback suggest that only the extrinsically motivated children were susceptible to helplessness effects. Since previous research indicates that extrinsically motivated children have higher perceptions of uncontrollability over outcome (Harter, 1981), which have been found to moderate helplessness deficits (see Pittman & Pittman, 1979), perceptions of control are assumed to account for the pattern of data obtained in the present study. This analysis may also explain the performance differences shown between these two groups when success feedback was provided. Like the helpless children in Dweck's (1975) research, success feedback had no positive effect on subsequent performance for extrinsically motivated children. Perhaps the perception of uncontrollability over outcomes led the extrinsically motivated children to view the positive feedback as not contingent on their own responses. Alternatively, it may be that extrinsically motivated children, characterized by low perceptions of competence (Deci et al., 1981), tend to avoid exerting effort in

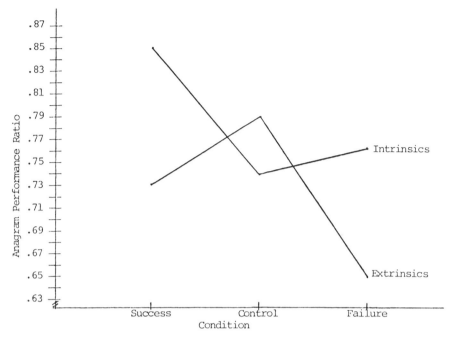

FIG. 11.4.   Ratio of number of anagrams correctly solved to number of anagrams attempted as a function of motivational orientation (initial performance covaried out).

activities that may be diagnostic of ability level. Thus, the possibility of obtaining information discrepant with previous positive feedback may have led the extrinsically motivated children to avoid increased effort as a kind of self-handicapping strategy (cf. Trope, 1983). We are presently testing this explanation of our findings by means of scales examining perceptions of competence and control recently developed by Harter and Connell (see Harter, 1981).

Summary and Directions for Future Research

In this chapter, we have reviewed studies relevant to a wide variety of paradigms concerned with children's reactions to being evaluated: learned helplessness, overjustification, mastery motivation, and information-seeking. We have argued that lack of perceived competence and controllability may play a major role in affecting such reactions as decreased interest in ability evaluation, helplessness deficits, susceptibility to overjustification effects, and reduced mastery motivation. Moreover, we have begun to explore potential antecedents of emerging self-conceptions about control and competence, with an emphasis on the role of a child's motivational orientation toward learning.

Our primary interest in the relationship among the variables presented in our model is based on the assumption that they may ultimately have negative effects on overall achievement level in school age children. However, inferences about achievement-related behaviors based on the constructs presented in the model appear limited, since studies have focused on the relationship between *pairs* of constructs rather than the pattern of relationships within this network of constructs. For example, studies indicate that an extrinsic motivational orientation has a detrimental effect on performance in children in laboratory settings, providing indirect support for links B and F in the proposed model. In addition, a significant relationship has been demonstrated in previous research between teacher strategy (controlling versus autonomous) and student motivational orientation and perceptions of competence (links A, B and C depicted in the model). Moreover, research in the learned helplessness literature suggests that low perceptions of controllability is an important factor mediating performance (links D and F), and that perceptions of uncontrollability as well as perceptions of incompetence produce anxiety (links C, D, and E). Finally, perceptions of competence have been shown to affect information-seeking about ability level (links C and H).

We are presently employing the paradigm developed by Deci et al., (1981) in a longitudinal study (Boggiano & Barrett, in progress) to examine the effect of teacher strategy (controlling versus autonomus) on subsequent student achievement, as well as the impact of a student's motivational orientation, perceptions of competence and control on indices of achievement (grades and national tests). This research should provide us with a more comprehensive understanding of the causal relationship among the variables presented in the model proposed.

ACKNOWLEDGMENTS

The authors would like to acknowledge the assistance of a number of students who have collaborated in the studies described in this chapter and/or who have made helpful suggestions on an earlier draft: Marty Barrett, Marcy Cooper, David Conner, Lois Feldman, Gordon Flett, Karin Frey, Audrey Kast, Terri Macey, Deborah Main, Becky Miller, and Fred Stern.

The research reported in this paper was supported by Grant No. 35005 to the first author and Grant No. 37215 to the second author, both from the National Institute of Mental Health.

REFERENCES

Abramson, L. Y., Seligman, M. E. P., & Teasdale, J. D. Learned helplessness in humans: Critique and reformulation. *Journal of Abnormal Psychology,* 1978, *87,* 49–74.

Allport, G. W. *Pattern and growth in personality.* New York: Holt, Rinehart & Winston, 1961.

Amabile, T. M. Effects of external evaluation on artistic creativity. *Journal of Personality and Social Psychology,* 1979, *37,* 221–233.

Amabile, T. M., Dejong, W., & Lepper, M. Effects of externally imposed deadlines on subsequent intrinsic motivation. *Journal of Personality and Social Psychology,* 1976, *34,* 92–98.

Arkes, H. R. Competence and the overjustification effect. *Motivation and Emotion,* 1979, *3,* 143–150.

Atkinson, J. W. *An Introduction to motivation.* Princeton, NJ: Van Nostrand, 1964.

Atkinson, J. W., & Feather, N. T. (Eds.) *A theory of achievement motivation.* New York: Wiley, 1966.

Bandura, A. Self-efficacy: Toward a unifying theory of behavior change. *Psychological Review,* 1977, *84,* 191–215.

Bandura, A. Self-referent thought: The development of self-efficacy. In J. H. Flavell & L. Ross (Eds.), *Development of social cognition.* New York: Academic Press, 1982.

Boggiano, A. K., & Barrett, M. *A longitudinal study of the effect of a child's motivational orientation on changes in achievement level.* In preparation.

Boggiano, A. K., & Barrett, M. Performance and motivational deficits of helplessness: The role of motivational orientations. *Journal of Personality and Social Psychology.* In press.

Boggiano, A. K., Harackiewicz, J. M., Main, D. S., & Bessette, J. M. Increasing children's intrinsic interest through performance contingent reward. *Social Cognition.* In press.

Boggiano, A. K., & Hertel, P. T. Bonuses and bribes: Mood effects in memory. *Social Cognition,* 1983.

Boggiano, A. K., Main, D. S., & Katz, P. *The effect of verbal controlling feedback on sex differences in preference for challenge.* Unpublished Manuscript, University of Colorado, 1983.

Boggiano, A. K., Pittman, T. S., & Ruble, D. N. The mastery hypothesis and the over-justification effect. *Social Cognition,* 1982, *1*(1), 38–49.

Boggiano, A. K., & Ruble, D. N. Competence and the overjustification effect: A developmental study. *Journal of Personality and Social Psychology,* 1979, *37,* 1462–1468.

Boggiano, A. K., & Ruble, D. N. *Self-perception versus cued expectancy: Analyses of the effects of reward on task interest.* Paper presented at the American Psychological Association Convention, 1981.

Brickman, P., & Bulman, R. J. Pleasure and pain in social comparison. In J. Suls & R. L. Miller (Eds.), *Social comparisons processes.* New York: Hemisphere, 1977.

Calder, B. J., & Staw, B. M. Self-perception of intrinsic and extrinsic motivation. *Journal of Personality and Social Psychology,* 1975, *31,* 599–605.

Cofer, C. N., & Appley, M. H. *Motivation: Theory and research.* New York: Wiley, 1964.

Condry, J. C., & Chambers, J. C. Intrinsic motivation and the process of learning. In M. R. Lepper & D. Greene (Eds.), *The hidden costs of reward.* Hillsdale, NJ: Lawrence Erlbaum Associates, 1978.

Crandall, V. C. Achievement behavior in the young child. In W. W. Hartup (Ed.), *The young child: Reviews of research.* Washington, DC: National Association for the Education of Young Children, 1967.

Crandall, V. J., Katkovsky, W., & Preston, A. A conceptual formulation for some research on children's achievement development. *Child Development,* 1960, *31,* 787–797.

Danner, F. W., & Lonky, E. A. Cognitive-developmental approach to the effects of rewards on intrinsic motivation. *Child Development,* 1981, *52,* 1043–1052.

Deci, E. L. *Intrinsic Motivation.* New York: Plenum, 1975.

Deci, E. L., Cascio, W. F., & Krusell, J. Cognitive evaluation theory and some comments on the Calder-Staw critique. *Journal of Personality and Social Psychology,* 1975, *40,* 1–10.

Deci, E. L., Nezlek, J., & Sheinman, L. Characteristics of the rewarder and intrinsic motivation of the rewardee. *Journal of Personality and Social Psycology,* 1981, *40,* 1–10.

Deci, E. L., & Ryan, R. M. The empirical exploration of intrinsic motivational processes. In L. Berkowitz (Ed.), *Advances in experimental social psychology* (Vol. 13). New York: Academic Press, 1980.

Deci, E. L., & Ryan, R. M. Intrinsic motivation and self-determination in human behavior. New York: Plenum, in press.

Diener, C. I., & Dweck, C. S. An analysis of learned helplessness: Continuous changes in performance, strategy, and achievement cognitions following failure. *Journal of Personality and Social Psychology,* 1978, *36,* 451–462.

Diener, C. I., & Dweck, C. S. An analysis of learned helplessness: II. The processing of success. *Journal of Personality and Social Psychology,* 1980, *39,* 940–952.

Dweck, C. S. The role of expectations and attributions in the alleviation of learned helplessness. *Journal of Personality and Social Psychology,* 1975, *31,* 674–685.

Dweck, C. S., & Bempechat, J. To appear in S. G. Paris, G. M. Olson, & H. W. Stevenson (Eds.), *Learning and motivation in the classroom.* Hillsdale, NJ: Lawrence Erlbaum Associates, 1983.

Dweck, C. S., Davidson, W., Nelson, S., & Enna, B. Sex differences in learned helplessness: II. The contingencies of evaluative feedback in the classroom, and III. An experimental analysis. *Developmental Psychology,* 1978, *14,* 268–276.

Dweck, C. S., & Elliot, E. S. Achievement motivation. In P. Mussen (General Editor) and E. M. Hetherington (Volume Editor). *Carmichael's manual of child psychology: Social and personality development.* New York: Wiley, in press.

Dweck, C. S., & Reppucci, N. D. Learned helplessness and reinforcement responsibility in children. *Journal of Personality and Social Psychology,* 1973, *25,* 109–116.

Eccles, J., Midgley, C., & Adler, T. F. In J. H. Nicholls (Ed.), *The development of achievement motivation.* Greenwich, CT, JAI Press, in press.

Enzle, M. E., & Ross, J. M. Increasing and decreasing intrinsic interest with contingent rewards: A test of cognitive evaluation theory. *Journal of Experimental Social Psychology,* 1978, *14,* 588–597.

Fisher, C. D. The effects of personal control, competence and extrinsic reward systems on intrinsic motivation. *Organizational Behavior and Human Performance,* 1978, *21,* 273–288.

Flett, G. L., & Ruble, D. N. *Perceptions of ability and self-evaluation information seeking: A developmental analysis.* Unpublished manuscript, New York University, 1983.

Frey, K. S., & Ruble, D. N. *What children say to one another when the teacher is not around: Self-evaluation and social comparison in the classroom.* Manuscript submitted for publication, 1983.

Glass, D. C., & Carver, C. S. Helplessness and the coronary-prone personality. In J. Garber & M. E. P. Seligman (Eds.), *Human helplessness: Theory and application.* New York: Academic Press, 1980.

Greene, D., & Lepper, M. R. Effects of extrinsic rewards on children's subsequent intrinsic interest. *Child Development,* 1974, *45,* 1141–1145.

Harackiewicz, J. M. The effects of reward contingency and performance feedback on intrinsic motivation. *Journal of Personality and Social Psychology,* 1979, *37,* 1352–1363.

Harter, S. Effectance motivation reconsidered: Toward a developmental model. *Human Development,* 1978, *1,* 34–64.

Harter, S. A new self-report scale of intrinsic versus extrinsic orientation in the classroom: Motivational and informational components. *Developmental Psychology,* 1981, *17,* 300–312.

Harter, S., & Connell, J. P. A model of the relationship among children's academic achievement and their self-perceptions of competence, control, and motivation. In J. Nicholls (Ed.), *The development of achievement motivation.* Greenwich, CT: JAI Press, 1981.

Hill, K. T. The relation of evaluative practices to test anxiety and achievement motivation. *Educator*, 1977, *19*, 15–22.

Hill, K. T., & Sarason, S. B. The relation of test anxiety and defensiveness to test and school performance over the elementary school years: A further longitudinal study. *Monographs of the Society for Research in Child Development*, 1966, *31*, (2).

Hunt, J. Intrinsic motivation and its role in psychological development. In D. Lewis (Ed.), *Nebraska Symposium on Motivation*, (Vol. 13). Lincoln: University of Nebraska Press, 1965.

Karniol, R., & Ross, M. The effect of performance-relevant and performance irrelevant rewards on children's intrinsic motivation. *Child Development*, 1977, *48*, 482–487.

Kast, A. C. *Sex differences in intrinsic motivation: A development analysis of the effects of social rewards.* Unpublished dissertation, 1983.

Kohlberg, H. L. A cognitive-developmental analysis of children's sex-role concepts and attitudes. In E. E. Maccoby (Ed.), *The development of sex differences.* Stanford: Stanford University Press, 1966.

Kruglanski, A. W., Friedman, I., & Zeevi, G. The effects of extrinsic incentives on some qualitative aspects of task performance. *Journal of Personality*, 1971, *39*, 606–617.

Kukla, A. An attributional theory of choice. In L. Berkowitz (Ed.), *Advances in experimental social pshchology* (Vol. II). New York: Academic Press, 1978.

Lepper, M. R., & Greene, D. Turning play into work: Effects of adult surveillance and extrinsic rewards on children's intrinsic motivation. *Journal of Personality and Social Psychology*, 1975, *31*, 479–486.

Lepper, M. R., & Greene, D. *The hidden costs of rewards.* Hillsdale, NJ: Lawrence Erlbaum Associates, 1978.

Lepper, M. R., Greene, D., & Nisbett, R. E. Undermining children's intrinsic interest with extrinsic reward: A test of the "overjustification" hypothesis. *Journal of Personality and Social Psychology*, 1973, *28*, 129–137.

Lepper, M. R., Sagotsky, G., Dafoe, J., & Greene, D. Consequences of superfluous social constraints: Effects on young children's social inferences and subsequent intrinsic interest. *Journal of Personality and Social Psychology*, 1982, *42*, 51–65.

Levine, J. Social Comparison and education. In J. M. Levine & M. C. Wang (Eds.), *Teachers and student perceptions: Implications for learning.* Hillsdale, NJ: Lawrence Erlbaum Associates, 1983.

Licht, B. G., & Dweck, C. S. Sex differences in achievement orientations: Consequences for academic choices and attainments. In M. Marland (Ed.), *Sex differentiation and schooling.* London: Heineman, 1983.

Luyten, H., & Lens, W. The effect of earlier experience and reward contingencies on intrinsic motivation. *Motivation and Emotion*, 1981, *5*, 25–36.

Macey, T. J., & Boggiano, A. K. *The effect of universal versus personal helplessness on performance: A developmental study.* Unpublished manuscript, University of Colorado, 1983.

Maehr, M. L., & Stallings, W. M. Freedom from external evaluation. *Child Development*, 1972, *43*, 177–185.

Main, D. S., & Boggiano, A. K. The effects of extrinsic constraints on intrinsic interest in children. Paper presented at the conference for Society of Research and Child Development, Southwest Region, 1984.

McGraw, J. C. Issues in learning and motivation. In M. R. Lepper & D. Greene (Eds.), *The hidden costs of reward.* Hillsdale, NJ: Lawrence Erlbaum Associates, 1978.

McGraw, K. O., & McCullers, J. C. Evidence of a detrimental effect of extrinsic incentives on breaking a mental set. *Journal of Experimental Social Psychology*, 1979, *15*, 285–294.

Miller, I. W., & Norman, W. H. Learned helplessness in humans: A review and attribution theory model. *Psychological Bulletin*, 1979, *86*, 93–118.

Miller, W. R., & Seligman, M. E. P. Depression and learned helplessness in man. *Journal of*

Abnormal Psychology, 1975, *84,* 228–238.

Nicholls, J. G., & Miller, A. J.   Development and its discontents: The differentiation of the concept of ability. In J. G. Nicholls, (Ed.), *The development of achievement motivation.* Greenwich, CT: JAI Press, in press.

Pittman, T. S., Davey, M. E., Alafat, K. A., Wetherill, K. V., & Kramer, N. A.   Information versus controlling verbal rewards. *Personality and Social Psychology Bulletin,* 1980, *6,* 228–233.

Pittman, T. S., Emery, J., & Boggiano, A. K.   Intrinsic and extrinsic motivational orientations: Reward induced changes in preferences for complexity. *Journal of Personality and Social Psychology,* 1982, *42,* 789–797.

Pittman, N. L., & Pittman, T. S.   Effects of amount of helplessness training and internal-external locus of control on mood and performance. *Journal of Personality and Social Psychology,* 1979, *37,* 39–47.

Rheinberg, F.   Achievement evaluation: A fundamental difference in motivational consequences. *Studies in Educational Evaluation,* 1983, *2,* in press.

Rheinberg, F., Lührmann, J. V., & Wagner, H.   Bezugsnorm-Orientievung von Schulern der 5–13. Klasse bei der Leistungsbeurteilung. *Zeitschrift fur Entwicklungspsychologie und Padagogische Psychologie,* 1977, *9,* 90–93.

Rholes, W. S., Blackwell, J., Jordan, C., & Walters, C.   A developmental study of learned helplessness. *Developmental Psychology,* 1980, *16,* 616–624.

Ross, M.   Salience of reward and intrinsic motivation. *Journal of Personality and Social Psychology,* 1975, *33,* 245–254.

Ruble, D. N.   The role of social comparison processes and their role in achievement-related self-socialization. In E. T. Higgins, D. N. Ruble, & W. W. Hartup (Eds.), *Social cognition and social development: A sociocultural perspective.* New York: Cambridge University Press, 1983.

Ruble, D. N., & Boggiano, A. K.   Optimizing motivation in an achievement context. In B. K. Keogh (Ed.), *Advances in special education* (Vol. 1). JAI Press, 1980.

Ruble, D. N., Boggiano, A. K., Feldman, N. S., & Loebl, J. H.   The concept of competence: A developmental analysis of self-evaluation through social comparison. *Developmental Psychology,* 1980, *16,* 105–115.

Ruble, D. N., Feldman, N. S., & Boggiano A. K.   Social comparison between young children in achievement situations. *Developmental Psychology,* 1976, *12,* 192–197.

Ruble, D. N., Parsons, J. E., & Ross, J.   Self-evaluative responses of children in an achievement setting. *Child Development,* 1976, *47,* 990–997.

Ruble, D. N., & Rholes, W. S.   The development of children's perceptions and attributions about their social world. In J. H. Harvey, W. Ickes, & R. Kidd (Eds.), *New Directions in attribution research* (Vol. 3). Hillsdale, NJ: Lawrence Erlbaum Associates, 1981.

Ryan, R. M.   Control and information in the interpersonal sphere: An extension of cognitive evaluation theory. *Journal of Personality and Social Psychology,* 1982, *43,* 450–461.

Ryan, R. M., Chandler, C. L., Connell, J. P., & Deci, E. L.   *Internalization and motivation: Some preliminary research and theoretical assumptions.* Presented at the conference for Society of Research and Child Development, 1983.

Ryan, R. M., & Deci, E. L.   *The importance of intrinsic motivation for maintenance and transfer of treatment gains in psychotherapy.* Unpublished manuscript, University of Rochester, 1980.

Seligman, M. E. P.   Fall into helplessness. *Psychology Today,* June, 1973, *88,* 43–48; 51–54.

Seligman, M. E. P.   Depression and learned helplessness. In R. J. Friedman & M. M. Katz (Eds.), *The psychology of depression: Contemporary theory and research.* Washington, DC: Winston, 1974.

Seligman, M. E. P.   *Helplessness: On depression, development, and death.* San Francisco: Freeman, 1975.

Seligman, M. E. P., & Maier, S. F. Failure to escape traumatic shock. *Journal of Experimental Psychology,* 1967, *74,* 1–9.

Shapira, Z. Expectancy determinants of intrinsically motivated behavior. *Journal of Personality and Social Psychology,* 1976, *34,* 1235–1244.

Stevens, L., & Jones, E. E. Defensive attribution and the Kelly cube. *Journal of Personality and Social Psychology,* 1976, *34,* 809–820.

Trope, Y. Self-assessment in achievement behavior. In J. Suls & A. G. Greenwald (Eds.), *Psychological perspectives on the self* (Vol.2). Hillsdale, NJ: Lawrence Erlbaum Associates, 1983.

Trope, Y. Uncertainty reducing properties of achievement task. *Journal of Personality and Social Psychology,* 1979, *37,* 1505–1518.

Veroff, J. Social comparison and the development of achievement motivation. In J. P. Smith (Ed.), *Achievement-related motives in children.* New York: Russell Sage Foundation, 1969.

Weiner, B. Achievement motivation and attribution theory. Morristown, NJ: General Learning Corporation, 1974.

Weiner, B., Frieze, J., Kukla, A., Reed, L., Rest, S., & Rosenbaum, R. *Perceiving the causes of success and failure.* New York: General Learning Press, 1971.

Weiner, M. J., & Mander, A. M. The effects of reward and perception of competency upon intrinsic motivation. *Motivation and Emotion,* 1978, *2,* 67–73.

White, R. W. Motivation reconsidered: The concept of competence. *Psychological Review,* 1959, *66,* 297–333.

Wine, J. Test anxiety and direction of attention. *Psychological Bulletin,* 1971, *76,* 92–104.

Wortman, C. B., & Dinzer, L. Is an attributional analysis on the learned helplessness phenomenon viable? A critique of the Abramson-Seligman-Teasdale Reformation. *Journal of Abnormal Psychology,* 1978, *87,* 75–90.

Zuckerman, M., Brown, R. H., Fischler, G. L., Fox, G. A., Lathin, D. R., & Minesiran, A. J. Determinants of information seeking behavior. *Journal of Research in Personality,* 1979, *13,* 161–172.

12 Conceptions of Motivation Within Competitive and Noncompetitive Goal Structures

Carole Ames
University of Maryland

For many children, success in school means getting more answers right than others and loathing those students who do better than themselves. In the following example, where a teacher is using a boys-against-girls game of tic-tac-toe with addition problems, we can see how such competitive behavior is socialized:

> A small boy comes forward for 7 + 2 and guesses at 8. The boys groan, the girls cheer; and the teacher looks pained . . . It seems the girls frequently win. The chagrined boy returns to his seat and . . . punches the little girl next to him as hard as he can saying "I hate you, I hate you." (Campbell, 1974, p. 182)

While this example may seen severe, the "curriculum" is similar across many American classrooms where only a few students win (being in the top ability group, getting As, finishing first and so forth), and losers predominate and must be prepared for the possibility of continued failure. "Since all but the brightest children have the constant experience that others succeed at their expense, they cannot help but develop an inherent tendency to hate — to hate the success of others, to hate others who are successful, and to be determined to prevent it" (Henry, 1969, p. 83).

As can be seen in any classroom, children are motivated toward a variety of goals, some of which are desirable and others less desirable. While there are certainly a variety of factors that impinge upon a child's motivation in any achievement situation, one central factor concerns the situational context in a broad sense and the goal structure, more specifically. Goal structure defines how students are to be evaluated in relation to each other and to a goal. In general, we can describe the structure of an achievement setting as either predominantly competitive (where students work against each other for a reward or recognition), cooperative (where students work toward a shared goal), or individualistic (where students work toward independent goals) (cf. Johnson & Johnson, 1974, for example). Although there has been extensive research on competitive versus alternative noncompetitive goal structures in relation to achievement gains and social relationships as outcome variables (for reviews, see Johnson & Johnson, 1974; Michaels, 1977; Slavin, 1977), the motivational consequences of these different goal structures has rarely been directly assessed. Instead, the presence or level of motivation has typically been inferred from achievement gains. As such, motivation is presumed to covary with achievement and performance indices. In fact, in explaining findings of achievement differences, authors have often referred to motivational constructs without measuring these variables. Thus, although motivation has been regarded as one of the mediating constructs in achievement, the research on goal/reward structures has tended to focus on the question "Which type of structure leads to greater or lesser achievement?"

As implied above in the achievement literature, motivation has often been viewed as a quantitative variable especially when constructs such as activity level, energy, and persistence are employed. Motivation, however, can also be viewed as a qualitative construct that reflects different value orientations, behavioral choices, meanings assigned to success and failure, and goals (see e.g., Maehr, 1984). Thus, on the one hand, we may want students to persist longer, work harder, or spend more time on a task, and on the other hand, we may be equally concerned about getting students to focus on one set of information and not another, to value certain goals and objectives over others, to choose certain activities, and to implement certain cognitive and task strategies. When motivation is viewed in the latter manner, that is, as a qualitative variable, it is my contention that competitive, cooperative, and individualistic goal structures can be shown to involve qualitatively different motivational systems. Thus, what I am proposing is that these goal structures differ qualitatively, whether or not they differ quantitatively. The motivational processes implicit in each structure can be described as reflecting different motivational systems that have different origins, meanings, and cognitive-motivational consequences (see also Ames, 1984).

A cognitive-attributional approach to studying how students interpret and react to success and failure outcomes provides one qualitative framework for examining motivatonal processes within different goal structures. We might ask, for example, how students' cognitions about their performance, themselves, and the task differ according to how the achievement situation is structured. That students may be differentially focused on how smart they are versus how much effort is needed has significant implications for their self-esteem as well as future achievement behaviors. In other words, the goal structure influences how students evaluate their ability and/or effort and how they interpret the causes of their own success and failure, and the importance of these cognitions is documented by their impact on subsequent achievement-related affect, as well as on short- and long-term achievement strategies. In this paper, I examine how differing goal structures influence attributional patterns and other cognitive-based motivational variables. I propose that each goal structure elicits a motivational system that differentially affects children's attributions and self-cognitions and has different affective and action consequences. In Table 12.1, three motivational systems are proposed as relating to competitive, cooperative, and individualistic structures. An interpersonal competitive structure involves a motivation that impacts self-evaluation where social comparison information is dominant and ability is the focus of self-evaluation. A cooperative structure elicits a moral orientation where the focus is on group performance information and effort is directed toward the group goal. An individualistic structure evokes a task-mastery motivation system where performance change/improvement over time is salient and effort-related strategies are the focus of attention. The point I'm trying to make is not that one structure produces higher or lower motivation levels than another, rather, the resulting motivational systems are qualitatively different. I now outline how I see these systems as relating to each goal structure, although this task will be done briefly since I have elaborated on them in more detail elsewhere (Ames, 1984).

MOTIVATIONAL SYSTEMS

Competition as a pervasive phenomenon in American schools has been repeatedly documented by investigative observers of the classroom (Crockenberg & Bryant, 1978; Johnson & Johnson, 1975; Levine, 1983) as

TABLE 12.1
Motivational Systems

Motivational System	Eliciting Goal Structure	Salient Performance Information	Attributional Focus
Egoistic	Competitive	Own performance relative to other's	Ability
Moral Responsibility	Cooperative	Group Performance	Effort
Task Mastery	Individualistic	Own performance change/ improvement over time	Effort

Based on C. Ames & R. Ames. Goal structures as motivational systems. *Elementary School Journal,* in press.

well as by critics of the American educational system (e.g., Henry, 1969; Holt, 1964). In competition, students work against each other toward some goal such that the probability of one individual receiving a reward is reduced by the presence of more capable individuals. That competition produces irreverent and sometimes irrational behavior is an empirical reality when we find, for example, that children will deny themselves rewards to prevent another child getting any reward (Nelson & Kagan, 1972), that children value winning over fairness in sports activities (Kleiber & Roberts, 1981), and that even young children believe that being happy, smart, and deserving of reward is more related to winning than to performing well (Ames & Felker, 1979). Standardized tests, grading curves, ability grouping, and teacher's communications (e.g., "I like the way Allan is working." "Who can help _____ with the answer?" "Who can be first to . . . .") all invite social comparison, and there is reason to believe that these practices contribute to increases in children's interest in social comparison as they progress through school (Rosenholtz & Simpson, 1983). In essence, a competitive system of motivation can be depicted as a situation of forced social comparison where students are bombarded with information about their peers' performance and where their "survival" is based on their ability to compete, be better or the best, and to win. In competition, social comparison information is highly salient and we have found that students' evaluations of their ability fluctuate as a function of how they are performing relative to others. Not only do self-perceptions of ability differentiate winners and losers, ability appears to be the factor that is most related to achievement-related affect. The bottom line in a competitive structure is whether one is a winner or loser.

Central to cooperative structures are concepts of shared effort: positive interdependence among students, and a responsibility to do one's part. Cooperative structures create a social interdependency among students and a valuing of effort directed toward attaining a common gaol. Both cooperative and moral situations (cf. Ames, 1984) are social in nature, involve interdependency, and impart a responsibility for helping, either by doing one's share of the work or by directly assisting another. Implicit in both moral and cooperative situations, then, are norms for helping; and, in an achievement context, helping another benefits the group. Even when students have little opportunity to directly assist each other, the social interdependency among group members, nevertheless prevails. Unlike competitive structures, within cooperative structures, children's self-perceptions are not entirely, nor even primarily, a function of their own personal achievement. Children are focused on the group performance and the group performance affects the meaning of an individual's performance. Cooperative groups that have successful outcomes have been found to alleviate the potentially negative self-evaluations of a low performer, but group failure has been found to diminish the positive self-evaluations of a high performer (Ames, 1981). Further, similar to a morally-based evaluation system, in a cooperative structure, blame tends to be imparted for negative outcomes (Ames, 1981). Negative sanctions tend to be directed toward those who fail to fulfill their obligation when the group fails. The implication here is that motivation is aimed toward fulfilling the group goal, implying a concept of *ought* — that one ought to put forth effort for the group.

By contrast, individualized structures imply an independence of goals among individuals where the criteria for success are defined in relation to some preestablished standard. Often, however, individualism has been equated with "self-competition" in that performance evaluations are based on external criteria. The implication is that an individualistic structure may elicit a self or norm-referenced competition which is, in effect, much like interpersonal competition (e.g., Ames & Felker, 1979; Garibaldi, 1979; Johnson, Johnson, Johnson, & Anderson, 1976). Alternative conceptions of individualized structures, however, suggest that an opportunity for self-improvement and self-perception of "I can" may be necessary to define an individualistic goal structure that is also noncompetitive (Ames & Ames, 1981; Covington, 1984). An implied request for self-improvement embodies what has been called success or mastery-oriented structures (Covington & Beery, 1976) and origin-like classrooms (deCharms, 1976). When individualistic structures solicit a "task engagement" (e.g., try to do your best, try to improve upon your performance) and incorporate an opportunity for self-improvement, they have a stronger task focus, and the self-awareness that is endogenous to competitive structures is minimized. A noncompetitive-individualistic structure, then, is presumed to foster a task-mastery orientation where students are focused on effort-related strategies for improving their performance.

Thus, competitive, cooperative, and individualistic structures are conceived as reflecting different motivational systems which result in different ways of attending to performance information, different meanings attached to success and failure, and different action consequences (see Table 12.1). I now examine two of these motivational systems in more detail: a competitive versus an individualistic goal structure. I have chosen to focus on the competitive-individualistic comparison and to describe some explicit differences in the self-cognitions that result from these two structures, because they have often been inappropriately equated in the literature.

ATTENTION TO PERFORMANCE INFORMATION

How students evaluate their performance certainly depends on whether they perceive themselves as successful or not. However, in most performance situations there are several sources of performance information (e.g., past performance on related tasks, current performance on the current task, and relevant others' performance) that impinge upon children's subjective evaluation of their performance. In one recent study (Ames & Ames, 1981), we looked at how children attend to different sources of performance information in competitive as compared to individualistic structures. In this study, fifth- and sixth-grade children worked on a novel achievement task over several trials so that a performance history of success or failure could be established. Success evolved from a task of predominantly solvable puzzles and failure from a task of predominantly unsolvable puzzles. Upon completion of these preliminary trials, children either competed with another child or continued to work alone with the challenge to try to do their best. Thus, the study involved two phases; the first established a performance history and the second imposed a goal structure for the final performance. In a completely crossed design, all children had information about their prior performance (success or failure) and then performed either successfully or unsuccessfully at a similar task in a competitive or individualistic structure. At the conclusion of the task, all children were asked to assess and evaluate their performance on a number of dimensions. Central to the issue raised here is the question of whether past performance or current (social comparison) performance information was more salient to children's self-evaluations. Do children attend to the changes (improvement or decline) in their performance over time or is this information outweighed by the salience of their immediate performance? Our findings showed that in the competitive structure, social comparison information was dominant and performance history information was little utilized. That is, children's tendencies to reward themselves and their feelings of satisfaction were based on whether or not they won or lost in the competition and were not affected by the quality of their past performance. The performance history information, however, was important to children's self-perceptions in the individualistic structure where past and current performance accounted for equal proportions of the variance in children's self-reward and feelings of satisfaction. As a consequence, among those children who had performed well in the past, those in the individual setting weathered a poor performance better than did children in the competitive situation. In sum, we found strong evidence for differential focusing on performance cues as a function of the imposed goal structure. Social comparison information, to the exclusion of other performance information that was available, was the central focus in the competitive structure; and only in the individual setting was the child's past performance a salient source of information.

Related to the issue of how performance information is utilized, we might also ask if the value or importance attached to success and failure outcomes differs as a function of the imposed goal structure. Obviously, individuals prefer success over failure and they feel better about themselves after succeeding; nevertheless, research findings do suggest that success is more positively valued and failure more reproached in some contexts than in others. In fact, in achievement-related situations, we have found that outperforming another student is more prized by students than is merely performing a task well (Ames & Felker, 1979). In this latter study, children were asked to reward hypothetical others who were described as performing in competitive or alternatively noncompetitive situations. Although successful children were described as achieving the same level of performance in each goal structure situation, this information was subordinate to the information that one performance occasioned a win (competition) and the others did not. In other words, success was more valued when it involved winning.

Not only is winning more prized by others, winning also appears to engender self-interest motives and self-aggrandizing behaviors. Self-interest motives are apparent when we examine the interpersonal behaviors of competitors versus noncompetitors. A consistent finding of ours has been that winners tend to give themselves more reward than they give to their losing competitors (Ames, 1978; Ames & Ames, 1981; Ames, Ames, & Felker, 1977). Further, children tend to reward themselves more when they are the winners than when they are rewarding another for winning (Ames, 1981). No evidence of these motives has been found in noncompetitively-structured social settings.

In contrast to these self-enhancement motives that are associated with winning, losing appears to accentuate the self-directed negativity that typically results from a poor performance (Ames, 1978; 1981; Ames et al., 1977). Not only do children perceive the poor performances of others as least satisfying when it involves losing to another, they report significantly lower levels of personal satisfaction after losing (Ames et al., 1977). There is also evidence to suggest that losing is more affectively salient than is winning (Ames, 1984). What this means is that the negative affect that follows losing is greater than the positive affect following a win. Basically, competition creates a situation of high vulnerability to self-imposed criticism. This self-negativism is not limited to children who hold a priori negative self-views, since even children who have been classified as having a positive self-concept have been found to become self-punitive when they fail in competitive settings. Specifically, we have found that while children low in self-concept are more self-punitive than high self-concept children in noncompetitively-defined settings, the high group becomes equally self-critical in a competitive setting (Ames, 1978). In general, we have consistently found that failing elicits more negative affect, reduced self-reward, and increased self-criticism in competitive than in noncompetitive settings. Thus while failure contributes to general feelings of dissatisfaction, the added constraint of losing appears to magnify these consequences.

In comparison, competitive and noncompetitive-individualistic structures appear to differentially affect the perceived value of success and failure and the salience of certain informational cues. Consistency or changes in one's performance over time is salient to a child's self-perceptions in individualistic structures, but social comparison information is clearly a more important cue in competitive structures. Thus, children who are quite similar in achievement may have markedly different self-views as a function of their experiences in different goal structure settings. Further, the attentional focus in competitively-structured settings may make children impervious to requests to monitor their performance change over time.

ATTRIBUTIONAL FOCUS

Covington and Beery (1976) have described competition as a system of differential motivation such that sense of self-worth and motivation are directly tied to self-perceptions of ability. Students' self-worth is threatened when they size up their ability as not competitive, and a self-attribution of low ability results if they continue to try and perform poorly relative to others. That self-attributions of high ability following success and low ability following failure prevail in competitive situations is also consistent with Nicholls' (1979) description of ego-involving situations where students' attention is focused on their ability to perform (better than others), rather than on how to do the task at hand. The basis of a competitive system of motivation, then, is that a competitive structure focuses children on their ability, and these self-perceptions are uniquely a function of how they perform relative to others. There are now a number of empirical investigations to support this position.

In several studies (e.g., Ames, 1978; Ames & Ames, 1981; Ames et al., 1977) we have contrasted competitive and noncompetitive structures and assessed children's self-attributions of ability and effort as well as their perceived satisfaction with their performance. In each study, children performed in pairs at a novel achievement task in which both the structure and the task performance were experimentally manipulated. The task performance of each child in each pair was always discrepant such that while one child performed at a high level (winning in the competition) the other child performed at a low level (losing). The goal structure was conveyed through promised rewards for winning (competitive) or performing well (noncompetitive) or merely through an instructional set to try to win or to do well. Consistent across this research has been the finding that competition increases the salience of ability as a factor that differentiates winning and losing. Competitive winners judge themselves as smarter than their competitors, and losers self-attribute low ability relative to others who are successful or who perform equally poor in a noncompetitive condition. Self-attributions of high or low ability tend to be accentuated by the occurrence of winning and losing. Even when children have been asked to evaluate hypothetical others, the ascription of ability to high and low performers has been found more discrepant in competitive than in alternative noncompetitive structures (Ames & Felker, 1979).

Why do competitive situations make ability such a salient factor in judging one's performance? From a rational point of view, social comparison information provides the most information about the task difficulty and one's ability; and when one's performance is better or worse than others on the same task, ability becomes the logical focus of one's attention. Competition is necessarily a situation of winners and losers on the same task, thus a logical inference would be that differences in performance must reflect differences in ability. Ability is even more assuredly the salient attribution when effort is presumed to be high and it can be argued that competitive situations are perceived as generally difficult or even uncertain such that both effort and ability are perceived as necessary. In support of this point, perceptions of ability and effort have been found to be positively correlated as perceived causes of success in competitive, but not in individualistic, structures (Ames, submitted for publication). In other words, competition may be more a question of "can," where trying is presumed.

Our research further suggests that it is not the presence of another for comparison or the social nature of a performance setting that contributes to an ability focus, for when children have been rewarded for participating, trying, or cooperating, ability has not emerged as a self-evaluative factor that differentiates winners' and losers' self- and interpersonal perceptions. Because competition apparently highlights social comparison information, we might expect such a condition to elicit motivational biases. Self-worth or ego-involving biases become evident when we find, for example, that ability attributions mediate achievement-related affect in competitive situations. In the Ames et al. study, affective reactions to success and failure were related to self-attributions of ability in competitive situations, but the ability-affect linkage was not apparent in a non-competitively structured setting. In related research where normative feedback has been involved, a positive relationship between ability attributions and affect has also been reported. Nicholls (1975), for example, had children compare their performance to a norm-referenced chart; and Covington and Omelich (1979a) asked college students to imagine they had taken an exam and then provided a mock normal distribution of exam scores for comparison. In each case, normative comparisons were available and ability was found to mediate achievement affect. Positive feelings associated with winning evolved from the attribution of high ability and negative feelings from attributions of low ability. Winning enhances self-worth and losing triggers a negative self-attribution-affect system. It seems plausible to suggest that an ability-mediated motivational system may typify any achievement situation that is perceived as important, and the cultural value placed on winning may make all or most competitive encounters important ones. Nevertheless, noncompetitive structures may, at times, also elicit an ability-affect covariation when, for example, ability has instrumental value; and this effect has been found when future performances are anticipated (Ames, submitted for publication).

Unlike competitive situations where the focus is on external norms and where perceptions of task difficulty involve a self-assessment of ability relative to others, in individualized settings, perceptions of task difficulty should depend on a determination of the amount of effort that is needed to achieve success relative to one's prior achievements and the goal. It is presumed that a perception of "can" is necessary for an individualized structure to be noncompetitive in nature ("I can do this if I try." "How can I go about doing this?"). Thus, individualized structures that emphasize trying and/or self-improvement should make effort the focus of self-attribution. In comparison, the focus in competitive structures is on "can" where trying is presumed, but in individualistic structures, "trying" is more salient because the presumption is that one has the ability to do the task.

In an early study (Ames et al., 1977) we used a noncompetitive situation that in many respects involved an individualistic orientation. Although it was a social situation, children worked independently and there were no external performance criteria. Instead, children were rewarded for their participation which they may have interpreted as a "request" to become involved in the task and to try. In contrast to an ability-affect linkage that occurred in the competitive condition, self-attributions of effort mediated affect in this noncompetitive situation. That is, feelings of satisfaction or dissatisfaction were related to a belief that one had tried or had not tried enough. In a subsequent study (Ames & Ames, 1981), we looked at children's causal attributions for success and failure in an individualized versus a competitive setting. The individualistic structure was defined as "try to solve as many puzzles as you can" and also included an opportunity for self-improvement on a second set of tasks. The findings from this study showed that effort attributions were associated more with individualistic than with competitive outcomes. Children believed that effort accounted for both high and low performances more in the individual condition. A more recent study (Ames, submitted for publication), which is discussed in more detail in the next section, also provides strong support for an effort-outcome linkage in an individualistic structure when trying is emphasized. Additionally, Covington (1984) has reported on a field study in which a mastery-based learning approach was used with college students and the results rather decidedly demonstrated how an opportunity for self-improvement through multiple test options was a critical factor for eliciting perceptions of personal control through effort.

A belief that effort and achievement outcomes covary is the basis for Weiner's model of achievement-motivated behavior (Weiner, 1979) and this effort-outcome covariation appears evident in individualistic structures when students are encouraged to try, when there is an opportunity for self-improvement, and/or when students are not focused on externalized goals. When students become focused on social norms, effort is less salient and students become engaged in self-evaluations of their ability relative to their peers.

ATTRIBUTIONS AND OTHER ACHIEVEMENT-RELATED COGNITIONS

The research described thus far suggests that competitive versus noncompetitive-individualistic structures differently influence the salience of ability versus effort cues. It has also been suggested that competitive structures focus children more on evaluations of their ability on *how* to do the task, but we have not yet provided explicit evidence to support this point. The following study was an attempt to address this issue, that is, to examine the prevalence of attributions and other achievement-related cognitions in children's thoughts as a function of goal structure conditions. The presumption has been that a preeminent concern with one's ability in competitive structures obviates what might be called a task orientation, that is, children are less focused on strategies for solving a problem or completing a task. In contrast, we have described individualistic structures as noncompetitive such that thoughts about winning and losing do not prevail; as such, children should be free to become more task-focused and task or cognitive strategies should become more prevalent in their thoughts.

Although individual differences in a task-focus (i.e., children use of general strategies such as self-instructions and self-monitoring) has been reported by Diener & Dweck (1978), we might also ask whether a similar task mastery orientation can be induced by a noncompetitive-individualistic structure. Diener and Dweck found that while some children viewed failure as indicative of low ability, other children (those they labeled mastery-oriented) responded with strategies for improving their performance (e.g., "I should slow down and try to figure this out." "I need to concentrate." "The harder this gets the harder I try."). Their research suggested that a variety of achievement cognitions are associated with positive versus negative achievement orientations, so we might also ask whether similar cognitive-motivational differences distinguish competitive and individualistic structures. Based on Table 12.1, we should expect that the achievement cognitions associated with a mastery orientation occur more within an individualistic than a competitive structure. Thus, the intent of this study was to look at a wider range of achievement cognitions and to directly test the salience of different cognitions as a function of contrasting goal structures.

In this study, fifth- and sixth-grade children were assigned to competitive and individualistic goal structure conditions and were given a sequence of two separate tasks, each involving several line-drawn puzzles that were to be traced. Half the children were given tasks of predominantly solvable puzzles and the other half were given predominantly unsolvable puzzles. The task was presented with either competitively-oriented or challenge-oriented instructions (e.g., "try to solve as many as you can . . . try to improve . . ."). In brief, the children were given two tasks in competitive or individually-structured conditions and each child's performance remained consistent over the two tasks such that the same child won (or lost) on both competitive tasks or performed at a high (or low) level on both tasks in the individual condition.

After the second task, and while anticipating a third task, each child was asked to respond to a questionnaire and identify those statements that reflected what he or she was "thinking right now." The variety of statements reflected a range of achievement cognitions and affective responses that a child might have about his or her task performance. These statements were based, in part, on the categories generated by Diener and Dweck (1978) and the attributional schema of Weiner (1979). The categories included: (1) effort-related attributions, including both typical and immediate effort, (2) ability-related attributions, (3) self-instructions and self-monitoring strategies, and (4) affective responses. The statements in the self-instruction category included instructions children might give to themselves as well as strategies they might use to become more effective in their task behavior. By looking at the statements the child selected, we could see if he or she was thinking about responses to any of the following questions: Why did I perform well (poorly)? (Categories 1 and 2), How can I go about working this next task? (Category 3), How do I feel about my performance? (Category 4). Thus, while we have considerable knowledge about the variety of cognitions that students may have about themselves, the task, and their performance, we know a lot less about the relative dominance of certain cognitions over others and we know even less about the situational factors that influence the direction of students' thoughts.

A "thought-matching" methodology that was used in this study involved asking children to report what they were thinking by identifying specific statements that matched their thoughts. This method differed considerably from prior efforts that have either encouraged children to think aloud while they were performing a task, directly posed "why" questions, or asked subjects to ask themselves questions. Children were free to select as few or as many of the statements as they wished; a method that is less confounded by children's ability or willingness to express themselves. In fact, this "thought-matching" methodology for assessing self-related cognitions proved to be an effective way of tapping children's thoughts, and permitted the testing of competing hypotheses about the types of cognitions in children's thoughts.

There were clear differences in what children reported they were thinking in the competitive and individualistic structures. Competing children selected more ability statements than did children performing individually. In contrast, children in the individual condition selected more effort statements and self-instructions than those in the competitive condition. Figure 12.1 illustrates the differences and analysis of variance effects between these conditions across the categories of statements. The differences in the use of the strategy statements was quite striking considering that children in the individualistic structure not only selected more of these statements than did children in the competitive structure, they utilized more self-instructional statements than any other category of statements. Further, this focus on self-instructions and self-monitoring thoughts was not limited to only those children who were performing poorly nor to those children who were typically high achievers in their classrooms (those most likely to have high self-concept of ability). Self-instructions figured prominently in the thoughts of all children who were performing in the individually-structured setting. Unlike children in the competitive structure who seemed to be thinking about the question "Was I smart," in the individualistic structure where trying and self-improvement were emphasized, children's thoughts reflected a stronger focus on "Did I try hard enough?" and "How am I going to approach this next task?" Like the mastery children studied by Diener and Dweck, the children in the individualistic structure, particularly those who were performing poorly, were more future-oriented in their thoughts, thinking about how to channel their efforts on the next task.

Looking at Figure 12.2 now, goal structure has been shown to be an important factor that affects processing of performance information and the sali-

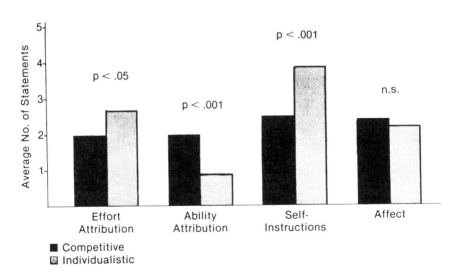

FIG. 12.1   Self-Cognitions as a Function of Goal Structure.

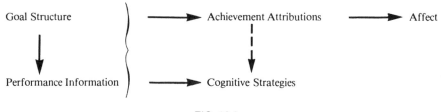

FIG. 12.2

ence of specific attribution cues. The intent here is to illustrate the role of goal structure as a situationaal factor in the formation of self-cognitions. Also depicted in this figure is the influence of goal structure on cognitive strategies and affect as well as achievement-related attributions. The linkage between attributions and affective reactions has been well-documented in the attribution literature, but the relationship between attributions and cognitive strategies is less clear. Additional data from the Ames (submitted for publication) study suggest a modest positive but significant relationship between attributions and self-instructions. That is, children who used effort attribution statements were more likely to employ self-instructional statements. Clearly, these data only suggest a correlational relationship; and the specific question of whether cognitive strategies are mediated by attributions or the more general issue of whether certain types of cognitions are necessary for the activation of strategies is in need of further study. These findings further showed no significant relationship between self-instructions and affect, that is, they appeared to be relatively independent. While there is some evidence for some of the linkages outlined in Figure 12.1, the mediational role of attributions for other achievement cognitions remains fairly unclear. It seems reasonable to suggest that the use of cognitive strategies may be premised on the assumption that one's performance is attributed to some unstable cause. These attributions, however, may at times be more implicit than explicit or may have occurred further back in the thought process (cf. Weiner, 1979). Nevertheless, while the right-hand side of Figure 12.2 raises new questions, goal structure has been shown to be an important influence on the entire cognitive-motivational sequence.

CONCLUSION

To review, competitive structures have been described as social comparative motivational systems. Students' "natural" interest in social comparison cues is given added relevance and importance by the competitive structure. Evaluations of one's ability becomes the focus of attention and such a focus may be "enabling" in as much as predicting future outcomes is singularly important for protecting or enhancing one's self-worth. By contrast, students in an individualistic structure seem to be focused more on the process of mastering the task; they seem to be attending to "How have I been doing?" "Was I working hard enough?" "How am I doing now?" "How can I do this next task?"

It has been argued that differing goal structures elicit qualitatively different types of motivation. An analysis has been made of the differences in self-evaluations and self-related cognitions that evolve from competitive and individualistic goal structures, in particular. Not only do children focus on different types of performance information as a function of the goal structure, the resulting attributional differences have markedly different implications for subsequent cognitions and affective responses. When goal structures are analyzed qualitatively, we can see how many students may be socialized into a preferred motivational system, may develop certain components of a self-evaluation and self-monitoring system at the expense of others, and may become dependent on certain sources of performance information. Whether students learn more or less in one structure or another has not been a concern of this paper, but when we look at the differential focusing of students' thoughts, it seems clear that the motivational outcomes of these different goal structures should have long term implications for goals of continuing motivation, successful learning, and self-directed achievement behavior.

REFERENCES

Ames, C. Children's achievement attributions and self-reinforcement: Effects of self-concept and competitive reward structure. *Journal of Educational Psychology,* 1978, *70,* 345–355.

Ames, C. Competitive versus cooperative reward structures: The influence of individual and group performance factors on achievement attributions and affect. *American Educational Research Journal,* 1981, *18,* 273–287.

Ames, C. Competitive, cooperative and individualistic goal structures: A cognitive-motivational analysis. In R. Ames & C. Ames (Eds.), *Research on motivation in education: Student motivation,* New York: Academic Press, 1984.

Ames, C. Achievement attributions and self-instructions under competitive and individualistic goal structures. Manuscript submitted for publication.

Ames, C., & Ames, R. Competitive versus individualistic goal structures: The salience of past performance information for causal attributions and affect. *Journal of Educational Psychology,* 1981, *73,* 411–418.

Ames, C., & Ames, R. Goal structures as motivational systems. *Elementary School Journal,* in press.

Ames, C., Ames, R., & Felker, D. Effects of competitive reward structure and valence of outcome on children's achievement attributions. *Journal of Educational Psychology,* 1977, *69,* 1–8.

Ames, C., & Felker, D. An examination of children's attributions and achievement-related evaluations in competitive, cooperative, and individualistic reward structures. *Journal of Educational Psychology,* 1979, *71,* 413–420.

Aronson, E. *The jigsaw classroom.* Beverly Hills, CA: Sage, 1978.

Campbell, D. On being number one: Competition in education. *Phi Delta Kappan,* 1974, *56,* 143–146.

Covington, M. The motive for self-worth. In R. Ames & C. Ames (Eds.), *Research on motivation in education.* New York: Academic Press, 1984.

Covington, M., & Beery, R. *Self-worth and school learning.* New York: Holt, Rinehart & Winston, 1976.

Covington, M., & Omelich, C. Effort: The double-edged sword in school achievement. *Journal of Educational Psychology,* 1979, *71,* 169–182. (a)

Covington, M., & Omelich, C. It's best to be able and virtuous too: Student and teacher evaluative responses to successful effort. *Journal of Educational Psychology,* 1979, *71,* 688–700. (b)

Crockenberg, S., & Bryant, B. Socialization: The implicit curriculum of learning environments. *Journal of Research and Development in Education,* 1978, *12,* 69–78.

deCharms, R. *Enhancing motivation: Change in the classroom.* New York: Irvington, 1976.

Deci, E. *Intrinsic motivation.* New York: Plenum, 1975.

Deci, E. When trying to win: Competition and intrinsic motivation. *Personality and Social Psychology Bulletin,* 1981, *7,* 79–83.

Diener, C., & Dweck, C. An analysis of learned helplessness: Continuous changes in performance, strategy, and achievement cognitions following failure. *Journal of Personality and Social Psychology,* 1978, *36,* 451–462.

Garibaldi, A. Affective contributions of cooperative and group goal structures. *Journal of Educational Psychology,* 1979, *71,* 788–794.

Henry, J. In suburban classrooms. In R. Gross & B. Gross (Eds.), *Radical school reform.* New York: Simon & Schuster, 1969.

Holt, J. *How children fail.* New York: Pittman, 1964.

Johnson, D., & Johnson, R. Instructional goal structure: Cooperative, competitive or individualistic. *Review of Educational Research,* 1974, *44,* 213–240.

Johnson, D., & Johnson, R. *Learning together and alone: Cooperation, competition and individualization.* Englewood Cliffs, NJ: Prentice Hall, 1975.

Johnson, D., Johnson, R., Johnson, J., & Anderson, D. The effects of cooperative vs. individualized instruction on student prosocial behavior, attitudes toward learning and achievement. *Journal of Educational Psychology,* 1976, *68,* 446–452.

Johnson, D., Maruyama, G., Johnson, R., Nelson, D., & Skon, L. Effects of cooperative, competitive, and individualistic goal structures on achievement: A meta-analysis. *Psychological Bulletin,* 1981, *89,* 47–62.

Kelley, H. The process of causal attribution. *American Psychologist,* 1973, *28,* 107–128.

Kleiber, D. & Roberts, G. The effects of sport experience in the development of social character: An exploratory investigation. *Journal of Sport Psychology,* 1981, *3,* 114–122.

Levine, J. Social comparison and education. In J. Levine & M. Wang (Eds.), *Teacher and student perceptions: Implications for learning.* Hillsdale, NJ: Lawrence Erlbaum Associates, 1983.

Maehr, M. Continuing motivation: An analysis of a seldom considered educational outcome. *Review of Educational Research,* 1976, *46,* 443–462.

Maehr, M. Meaning and motivation: Toward a theory of personal investment. In R. Ames & C. Ames (Eds.), *Research on motivation in education: Student motivation* (Vol. 1). New York: Academic Press, 1984.

Michaels, J. Classroom reward structures and academic performance. *Review of Educational Research,* 1977, *47,* 87–99.

Nelson, L., & Kagan, S. Competition: The star-spangled scramble. *Psychology Today,* 1972, September, 58–91.

Nicholls, J. Causal attributions and other achievement-related cognitions: Effects of task outcome, attainment value, and sex. *Journal of Personality and Social Psychology,* 1975, *31,* 379-389.

Nicholls, J. Quality and equality in intellectual development: The role of motivation in education. *American Psychologist,* 1979, *34,* 1071-1084.

Nicholls, J. Motivation theory and its applications to education. In S. Paris, G. Olson, & H. Stevenson (Eds.), *Learning and motivation in the classroom.* Hillsdale, NJ.: Lawrence Erlbaum Associates, 1983.

Pepitone, E. *Children in cooperation and competition: Toward a developmental social psychology.* Lexington, MA: Heath, 1980.

Rosenholtz, S., & Simpson, C. The formation of ability conceptions: Developmental trend or social construction? Paper presented at the American Educational Research Association annual meeting, Montreal, 1983.

Slavin, R. Classroom reward structure: Analytical and practical review. *Review of Educational Research,* 1977, *47,* 633-650.

Weiner, B. A theory of motivation for some classroom experience. *Journal of Educational Psychology,* 1979, *71,* 3-25.

13 Anatomy of Failure-Induced Anxiety: The Role of Cognitive Mediators

Martin V. Covington
University of California, Berkeley

Three major research foci can be discerned from the voluminous literature on test anxiety which, in effect, track the temporal course of anxiety in its various relationships to achievement behavior, from the test-preparation phase, to test-taking itself, and finally to the inevitable self-evaluative reactions to test outcome. As to the first of these emphases, it is clear that anxiety predates the event of test-taking as reflected in the amount, timing, and quality of test preparation (Becker, 1982). For example, Culler & Holahan (1980) propose a learning deficit model suggesting that high-anxious individuals have ineffectual study habits which lead to deficiencies in test preparation such that these students exhibit less task involvement despite describing themselves as spending more time studying than do low-anxious students (Vagt & Kühn, 1976), and often appear to sabotage their own study efforts through procrastination and other self-defeating strategies (Beery, 1975). As to the second focus, the bulk of research over the years has centered on the effects of anxiety on performance in the immediate testing situation (for a review, see Tryon, 1980), and more recently on the mechanisms by which anxiety arousal interferes with achievement (Hagtvet, 1983; Liebert & Morris, 1967; Sarason, 1978; Wine, 1971, 1980). Generally speaking, the deficiencies underlying poor achievement among high test-anxious students appear to be attentional in nature. These individuals are easily diverted from a task orientation and are prone to self preoccupation and worry (Marlett & Watson, 1968; Stephan, Fischer, & Stein, 1983). For example, test-anxious persons worry about their performance, speculate about how well others are doing, and wonder if they are falling behind, all to the neglect of the task at hand. The third and least studied focus concerns the nature and causes of anxiety elicited by test-failure feedback. While little is known about such anxiety re-actions, we suspect that they may be associated with self-perceptions of ina-bility that invariably accompany failure (Covington & Omelich, 1982a).

In reviewing these accumulated findings, it seems reasonable to conclude that anxiety as a generic phenomenon is manifest in different ways as the hap-less learner moves from one phase of the achievement cycle to the next, with the role of anxiety — and perhaps its very nature — changing with respect to those factors that sustain and mediate it, and to the behaviors that it in turn initiates. If this observation is essentially correct, then an important, if not overarching question becomes, "What is the ultimate nature and source of test anxiety?"; or stated differently, "What is it about the achievement process itself that elicits anxiety in the first place, causing maladaptive study patterns, disruption of a task orientation, and finally acute distress following the disclosure of test failure?" If, as many observers contend (e.g., Covington, 1983; Liebert & Morris, 1967; Schwarzer & Cherkes-Julkowski, 1982; Spielberger, 1972, 1975), anxiety is basically a reaction to and an antici-pation of failure, then, heuristically, the third research focus on anxiety reac-tions following failure would seem a most appropriate starting point to ex-plore these questions. Specifically, because the individual is confronted directly with failure, it is here that the correlates, mediators, and conse-quences of anxiety should be most available to observation. In effect, the test-preparation and test-taking aspects of the anxiety experience become subordinated to failure-arousal mechanisms, with maladaptive study pat-terns being largely the result of anticipating failure and task disruption repre-senting a tangible, behavioral manifestation of the threat of failure.

But, then, what is the nature of the threat of failure, and *how* and *why* does it elicit anxiety? To anticipate some answers, one body of thought suggests that emotional disruption following test failure arises primarily from a recog-nition that try as one might, outcomes are seen as beyond the control of all in-dividuals. This interpretation faults the unresponsiveness and inequities of the achievement setting. By contrast, an equally well-documented position holds that failure-induced anxiety results from the realization that the indi-vidual is personally incompetent to influence events, thereby focusing on self-perceived limitations of the learner as the main source of achievement anxiety. In effect, both explanations stress a sense of powerlessness, but from different sources. The first view places emphasis on universal helplessness, that is, situations in which no one has control; whereas the second view em-phasizes personal, individual limitations (Abramson, Seligman, & Teasdale, 1978).

It is likely that the distinction between universal uncontrollability and per-sonal inadequacy lies at the heart of questions regarding the ultimate nature of test anxiety and why it permeates achievement dynamics. Consequently, this distinction is the major focus of the present study, which involves an analysis of the causes of anxiety reactions following achievement failure. More specifically, the purpose is three-fold: (1) to explore the extent to which test anxiety involves an undifferentiated reaction of individuals to achievement failure as contrasted to a more differential reaction mediated by self cognitions that can vary depending on circumstances; (2) to consider which specific self-cognitions, either those related to perceived uncontrollability or to a sense of personal incompetency, are involved and their relative importance in causing anxiety reactions; and (3) to explore the question of whether or not these cognitive mechanisms differ among high-anxious and low-anxious students.

Anxiety as an Undifferentiated Emotion

To what extent are anxiety reactions produced simply by the occurrence of test failure as a cognitively undifferentiated emotion, and thus possibly reflect a trait-like disposition? Evidence concerning the possibility that achievement anxiety is merely a global, diffused reaction to *any* failure irrespective of circumstances is sparse, and what data exist come largely from a series of studies that relate various achievement-linked emotions to success and failure outcomes (Weiner, Russell, & Lerman, 1978, 1979). This research suggests that certain emotional reactions to success and failure, such as happiness/unhappiness, occur independent of any particular internal, causal attributions that may be made by the learner and hence have been dubbed, "outcome-independent emotions." In contrast, other achievement affect, primarily pride, guilt, and shame, depend heavily on achievement circumstances. Pride is maximized when success occurs through a combination of high effort and ability (Covington & Omelich, 1979c), whereas shame and guilt intensify as self ascriptions to low ability and to low effort increase, respectively (Covington & Omelich, 1979b, 1984; Covington, Spratt, & Omelich, 1980; Nicholls, 1976; Weiner & Kukla, 1970). Unfortunately, little of this research has focused on anxiety reactions per se. Thus, the more refined research question becomes, "Are anxiety reactions to failure primarily outcome-independent, and conditioned largely by predispositions to anxiety; or are they in part the product of cognitive mediators that change with achievement circumstances?" The present research addresses these questions.

Anxiety and Self Cognitions

Assuming that anxiety reactions to test failure are mediated in part by self-generated cognitions, then the second main inquiry involves identifying these cognitions and their relative importance as causal agents. As already anticipated, two general explanations have been offered for the causes of achievement distress.

Effort-Linked Affect. One possibility is that anxiety reactions are a product of a sense of universal powerlessness. There is a substantial body of evidence suggesting that negative affect, especially a sense of despair, is largely the result of a sense of futility whenever outcomes appear independent of one's actions or efforts (for a review, see Coyne & Gotlib, in press). This emphasis on distress as a product of an effort/outcome noncontingency has its clearest expression in the learned helplessness model as it applies to clinical depression (Seligman, 1975). In its earliest form, this model proposed that affective and behavioral manifestations of depression (e.g., anxiety, despair, inaction) were the result of the individual having learned that events (rewards, punishment) cannot be controlled as when, say, a student studies hard on one occasion and still fails, whereas at another time, little or no effort is rewarded by success. Here, the culprit is assumed to be the vagaries of achievement testing, not personal limitations. Stated in attributional terms, ascriptions to *high* effort following failure lead to lowered expectations of future success, which in turn cause distress, anxiety, and depression. In contrast, ascriptions to *low* effort following failure should encourage optimism regarding future success, and thereby forestall distress, because degree of task controllability cannot be evaluated unless one attempts seriously to influence events. These hypothesized effort/affect linkages and their directions of influence are presented in Figure 13.1a.

We know that variations in effort level (either high or low) influence subjective estimates of future success in ways consistent with these predictions (Fontaine, 1974; Valle, 1976). However, we are still essentially uninformed regarding the nature and strength of these linkages as they apply to anxiety reactions following failure.

Ability-Linked Affect. A different body of research literature suggests that achievement distress, especially self-blame, humiliation, and self-derogation, follow from a realization that the individual is personally unable to manage events that are controllable by others. This position rests on the well-documented observation that individuals accept personal responsibility for their failure to achieve desired goals and tend to interpret such failures as the result of personal defects, especially low ability (Beck, 1967; Lichtenberg, 1957; Wortman & Brehm, 1975). Thus, by this reasoning, self-disclosure of incompetency becomes a potent trigger for achievement distress. Moreover, ascriptions to inability are also likely to dampen one's expectations for future success (Covington & Omelich, 1981), thereby compounding distress at failure. Finally, another affective factor, that of humiliation, is likely to be implicated in this process. Humiliation has been shown to be an ability-linked reaction to failure (Covington & Omelich, 1984) and is therefore also likely to mediate the hypothesized ability demotion/anxiety axis. Overall, then, the logic of this position argues that to the degree failure causes a diminution in

a.) EFFORT-LINKED

Effort ⟶ Future expectancy ⟶ Anxiety

b.) ABILITY-LINKED

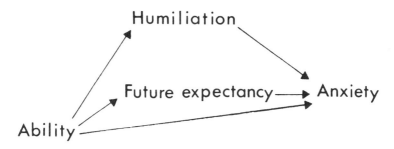

FIG. 13.1.   Hypothesized causal linkages in failure-induced anxiety.

ability ascriptions, failure leads to distress both directly (low ability → distress) and indirectly through lowered future expectations (low ability → expectancy → distress) as well as through humiliation (low ability → humiliation → distress). These various linkages associated with ability demotion and their direction of influence on achievement anxiety are presented in Figure 13.1b. Note that both the effort-linked, powerlessness interpretation of achievement distress and the ability-linked view share a common mediator in the form of expectations for future success, and that ascriptions to low effort and to low ability work in essentially opposite ways: attributions to low effort increase future optimism, whereas attributions to low ability dampen it.

Evidence on the perceived centrality of ability ascriptions as causes of achievement affect, especially pride, shame, and humiliation, come largely from research generated under the self-worth theory of achievement motivation (Beery, 1975; Covington & Beery, 1976). The basic assumption of this model is that achievement behavior is largely the result of the learner's efforts to protect his or her sense of personal esteem because in our society self-worth depends heavily on one's accomplishments and on one's ability to achieve competitively. Indeed, the perceived instrumental value of ability in success makes the maintenance of a sense of competency of the highest priority — sometimes even higher than achievement itself — as when individuals handicap themselves by studying only at the last minute. Failure following procrastination permits explanations of little or ineffectual effort, not low ability, and if procrastinators succeed they will appear highly able because they achieved with so little effort.

Research using different methodologies — ranging from multivariate analyses of actual classroom achievement, to student role-playing paradigms, and to achievement preference studies — provide a broad empirical consensus (for review, see Covington & Omelich, 1984). Self-perception of ability is the dominant mediating cognition in competitively-oriented achievement settings among adults and older students. These individuals prefer to achieve via ability, not effort (Covington & Omelich, 1979c; Nicholls, 1976; Sohn, 1977). Moreover, variations in self-perceived ability account for the bulk of explained variance in pride reactions in success (Covington & Omelich, 1979c) and in humiliation reactions to failure (Covington & Omelich, 1979a, 1979b, 1982b). Finally, ability is seen as a major contributor to feelings of self-regard, especially when ability is perceived as instrumental to subsequent achievement (Covington & Omelich, 1984, 1982c).

Although the central role of ability as a causal agent is well understood for some achievement affect, once again, as in the case of the literature on effort cognitions, we lack firm evidence on how these ability dynamics apply to anxiety reactions, although there is some preliminary evidence that anxiety may behave similarly to shame in that both are mediated by attributions to incompetency (Covington & Omelich, 1982c; Schwarzer & Cherkes-Julkowski, 1982). However, while it is reasonable to suppose the importance of a low-ability linkage, no research has yet been conducted that tracks the various indirect pathways via expectation and humiliation, nor is there any analysis of the *relative* importance of effort and ability cognitions in triggering anxiety reactions to failure. The present research provides evidence on these points.

Individual Differences and Causal Mechanisms

A third related inquiry concerns the question of whether or not the cognitive mechanisms that underlie failure-induced anxiety differ for high-anxious and for low-anxious students. This query is best understood in terms of a level/process distinction (Covington, 1983b). High-anxious and low-anxious individuals differ, of course, by definition, in level or degree of anxiety proneness, and also presumably in the extent to which they experience anxiety reactions following failure. Yet, to what degree are the mechanisms (processes) by which anxiety proneness gets translated into distress the same or different for these students? For example, it may be (Covington & Omelich,

1981) that perceptions of inability play a more important role in causing humiliation at failure for high-anxious than for low-anxious students (process difference). Concommitantly, high-anxious students may also perceive themselves as less able (level difference). Thus, it follows from this level × process analysis that high-anxious students are placed in double jeopardy by failure, that is, not only may they be less sure of their capabilities to begin with, but also for them, inability cognitions may exercise greater weight as a causal factor in anxiety reactions.

METHOD

Subjects and Procedures

Subjects were 114 undergraduates enrolled in an introductory psychology course at the University of California, Berkeley. Following a regular midterm examination which featured an objective multiple-choice format, students were given grade-equivalent feedback (e.g., A, B, C) as well as the number of items correct. Students were then asked to rate the degee to which they were satisfied or dissatisfied with their performance on a Likert-type scale with a neutral point and anchored at the extremes (5 = very satisfied; − 5 = very dissatisfied). The present sample consisted of those subjects who rated their performance as unsatisfactory to one degree or another. These students also made several additional ratings:

Postdictive Attributions.   Students indicated the extent to which their disappointing performance was due to a lack of ability or to a lack of effort (insufficient study) using a 7-point scale (1 = not at all a cause; 7 = very much a cause) that is consistent with a widely-used format in attribution research (e.g., Covington & Omelich, 1979a, 1979b; Feather & Simon, 1971). Care must be exercised in interpreting the direction and meaning of relationships among variables gathered in this manner. Subjects rated the extent (from high to low) to which they ascribed attributions either to low effort or to low ability. Thus, a significant positive relationship between, say, effort ascriptions and probability of future success means that the more an individual attributed failure to low effort, the higher his or her expectations were for future success.

Attributions to bad luck and task difficulty were not gathered since they are irrelevant to the present theoretical concerns, and have been shown to play little or no role as mediators of failure affect in actual classrooms where comparison tasks are typically unavailable (Covington & Omelich, 1979a; 1981).

Postdictive Reactions.   Students also judged degree of humiliation experienced, anxiety over their disappointing performance, and the subjective likelihood of achieving success on similar examinations in the future, all on a 7-point scale (1 = not at all; 7 = very much).

Individual Difference Measure.   Prior to the first lecture period all students were administered a precourse questionnaire that included the Debilitating Anxiety subscale of the Achievement Anxiety Test (AAT) (Alpert & Haber, 1960).

Design and Analysis of Data

The method chosen for analyzing this set of non-manipulated variables, and for testing the hypothesized causal linkages and their relative importance was path analysis (Duncan, 1966; Heise, 1975). The assumptions of path analysis permit a causal interpretation of correlational data as long as they are generated from a well specified model of behavior that assumes at least a weak causal ordering among the variables. Questions regarding the similarity of causal dynamics for students differing in degree of initial test anxiety were assessed by comparing the differences in magnitude of regression slopes for each anxiety group.

RESULTS

The means, standard deviations, and intercorrelations among the variables gathered are presented in Table 13.1. No assumptions are made in this model regarding the causal reciprocity between same level variables. In path analytic terms, any observed residual covariation (e.g., $-.267$ between humiliation and future expectations for success) is assumed to be noncausal and may originate from a common dependency on antecedent variables or on variables outside the model.

Figure 13.2 presents the results of the total path analysis. The values associated with unidirectional arrows are path (standardized regression) coefficients (P). Epsilon $[E = (1 - R^2)^{1/2}]$ represents the path coefficient value of all sources of variation not specified by the model. Preliminary path analyses by sex produced virtually identical results, hence male and female data are combined in this analysis. These null results point to the relatively modest role played by sex when a number of achievement-related variables are allowed to vary naturally.

Table 13.2 presents the results of decomposing the relationship between AAT and anxiety reactions following failure into direct and indirect effects. Indirect effects indicate the degree to which a change in an independent, ante-

TABLE 13.1

Means, Standard Deviations, & Product-Moment Correlations for Variables in
Failure-induced Anxiety (N = 114)

Variable	AAT	Low Effort	Low Ability	Humil-iation	Probability of Success	Experienced Anxiety
AAT	—	−.070	.219*	.270*	−.120	.253*
Low Effort		—	.048 (.063)[a]	.082	.134	−.063
Low Ability			—	.603*	−.369*	.484*
Humiliation				—	−.271* (−.267)[a]	.534*
Probability of Success					—	−.147
M	28.62	3.29	2.98	2.85	4.47	4.20
SD	6.27	1.90	1.41	1.69	1.67	1.75

[a]Coefficient of residual covariation
*$p < .05$.

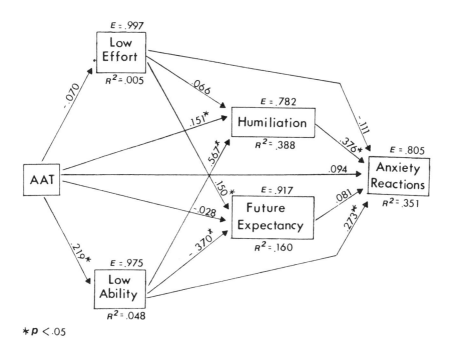

$\star p < .05$

FIG. 13.2. Path diagram of the effects of AAT, causal attributions, expectancy, and humiliation on failure-induced anxiety.

255

TABLE 13.2
Decomposition of Zero-Order Correlation of AAT with
Anxiety Reactions

Relationship	Anxiety Reactions
Zero-order correlation	.253*
Direct effect	.094
Total indirect effect	.160
Effort	.008
Ability	.060
Humiliation	.057
Expectancy	− .002
Effort and humiliation	− .002
Effort and expectancy	− .001
Ability and humiliation	.047
Ability and expectancy	− .007

*$p < .05$

cedent variable (AAT) influences an intervening variable (e.g., effort or ability cognitions) which in turn results in variations in the dependent variable of interest (anxiety reactions). They are estimated by summing the products of the path coefficients of all the paths that intervene. At present no significance tests are available for indirect effects except by evaluating the overall goodness of fit to the model.

Inspection of the initial entry in the first column of Table 13.2 indicates a significant zero-order correlation between AAT and anxiety reactions to failure of .253 ($p < .05$) that decomposes into a non-significant direct effect (AAT → anxiety) of .094, and into a total indirect influence on anxiety reactions from AAT mediated through all the various pathways of .160. The nominal impact of AAT on anxiety reactions, most of which are mediated by cognitions, suggests that anxiety reactions to failure may depend far less on individual differences in anxiety-proneness than has commonly been assumed. In contrast, the vast majority of explained variance was accounted for by cognitions and by cognitively-linked affect, both as conveyors of anxiety-proneness and also as substantial instigators of anxiety reactions in their own right.

Given this preliminary evidence for the importance of cognitions as mediators of anxiety reactions, we can now turn to the second main inquiry concerning the relative saliency of effort versus ability cognitions in this dynamic, and to a consideration of the importance of the various causal pathways they mediate. One approach is to compare the magnitude of those indirect linkages listed in Table 13.2 that involve effort and ability cognitions:

AAT → Effort → Anxiety.   The negligible value associated with the AAT → effort → anxiety linkage (.008; Table 13.2) represented only 1% of the total indirect effect of all mediators on anxiety reactions. Thus, perceived effort level as mediator of AAT made only a marginal contribution to subsequent anxiety reactions. Moreover, as can be seen from Figure 13.2, the direct influence of effort cognitions on anxiety reactions, independent of AAT dispositions (effort → anxiety), was nonsignificant as well ($P = -.111$, $p > .05$). Other attempts to establish that anxiety-prone individuals tend to ascribe failure to low effort have also met with disappointment (e.g., Weiner, Frieze, Kukla, Reed, Rest, & Rosenbaum, 1971; Weiner & Kukla, 1970; Weiner & Potepan, 1970). Indeed, some evidence suggests that far from being disengaged, anxious students may actually study more than low-anxious students, but less efficiently (Goldman, Hudson, & Daharsh, 1973). The mechanisms responsible for degree and quality of effort expenditure among both high- and low-anxious individuals have yet to be the subject of systematic study.

We note that all other indirect linkages involving effort (Table 13.2) were also negligible. This is not surprising in the case of the AAT → effort → humiliation → anxiety pathway ($-.002$) since it has been shown elsewhere (Covington & Omelich, 1984) that low effort elicits guilt-like reactions associated with not trying rather than with humiliation, an emotion more closely linked to disclosure of incompetency. By contrast, however, what *is* surprising was the failure to confirm the presence of an effort/outcome noncontingency mechanism related to learned helplessness phenomena (AAT → effort → expectancy → anxiety: Table 13.2; $-.001$). Moreover, leaving AAT aside, Figure 13.2 indicates that expectations of future success did not depend significantly on variations in effort expenditure ($P = .150$, $p < .10$) such that a combination of high effort and failure would trigger low expectations. Nor did anxiety reactions in turn depend on variations in future expectations (Fig. 13.2; $P = .081$, $p > .05$). Thus, none of the pathways implied in the effort-linked explanation for distress were substantiated, at least in the case of anxiety reactions. In summary, pessimism about attaining one's future goals appears not to be an important source of anxiety following test failure. What is important, by contrast, are self-cognitions of inability, a point to which we now turn.

AAT → Ability → Anxiety.   Of the two cognitions — effort and ability — ability was by far the more powerful mediating contributor to anxiety reactions. We note from Figure 13.2 that high-anxious students tend to attribute their failures to low ability ($P = .219$, p < .05), a cognition that in turn triggered anxiety reactions ($P = .273$, p < .05). This AAT → ability → anxiety linkage accounted for most of the total indirect effect (Table 13.2; .060). Also, as a co-mediator with humiliation (AAT → ability → humiliation → distress) ability also exerted an additional and substantial impact on anxiety reactions (.047). The relative strength of this particular linkage was expected since, as mentioned earlier, humiliation is an ability-linked affect triggered exclusively by the disclosure of incompetency (Covington & Omelich, 1984). Indeed, humiliation itself, regardless of ability attributions, was a substantial mediator of anxiety, accounting for the remainder of the indirect effect. Finally, regarding the ability → anxiety linkage via expectancy, we note in Table 13.2, a negligible impact since, as already discussed, expectancies exert a non-significant influence on anxiety reactions. The presence of these several substantial indirect linkages involving ability ascriptions supports the self-worth position regarding the centrality of ability cognitions in achievement dynamics.

Now consider the third inquiry regarding individual differences in these anxiety dynamics. Specifically, we inquire whether or not the mechanisms that underlie failure-induced anxiety are different for high-anxious and low-anxious students. As to *level* differences among the causal variables of interest, high-anxious and low-anxious subjects did not differ significantly in the degree to which they attributed failure either to low effort or to low ability, nor did they differ in their expectations for future success, although the trends were in the expected directions with high-anxious students anticipating future failure to a greater degree (d = .36, p < .275) and more likely to attribute failure to low ability (d = .36, p < .178). Degree of humiliation experienced was significantly greater among high-anxious students (d = .888, p < .004) as was magnitude of anxiety reaction (d = .65, p < .05). As to *process* differences, the present path analysis (Fig. 13.2) was recalculated separately for both high-anxious and low-anxious subjects. Students were assigned to either high-anxious or low-anxious categories on the basis of a median split in the AAT distribution. Comparison of the resulting regression slopes for all 13 possible pathways reveals no significant differences. We can therefore conclude that the mechanisms that evoke anxiety reactions to failure are similar for all individuals, irrespective of initial differences in proneness to disabling anxiety.

DISCUSSION

The present data support the view that anxiety reactions to failure are caused largely by a diminution in one's sense of competency. This conclusion holds implications both for learned helplessness theory, specifically, and for the nature of achievement anxiety, generally.

First, consider learned helplessness phenomena. The present data help re-solve an apparent contradiction in the original learned helplessness paradigm (effort/outcome noncontingency) whose logic required that individuals ex-press despair at an event (e.g., failure) over which they perceived themselves as having little, if any, control. This formulation appears to violate common sense. Why, as Abramson and Sackeim (1977) asked, should a person feel re-sponsible for events beyond their influence? This issue can now be resolved at an empirical level. We now know that negative affect such as anxiety — and most likely despair and helplessness as well — are not so much reactions to uncontrollable events as they are the result of a realization that the individual is personally incompetent to alter events. In this connection, it is well known that individuals blame themselves for personal inadequacies such as insuffi-cient ability even though, logically speaking, they cannot be faulted (Lichtenberg, 1975). Thus, the issue is not lack of control per se, but rather the *source* of uncontrollability: whether failure is perceived as caused by per-sonal deficiencies or by environmental unresponsiveness. This is precisely why individuals often attempt to avoid personal responsibility for their fail-ures, and the anxiety that follows, by resorting to self-handicapping tactics such as procrastination or blaming others (Birney, Burdick, & Teevan, 1969). This interpretation is entirely compatible with the reformulated model of learned helplessness (Abramson, Seligman & Teasdale, 1978; which stresses a distinction between universal helplessness (when no one can be expected to succeed) and personal helplessness (where events are controllable but some individuals perceived themselves as inadequate to the task). According to this reformulation, personal helplessness arises out of an internalization of stable causes following failure (in attributional terms, low ability) that leads to a va-riety of negative behaviors such as indifference to learning, emotional de-spondency, and low self-esteem. Prior to the present research, little evidence was available regarding the causal role of ability ascriptions in influencing ex-pectations and achievement affect within this reformulated paradigm. Some of the most relevant earlier work (Klein, Fencil-Morse, & Seligman, 1976; Tennen & Eller, 1977) assumed that subjects would infer a state of low ability from experiment-induced failures at a simple task. Although subsequent per-formance was lowered following this manipulation, changes in ability self-ascriptions as causal agents could only be inferred.

From the larger perspective of self-worth theory, which stresses the role of ability cognitions in achievement dynamics, learned helplessness represents the final step in a process of demoralization in which individuals become *fail-ure accepting* after unsuccessful efforts to evade the implications of repeated failure that they lack ability (Covington & Omelich, 1981, 1984). The concep-tual formulations of Schwarzer and his colleagues (Schwarzer, Jerusalem, & Stiksrud, 1984) are consistent with this interpretation and with the present findings. They propose that a first failure, especially if unexpected, repre-sents a challenge to be overcome. However, subsequent failures, particularly as they become anticipated, elicit anxiety caused by implicit implications of low ability, until finally, the individual experiences a total loss of personal control that leads to helplessness and depression.

The second main implication of the current study concerns the essential nature of the achievement process and of test anxiety. These data corroborate an emerging view that achievement behavior, and in particular its motivational aspects, are mediated largely by self-cognitions of ability. Thus, to answer the questions posed earlier regarding what is so threatening about the achievement process, we can now say with some assurance that the threat emanates from risking failure with its implications for low ability. Moreover, the data also suggest that this dominant ability-diminution mechanism is common to all individuals, and that evaluative anxiety can be most properly viewed as largely the product of certain inevitable achievement events that befall all learners sooner or later (i.e., failure) rather than representing soleley a situation-specific trait-like property of certain individuals. Naturally, such an observation can be sustained only in the abstract since repeated failure, no matter what its interpretation, will eventually produce a generalized, stable fear of all achievement activities.

Seen in this broader context, anxiety reactions are the natural consequence of a threat to a sense of worth and to a positive self-definition that depends heavily on the maintenance of a reputation for competency. By this reasoning, the upcoming school test is perceived by many students as a measure of their ability to achieve competitively, and hence a clear indication of their worth. When one's subjective estimates of failure are high, maladaptive study patterns are often the result. This occurs not only because anxiety directly impairs rational, decision-making functions (Covington, 1983a), but also because the threat of failure promotes seemingly irrational study strategies, for defensive purposes (i.e., procrastination). From this perspective, anxiety, shame, and humiliation, as well as defensive maneuvering are all manifestations of a single threat to self worth, with anxiety acting variously as an initiator, amplifier, and sustainer of these negative processes.

REFERENCES

Abramson, L. Y., & Sackeim, H. A. A paradox in depression: Uncontrollability and self-blame. *Psychological Bulletin,* 1977, *84,* 838–851.

Abramson, L. Y., Seligman, M. E. P., & Teasdale, J. D. Learned helplessness in humans: Critique and reformulation. *Journal of Abnormal Psychology,* 1978, *87,* 49–74.

Alpert, R., & Haber, R. N. Anxiety in academic achievement situations. *Journal of Abnormal and Social Psychology,* 1960, *61,* 207–215.

Beck, A. T. *Depression: Clinical, experimental, and theoretical aspects.* New York: Harper & Row, 1967.

Becker, P. Towards a process analysis of test anxiety: Some theoretical and methodological observations. In R. Schwarzer, H. van der Ploeg, & C. D. Spielberger (Eds.), *Advances in test anxiety research* (Vol. 1). Lisse/Hillsdale, NJ: Swets & Zeitlinger/Erlbaum, 1982.

Beery, R. G. Fear of failure in the student experience. *Personnel and Guidance Journal,* 1975, *54,* 190–203.

Birney, R. C., Burdick, H., & Teevan, R. C. *Fear of failure.* New York: Van Nostrand, 1969.

Covington, M. V. Anxiety, task difficulty and childhood problem solving: A self-worth interpretation. In H. M. van der Ploeg, R. Schwarzer, & C. D. Spielberger (Eds.), *Advances in test anxiety research* (Vol. 2). Lisse/Hillsdale, NJ: Swets & Zeitlnger/Erlbaum, 1983. (a)

Covington, M. V. Motivated cognitions. In S. G. Paris, G. M. Olson, & H. W. Stevenson (Eds.), *Learning and motivation in the classroom.* Lawrence Erlbaum Associates, 1983. (b)

Covington, M. V. Anxiety management via problem-solution instruction. In H. van der Ploeg, R. Schwarzer, & C. Speilberger (Eds.), *Advances in test anxiety research* (Vol. 3). Lisse/Hillsdale, NJ: Swets & Zeitlinger/Erlbaum, 1984.

Covington, M. V., & Beery, R. *Self-worth and school learning.* New York: Holt, Rinehart & Winston, 1976.

Covington, M. V., & Omelich, C. L. Are causal attributions causal? A path analysis of the cognitive model of achievement motivation. *Journal of Personality and Social Psychology,* 1979, *37,* 1487–1504. (a)

Covington, M. V., & Omelich, C. L. Effort: The double-edged sword in school achievement. *Journal of Educational Psychology,* 1979, *71,* 169–182. (b)

Covington, M. V., & Omelich, C. L. It's best to be able and virtuous too: Student and teacher evaluative responses to successful effort. *Journal of Educational Psychology,* 1979, *71,* 688–700. (c)

Covington, M. V., & Omelich, C. L. As failures mount: Affective and cognitive consequences of ability demotion in the classroom. *Journal of Educational Psychology,* 1981, *73,* 796–808.

Covington, M. V., & Omelich, C. L. Achievement anxiety, performance and behavioral instruction: A cost/benefits analysis. In R. Schwarzer, H. van der Ploeg, & C. Spielberger (Eds.), *Advances in test anxiety research* (Vol. 1). Lisse/Hillsdale, NJ: Swets & Zeitlinger/Erlbaum, 1982. (a)

Covington, M. V., & Omelich, C. L. *The conflicting role of effort in student affective reactions to failure.* Unpublished manuscript, University of California, Berkeley, 1982. (b)

Covington, M. V., & Omelich, C. L. *The role of effort expenditure, ability inferences and achievement outcome in determining self worth.* Unpublished manuscript, University of California, Berkeley, 1982. (c)

Covington, M. V., & Omelich, C. L. Controversies or Consistencies: A reply to Brown and Weiner. *Journal of Educational Psychology,* 1984, *76,* 159–168.

Covington, M. V., Spratt, M. F., & Omelich, C. L. Is effort enough or does diligence count too? Student and teacher reactions to effort stability in failure. *Journal of Educational Psychology,* 1980, *72,* 717–729.

Coyne, J. C., & Gotlib, I. H. The role of cognition in depression: A critical appraisal. *Psychological Bulletin,* in press.

Culler, R. E., & Holahan, C. J. Test anxiety and academic performance: The effects of study-related behaviors. *Journal of Educational Psychology,* 1980, *73,* 816–824.

Duncan, O. D. Path analysis: Sociological examples. *American Journal of Sociology,* 1966, *72,* 1–16.

Feather, N. T., & Simon, J. G. Causal attributions for success and failure in relation to expectations of success based upon selective or manipulative control. *Journal of Personality,* 1971, *39,* 528–41.

Fontaine, G. Social comparison and some determinants of expected personal control and expected performance in a novel task situation. *Journal of Personality and Social Psychology,* 1974, *29,* 487–496.

Goldman, R., Hudson, D., & Daharsh, B. Self-estimated task persistence as a nonlinear predictor of college success. *Journal of Educational Psychology,* 1973, *65,* 216–221.

Hagtvet, K. A. A constant validation study of test anxiety: A discriminant validation of fear of failure, worry and emotionality. In H. M. van der Ploeg, R. Schwarzer, & C. D. Speilberger (Eds.), *Advances in test anxiety research* (Vol. 2). Lisse/Hillsdale, NJ: Swets & Zeitlinger/ Erlbaum, 1983.

Heise, D. R. *Causal analysis.* New York: Wiley, 1975.

Klein, D. C., Fencil-Morse, E., & Seligman, M. E. P. Learned helplessnes, depression, and the attribution of failure. *Journal of Personality and Social Psychology,* 1976, *33,* 508–516.

Lichtenberg, P. A. A definition and analysis of depression. *Archives of Neurology and Psychiatry,* 1957, *77,* 519–527.

Liebert, R. M., & Morris, L. W. Cognitive and emotional components of test anxiety: A distinction and some initial data. *Psychological Reports,* 1967, *20,* 975–978.

Marlett, N. J., & Watson, D. Test anxiety and immediate or delayed feedback in a test-like avoidance task. *Journal of Personality and Social Psychology,* 1968, *8,* 200–203.

Nicholls, J. G. Effort is virtuous, but it's better to have ability: Evaluative responses to perceptions of effort and ability. *Journal of Research in Personality,* 1976, *10,* 306–315.

Sarason, I. G. The test anxiety scale: Concept and research. In C. D. Spielberger & I. G. Sarason (Eds.), *Stress and anxiety.* Washington, DC: Hemisphere, 1978.

Schwarzer, C., & Cherkes-Julkowski, M. Determinants of helplessness and test anxiety: A path analysis. In R. Schwarzer, H. van der Ploeg, & C. D. Spielberger (Eds.), *Advances in test anxiety research* (Vol. 1). Lisse/Hillsdale, NJ: Swets & Zeitlinger/Erlbaum, 1982.

Schwarzer, R., Jerusalem, M. & Stiksrud, H. A. The developmental relationship between test anxiety and helplessness. In H. M. van der Ploeg, R. Schwarzer, & C. D. Spielberger (Eds.), *Advances in test anxiety research* (Vol. 3). Lisse/Hillsdale, NJ: Swets & Zeitlinger/Erlbaum, 1984.

Seligman,, M. E. P. *Helplessness: On depression, development and death.* San Francisco: W. H. Freeman, 1975.

Sohn, D. Affect-generating powers of effort and ability self attributions of academic success and failure. *Journal of Educational Psychology,* 1977, *69,* 500–505.

Spielberger, C. D. Anxiety as an emotional state. In C. D. Spielberger (Ed.), *Anxiety: Current trends in theory and research* (Vol. 1). New York: Academic Press, 1972.

Spielberger, C. D. Anxiety: State-trait-process. In C. D. Spielberger & I. G. Sarason (Eds.), *Stress and anxiety* (Vol. 1). Washington, DC: Hemisphere/Wiley, 1975.

Stephan, E., Fischer, M., & Stein, F. Self-related cognitions in test anxiety research: An empirical study and critical conclusions. In H. M. van der Ploeg, R. Schwarzer, & C. D. Spielberger (Eds.), *Advances in test anxiety research* (Vol. 2) (pp. 45–66). Lisse/Hillsdale: Swets & Zeitlinger/Lawrence Erlbaum Associates, 1983.

Tennen, H., & Eller, S. J. Attributional components of learned helplessness and facilitation. *Journal of Personality and Social Psychology,* 1977, *35,* 265–271.

Tryon, G. S. The measurement and treatment of test anxiety. *Review of Educational Research,* 1980, *50,* 343–372.

Vagt, G., & Kühn, B. Zum Zusammenhang zwischen Ängstlichkeit und Schulleistung. Die Berücksichtigung des häuslichen Vorbereitung auf schulische Prüfungssituationen. *Zeitschrift für Experimentelle und Angewandte Psychologie,* 1976, *23,* 163–173.

Valle, V. A. *Attributions of stability as a mediator in the changing of expectation.* Unpublished doctoral dissertation, University of Pittsburgh, 1974. (Reported in B. Weiner, R. Nierenberg, & M. Goldstein. Social learning [locus of control] versus attributional [causal stability] interpretations of expectancy of success. *Journal of Personality,* 1976, *44,* 52–68.)

Weiner, B., Frieze, I., Kukla, A., Reed, L., Rest, S., & Rosenbaum, R. Perceiving the causes of success and failure. In E. E. Jones et al. (Eds.), *Attribution: Perceiving the causes of behavior.* Morristown, NJ: General Learning Press, 1971.

Weiner, B., & Kukla, A. An attributional analysis of achievement motivation. *Journal of Personality and Social Psychology,* 1970, *15,* 1–20.

Weiner, B., & Potepan, P. A. Personality characteristics and effective reactions toward exams of superior and failing college students. *Journal of Educational Psychology,* 1970, *61,* 144–151.

Weiner, B., Russell, D., & Lerman, D. Affective consequences of causal ascriptions. In J. H. Harvey, W. J. Ickes, & R. F. Kidd (Eds.), *New directions in attribution research* (Vol. 2). Hillsdale, NJ: Lawrence Erlbaum Associates, 1978.

Weiner, B., Russell, D., & Lerman, D. The cognition-emotion process in achievement-related contexts. *Journal of Personality and Social Psychology,* 1979, *37,* 1211–1220.

Wine, J. Test anxiety and direction of attention. *Psychological Bulletin,* 1971, *76,* 92–104.

Wine, J. D. Cognitive-attentional theory of test anxiety. In I. G. Sarason (Ed.), *Test anxiety: Theory, research, and application.* Hillsdale, NJ: Lawrence Erlbaum Associates, 1980.

Wortman, C. B., & Brehm, J. W. Responses to uncontrollable outcomes: An integration of reactance theory and the learned helplessness model. In L. Berkowitz (Ed.), *Advances in experimental social psychology* (Vol. 8). New York: Academic Press, 1975.

14 Conceptions of Ability in Children and Adults

John G. Nicholls
Carolyn M. Jagacinski
Purdue University

Arden T. Miller
Morehead State University

Many theorists emphasize the importance of a sense of competence for effective personal functioning (Adler, 1912; Allport, 1961; deCharms, 1968; Deci, 1980; Smith, 1969; White, 1973). According to Allport (1961), for example, "It would be wrong to say that a need for competence is the simple and sovereign motive of life. It does, however, come as close as any . . ." (p. 214). Most empirical research on self-concept and self-esteem also embodies a belief in the significance of a positive appraisal of one's competence (Shrauger, 1975). We concur with this view, but in this chapter we show that there are age, situational, and individual differences in the way ability is inferred and conceived. For example, two individuals could gain similar scores on a measure of perceived ability, but have used different rules of inference to have formed this evaluation. They could also conceive of ability in different ways. That is to say, if we could get them to define what they mean by ability, they could give different definitions. Further, we show that these differences have significant consequences for affective or evaluative responses and for overt behavior.

DEVELOPMENT

The development of the concept of ability can be seen as a process of differentiation of the concept of ability from other achievement-related concepts

(Nicholls & Miller, 1984a). Specifically, in young children the concepts of task difficulty, luck, and effort are imperfectly differentiated from the concept of ability. For young children, the statements "That was easy," "I was lucky," and "I tried hard" do not have clearly different meanings from "I am smart." For adults, however, these statements usually have distinctly different meanings. In other words, if we could get them to give definitions of the concept of ability, we would find that adults and children give different definitions.

As Piaget discovered, asking children to define or explain the meaning of their concepts is a relatively ineffective way of studying these concepts. To overcome the problems with this clinical interview method, he developed the method of critical exploration, or the revised clinical method. We adopted this approach in which children are presented with concrete problem situations wherein it is possible to clearly establish whether or not mature concepts are present. It would not be advisable, for example, to present children with information indicating that someone tried very hard and got eight items of a test correct, and attempt by questioning to discern their concepts of effort and ability. This is because, for adults, such information is ambiguous. It does not enable us to make a precise ability judgment. We need to know how many items of the same test the individual's peers got right and whether they also tried hard before we can make an adequate judgment of the person's ability. To establish whether children's conceptions differ from those of adults, we must present them with problems that clearly require mature concepts and, thus, enable us to distinguish mature from less mature concepts.

Secondly, by varying stimuli and questions, it should be possible to clarify the meaning of children's responses. For example, because in initial interviews young children appeared to identify ability with effort they were presented with a further situation in which a child who worked harder than another scored less than the other (Nicholls, 1978). Questions were then presented to confront children with the logical implications of their initial responses — to clarify the meaning of these responses and to see if children are responsive to contradictions in their initial positions. This method is intended to avoid imposing adult meanings on children and to ensure that they are not taught to respond maturely but do display their fullest possible understanding.

Using this approach we have found age-related changes in children's conceptions (or implicit definitions) of ability, effort, task difficulty, and luck and associated changes in the way ability is inferred. These changes are summarized in Table 14.1. Evidence that different conceptions are associated with differences in evaluative judgments and overt behavior supports the validity of our assessment methods.

TABLE 14.1
Summary of Levels of Differentiation of the Concept of Ability from the Concepts of Difficulty, Luck, and Effort

Difficulty	*Luck*	*Effort*
1. Ego-centric: Own expectations of success the basis for judging task difficulty and ability indicated by outcomes.		
2. Objective: Properties of tasks (complexity) the basis for judging difficulty and ability indicated by outcomes.	1. Tasks not distinguished in terms of luck vs. skill. Visible complexity the basis for judging difficulty — luck tasks easier.	1. Effort or outcome is ability. Higher effort means higher ability. Effort and outcomes not seen as cause and effect.
3. Normative: Task difficulty and ability judged in relation to the performance of others. Tasks that few can do are hard and success on these indicates high ability.	2. Effort expected to improve performance on luck and skill tasks but more on skill.	2. Effort is the cause of outcomes. Equal effort is expected to lead to equal outcomes.
	3. As for 2 with addition of explanation that luck tasks do not offer a way to affect outcomes.	3. Ability is partially differentiated (as a cause of outcomes) from effort.
	4. Luck and skill clearly differentiated. Effort expected to have no impact on luck outcomes.	4. Complete differentiation: Ability conceived as capacity which limits the effect of effort on performance.

Difficulty and Ability

At the lowest level of differentiation of the concepts of difficulty and ability (about 5 years), children do not recognize that the most difficult of a series of jigsaw puzzles requires the most ability. Nevertheless, when allowed to attempt puzzles, they show consistent individual differences in difficulty level chosen (Nicholls & Miller, 1983). It seems that these 5- and 6-year-olds respond to task difficulty simply in terms of their own expectancies of success. They do not explicitly recognize a continuum of objective difficulty cues and a correlated continuum of ability that these difficulty levels demand. Nevertheless, they prefer tasks that are, from their subjective perspective, challenging — tasks that are neither very easy nor very hard for them (Heckhausen, 1967, 1984; Nicholls & Miller, 1983; Schneider, 1984). We call this lowest level, the ego-centric conception of difficulty. At this level, task difficulty is not distinguished from subjective probability of success, and children feel competent if they improve in performance or master something that appeared challenging.

At the second level, objective difficulty, children recognize that jigsaw puzzles with more pieces are harder and require more ability. Thus, their judgments of ability and task difficulty are more independent of their own expectancies of success. Their conceptions of ability and difficulty are, however, still partly confounded. Mastery of tasks that are personally challenging still indicates competence.

When there are no objective difficulty cues (puzzles are in covered boxes) and difficulty is communicated with performance norms alone, children at the objective level do not realize that normatively more difficult tasks require more ability. Understanding that tasks which fewer others can do, are more difficult and demand more ability marks the normative conception of difficulty, which is attained at about age 7. At this level, difficulty can be judged entirely independently of one's own perceived ability or expectancies of success. For example, a task is hard if few others can do it regardless of whether we can do it or whether it is "easy" or "hard" *for us*. Thus, the concepts of difficulty and ability are differentiated from each other. At this level, children, like psychometricians from Binet on, realize that an adequate judgment of ability depends on comparison of one's raw score with the scores of one's peers. Competence is no longer indicated by mastery of tasks that are personally challenging. To be smart, you must be smarter than others. At the lower levels, children feel competent if they succeed on tasks that are challenging for them. They also seek such tasks (Elkind, 1971; White, 1959). When the normative conception is attained, tasks that children find challenging could also be seen as normatively easy. Success on such tasks does not indicate high ability and is not highly valued by children at the normative level. Unlike children at the lower levels, they recognize that success is more impressive on normatively more difficult tasks (Nicholls, 1978, 1980).

Not surprisingly, attainment of the normative conception is accompanied by changes in preferences for different levels of difficulty when difficulty is indicated by normative cues only. Less mature children prefer normatively easy tasks, presumably either because they tend to imitate successful children or because they realize that success is more likely on these tasks (where many peers succeed) but do not feel that such successes are unimpressive (Nicholls, 1980). Most children with the normative conception choose tasks on which low or intermediate proportions of their peers are said to succeed. Such choices presumably maximize the level of ability they expect to demonstrate and the sense of accomplishment they hope to feel. Also, unlike less mature children, they show consistency in difficulty preferences across normative and objective cues. Those who prefer normatively more difficult tasks than do others also prefer objectively more difficult tasks. This indicates that mature children use both normative and objective difficulty cues to judge their ability, whereas less mature children use only objective cues. (See also, Ruble, 1984).

The differentiation of the concepts of difficulty and ability brings with it a decline in the likelihood that one's ability judgments will be self-referenced. Improving a skill or mastering a task that is personally challenging is, for older children, often not enough to show that one is able. The development of the normative conception means, therefore, that children who realize they regularly perform below average will feel incompetent even though they may gain in mastery every school day. It is probably fortunate that this realization does not have its full impact immediately. Children retain somewhat unrealistically favorable views of their academic standing relative to that of others for some years after the normative conception is attained (Nicholls, 1978, 1979a; Stipek, 1984). Nevertheless, this development seems bound to have largely negative effects on feelings of personal adequacy and achievement behavior for those who perform or believe they perform below average. This could account for age increases in associations between self-concept and self-esteem scores and academic attainment (Bloom, 1976).

Although the concepts of difficulty and ability are differentiated by about 7 years, at this age ability is still far from completely differentiated from luck and effort. It is not until about 11 years, that ability, effort, and luck are clearly differentiated from one another.

Luck and Skill

Like Weisz (1984), we found children's understanding of luck outcomes continues to change up to about 12 years of age (Nicholls & Miller, in press). We questioned children about the performance of actors on two forms of Matching Familiar Figures Test items. In the skill form, each item required finding one of six figures (which differed in small details) that was identical to a standard figure. On the luck or guessing items, the standard figures were visible but the other six figures were on cards that were turned face down. Thus, one could only guess which card had the matching figure.

At the lowest level of differentiation (below about 7 years), children did not distinguish the tasks in luck or skill-related terms. To them, the skill task with many figures to be compared appeared to be more difficult or to demand more effort. These responses parallel those indicating the lower levels of understanding of difficulty, where difficulty is judged on the basis of the subjective sense of challenge tasks present.

At the two intermediate levels, children expected effort to increase the possibility of success more on skill than on luck items, but they still expected effort to affect outcomes on luck items. Only at the highest level (4) did children realize that there was no way that effort could affect one's chances of success on the guessing items. Only at this level were the concepts of skill (implying ability and effort) and luck clearly differentiated.

The above levels of conceptions of luck and skill, established by Piagetian interviews, were paralleled by specific causal judgments children made about outcomes on further luck and skill tasks. Children with less differentiated concepts saw both effort and luck as causing outcomes on both skill and luck tasks. Children with differentiated conceptions saw effort as implicated in outcomes on skill but not luck tasks and luck as implicated in outcomes on luck but not skill tasks. These data provide independent support for the view that young children do not see skill and luck as distinctly different causal domains.

The validity of our index of differentiation is further supported by evidence on persistence in the face of "failure" on a series of luck tasks. Children at levels 2 and 3 (who expect effort to have some effect on luck outcomes) persisted longer than those at level 4, who believe that effort will not affect luck outcomes. On skill tasks, on the other hand, mature children persisted longer in the face of failure. Thus, the index of differentiation of luck and skill appears to tap cognitions that have a significant impact on children's own achievement behavior.

The consequences for achievement behavior and personal adaptation of the development of the understanding of luck appear more benign than the consequences of the development of the concept of difficulty. When luck is more fully understood, attribution of failure to bad luck would more clearly imply a lack of personal responsibility. Further, the differentiated conception leads children to apply less effort on luck tasks where effort is truly fruitless and to apply more on skill tasks where effort can have an impact.

Effort and Ability

To study the development of the concepts of effort and ability we showed children films (Nicholls, 1978), videotapes (Nicholls & Miller, 1984b), or a series of photographs (Miller, in press) of two children applying different amounts of effort on equivalent tasks. In most cases, the two children were shown as gaining the same score.

At the least differentiated level, children's concepts of effort, ability, and outcomes are confounded. Children see effort, ability, and outcomes as positively associated even if they are not. The harder worker of each pair of actors was usually judged more able even if he or she scored less. At the second level, effort is clearly differentiated from outcomes and seen as the cause of outcomes. Ability, however, is not conceived as a separate causal factor. Despite the fact that they saw two children gaining equal scores with very different levels of effort, children at level 2 attempt to explain the equal outcomes in terms of effort. For example, "At the end the lazy one tried really hard to catch up."

At level 3 the concept of ability begins to emerge as an independent causal factor. But only at level 4 is this differentiation complete and ability conceived as capacity which limits the effect of effort on performance. Like younger children, those at level 4 realize that more able students are usually more motivated. But unlike the younger children, they realize that students who can score as well as others with less effort are more able.

We term this differentiated conception of ability, ability as capacity. Not inherited capacity necessarily, but present developed level of capacity—an underlying trait that is inferred from both effort and outcomes. Children with this conception realize what is implicit in individual intelligence testing procedures. Namely, that one's present level of capacity is only manifest in performance when optimum effort is applied.

There are parallels between this trend of development and the previous two. The transition from level 1 to 2 of effort and ability occurs at about the same time as the development of the normative conceptions of difficulty and ability (Nicholls, 1978). We have not examined the other relationships empirically, but conceptual parallels are evident. At the lower levels of understanding of luck and skill and of effort and ability, effort is seen as having an influence that is, from a mature perspective, close to magical; it is more or less unconstrained by one's present capacity or by tasks that allow only guessing. The mature conceptions of ability and luck both involve a greater awareness of the limits of the impact that effort can have on outcomes.

The validity of our index of conceptions of ability and effort as a predictor of children's reasoning about their own ability and effort is supported by two forms of evidence. First, children show similar levels of maturity when reasoning about themselves (and a comparison other) and about two others (Nicholls & Miller, 1984b). Second, judgments of own effort and ability in test-like situations are positively related in less mature children and negatively related in those who have partially or fully attained the concept of capacity (Miller, in press). (See also, Rholes, Blackwell, Jordan, & Walters, 1980).

The validity of this index is also supported by evidence on expected teacher evaluations of outcomes said to reflect effort or ability. It was predicted that less mature children would be more inclined to see someone described as high in ability and low in effort as actually high in effort. Thus they would expect such individuals to be rewarded by teachers. When ability and effort are more clearly differentiated, the description of someone as high in ability and low in effort would mean just that. Thus, it was predicted that mature children would expect less reward for such individuals. These predictions were confirmed (Nicholls, 1978). Children at levels 1 and 2 expected almost the maximum possible reward for success whether it resulted from high effort or high ability. Those at level 3 and, to a greater extent, level 4, expected less reward from teachers when success was said to reflect high ability than when it was said to reflect high effort.

The differentiation of ability and effort means that effort is more likely to be a double-edged sword (Covington & Omelich, 1979) for adolesents than for younger children. Young children can face the problem that their effort may not produce success. Older children may face the added problem that if they try hard to reduce the chance of failure, but still fail, their high effort will convincingly indicate low ability. Further, adolescents are more likely to find themselves facing a conflict between reducing effort to minimize the extent to which failure indicates low ability and maintaining high effort to please teachers (Harari & Covington, 1981).

The development of the concept of ability as capacity was also predicted to lead to greater possibilities for impaired performance when individuals expect to demonstrate low ability. Three possible mechanisms could be involved. First, lack of capacity implies lack of an underlying personal characteristic that is difficult to change: It implies a fundamental personal deficiency. When ability and effort are less differentiated, perception of low ability should reflect on the person in a less fundamental way. When more mature children expect to demonstrate low ability, they would expect to be revealed as lacking a basic, stable, and valued personal quality. Anticipation of this revelation should produce more anxiety and self-derogatory affect than would occur for children who confound effort and ability. Thus, expectations of demonstrating low ability should produce more impaired performance when the concept of ability is more differentiated.

But anxiety is only one of the possible consequences of low perceived capacity that could lead to impaired performance (Nicholls, 1976b). Lack of capacity implies that effort will do little to prevent failure, which will, in turn, confirm one's perception of low ability. When ability and effort are confounded, the effect of effort is seen as less constrained by ability. Thus, more mature children are more likely to conclude that situations where they appear likely to demonstrate low ability are hopeless. They are, therefore, more likely to give up. (Anxiety need not be involved for performance to be impaired.) The term learned helplessness seems best applied to this phenomenon rather than, as has been the case, to impaired performance in general.

Third, the differentiation of the concept of ability means that when one expects to fail, and, thereby, demonstrate low ability, reduction of effort could be seen as a means of minimizing the extent to which failure implies low ability (Covington & Beery, 1976; Frankel & Snyder, 1978). Thus, effort-reduction in the interests of self-protection would be more likely to occur, and this would lower performance.

We have not separated these mechanisms empirically. Nor, we believe, has anyone else. (Indeed the third mechanism has not been empirically demonstrated.) However, Miller (in press) has supported the prediction that the expectation of demonstrating low ability is more likely to impair performance when the concepts of ability and effort are more differentiated. In a test-like setting, he gave sixth-graders a series of failures designed to make them all doubt their ability. They were then presented a further series of tasks that were said to be either highly or moderately normatively difficult — few or about half the children of the subject's age were said to be able to do the tasks. For sixth-graders, failure at moderate normative difficulty levels would indicate low (below average) ability. Thus, children in the moderately difficult condition would expect to demonstrate low ability. On the other hand, those told that the second series of tasks were normatively difficult were "safe." They would realize that failure on normatively difficult tasks cannot indicate low ability. As expected, impaired performance was found only in the moderate difficulty condition *and* only for those sixth-graders who had partially (Level 3) or completely (Level 4) differentiated concepts of effort and ability. Those at the lower levels of differentiation performed similarly in the moderate and high difficulty conditions (and in a control condition where initial success was followed by moderately difficult tasks).

This result indicates that impaired performance is a consequence of the expectation of demonstrating low ability rather than mere expectation of failure (Carver & Scheier, 1981) or non-contingency (Abramson, Seligman, & Teasdale, 1978). Expectations of failure and perception of non-contingency between effort and outcome would be higher in the difficult condition. Yet performance was not impaired in that condition. This study also indicates that the conception of ability as capacity may be the cognitive basis of many of the examples of impaired performance observed in adults (e.g., Frankel & Snyder, 1978).

Summary

The changes in children's inferences and conceptions of ability can be summarized as changes from a self-referenced perspective to a more external or social perspective. The less differentiated conception of young children embodies the notion that improved mastery or mastery of tasks one is uncertain of completing indicates competence. The more differentiated position of adolescents and adults is that high ability is indicated if one can accomplish more than others with equal effort or if one needs less time or effort for an equivalent accomplishment. For young children, mastery following high effort indicates high ability. For adolescents, the implications of one's own effort for one's ability depend on the effort and performance of others. Ability is conceived as capacity and the effect of effort on performance is seen as more limited by one's ability and the characteristics of tasks.

SITUATIONAL INFLUENCES

Conceptions of Ability

The methods we used to study children's conceptions of ability were designed to reveal their most complex thought processes. But people do not always function at their highest levels. Thought, like overt action, requires attention or effort and more complex thought presumably requires more effort. We are, therefore, unlikely to use complex concepts if simpler ones will serve our purposes satisfactorily. If our purpose is to learn or to increase our mastery of an activity, we can monitor our progress with regard to this goal without using the fully differentiated conception of ability. As many writers have observed, preschool children show a preference for tasks that are challenging for them, and gain a sense of competence from increasing their mastery (e.g., Deci, 1975; Elkind, 1971; Flavell, 1977; White, 1959). This form of motivation depends on availability of tasks that offer a moderate personal challenge in situations without extrinsic incentives. Adults, too, can gain a sense of competence while employing the more subjective, less differentiated conception of ability of young children. When learning or mastery is an end in itself we can judge whether we have attained that goal without reference to the effort and performance of others. If, in such instances, we choose a task we are uncertain of mastering—one that is personally challenging—and master it, we will feel competent. Because learning is assumed to depend on effort and more effort indicates more learning, mastery that requires higher effort will occasion greater feelings of competence in the undifferentiated sense.

We refer to states where our concern is to learn—where mastery is an end in itself—as states of task-involvement. It has been well demonstrated that introduction of task-extrinsic rewards can, by inducing a concern to attain the extrinsic rewards, transform such states so that learning becomes experienced as a means to the end of attaining task-extrinsic incentives (Kruglanski, 1975; Lepper & Greene, 1978). Our thesis is that test-like or evaluative achievement situations will make demonstration of high rather than low ability in the differentiated sense a goal. As a consequence, emotional reactions and performance will change and learning can become a means to the end of demonstrating high ability in the differentiated sense. First, we will examine the hypothesis that evaluative situations will engage the differentiated conception of ability.

Suppose you asked a friend who had recently joined a chess class how able she was at chess. If she said she was proud to have just learned two complex opening gambits, you could infer that she felt competent in the less differentiated sense—she had gained in mastery. You would not, however, have gained a conceptually adequate answer to your question about her ability.

You would have gained more adequate information if she said that she had beaten all those she had played who had been learning for the same length of time as she had. The purpose of this example, is to illustrate the inadequacy of the undifferentiated, subjective perspective on ability for providing a conceptually adequate evaluation of our own or another's ability. This means that if a test-like situation makes us concerned about evaluating our ability, we will employ the differentiated perspective. Given the concern in our society about being able relative to others or succeeding in competitive contests (Allport, 1961, Covington & Beery, 1976), situations that emphasize comparison with others should also lead us to employ the differentiated conception to evaluate ourselves.

We term the state where our goal is to demonstrate high capacity and avoid demonstrating low capacity, ego-involvement. In this state, our concern is to maintain a favorable view of our own ability relative to that of others. In common sense terms, the question individuals ask themselves when they are ego-involved is, "How can I show I am smart or avoid looking stupid?" This contrasts with task-involvement where the issue is "How can I do this?" or "How does this work?" (Nicholls, 1979b).

We conducted a series of studies to test our hypothesis that task- versus ego-involving conditions would engage less versus more differentiated conceptions of ability. We compared university students' ability judgments in a self-referenced situation on tasks they found intrinsically interesting with ability judgments on tasks where they desired to out-perform others and had information about others' effort and performance. Students judged they would feel more able if they had to try hard to master tasks they found intrinsically interesting. That is, higher effort indicated greater ability. On the other hand, on tasks where they felt interpersonally competitive and were compared to others, they judged they would feel more competent if they applied low effort and others applied high effort to master the task.

In short, these university students functioned rather like 5-year-olds in self-referenced, task-involving situations. But they employed the differentiated conception of ability when ego-involved and aware of others' effort and performance. This result has been replicated several times (Jagacinski & Nicholls, 1984).

Attributions and Emotion

There has been considerable interest on the part of researchers in the questions of whether perceptions of effort or ability are more important as mediators of achievement affect (e.g., Covington & Omelich, 1979; Nicholls, 1976a) and whether specific attributions are associated with specific affective responses (e.g., Weiner, Russell, & Lerman, 1978). These questions imply that the meanings of effort and ability (and other causal factors) are fixed. As we have shown, this is not the case. Accordingly, we expected the affective consequences of perceptions of effort to differ in task- and ego-involving situations.

Pride and a sense of accomplishment proved to be maximized by high effort in task-involving contexts where high effort also indicates high ability. In ego-involving contexts, where less effort indicates more ability, pride and a sense of accomplishment were higher when effort was lower. The reverse pattern was found for embarrassment. Lower effort reduced embarrassment in ego-involvement but increased it in task-involvement (Jagacinski & Nicholls, 1984).

Thus, in task-involving situations, the affective consequences of task mastery are enhanced by higher effort. In ego-involving situations, the reverse is true: Affective reactions are more favorable when mastery requires less effort. In both states, individuals expect effort to increase one's chances of mastery and only through mastery can one expect to convincingly demonstrate high ability. However, in ego- but not task-involvement, higher effort can diminish the positive value of success and increase the negative value of failure.

Performance

We assume that achievement behavior and, thus, level of performance on achievement tasks is a function of expectations that behavior will lead to demonstration of high rather than low ability. In task-involving situations, where mature individuals employ the less differentiated conception, they should expect to demonstrate or develop high ability if they expect to be able to improve their performance. The more effort they apply, the more competent they should feel — provided their effort does not prove fruitless or leave them exhausted. In this self-referenced framework, one might fail to demonstrate ability by failing to improve or to master any items. But one cannot demonstrate low ability in the conclusive manner that is possible in competitive situations where below average performance indicates low ability.

In ego-involvement, however, the higher one's effort, the more convincingly will failure indicate low ability. Further, when ability is conceived as capacity, demonstration of low ability implies that one lacks something more fundamental than when one concludes simply that one is unable to master a particular task.

Thus, when task-involved, individuals should expect to feel competent if they expect effort to lead to mastery of some (not necessarily a large proportion) of the items of a "test." They should not see such a situation as hopeless, feel anxious about demonstrating incompetence, or worry that higher effort might indicate lower ability. In ego-involving, test-like situations, however, an expectation of being able to gain or to complete items is not itself sufficient basis for expecting to demonstrate high ability. One must expect to do better than others with equivalent effort. Thus, especially on normatively moderately difficult tasks, students who believe their ability is below average would expect to demonstrate a lack of capacity. Their performance should, therefore, be impaired. They should perform worse than they would in a task-involving situation. In ego-involving situations they should also perform worse than those who believe their ability is above average. (See also Maehr, 1978).

A number of studies comparing performance on moderately difficult tasks in test-like and non-evaluative situations support these hypotheses (Nicholls, 1984). In task-involving situations, students with high and low perceived ability perform at similar levels. Those with high perceived ability perform similarly in ego-involving and task-involving conditions whereas those with low perceived ability show impaired performance in ego-involving conditions.

Recall that ego-involving conditions engage the conception of ability as capacity (Jagacinski & Nicholls, 1984) and that impaired performance in ego-involving conditions was found only in adolescents who expected to demonstrate low ability *and* who conceived of ability as capacity (Miller, in press). These two lines of evidence support the thesis that impaired performance of adults in evaluative achievement situations often depends on an expectation of demonstrating low ability and on use of the conception of ability as capacity. It is, of course, possible to get impaired performance when the differentiated conception of ability is lacking. Infants placed in unresponsive environments give up mastery behavior. It seems appropriate to explain such cases in terms of perception of non-contingency or learned helplessness (Nicholls, 1984). However, impaired performance in adolescents and adults appears usually to be a consequence of expectations of demonstrating low capacity rather than merely of expectations of failure or of non-contingency.

Learning as a Means or as an End

When we are task involved, our goal is to gain in mastery. Such gains are equivalent to demonstrations of competence. In other words, learning is an end in itself. In ego-involvement, however, our concern is whether what we can master will lead to demonstration of superior rather than inferior capacity. In this instance, we must calculate whether learning will serve our end. Thus, learning is more likely to be experienced as a means to an end. In other words, ego-involving conditions are likely to make learning less intrinsically satisfying.

Several studies support these predictions. Ryan (1982) found more interest in tasks after performance in a neutral setting than after an "intelligence test" condition. Deci, Betley, Kahle, Abrams, and Porac (1981) found higher interest after individual performance than after successful competition with another. Deci, Schwartz, Sheinman, and Ryan (1981) found that children of teachers who used social comparison (and coercion) to control students reported less intrinsic interest in their schoolwork. Csikszentmihalyi (1975) also reports less intrinsic involvement (flow) in competitive contexts.

From an educational point of view, the potential benefits of task-involvement seem clear. The problem of maintaining task-involvement is, unfortunately, a considerable one (Nicholls, 1979b, 1983).

INDIVIDUAL DIFFERENCES

By about 13 years of age, most of us have mastered the conception of ability as capacity. As we have shown, use of this conception varies across situations. There are also reasons for predicting individual differences in the tendency to use differentiated versus undifferentiated conceptions of ability for self-evaluation and to set goals. Some individuals tend to be task-involved: to be concerned about how to learn, understand, discover new things, or to be intrinsically motivated. Others are more inclined toward ego-involvement: concern about whether they can demonstrate that their capacity is higher than that of others. No doubt socialization practices can produce individual differences in dispositions toward task- and ego-involvement (and other forms of task-extrinsic involvement). However, we will discuss only the role of individual differences in perceived ability.

We start with the assumption that our society is relatively competitive (Covington & Beery, 1976; Nicholls, 1979b). This competitive pressure and, therefore, the likelihood of ego-involvement generally becomes more marked in the higher grades of school (Eccles, Midgley, & Adler, 1984). In highly or moderately ego-involving situations, individuals who believe their ability is below average are unlikely to be able to forget this fact. Any remotely test-like task is likely to raise the prospect that they will demonstrate a lack of capacity. Their only escape is to reject the goal of demonstrating high rather than low ability (Nicholls, 1984). If they do not opt out psychologically, they are likely to see many achievement situations as tests of their present capacity. That is, individuals with low perceived ability should be prone to ego-involvement or, if they have opted out, to other forms of extrinsic involvement.

Individuals who are confident their ability is high will expect to demonstrate high capacity in most situations. They should assume that, if they apply themselves, they will demonstrate high capacity. Even when they expect failure, this would be seen as a result of task difficulty, not low ability (Valle & Frieze, 1976). In other words, they will not often have to wonder whether they can demonstrate high ability. The question for them is how to master tasks or solve problems rather than whether the outcomes of their efforts will reflect on their ability. Thus, mastery is less likely to be seen as a means to the end of demonstrating superior ability. Further, as they are relatively free of concerns about the adequacy of their capacity, they will be more likely to become involved in the process of task mastery and to find mastery inherently satisfying. In other words, it may be easier for individuals who are confident their ability is high to become task-involved, even in otherwise ego-involving situations.

Evidence in support of this prediction comes from a comparison of the ability judgments of high and low resultant achievement motive individuals (Touhey & Villemez, 1980). Higher resultant motive individuals have higher expectancies of success (Atkinson, 1957). For this and other reasons (Kukla, 1978), resultant achievement motivation can be used as an index of perceived ability. Touhey and Villemez found that high resultant motive students judged themselves more able when they applied high effort than when they applied low effort. Low resultant motive students judged themselves as more able when they employed less effort. These results conform to our thesis. The high motive students' ability judgments are consistent with the description of task-involvement when the undifferentiated conceptions of effort and ability are employed. Low motive students' judgments indicate ego-involvement where higher effort indicates lower ability. Covington (1983) obtained analogous results with music students. Those high in perceived competence expected less shame after failure when effort was high than did students with low perceived competence.

Our thesis is also that higher perceived ability will be associated with higher levels of intrinsic motivation. Harter and Connell (1984) found perceived ability and intrinsic motivation positively correlated. Thus, students with higher perceived ability not only have the advantage of greater feelings of competence and of the consequent positive effects on performance in ego-involving settings. They have the added advantage of finding learning more intrinsically satisfying.

It is interesting that outstanding achievement appears to be fostered more by a disposition to task-involvement than by an ego-involved or competitive disposition (Nicholls, 1979b, 1983). It might be that in competitive settings, one must be assured of one's ability relative to that of others before one can become highly task-involved. It might also be that, paradoxically, the best strategy in competitive situations is to maintain task-involvement. In any event, the fact that outstanding performers can be task-involved is illustrated by Royal Robbins, who as a climber made many outstanding first ascents and as a kayaker still makes outstanding first descents. "Of course, there are some ego-maniacs who are only interested in how great they can look. But, like climbing, kayaking has put me in contact with many people . . . who aren't interested in making money or dominating others. They are out there for the joy of running the river. If that's the case, they can't have too cloudy a soul" (Clark, 1982, p. 8).

CONCLUSION

When starting the developmental research described above, it was not our intention to extend the resulting theoretical concepts to adults. The realization that different theories of motivation based on adults embodied different conceptions of ability suggested this step.

Kukla's theories of performance (1972) and task choice (1978) respectively embody the ego-centric and objective conceptions of difficulty and ability. Atkinson's theory (1957) holds that subjective probability of success and task difficulty are equivalent. Thus, it embodies the ego-centric conception of difficulty and ability. It seemed unlikely that theories that incorporate these undifferentiated conceptions could prove adequate for predicting adult behavior. Paradoxically, despite its incorporation of the least differentiated conception of ability and difficulty, Atkinson's theory applies better to adults in ego-involving contexts than to young children (Nicholls, 1984). For example, Atkinson predicts impaired performance for individuals who are low in resultant achievement motivation when subjective probability of success (task difficulty) is moderate. But, if difficulty and subjective probabilities of success are not distinguished it is difficult to see how performance could be impaired on tasks of moderate difficulty. Everyone would presumably have moderate expectancies of demonstrating high ability at moderate difficulty levels. They would, therefore, apply effort and perform effectively. As we noted, this does occur in task-involvement where subjective probabilities of success are not clearly distinguished from task difficulty. According to our position, the reason performance in ego-involvement can be impaired on tasks of moderate (normative) difficuty is that, at this difficulty level, some individuals have low subjective probabilities of success and, thus, have high expectations of demonstrating low capacity. The fact that Atkinson's theory does not distinguish probability of success and task difficulty, yet predicts behavior that appears to depend on this distinction, indicates the possibility of a lack of internal consistency in that theory.

Kukla's predictions apply better to young children and to adults in task-involving contexts. This is as we would expect given the undifferentiated conception of ability this theory embodies (Nicholls & Miller, 1983). This also suggests that Kukla's theory is more internally consistent than that of Atkinson. It is, however, of limited applicability because adults can employ either differentiated or undifferentiated conceptions of ability. We have reviewed part of the evidence showing that their behavior changes in predictable ways depending on which conception is activated. Thus, an unexpected outcome of our developmental research has been a highlighting of the limited applicability of previous theories of achievement behavior.

Unlike the above theories, attribution theory (Weiner, 1972, 1979) embodies a fully differentiated conception of ability. The suggestion that individuals attribute outcomes to effort, ability, difficulty, luck, or other factors implies that these factors have distinctly different meanings. This is not so for young children. We also argue that attribution theory, in its present form, applies better in ego- than task-involving situations. When they are task-involved, individuals do not need to clearly distinguish the contributions of effort and ability to outcomes to determine whether they have developed or demonstrated competence. If mastery is attained, higher effort indicates higher ability. Similarly, there is no need to determine whether one's gains in performance reflect high or low normative difficulty because improvement per se indicates high ability. Thus, task-involved individuals are unlikely to make causal attributions in the manner described by attribution theorists. They are more likely to focus on learning strategies or effort deployment than on distinguishing the contributions of effort, difficulty, and luck to outcomes from those of ability. Carole Ames (1984 has obtained results consistent with this thesis.

In summary, the child is father to the man and mother to the woman and can remain with them throughout life. If men and women become as little children they may or may not enter the kingdom of heaven. But they might more fully enjoy striving and their accomplishments might be more substantial (Nicholls, 1979b).

ACKNOWLEDGMENT

Preparation of this paper was supported in part by National Science Foundation Grant BNS 7914252, Harvard University Subcontract.

REFERENCES

Abramson, L. Y., Seligman, M. E. P., & Teasdale, J. D. Learned helplessness in humans: Critique and reformulation. *Journal of Abnormal Psychology,* 1978, *87,* 49–74.

Adler, A. Organminder-wertigkeit und ihre psychischen Kompensationen. *Nervous and Mental Disease Monograph Series,* No. 24. (1912, translation, 1917.)

Allport, G. W. *Pattern and growth in personality.* Holt, Rinehart & Winston, New York: 1961.

Ames, C. Competitive, cooperative, and individualistic goal structures: A motivational analysis. In R. Ames & C. Ames (Eds.), *Research on motivation in education: Student motivation.* New York: Academic Press, 1984.

Atkinson, J. W. Motivational determinants of risk-taking behavior. *Psychological Review,* 1957, *64,* 359–372.

Bloom, B. S. *Human characteristics and school learning.* New York: McGraw-Hill, 1976.

Carver, C. S., & Scheier, M. F. *Attention and self-regulation: A control-theory approach to human behavior*. New York: Springer-Verlag, 1981.

Clark, B. Royal Robbins: From first ascents to first descents. *Canoe*, 1982, *10*, (6), 8.

Covington, M. V. Musical chairs: Who drops out of music instruction and why? In *Motivation and creativity*. Reston, Virginia: Music Educators National Conference, 1983.

Covington, M. V., & Beery, R. *Self-worth and school learning*. New York: Holt, Rinehart & Winston, 1976.

Covington, M. V., & Omelich, C. L. Effort: the double-edged sword in school achievement. *Journal of Educational Psychology*, 1979, *71*, 169–182.

Csikszentmihalyi, M. *Beyond boredom and anxiety*. San Francisco: Jossey-Bass, 1975.

deCharms, R. *Personal causation: The internal affective determinants of behavior*. New York: Academic Press, 1968.

Deci, E. L. *Intrinsic motivation*. New York: Plenum, 1975.

Deci, E. L. *The psychology of self-determination*. Lexington, MA: Heath, 1980.

Deci, E. L., Betley, G., Kahle, J., Abrams, L., & Porac, J. When trying to win: Competition and intrinsic motivation. *Personality and Social Psychology Bulletin*, 1981, *7*, 79–83.

Deci, E. L., Schwartz, A. J., Sheinman, L., & Ryan, R. M. An instrument to assess adults' orientation toward control versus autonomy with children: Reflections on intrinsic motivation and perceived competence. *Journal of Educational Psychology*, 1981, *73*, 642–650.

Eccles (Parsons), J., Midgley, C., & Adler, T. Age-related environmental changes and their impact on achievement behavior. In J. G. Nicholls (Ed.), *The development of achievement motivation*. Greenwich, CT: JAI Press, 1984.

Elkind, D. Cognitive growth cycles in mental development. In J. K. Cole (Ed.), *Nebraska Symposium on Motivation*. Lincoln, NE: University of Nebraska Press, 1971.

Flavell, J. H. *Cognitive development*. Englewood Cliffs, NJ: Prentice-Hall, 1977.

Frankel, A., & Snyder, M. L. Poor performance following unsolvable problems: Learned helplessness or egotism? *Journal of Personality and Social Psychology*, 1978, *36*, 1415–1423.

Harari, O., & Covington, M. V. Reactions to achievement behavior from a teacher and student perspective: A developmental analysis. *American Educational Research Journal*, 1981, *18*, 15–28.

Harter, S., & Connell, J. P. A model of the relationship among children's academic achievement orientations. In J. G. Nicholls (Ed.), *The development of achievement motivation*. Greenwich, CT: JAI Press, 1984.

Heckhausen, H. *The anatomy of achievement motivation*. New York: Academic Press, 1967.

Heckhausen, H. Emergent achievement behavior: Some early developments. In J. G. Nicholls (Ed.), *The development of achievement motivation: Progress in motivation and achievement* (Vol. 2). Greenwich, CT: JAI Press, 1984.

Jagacinski, C. M., & Nicholls, J. G. *Conceptions of ability and related affects in task involvement and ego involvement. Journal of Educational Psychology*, 1984, *76*, 909–919.

Kruglanski, A. W. The endogenous-exogenous partition in attribution theory. *Psychological Review*, 1975, *82*, 387–406.

Kukla, A. Foundations of an attributional theory of performance. *Psychological Review*, 1972, *79*, 454–470.

Kukla, A. An attributional theory of choice. In L. Berkowitz (Ed.), *Advances in experimental social psychology* (Vol. 11). New York: Academic Press, 1978.

Lepper, M. R., & Greene, D. (Eds.). *The hidden costs of reward: New perspectives on the psychology of human motivation*. Hillsdale, NJ: Lawrence Erlbaum Associates, 1978.

Maehr, M. L. Sociocultural origins of achievement motivation. In D. Bar-Tal & L. Saxe (Eds.), *Social psychology of education: Theory and research*. Washington, DC: Hemisphere, 1978.

Miller, A. T. A developmental study of the cognitive basis of performance impairment after failure. *Journal of Personality and Social Psychology*, in press.

Nicholls, J. G. Effort is virtuous, but it's better to have ability: Evaluative responses to perceptions of effort and ability. *Journal of Research in Personality,* 1976, *10,* 306–315. (a)

Nicholls, J. G. When a scale measures more than its name denotes: The case of the Test Anxiety Scale for Children. *Journal of Consulting and Clinical Psychology,* 1976, *44,* 976–985. (b)

Nicholls, J. G. The development of the concepts of effort and ability, perception of own attainment, and the understanding that difficult tasks require more ability. *Child Development,* 1978, *49,* 800–814.

Nicholls, J. G. Development of perception of own attainment and causal attributions for success and failure in reading. *Journal of Educational Psychology,* 1979, *71,* 94–99. (a)

Nicholls, J. G. Quality and equality in intellectual development: The role of motivation in education. *American Psychologist,* 1979, *34,* 1071–1084. (b)

Nicholls, J. G. The development of the concept of difficulty. *Merrill-Palmer Quarterly,* 1980, *26,* 271–281.

Nicholls, J. G. Conceptions of ability and achievement motivation: A theory and its implications for education. In S. G. Paris, G. M. Olsen, & H. W. Stevenson (Eds.), *Learning and motivation in the classroom.* Hillsdale, NJ: Lawrence Erlbaum Associates, 1983.

Nicholls, J. G. Achievement motivation: Conceptions of ability, subjective experience, task choice, and performance. *Psychological Review,* 1974, *91,* 328–346.

Nicholls, J. G., & Miller, A. T. The differentiation of the concepts of difficulty and ability. *Child Development,* 1983, *54,* 951–959.

Nicholls, J. G., & Miller, A. T. The differentiation of the concepts of luck and skill. *Developmental Psychology,* in press.

Nicholls, J. G., & Miller, A. T. Development and its discontents: The differentiation of the concept ability. In J. G. Nicholls (Ed.), *The development of achievement motivation.* Greenwich, CT: JAI Press, 1984. (a)

Nicholls, J. G., & Miller, A. T. Reasoning about the ability of self and others: A developmental study. *Child Development,* 1984, *55,* 1990–1999. (b)

Rholes, W. S., Blackwell, J., Jordan, C., & Walters, C. A developmental study of learned helplessness. *Developmental Psychology,* 1980, *16,* 616–624.

Ruble, D. N. The development of social comparison processes and their role in achievement-related self-socialization. In E. T. Higgins, D. N. Ruble, & W. W. Hartup (Eds.), *Developmental Social Cognition: A socio-cultural perspective.* New York: Cambridge University Press, 1984.

Ryan, R. M. Control and information in the intrapersonal sphere: An extension of cognitive evaluation theory. *Journal of Personality and Social Psychology,* 1982, *43,* 450–461.

Schneider, K. Subjective uncertainty and achievement and exploratory behavior in preschool children. In J. G. Nicholls (Ed.), *The development of achievement motivation: Progress in motivation and achievement* (Vol. 2). Greenwich, CT: JAI Press, 1984.

Shrauger, J. S. Responses to evaluation as a function of initial self perceptions. *Psychological Bulletin,* 1975, *82,* 581–596.

Smith, M. B. *Social psychology and human values.* Chicago: Aldine, 1969.

Stipek, D. J. Young children's performance expectations: Logical analysis or wishful thinking? In J. G. Nicholls (Ed.), *The development of achievement motivation.* Greenwich, CT: JAI Press, 1984.

Touhey, J. C., & Villemez, W. J. Ability attribution as a result of variable effort and achievement motivation. *Journal of Personality and Social Psychology,* 1980, *38,* 211–216.

Valle, V. A., & Frieze, I. H. Stability of causal attributions as a mediator in changing expectations of success. *Journal of Personality and Social Psychology,* 1976, *33,* 579–587.

Weiner, B. *Theories of motivation: From mechanism to cognition.* Chicago: Markham, 1972.

Weiner, B. A theory of motivation for some classroom experiences. *Journal of Educational Psychology,* 1979, *71,* 3–25.

Weiner, B., Russell, D., & Lerman, D. Affective consequences of causal ascriptions. In J. H. Harvey, W. J. Ickes, & R. F. Kidd (Eds.), *New directions in attribution research* (Vol. 2). Hillsdale, NJ: Lawrence Erlbaum Associates, 1978.

Weisz, J. R. Contingency judgments and achievement behavior: Deciding what is controllable and when to try. In J. G. Nicholls (Ed.), *The development of achievement motivation.* Greenwich, CT: JAI Press, 1984.

White, R. W. Motivation reconsidered: The concept of competence. *Psychological Review,* 1959, *66,* 297–333.

White, R. W. The concept of healthy personality: What do we really mean? *Counseling Psychologist,* 1973, *4*(2), 3–12.

15 Outcome Comparisons in Group Contexts: Consequences for the Self and Others

John M. Levine
Richard L. Moreland
University of Pittsburgh

There is little question that people spend a good deal of time evaluating themselves and others. These self- and other-evaluations are often closely intertwined, because information about oneself can be gained through social comparison. A large body of evidence indicates that people assess their opinions, abilities, and emotions by comparing their own and others' characteristics (e.g., Festinger, 1954; Levine, 1983; Schachter, 1959; Suls & Miller, 1977). People also use social comparison to evaluate their outcomes (e.g., Austin, 1977; Cook, Crosby, & Hennigan, 1977; Walster, Walster, & Berscheid, 1978). Previous work on outcome evaluations has often neglected the fact that these judgments occur in group contexts. Recent analyses suggest, however, that group membership can play an important role in outcome comparisons (e.g., Crosby, 1984; deCarufel, 1981; Deutsch, 1974, 1981; Greenberg, 1982; Jasso, 1983; Leventhal, 1979; Levine & Moreland, in press).

The goal of this chapter is to clarify the consequences of outcome comparisons in group contexts. First, we present a recently developed typology of alternative forms of outcome comparisons. This typology is based on the identities of the source and the target of comparison, their group identifications, and the time period(s) during which the outcomes under consideration occur. Second, we discuss the consequences of outcome comparisons at a general level, focusing on how the source interprets comparison information and how this interpretation influences subsequent responses to the comparison. Finally, we analyze the consequences of outcome comparisons at a more specific level, showing how these consequences can depend on the particular form of comparison that occurs. This analysis will reveal that changes in self-

and other-related cognitions often occur as a function of outcome comparison.

ALTERNATIVE FORMS OF COMPARISON ˙

Although the literature on the social comparison of outcomes is large and diverse, certain general themes are apparent (Levine & Moreland, in press). Comparisons between oneself and another person have received the most theoretical and empirical attention (e.g., Adams, 1965; Austin, 1977; Cook et al., 1977; Crosby, 1976; Davis, 1959; Goodman, 1974, 1977; Martin, 1981; Merton & Kitt, 1950; Patchen, 1961, Walster et al., 1978). In some cases the two people involved in such comparisons are identified as members of the same group; in other cases they are identified as members of different groups; in still other cases their group memberships are not specified. Self/ other comparisons are usually assumed to occur at one point in time, generally the present. Work has also been done on self/self comparisons involving a single individual's outcomes at two points in time (e.g., Cook et al., 1977; Davies, 1962, 1969; Feierabend, Feierabend, & Nesvold, 1969; Goodman, 1974, 1977; Gurr, 1970). Usually the present is compared with the past, but sometimes the present and the future are compared. Finally, some attention has been devoted to group/group comparisons in which the outcomes of two groups are compared (e.g., Abeles, 1976; Crosby, 1982; Guimond & Dube-Simard, 1983; Martin & Murray, 1983, 1984; Runciman, 1966; Williams, 1975). Group/group comparisons, like self/other comparisons, are typically assumed to occur at one point in time, usually the present.

Because social comparison is clearly an important aspect of outcome evaluation, it is surprising that no general framework has been offered to integrate the various approaches mentioned above. In an effort to conceptualize alternative forms of comparison, we have recently developed a three-dimensional typology of outcome comparisons in group contexts (Levine & Moreland, in press). As Figure 15.1 indicates, the three dimensions are labeled "Type of Comparison," "Social Context," and "Temporal Context." Type of Comparison refers to the identities of the source and target of comparison: *self/self* comparisons involve the outcomes of a single individual; *self/other* comparisons involve the outcomes of different individuals; *group/group* comparisons involve the outcomes of one or more groups. Social Context refers to the group identification of the source and target of comparison: *intragroup* comparisons occur when the source and target are identified with a single group; *intergroup* comparisons occur when the source and target are identified with different groups. Finally, Temporal Context refers to the time period(s) during which the two outcomes under consideration occur: in *intratemporal* comparisons, the two outcomes occur during the

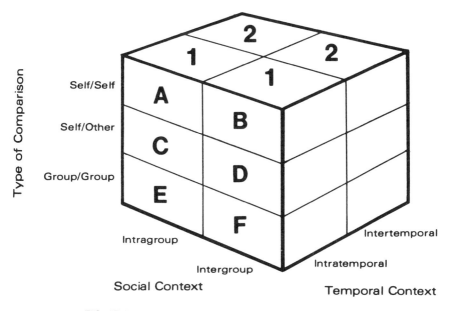

FIG. 15.1.   Varieties of outcome comparison in group contexts.

same time period (i.e., past-past, present-present, future-future). In *intertemporal* comparisons, the two outcomes occur during different time periods (i.e., past-present, past-future, present-future).

The four cells in the top layer of the figure illustrate comparisons involving the outcomes of a single individual. The cells differ regarding whether the outcomes involved occur within one group or two groups and at one point in time or two points in time. Examples of comparisons in the four self/self cells are:

A1   A faculty member comparing the compliments that he receives from his departmental chairperson with the raise that the chairperson recommends for him.

A2   A faculty member comparing her current salary to her anticipated salary next year

B1   A faculty member comparing his current salary at the university with the income that he currently receives as a member of a local consulting firm.

B2   A faculty member comparing her current fringe benefits to those that she received last year at another university.

The four cells in the middle layer of the figure illustrate comparisons involving the outcomes of two people. The cells differ regarding whether the comparison is intragroup or intergroup and intratemporal or intertemporal. Examples of comparisons in the four self/other cells are:

C1   A faculty member comparing his current salary to the current salary of a colleague at his own university

C2   A faculty member comparing her current teaching load to that endured last year by a colleague at her own university

D1   A faculty member comparing his current fringe benefits to those of a colleague at another university

D2   A faculty member comparing her current salary to that earned last year by a colleague at another university

The four cells in the bottom layer of the figure illustrate comparisons involving the outcomes of groups. Again, the cells differ regarding whether the comparison is intragroup or intergroup and intratemporal or intertemporal. Examples of comparisons in the four group/group cells are:

E1   A faculty member comparing his university's current prestige with the size of its current endowment.

E2   A faculty member comparing her university's current endowment to its endowment last year

F1   A faculty member comparing his university's current prestige to the current prestige of another university

F2   A faculty member comparing her university's current endowment to that of another university last year

We have also considered the issue of when the different forms of outcome comparison illustrated in Figure 15.1 will occur (Levine & Moreland, in press). Two general determinants of comparison choice were identified (cf. Austin, 1977; Goodman, 1977; Singer, 1981). The first determinant is the salience of an individual or a group as a possible target of comparison. Salience depends on the availability of information regarding the target's standing on two dimensions: (a) the outcome under consideration (e.g., salary) and (b) personal characteristics (related attributes) that are assumed to influence the probability of receiving the outcome (e.g., seniority). The second determinant of comparison choice is the attractiveness of the target as a source of comparison information. Attractiveness depends on the source's motive for seeking comparison information and the target's assumed instrumentality in satisfying this motive. Three motives for outcome comparison have received extensive research attention. One motive is the desire for *equity,* that is, equal ratios of outcomes to related attributes for oneself and the target of comparison (cf. Adams, 1965; Walster et al., 1978). A second motive is the desire for *self-enhancement,* that is, a higher ratio of outcomes to related attributes for oneself than for the target of comparison (cf. Gruder, 1977; Hyman, 1942; Levine, 1983). Finally, a third motive is the desire for *self-depreciation,* that is, a lower ratio of outcomes to related attributes for oneself than for the target of comparison (cf. Hyman, 1942; Martin, 1981; Patchen, 1961). The target's assumed instrumentality for satisfying these motives depends on information about one's own and the target's outcomes and related attributes. When equity motivation is dominant, targets whose outcomes and related attributes allow "equal" comparisons are preferred. When self-enhancement motivation is dominant, targets whose outcomes and related attributes allow "downward" comparisons (Wills, 1981) are preferred. When self-depreciation motivation is dominant, targets whose outcomes and related attributes allow "upward" comparisons are preferred.

The salience and attractiveness of an individual or a group as a potential target of comparison can be influenced by a variety of factors. These factors in turn affect which of the comparison options illustrated in Figure 15.1 will be chosen. Levine and Moreland (in press) have provided a detailed discussion of the factors that influence the probability of (a) self/self versus self/other versus group/group comparisons, (b) intragroup versus intergroup comparisons, and (c) intratemporal versus intertemporal comparisons. For example, self/self comparisons are likely when information about others' outcomes and related attributes is unavailable and when the self is highly salient, perhaps because of objective self-awareness (Carver & Scheier, 1981; Wicklund, 1980). Self/other comparisons are probable when information about one's own outcomes or related attributes is unavailable, when others are salient comparison objects, when one has a chronic concern about others' evaluations of oneself (Fenigstein, Scheier, & Buss, 1975), or when one desires to see oneself as unique (Lemaine, 1974; Snyder & Fromkin, 1980). Group/group comparisons are likely when group membership is salient because of group competition, group dissimilarity, or status differentials between groups (Brewer, 1979), when group members seek to enhance their social identity through intergroup comparisons (Tajfel, 1978), or when group members seek to demonstrate their group's inferior outcomes in order to produce social change (Austin, 1977; Patchen, 1961). Regarding intragroup versus intergroup comparisons, the former are more likely than the latter when information about the outcomes or related attributes of targets associated with other groups is unavailable or likely to yield unsatisfying results or when an individual is highly identified with one group, perhaps because of minority group membership (Gerard & Hoyt, 1974; McGuire & McGuire, 1981; Mullen, 1983). Finally, with some exceptions, intratemporal comparisons are more common than intertemporal comparisons, because outcomes and related attributes that occur at the same point in time are easier to compare than are those that occur at different points in time.

GENERAL CONSEQUENCES OF COMPARISON

As we have already suggested, the source's ratio of outcomes to related attributes can be higher than, equal to, or lower than the target's ratio. Therefore, following social comparison the source learns that he or she is relatively advantaged, neither advantaged nor disadvantaged, or relatively disadvantaged vis-à-vis the target. The crucial issue, of course, is not the objective relationship between the source's and the target's ratios, but rather the source's interpretation of this relationship (cf. Adams, 1965; Martin & Murray, 1984; Walster, et al., 1978).

Four dimensions of the source's interpretation of his or her superiority, equality, or inferiority, seem especially important. One such dimension is the *confidence* with which a comparison is made. A source will be confident about a comparison to the extent that he or she has subjectively valid information about (a) his or her own and the target's absolute outcomes and related attributes and (b) the similarity between his or her own and the target's ratio of outcomes to related attributes. Several factors can influence a source's confidence in information about absolute outcomes and related attributes. One such factor is the sheer amount of information that is available. A second and related factor is the presumed accuracy of this information. A source will feel more confident when he or she has a large amount of accurate information than when he or she has a small amount of inaccurate information. A third factor that can influence a source's confidence regarding his or her own and a target's absolute outcomes and related attributes is the ease with which information can be quantified. For example, the source is likely to feel more confident in assessing salary than prestige. Finally, a fourth determinant of the source's confidence is the consistency of information regarding outcomes or related attributes. The source will be more confident in assessing his or her own related attributes, for example, when his or her seniority and job skills are both high than when one is high and the other is low.

Even when the source is confident about his or her own and the target's absolute outcomes and related attributes, the source may have difficulty calculating the similarity between his or her own and the target's ratio of outcomes to related attributes. This calculation presumably is easier when the source's and the target's outcomes and related attributes are on the same metric than when they are on different metrics. Thus, it is probably easier for a source to compare his or her salary and seniority to a target's salary and seniority than to compare his or her salary and seniority to a target's fringe benefits and job skills. Even when the same metric is used for both the source and the target, it is presumably easier for the source to calculate the similarity between ratios of outcomes to related attributes when the source and the target have similar absolute outcomes and related attributes than when they do not. For example, the source will probably find it easier to compare his or her high salary and high seniority to a target's high salary and high seniority than to compare his or her high salary and high seniority to a target's low salary and low seniority.

A second dimension of the source's interpretation of his or her relative outcomes and related attributes is the *importance* attached to the comparison. Importance is primarily affected by the degree to which the source's outcomes and related attributes are relevant to his or her self-concept (cf. Adams, 1965). A comparison is more important when the outcomes and related attributes under consideration are relevant to how the source wishes to define himself or herself than when they are irrelevant to self-definition. Relevance, in turn, can be affected by an enduring desire to see oneself as possessing particular outcomes (e.g., wealth) or related attributes (e.g., intelligence), a wish to gain the esteem of people who value these particular outcomes or related attributes, or a belief that other desirable outcomes (e.g., political power) can only be achieved if one possesses these outcomes or related attributes. When a difference exists between the source's and the target's ratios of outcomes to related attributes, the absolute size of this difference can also affect its importance. Large differences will be viewed as more important than small differences.

The *causal attribution* that a source makes for a particular comparison is a third dimension of interpretation. Weiner (1979, 1980) has suggested that causal explanations for performance can be analyzed in terms of three attributional dimensions: locus, stability, and controllability. Locus refers to whether the cause of the performance resides within the actor (internal) or lies outside the actor (external). Stability refers to whether the cause of the performance is relatively constant (stable) or varies over time (unstable). Controllability refers to whether the cause of the performance is amenable to personal control (controllable) or is not amenable to such control (uncontrollable). These three dimensions also seem useful in analyzing causal attributions for outcome comparisons. Regardless of whether a source discovers that his or her ratio of outcomes to related attributes is superior, equal, or inferior to a target's ratio, the source is likely to seek an explanation for this state of affairs. In so doing, the source will probably consider the locus, stability, and controllability of his or her own and the target's related attributes. According to Weiner's analysis, for example, the related attribute of effort would be seen as internal, unstable, and controllable, whereas the related attribute of ability would be seen as internal, stable, and uncontrollable. Other related attributes, such as educational background and seniority, can also be analyzed in terms of locus, stability, and controllability, although general statements about their placement on the three attributional dimensions are more difficult to make. The source's attribution for an outcome will be influenced by the presumed cause of the related attribute that determines the outcome. Thus, a salary that is presumably determined by effort will itself be seen as less stable and more controllable than a salary that is determined by ability.

The final dimension that we will discuss is the *acceptability* of the comparison information. Acceptability is based on the source's motive for seeking comparison information and the relationship between the source's and the target's ratios of outcomes to related attributes. As mentioned earlier, three major motives for outcome comparison are equity, self-enhancement, and self-depreciation. For each motive, the source has a particular preference for the relationship between his or her own and the target's ratios of outcomes to related attributes. The acceptability of comparison information thus depends on its congruence with a motive-based preference. According to this analysis, a source who is motivated to achieve equity will find an "equal" comparison acceptable and an advantageous or a disadvantageous comparison unacceptable. A source who is motivated to achieve self-enhancement will find an advantageous comparison acceptable and an equal or a disadvantageous comparison unacceptable. A source who is motivated to achieve self-depreciation will find a disadvantageous comparison acceptable and an equal or an advantageous comparison unacceptable[1].

Our discussion of the four dimensions of interpretation has implicitly assumed that these dimensions are orthogonal. This assumption, although plausible in many cases, is not always valid. For example, comparisons in which a source has little confidence are unlikely to be perceived as very important. The causal attribution that a source makes for comparison information can also be influenced by the acceptability of the information. Sources may be more inclined, for example, to take responsibility for acceptable than for unacceptable comparisons. If so, then internal and controllable attributions will be more prevalent in the former than in the latter case. Because of a desire to believe that acceptable comparisons will persist whereas unacceptable comparisons will change, sources may also make more stable attributions for acceptable comparisons.

A source's interpretation of a comparison will affect how he or she responds to it. Responses to comparison information can be classified as affective, behavioral, or cognitive in nature (Levine, 1983). A number of specific affective responses to comparison information have been identified, including satisfaction, happiness, pride, guilt, anger, and envy (Adams, 1965; Crosby, 1976; Singer, 1981). For present purposes, we will collapse these specific responses into two general affective categories: positive responses and

---

[1] When a source is motivated to achieve equity, an advantageous comparison is preferred to a disadvantageous comparison (e.g., Deutsch, 1974; Homans, 1961; Singer, 1981). When a source is motivated to achieve self-enhancement, an equal comparison is preferred to a disadvantageous comparison. Finally, when a source is motivated to achieve self-depreciation, an equal comparison is preferred to an advantageous comparison.

negative responses. We will also assume, as have others (e.g., Adams, 1965; Homans, 1961; Walster et al., 1978), that affective responses mediate behavioral and cognitive responses. Behavioral responses refer to efforts on the part of the source to maintain, increase, or decrease his or her actual outcomes or related attributes or those of the target. Additional behavioral responses, such as changing the target of comparison or leaving the field, can also occur. Finally, cognitive responses refer to the source's distortions of his or her own outcomes or related attributes or those of the target. These distortions can involve changing the perceived level, relevance, or cause of outcomes or related attributes.

The confidence, importance, causality, and acceptability associated with a comparison can have complex effects on the *latency, strength,* and *duration* of a source's response and on the specific *type of response* that he or she makes. For example, responses to a confident and important comparison will generally have shorter latency, higher strength, and longer duration than responses to an unconfident and unimportant comparison. The confidence of a comparison can also affect the perceived ease of distorting relevant outcomes and related attributes, which in turn influences the probability that cognitive distortion will be used in response to an unacceptable comparison. Regarding causal attributions, we would expect that a source who perceives that he can control his own or a target's outcomes or related attributes will view these as relatively easy to actually change. In contrast, a source who perceives that she cannot control her own or a target's outcomes or related attributes will view these as relatively difficult to change. In responding to an unacceptable comparison, a source who views outcomes or related attributes as controllable is thus more likely to try to actually change these outcomes or related attributes (Martin, Brickman, & Murray, 1984). Finally, the acceptability of a comparison will affect whether a source's affective response is positive or negative and whether behavioral and cognitive responses are designed to maintain, increase, or decrease his or her own or the target's outcomes or related attributes. As previously discussed, acceptability is based on the source's motive for seeking comparison information and the relationship between the source's and the target's ratios of outcomes to related attributes.

When equity motivation is dominant, the source will have a positive affective response to information indicating equality between his or her own and the target's ratio of outcomes to related attributes. The source will also attempt to ensure that this ratio remains stable over time. If one party's outcomes or related attributes seem likely to change, thereby threatening to produce an advantageous or a disadvantageous comparison, then the source will seek to prevent this change by engaging in behavior designed to maintain the potentially troublesome element at its current level. If this tactic fails (or is too costly to try) and inequity actually occurs, then the source will experience negative affect and attempt to change his or her own outcomes or related attributes or those of the target to restore "actual" equity (Adams, 1965; Walster et al., 1978). For example, if the target's outcomes rise, then the source may try to (a) increase his or her own outcomes, (b) decrease his or her own related attributes, (c) decrease the target's outcomes, or (d) increase the target's related attributes. In addition, the source may cognitively distort the level, relevance or cause of his or her own outcomes or related attributes or those of the target to restore "psychological" equity (Adams, 1965; Walster et al., 1978). If neither overt behaviors nor cognitive distortions produce equity, then the source may change the target of comparison, leave the field, or endure the inequity and experience stress symptoms as a result (Crosby, 1976).

Adams (1965) has described some of the specific ways in which people respond to inequity. He hypothesizes that sources maximize their positive outcomes and minimize increases in costly related attributes (inputs). He also suggests that sources resist real and cognitive changes in outcomes and related attributes that are central to their self-concept and that they tend to distort the target's outcomes and related attributes rather than their own. Finally, Adams states that sources resist both changing the target of comparison and leaving the field.

Few investigators have studied responses to outcome comparisons when self-enhancement or self-depreciation motivation is dominant, but some general predictions can be made. When self-enhancement motivation is dominant, the source will have a positive affective response to information indicating that his or her ratio of outcomes to related attributes is higher than the target's ratio. The source will attempt to ensure that this ratio remains stable over time, responding more strongly to a probable disadvantageous comparison than to a probable equal comparison. If an equal or a disadvantageous comparison actually occurs, then the source will experience negative affect and attempt to restore actual or psychological superiority, again responding more vigorously in the disadvantageous than in the equal case. If superiority cannot be produced, then the source may change the comparison target, leave the field, or endure the unpleasant situation. The selection of a specific tactic for producing self-enhancement will be influenced by the same factors that affect responses to inequity.

When self-depreciation motivation is dominant, the source will have a positive affective response to information indicating that his or her ratio of outcomes to related attributes is lower than the target's ratio. The source's reactions to equal and advantageous comparisons will parallel reactions to equal and disadvantageous comparisons when self-enhancement motivation is dominant, except that inferiority rather than superiority will be sought. An important difference exists, however, between equity and self-enhancement motivation on the one hand and self-depreciation motivation on the other hand. If self-depreciation motivation is based on the desire to increase one's bargaining power (Patchen, 1961), then this motive may be more transient than equity or self-enhancement. If bargaining is successful, then the source's outcomes will increase and there will be no reason to seek out information indicating inferiority. If bargaining is unsuccessful, then the source's continued attention to his or her inferiority will be distressing and serve no useful purpose. Therefore, unless self-depreciation motivation is due to a chronic "need" to feel inferior, this motive will probably be replaced by equity or self-enhancement motivation after a bargaining attempt has been made, regardless of the outcome of this attempt.

Specific Consequences of Comparison

The source's interpretation of a comparison clearly influences how he or she responds to it. For example, the confidence of a comparison is likely to affect the latency, strength, and duration of a source's responses, as well as the probability that the source will use cognitive distortion to deal with an unacceptable comparison. Moreover, the source's perceived control over his or her own and the target's outcomes and related attributes is likely to influence attempts to actually change these outcomes and related attributes. In this section we suggest some elaborations of these hypotheses, elaborations that are required because different forms of comparison can elicit different responses. In discussing specific consequences of outcome comparisons, we will make use of the three-dimensional typology (Type of Comparison, Social Context, and Temporal Context) discussed earlier.

Regarding the Type of Comparison dimension, self/self comparisons are made more confidently than self/other comparisons, which in turn are made more confidently than group/group comparisons. This is because sources typically believe that they have more accurate information (a) about their own absolute outcomes and related attributes than about those of other persons and (b) about the absolute outcomes and related attributes of individuals than about those of groups.

In the case of his or her own outcomes and related attributes, the source has access to information through self-observation, which is generally viewed as a reliable means of acquiring information. In the case of other persons' outcomes and related attributes, the source must rely on direct observations of the target or the report of an informant (either the target or a third party). The source may have relatively little confidence in his or her own observations because the source knows that he or she does not have complete information about the target. In addition, the source may lack confidence in an informant's report because the informant is perceived to have incomplete information or to be biased. Finally, in the case of a group's outcomes and related attributes, the source almost always lacks detailed knowledge about every member of the group, whether information is obtained through direct observation or the report of an informant. Moreover, the source is often confronted with the difficult task of aggregating inconsistent information across those group members for whom information is available. The absence of information about all group members and the difficulty of aggregating available information are likely to reduce the source's confidence regarding a group's absolute outcomes and related attributes. If comparisons are generally rank-ordered self/self > self/other > group/group in terms of confidence and importance is held constant, then responses to self/self comparisons should have shorter latency, higher strength, and longer duration than responses to self/other comparisons, which in turn should have shorter latency, higher strength, and longer duration than responses to group/group comparisons.

The differential confidence associated with comparisons involving the self, other persons, and groups can also be expected to influence the degree to which cognitive distortion is used to deal with unacceptable comparisons. The perceived ease of distorting information probably varies inversely with confidence. We would thus expect more efforts to distort outcomes and related attributes in group/group comparisons than in self/other or self/self comparisons. Self/other comparisons should also produce more attempts at distortion than self/self comparisons.

Efforts to change actual outcomes and related attributes are presumably based on the perceived ease of making these changes, rather than on the confidence associated with the outcomes and related attributes. Therefore, efforts to make actual changes are not expected to parallel the cognitive distortions discussed above. In general, the perceived ease of making real changes should be highest when the self is involved, intermediate when another individual is involved, and lowest when a group is involved. This is because most people believe that they have more control over themselves than over others and can exert more influence on individual persons than on groups. We would thus expect more overt efforts to increase or decrease outcomes or related attributes in self/self comparisons than in self/other or group/group comparisons. Self/other comparisons should also produce more attempted changes than group/group comparisons.

Turning now to the Social Context dimension, intragroup comparisons are probably made with more confidence than intergroup comparisons. In the case of self/other comparisons, a source is likely to feel that he or she has more accurate information about the absolute outcomes and related attributes of another ingroup member (intragroup comparison) than about those of an outgroup member (intergroup comparison). Similarly, in the case of group/group comparisons, a source probably feels that he or she has more accurate information about the absolute outcomes and related attributes of the ingroup (intragroup comparison) than about those of an outgroup (intergroup comparison). The source may also find it easier to calculate the similarity between ratios of outcomes to related attributes when an intra-group rather than an intergroup comparison is involved. This is because outcomes and related attributes are more likely to be on the same metric in the former than in the latter case. For this reason, in a self/self comparison the source should also find it easier to calculate the similarity between ratios of outcomes to related attributes when one group rather than two groups is involved. Assuming that intragroup comparisons are generally made more confidently than intergroup comparisons and that importance is held constant, responses to intragroup comparisons should have shorter latency, higher strength, and longer duration than responses to intergroup comparisons.

The differential confidence associated with intragroup and intergroup comparisons can again be expected to influence the degree to which cognitive distortion is used to deal with unacceptable comparisons. As in the case of self/self, self/other, and group/group comparisons, the perceived ease of distorting information should vary inversely with confidence. We would thus expect more attempts to distort outcomes and related attributes in intergroup than in intragroup comparisons.

As before, efforts to change actual outcomes and related attributes will not parallel cognitive distortions. The perceived ease of making real changes should be higher when intragroup rather than intergroup comparisons are involved, at least in the self/other and group/group cases. This is because most people believe that they have more influence over members of their own group than over members of other groups. As a result, we would expect more overt efforts to increase or decrease outcomes or related attributes in intragroup than in intergroup comparisons.

In regard to the Temporal Context dimension, we assume that comparisons involving present outcomes and related attributes are generally made more confidently than those involving past outcomes and related attributes, which in turn are generally made more confidently than those involving future outcomes and related attributes. This is because (a) present information is not subject to memory errors, as is past information, or to disconfirmation, as is expected future information, and (b) memory errors generally pose less threat to confidence than does the possibility of future disconfirmation. These assumptions lead to straightforward predictions for both intratemporal comparisons, which occur within time periods, and intertemporal comparisons, which occur across time periods. Regarding intratemporal comparisons, present-present comparisons should be made more confidently than past-past comparisons, which should be made more confidently than future-future comparisons. Regarding intertemporal comparisons, present-past comparisons should be made more confidently than present-future comparisons, which should be made more confidently than past-future comparisons. Predictions about the relative confidence of intratemporal versus intertemporal comparisons can be made if we assume that the source finds it easier to calculate the similarity between ratios of outcomes to related attributes when an intratemporal rather than an intertemporal comparison is involved. This is because outcomes and related attributes are more likely to be on the same metric in the former than in the latter case. We tentatively suggest that the six intratemporal and intertemporal comparisons will be rank-ordered in terms of confidence as follows: present-present > present-past > past-past > present-future > past-future > future-future. To the extent that this rank-order is correct and importance is held constant, the latency, strength, and duration of responses will follow a parallel ordering.

In the case of unacceptable comparisons, attempts to cognitively distort outcomes and related attributes will again be determined by the confidence associated with the comparisons. Assuming that the perceived ease of distorting information varies inversely with confidence, the six comparisons should be rank-ordered in terms of distortion effort as follows: future-future > past-future > present-future > past-past > present-past > present-present.

We assume that the perceived ease of changing actual outcomes and related attributes is highest when present information is involved, intermediate when future information is involved, and lowest when past information is involved. This is because the difficulties of altering present outcomes and related attributes are typically known, whereas the difficulties of altering future outcomes and related attributes can only be estimated. It is impossible, of course, to change past outcomes and related attributes. We would thus expect more overt efforts to increase or decrease outcomes or related attributes (a) in present-present than in future-future than in past-past comparisons and (b) in present-future than in present-past than in past-future comparisons. We would expect the six intratemporal and intertemporal comparisons to be rank-ordered in terms of overt effort as follows: present-present > present-future > present-past > future-future > past-future > past-past.

SUMMARY AND CONCLUSIONS

The goal of this chapter was to clarify the consequences of outcome comparisons in group contexts. To this end we first presented a three-dimensional typology of alternative forms of comparisons. In discussing the typology, we differentiated between (a) self/self, self/other, and group/group comparisons, (b) intragroup and intergroup comparisons, and (c) intratemporal and intertemporal comparisons. We also mentioned two general determinants of comparison choice — the salience of a possible target of comparison and its attractiveness. Salience depends on the availability of information regarding the target's standing on outcome and related attributes dimensions. Attractiveness depends on the source's motive for seeking comparison information (equity, self-enhancement, self-depreciation) and the target's assumed instrumentality in satisfying this motive, which is based on the relationship between the source's and the target's ratio of outcomes to related attributes. Finally, we briefly described a number of factors that can affect a potential target's salience and attractiveness.

In the second section of the chapter, we discussed the consequences of outcome comparisons at a general level, emphasizing how the source interprets comparison information and how this interpretation influences his or her subsequent responses. Four dimensions of interpretation were identified: confidence, importance, causality, and acceptability. Confidence reflects the source's perception of the validity of information about his or her own and the target's absolute outcomes and related attributes and the similarity between his or her own and the target's ratio of outcomes to related attributes. Importance is affected by the degree to which the source's outcomes and related attributes are relevant to his or her self-concept and by the absolute difference between the source's and the target's ratio of outcomes to related attributes. Causality is determined by the source's perception of the locus, stability, and controllability of his or her own and the target's outcomes and related attributes. Finally, acceptability is based on the source's motive for seeking comparison information and the relationship between the source's and the target's ratios of outcomes to related attributes.

Responses to comparison information were classified as affective, cognitive, and behavioral in nature, and it was assumed that affective responses mediate behavioral and cognitive ones. Affective responses involve positive or negative emotional reactions. Behavioral responses involve efforts on the part of the source to maintain, increase, or decrease his or her actual outcomes or related attributes or those of the target. Cognitive responses involve the source's distortions of his or her own outcomes or related attributes or those of the target. The source's intepretation of a comparison influences how he or she responds to it. The confidence, importance, causality, and acceptability of a comparison affect the latency, strength, and duration of the source's responses and the specific type of response that he or she makes.

In the third section, we analyzed the consequences of outcome comparisons at a more specific level, showing how these consequences depend on the particular form of comparison that occurs. This analysis was organized around our three-dimensional typology of outcome comparisons. Regarding the Type of Comparison dimension, we argued that (a) efforts to cognitively distort outcomes and related attributes will generally be rank-ordered:

group/group > self/other > self/self and (b) efforts to change actual outcomes and related attributes will generally be rank-ordered: self/self > self/other > group/group. Regarding the Social Context dimension, we suggested that (a) cognitive distortion efforts will be rank-ordered: intergroup > intragroup and (b) efforts to produce actual changes will be rank-ordered: intragroup > intergroup. Finally, regarding the Temporal Context dimension, we predicted that (a) cognitive distortion efforts will be rank-ordered: future-future > past-future > present-future > past-past > present-past > present-present and (b) efforts to produce actual changes will be rank-ordered: present-present > present-future > present-past > future-future > past-future > past-past. For all three dimensions, predicted efforts to cognitively distort outcomes and related attributes are based on assumptions about the confidence associated with comparison information, and predicted efforts to change actual outcomes and related attributes are based on assumptions about the perceived ease of making these changes.

Our analysis has suggested a number of interesting theoretical and empirical questions regarding the consequences of outcome comparisons in group contexts. Two additional issues that warrant attention have not been mentioned, however. One of these concerns the precise manner in which a source attempts to increase or decrease actual outcomes or related attributes. This issue is particularly interesting for group/group comparisons, in which changes are generally difficult to make and require the cooperation of other individuals. How does an individual mobilize support for efforts to alter his or her own group's or another group's outcomes or related attributes? Although partial answers to this question have been offered (e.g., Cook & Parcel, 1977; deCarufel, 1981; Martin & Murray, 1984; Williams, 1975), a good deal of additional work is needed. A second issue that deserves further attention concerns the way in which a source cognitively distorts outcomes or related attributes. Evidence indicates, for example, that an individual who feels responsible for another person's relatively low outcomes often cognitively lowers the target's related attributes through derogation (Walster et al., 1978). It would be interesting to analyze this and other cognitive distortion strategies in contexts in which members of one group feel responsible for the outcomes of members of another group. Schlenker's (1980) recent discussion of remedial behaviors in predicament situations might prove useful in clarifying changes in self- and other-related cognitions in these contexts.

ACKNOWLEDGMENTS

Preparation of the paper was supported by funds from the National Institute of Education to the Learning Research and Development Center at the University of Pittsburgh.

REFERENCES

Abeles, R. P. Relative deprivation, rising expectations, and black militancy. *Journal of Social Issues,* 1976, *32,* 119–137.

Adams, J. S. Inequity in social exchange. In L. Berkowitz (Ed.), *Advances in experimental social psychology* (Vol. 2). New York: Academic Press, 1965, pp. 267–299.

Austin, W. Equity theory and social comparison processes. In J. M. Suls & R. L. Miller (Eds.), *Social comparison processes: Theoretical and empirical perspectives.* Washington, DC: Hemisphere, 1977, pp. 279–305.

Brewer, M. B. In-group bias in the minimal intergroup situation: A cognitive-motivational analysis. *Psychological Bulletin,* 1979, *86,* 307–324.

Carver, C. S., & Scheier, M. F. *Attention and self-regulation: A control-theory approach to human behavior.* New York: Springer-Verlag, 1981.

Cook, K. S., & Parcel, T. L. Equity theory: Directions for future research. *Sociological Inquiry,* 1977, *47,* 75–88.

Cook, T. D., Crosby, F., & Hennigan, K. M. The construct validity of relative deprivation. In J. M. Suls & R. L. Miller (Eds.), *Social comparison processes: Theoretical and empirical perspectives.* Washington, DC: Hemisphere, 1977, pp. 307–333.

Crosby, F. A model of egoistical relative deprivation. *Psychological Review,* 1976, *83,* 85–113.

Crosby, F. J. *Relative deprivation and working women.* New York: Oxford, 1982.

Crosby, F. Relative deprivation in organizational settings. In B. M. Staw (Ed.), *Research in organizational behavior* (Vol. 6). Greenwich, CT.: JAI Press, 1984, pp. 51–93/.

Davies, J. C. Toward a theory of revolution. *American Sociological Review,* 1962, *27,* 5–19.

Davies, J. C. The J-curve of rising and declining satisfactions as a cause of some great revolutions and a contained rebellion. In H. D. Graham & T. R. Gurr (Eds.), *Violence in America: Historical and comparative perspectives.* New York: New American Library, 1969, pp. 671–709.

Davis, J. A. A formal interpretation of the theory of relative deprivation. *Sociometry,* 1959, *22,* 280–296.

deCarufel, A. The allocation and acquisition of resources in times of scarcity. In M. J. Lerner & S. C. Lerner (Eds.), *The justice motive in social behavior: Adapting to times of scarcity and change.* New York: Plenum, 1981, pp. 317–341.

Deutsch, M. Awakening the sense of injustice. In M. Lerner & M. Ross (Eds.), *The quest for justice: Myth, reality, ideal.* Toronto/Montreal: Holt, Rinehart & Winston of Canada, 1974, pp. 19–41.

Deutsch, M. Justice in "the crunch." In M. J. Lerner & S. C. Lerner (Eds.), *The justice motive in social behavior: Adapting to times of scarcity and change.* New York: Plenum, 1981, pp. 343–357.

Feierabend, I. K., Feierabend, R. L., & Nesvold, B. A. Social change and political violence: Cross-national patterns. In H. D. Graham & T. R. Gurr (Eds.), *Violence in America: Historical and comparative perspectives.* New York: New American Library, 1969, pp. 606–668.

Fenigstein, A., Scheier, M. F., & Buss, A. H. Public and private self-consciousness: Assessment and theory. *Journal of Consulting and Clinical Psychology,* 1975, *43,* 522–527.

Festinger, L. A theory of social comparison processes. *Human Relations,* 1954, *7,* 117–140.

Gerard, H. B., & Hoyt, M. F. Distinctiveness of social categorization and attitude toward ingroup members. *Journal of Personality and Social Psychology,* 1974, *29,* 836–842.

Goodman, P. S. An examination of referents used in the evaluation of pay. *Organizational Behavior and Human Performance,* 1974, *12,* 170–195.

Goodman, P. S. Social comparison processes in organizations. In B. M. Staw & G. R. Salancik (Eds.), *New directions in organizational behavior.* Chicago: St. Clair, 1977, pp. 97–132.

Greenberg, J. Approaching equity and avoiding inequity in groups and organizations. In J. Greenberg & R. L. Cohen (Eds.), *Equity and justice in social behavior*. New York: Academic Press, 1982, pp. 389–435.

Gruder, C. L. Choice of comparison persons in evaluating oneself. In J. M. Suls & R. L. Miller (Eds.), *Social comparison processes: Theoretical and empirical perspectives*. Washington, DC: Hemisphere, 1977, pp. 21–41.

Guimond, S., & Dube-Simard, L. Relative deprivation theory and the Quebec Nationalist Movement: The cognition-emotion distinction and the personal-group deprivation issue. *Journal of Personality and Social Psychology*, 1983, *44*, 526–535.

Gurr, T. R. *Why men rebel*. Princeton, NJ: Princeton University Press, 1970.

Homans, G. *Social behavior: Its elementary forms*. New York: Harcourt Brace, 1961.

Hyman, H. H. The psychology of status. *Archives of Psychology*, 1942, No. 269, 5–94.

Jasso, G. Social consequences of the sense of distributive justice: Small-group applications. In D. M. Messick & K. S. Cook (Eds.), *Equity theory: Psychological and sociological perspectives*. New York: Praeger, 1983, pp. 243–294.

Lemaine, G. Social differentiation and social originality. *European Journal of Social Psychology*, 1974, *4*, 17–52.

Leventhal, G. S. Effects of external conflict on resource allocation and fairness within groups and organizations. In W. G. Austin & S. Worchel (Eds.), *The social psychology of intergroup relations*. Monterey, CA: Brooks/Cole, 1979, pp. 237–251.

Levine, J. M. Social comparison and education. In J. M. Levine & M. C. Wang (Eds.), *Teacher and student perceptions: Implications for learning*. Hillsdale, NJ: Lawrence Erlbaum Associates, 1983, pp. 29–55.

Levine, J. M., & Moreland, R. L. Social comparison and outcome evaluation in group contexts. In J. C. Masters & W. P. Smith (Eds.), *Social comparison and social justice*. Hillsdale, NJ: Lawrence Erlbaum Associates, in press.

Martin, J. Relative deprivation: A theory of distributive injustice for an era of shrinking resources. In L. L. Cummings & B. M. Staw (Eds.), *Research in organizational behavior* (Vol. 3). Greenwich, CT: JAI Press, 1981, pp. 53–107.

Martin, J., Brickman, P., & Murray, A. Moral outrage and pragmatism: Explanations for collective action. *Journal of Experimental Social Psychology*, 1984, *20*, 484–496.

Martin, J., & Murray, A. Distributive injustice and unfair exchange. In D. M. Messick & K. S. Cook (Eds.), *Equity theory: Psychological and sociological perspectives*. New York: Praeger, 1983, pp. 169–205.

Martin, J., & Murray, A. Catalysts for collective violence: The importance of a psychological approach. In R. Folger (Ed.), *The sense of injustice: Social psychological perspectives*. New York: Plenum, 1984, pp. xxx–yyy.

McGuire, W. J., & McGuire, C. V. The spontaneous self-concept as affected by personal distinctiveness. In M. D. Lynch, A. A. Norem-Hebeisen, & K. J. Gergen (Eds.), *Self-concept: Advances in theory and research*. Cambridge, MA: Ballinger, 1981, pp. 147–172.

Merton, R. K., & Kitt, A. S. Contributions to the theory of reference group behavior. In R. K. Merton & P. F. Lazarsfeld (Eds.), *Continuities in social research: Studies in the scope and method of "The American Soldier."* Glencoe, IL: Free Press, 1950, pp. 40–105.

Mullen, B. Operationalizing the effect of the group on the individual: A self-attention perspective. *Journal of Experimental Social Psychology*, 1983, *19*, 295–322.

Patchen, M. A conceptual framework and some empirical data regarding comparisons of social rewards. *Sociometry*, 1961, *24*, 136–156.

Runciman, W. G. *Relative deprivation and social justice: A study of attitudes to social inequality in twentieth-century England*. London: Routledge and Kegan Paul, 1966.

Schachter, S. *The psychology of affiliation: Experimental studies of the sources of gregariousness*. Stanford, CA: Stanford University Press, 1959.

Schlenker, B. R. *Impression management: The self-concept, social identity, and interpersonal relations.* Monterey, CA: Brooks/Cole, 1980.

Singer, E. Reference groups and social evaluations. In M. Rosenberg & R. H. Turner (Eds.), *Social psychology: Sociological perspectives.* New York: Basic Books, 1981, pp. 66–93.

Snyder, C. R., & Fromkin, H. L. *Uniqueness: The human pursuit of difference.* New York: Plenum, 1980.

Suls, J. M., & Miller, R. L. (Eds.). *Social comparison processes: Theoretical and empirical perspectives.* Washington, DC: Hemisphere, 1977.

Tajfel, H. Social categorization, social identity, and social comparison. In H. Tajfel (Ed.), *Differentiation between social groups: Studies in the social psychology of intergroup relations.* London: Academic Press, 1978, pp. 61–76.

Walster, E., Walster, G. W., & Berscheid, E. *Equity: Theory and research.* Boston: Allyn and Bacon, 1978.

Weiner, B. A theory of motivation for some classroom experiences. *Journal of Educational Psychology,* 1979, *71,* 3–25.

Weiner, B. *Human motivation.* New York: Holt, Rinehart & Winston, 1980.

Wicklund, R. A. Group contact and self-focused attention. In P. Paulus (Ed.), *Psychology of group influence.* Hillsdale, NJ: Lawrence Erlbaum Associates, 1980, pp. 189–208.

Williams, R. M., Jr. Relative deprivation. In L. A. Coser (Ed.), *The idea of social structure: Papers in honor of Robert K. Merton.* New York: Harcourt, Brace, Jovanovich, 1975, pp. 355–378.

Wills, T. A. Downward comparison principles in social psychology. *Psychological Bulletin,* 1981, *90,* 245–271.

16 On the Structure of Self-Concept

Richard J. Shavelson
*University of California, Los Angeles,
and The Rand Corporation*

Herbert W. Marsh
The University of Sydney

The enhancement of students' self-concepts is valued both as a goal of education and as a moderator and perhaps cause of scholastic achievement. Nevertheless, conceptual and methodological problems have plagued research and evaluations involving self-concept. In an attempt to help remedy this situation conceptually and methodologically, Shavelson, Hubner, and Stanton (1976) posited a multifaceted, hierarchical self-concept (see Fig. 16.1) with the facets becoming increasingly differentiated with age. This chapter brings recent research to bear on these properties of self-concept structure.

SELF-CONCEPT

Self-concept, broadly defined, is a person's perception of him- or herself (Shavelson et al., 1976). Those perceptions are formed through one's experience with and interpretations of one's environment and are influenced especially by evaluations of significant others, reinforcements, and one's attributions for one's own behavior.

The construct, self-concept, can be further defined by seven major features (Shavelson et al., 1976; Fig. 16.1): (1) It is organized or structured, in that people categorize the vast amount of information they have about themselves and relate the categories to one another. (2) It is multifaceted, and the particular facets reflect the category system adopted by a particular individ-

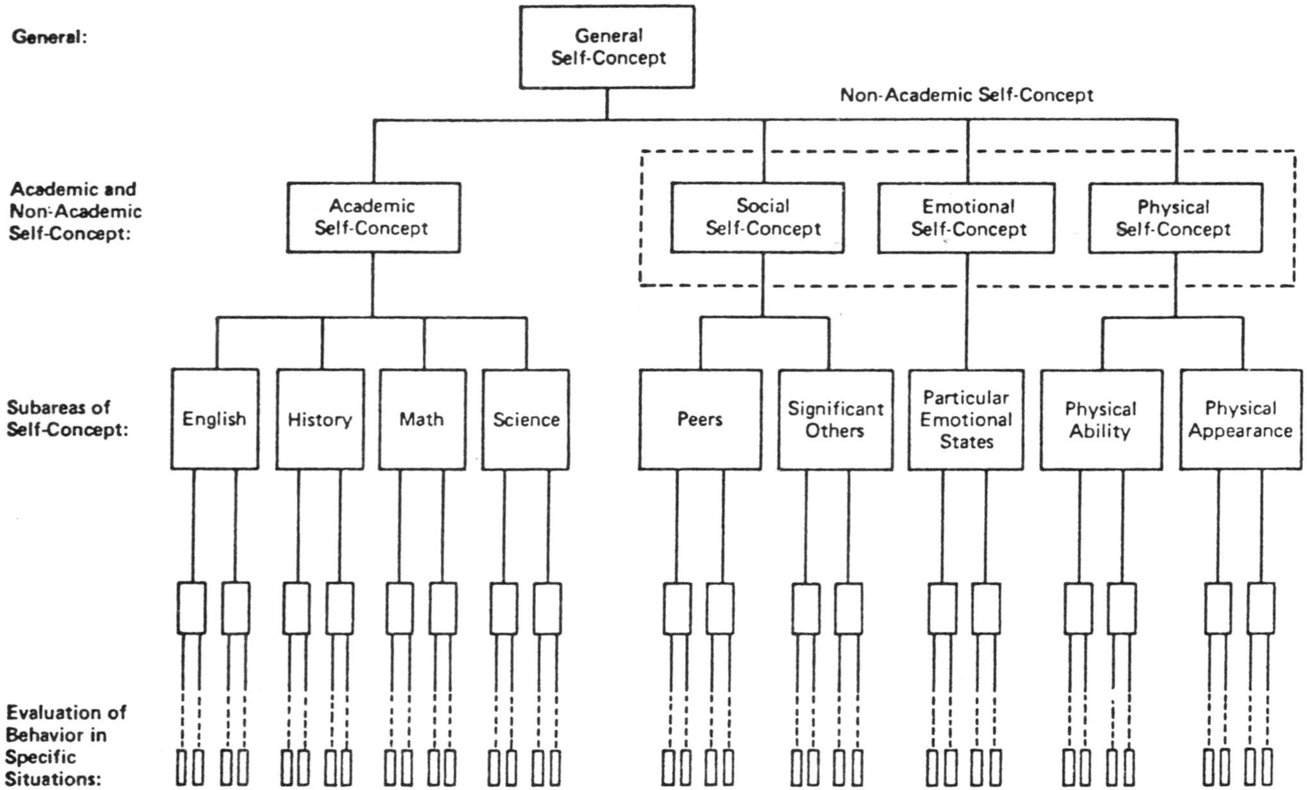
General:
Academic and Non-Academic Self-Concept:
Subareas of Self-Concept:
Evaluation of Behavior in Specific Situations:
General Self-Concept
Non-Academic Self-Concept
Academic Self-Concept
Social Self-Concept
Emotional Self-Concept
Physical Self-Concept
English
History
Math
Science
Peers
Significant Others
Particular Emotional States
Physical Ability
Physical Appearance

FIG. 16.1. Structure of self-concept (Shavelson, Hubner, & Stanton, 1976).

ual and/or shared by a group. (3) It is hierarchical, with perceptions of behavior at the base moving to inferences about self in subareas (e.g., academic — English, science, history, mathematics), then to inferences about self in academic and nonacademic areas, and then to inferences about self in general. (4) General self-concept is stable, but as one descends the hierarchy, self-concept becomes increasingly situation specific and as a consequence, less stable. (5) Self-concept becomes increasingly multifaceted as the individual develops from infancy to adulthood. (6) It has both a descriptive and an evaluative dimension such that individuals may describe themselves ("I am happy") and evaluate themselves ("I do well in mathematics"). And (7), it can be differentiated from other constructs such as academic achievement.

STUDIES OF THE HIERARCHICAL, MULTIFACETED NATURE OF SELF-CONCEPT

Until recently, the notion that self-concept is multifaceted has been more implicit than explicit in research on and reviews of self-concept. Of the studies that systematically examined this aspect of self-concept, most support a multifaceted interpretation of the construct (e.g., Fernandes, 1978; Fernandes, Michael, & Smith, 1978; Fleming & Watts, 1980; Kokenes, 1974; Marsh, Parker, & Smith, 1983; Marsh, Relich, & Smith, 1983; Marsh, Smith, & Barnes, 1983; Michael, Smith, & Michael, 1975; Piers & Harris, 1964; Shavelson & Bolus, 1982; Shepard, 1979; Wylie, 1979).

Studies by Marx and Winne (1978) and Winne, Marx, and Taylor (1977) are noteworthy because they purported not to support the multifaceted interpretation of self-concept. However, Shavelson and Bolus (1982) identified methodological problems in a reanalysis of the data and suggested that a multifaceted intepretation could be supported.

Most of the research on the facets of self-concept focused on a particular area (e.g., academic or social). Moreover, until recently, the assumption of a hierarchical structure of self-concept had not been tested. Finally, little attention has been paid to the assumption that self-concept becomes increasingly multifaceted with age. The purpose of this paper, then, is to bring recent and new data to bear on these assumptions underlying the conceptual structure presented in Figure 16.1.

THE SHAVELSON-BOLUS STUDY

Shavelson and Bolus (1982) examined the multifaceted, hierarchical structure of academic self-concept. They compared a structure having only general self-concept underlying all of the observed self-concept measurements with alternative structures that posited several distinguishable but correlated dimensions of self-concept. For example, the single facet (general self-concept) model was tested against the five-facet model of academic self-concept shown in Figure 16.2.

A sample of 99 seventh- and eighth-grade boys (n = 50) and girls (n = 49) participated from an intermediate school located in a predominantly white, upper middle-class, suburban community outside of greater Los Angeles. The students received a battery of self-concept tests during a 50-minute class session in Feburary 1980 and again in June 1980. General self-concept was measured by the Piers-Harris (WIFM; Piers & Harris, 1964) and Tennessee (TSC; Fitts, 1965) scales. The 8-item Michigan State Self-Concept of Ability scale, Forms A and B (Brookover, Le Pere, Hamachek, & Erickson, 1965), was divided into two parallel composites such that two measures of self-concept of academic ability (SCA) and ability in subject-matter areas (English — SCE, science — SCS and mathematics — SCM) were obtained.

An analysis of the covariance structure of the data, using LISREL IV (Joreskog & Sorbom, 1978), was conducted to examine the structure of self-concept. The boxes in Figure 16.2 represent the observed measurements, the circles represent the unobserved constructs underlying the measurements, and the e's represent residuals which are estimated in the data analysis. The straight arrows indicate that the underlying facets (constructs) give rise to the performance observed on the measurements and the relation between the measurement and the facet is estimated in a manner akin to estimating factor loadings. In Figure 16.2, for example, each observed measurement is expected to load on only one facet of self-concept (all other possible loadings for a particular measurement are constrained to zero). The curved arrows indicate that the facets of self-concept are correlated; these correlations are estimated in the data analysis. A nested set of models was examined: (0) a "null model" of complete independence of all observed measurements — this provides a measure of the total covariation in the data; (1) a single-facet, general self-concept model; (2) a two-facet, general- and academic self-concept model; and (3) a five-facet model as shown in Figure 16.2.

The results of fitting each of the four models to the data collected in February and again in June are presented in Table 16.1. Before interpreting the findings, a word about the methods used to evaluate the alternatives models is warranted. Covariance structure analysis has traditionally relied on a chi-square significance test to determine the degree to which a proposed model fits the observed data. However, as Bentler and Bonett (1980) have pointed out, chi-square goodness-of-fit tests are often inadequate because they are contingent on sample size. One alternative has been to express the adequacy of fit as a ratio of chi-square to degrees of freedom. This is the tack taken here (for alternative methods of evaluating models, see, for example, Bentler & Bonett, 1980).

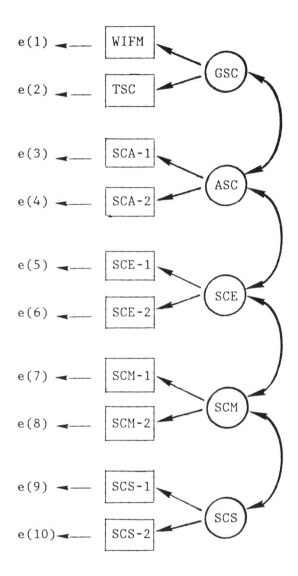

FIG. 16.2. Model of the structure of self-concept based on Fig. 16.1. (All proposed correlations among constructs — curved arrows — have not been drawn to permit clarity. GSC = general self-concept measured by the Way I Feel About Myself scale and the Tennessee Self-concept scale; ASC = academic self-concept measured by Self-concept of Ability scale halves 1 and 2; SCE = self-concept in English measured by Self Concept of Ability in English Scale halves 1 and 2; SCM = self concept in math measured by Self-concept of Ability in Math scale halves 1 and 2; SCS = self-concept in science Scale halves 1 and 2.)

TABLE 16.1
Test of the Assumption of a Hierarchical, Multifaceted Structure of Self-Concept

	Time 1			Time 2		
Competing Models	χ^2	df	χ^2/df	χ^2	df	χ^2/df
0. Null model	718.84	45	15.97	791.54	45	17.58
1. General self-concept	354.42	35	10.10	352.90	35	10.08
2. General & academic	272.50	34	8.01	272.90	34	8.02
3. General, academic & subject-matter	98.80	25	3.95	116.40	25	4.65

We interpret the data in Table 16.1 to mean that the hierarchical, multifaceted model shown in Figure 16.2 provides the best fit to the data at time 1 and this finding was replicated at time 2. For Model 1, the ratio of chi-square to its degrees of freedom exceeded 10, indicating a poor fit. Moreover, this ratio was more than twice as large for Model 2 as for Model 3.

The correlations among the self-concept facets of Model 3 are presented in Table 16.2. They may be interpreted as supporting a hierarchical structure in the data. That is, a hierarchical structure should produce a pattern of correlations such that GSC correlates highest with ASC, and next with subject-matter self-concepts. Note, however, that the relationship among the subject-matter facets are not of equal magnitude. As might be expected, the mathematics and science facets correlate moderately high (0.58) and both correlate substantially lower with the English facet (0.33 and 0.38, respectively). This suggests that the academic facet of self-concept might be divided into subareas (math and science versus English), a possibility not entertained by Shavelson et al. (1976, see Fig. 16.1). The studies reported in the remainder of this paper shed further light on this possibility.

In summary, then, the Shavelson-Bolus study provided substantial evidence for a multifaceted, hierarchical interpretation of *academic* self-concept. The study, however, does not bear on nonacademic aspects of self-concept. Nor does it bear on the development of self-concept.

THE STRUCTURE OF SELF-CONCEPT: GRADES 2-5

The model of self-concept (Fig. 16.1) posits that self-concept is multifaceted, hierarchically ordered, and the facets become more distinct with age. These assumptions are tested here with 662 respondents to the Self-Description Questionnaire (SDQ) in Grades 2-5 (for methodological details, see Marsh, Barnes, Cairne, & Tidman, 1983). More specifically, this analysis examines the (first-order factor) structures underlying responses to items on the SDQ at each grade level, separately. It also tests the consistency of this structure across the grade levels. And it examines the hierarchical structure of self-concept. Based upon previous research with the SDQ and the self-concept model, we expect:

1. to identify the 7 factors corresponding to the facets of Physical Appearance, Physical Abilities, Peer Relations, Parent Relations, Reading, Mathematics, and school subjects (cf. Fig. 16.1 at each grade level);
2. to find that the factor loadings are the same for each grade level;
3. to show that the size of the relationships among the facets (factors) varies systematically with grade level;
4. to identify the hierarchical structure among facets.

In examining the data from SDQ, four item-pairs were formed from the eight items designed to measure each of the 7 facets of self-concept on which the SDQ is based. (This collapsing of items was necessary in order to meet size and cost limitations of computer analysis.) Responses to these item-pairs were factor analyzed separately at each grade level with the result that the seven facets (factors) were identified at each of the four grade levels (Table 16.3). The factor loadings for each variable are consistently high on the factor they are designed to measure and low on other factors (Table 3). The factors are particularly well defined for grades 4 and 5, while the separation among the various academic factors is less clear for Grades 2 and 3. The pattern of correlations among the seven oblique factors offers support for other hypotheses based on the self-concept model. At each grade level, the highest correlations tend to occur between the general school factor and the other academic dimensions, and among the nonacademic dimensions. Despite the similarity in this pattern of correlations, there is a consistent decline in the size of the correlations among facets with increasing grade level (age). The median correlations among the factors decrease with increasing grade level (0.27 in Grade 2, 0.19 in Grade 3, 0.18 in Grade 4, and 0.14 in Grade 5) even when coefficient alpha for the measurements are somewhat higher for the

TABLE 16.2
Intercorrelations Among Latent Self-Concept Facets Time 1

Measure	GSC	SCA	SCE	SCM	SCS
GSC	—	.48	.26	.34	.30
SCA		—	.52	.62	.73
SCE			—	.33	.38
SCM				—	.58

TABLE 16.3

Separate Factor Analyses of Responses to the SDQ at Grades 2 (n = 176), 3 (n = 103), 4 (n = 134), and 5 (n = 241)

Self-Concept Facets	Item Pairs	Grade 2 Factor Pattern Matrix Factor Loadings							Grade 3 Factor Pattern Matrix Factor Loadings						
		I	II	III	IV	V	VI	VII	I	II	III	IV	V	VI	VII
Physical Abilities	1	50	05	06	08	-06	14	09	31	04	08	30	-04	07	-24
	2	62	02	-04	22	04	-03	09	70	14	-14	-12	11	-06	-05
	3	64	10	-05	13	-08	14	16	58	09	20	07	-05	12	-05
	4	69	-10	22	05	15	-01	-11	48	14	29	01	02	01	01
Physical Appearance	1	01	67	03	16	-01	06	02	-10	73	-02	05	20	01	-17
	2	-15	70	04	18	04	01	-08	09	69	-15	01	13	00	10
	3	19	47	11	03	-01	36	-26	06	59	22	04	-20	06	12
	4	00	55	00	21	09	32	-13	17	65	24	-07	-13	06	08
Peer Relations	1	05	-01	60	16	-11	12	-11	39	-05	08	14	-03	04	02
	2	-16	-12	47	39	20	28	-13	27	04	42	-26	31	07	-08
	3	13	06	27	20	-05	45	-12	18	-14	42	00	30	02	-10
	4	25	10	39	16	15	29	-29	07	16	74	-03	25	-04	-06
Parent Relations	1	29	22	21	34	-08	-16	13	14	20	-10	69	11	12	-35
	2	18	-06	05	34	29	-02	13	04	-06	21	37	-11	-04	40
	3	01	17	12	49	16	05	07	-04	-04	16	49	05	13	14
	4	15	13	-04	52	39	01	-05	06	13	17	20	31	-25	12

		I	II	III	IV	V	VI	VII	I	II	III	IV	V	VI	VII
Reading	1	05	22	34	−16	49	−13	20	08	−13	03	04	45	09	13
	2	19	28	27	−09	40	−04	02	09	−18	−05	44	37	02	13
	3	07	23	38	10	40	−10	12	06	18	−15	28	28	10	56
	4	08	07	00	18	50	11	05	02	−03	18	35	23	11	51
Mathematics	1	11	10	12	00	−08	51	33	05	14	−10	−07	50	53	01
	2	08	−05	−09	11	32	50	39	08	05	06	−03	13	73	13
	3	−02	10	16	24	00	39	59	−01	−09	37	27	−05	57	09
	4	14	−06	06	−07	20	58	32	10	−23	44	08	−01	66	07
All School	1	04	20	46	01	−06	−11	49	25	04	−09	−03	−03	43	37
Subjects	2	14	17	07	01	21	17	36	00	24	−03	10	10	59	20
	3	−09	05	09	−02	46	19	35	07	02	−02	−03	27	31	53
	4	14	21	12	−24	29	21	41	17	−13	16	13	28	25	32

Factor Pattern Correlations

	I	II	III	IV	V	VI	VII	I	II	III	IV	V	VI	VII
Factor I	(78)							(71)						
Factor II	18	(95)						17	(81)					
Factor III	29	34	(83)					28	15	(72)				
Factor IV	34	32	36	(80)				11	13	18	(66)			
Factor V	19	26	31	28	(84)			09	20	21	17	(74)		
Factor VI	26	27	28	27	24	(85)		09	19	19	19	22	(86)	
Factor VII	20	12	15	00	33	23	(82)	−12	14	12	26	19	33	(83)

(continued)

313

TABLE 16.3 (continued)

Self-Concept Facets	Item Pairs	Grade 4 Factor Pattern Matrix Factor Loadings							Grade 5 Factor Pattern Matrix Factor Loadings						
		I	II	III	IV	V	VI	VII	I	II	III	IV	V	VI	VII
Physical Abilities	1	77	−01	08	10	07	02	−09	65	00	08	−02	05	−05	−08
	2	50	12	08	−05	−07	03	14	44	23	−06	08	−06	23	09
	3	68	08	08	05	−01	10	01	77	04	12	01	−01	10	06
	4	62	16	11	06	−04	02	07	83	00	04	04	02	−03	04
Physical Appearance	1	08	77	03	17	−09	00	02	00	80	04	09	02	10	−05
	2	12	77	−03	08	21	07	−03	−05	80	05	10	06	02	−05
	3	18	60	27	−04	05	−09	15	12	66	19	−08	−03	−07	14
	4	−03	57	38	−05	04	03	08	21	55	19	04	05	−09	14
Peer Relations	1	20	−05	66	11	07	04	00	09	01	61	02	13	−03	−05
	2	14	32	41	02	08	00	22	02	19	49	06	−01	10	07
	3	02	13	69	03	07	−08	10	09	09	62	14	−07	−14	32
	4	13	21	63	07	−07	00	02	07	11	66	04	01	10	−02
Parent Relations	1	10	02	−11	62	−03	−08	11	05	08	06	50	09	04	−11
	2	07	03	13	45	11	18	−05	−10	−10	25	49	11	09	−10
	3	11	00	22	75	15	01	−07	10	05	01	75	01	−06	14
	4	−10	13	08	71	−06	02	04	−02	09	−04	76	01	−02	17

		I	II	III	IV	V	VI	VII	I	II	III	IV	V	VI	VII
Reading	1	-04	05	-11	00	85	05	10	-05	06	03	06	78	03	10
	2	-02	05	11	00	75	04	10	02	04	-05	13	76	-14	21
	3	08	06	01	14	53	06	29	02	08	11	04	79	04	11
	4	00	02	18	04	76	02	-05	06	-07	06	06	77	10	06
Mathematics	1	11	07	-02	01	-03	66	22	00	03	-08	05	00	79	11
	2	14	-04	02	03	-05	69	27	08	02	13	04	07	72	16
	3	-01	04	02	02	-05	82	10	01	01	04	-04	02	76	28
	4	13	01	01	02	02	85	13	03	01	07	-01	00	76	24
All School	1	01	07	-04	06	15	10	68	-09	03	07	-04	12	12	65
Subjects	2	01	15	15	04	-05	12	62	16	10	05	-05	16	23	38
	3	01	-07	-03	04	20	48	36	-05	-05	00	19	20	25	52
	4	05	-06	07	03	11	17	71	07	-04	02	10	19	12	64

Factor Pattern Correlations

	I	II	III	IV	V	VI	VII	I	II	III	IV	V	VI	VII
Factor I	(80)							(78)						
Factor II	29	(90)						23	(87)					
Factor III	35	43	(87)					22	30	(81)				
Factor IV	19	18	20	(77)				06	15	23	(79)			
Factor V	03	12	15	14	(85)			05	05	16	24	(90)		
Factor VI	19	03	08	09	19	(90)		10	08	09	11	12	(91)	
Factor VII	18	22	18	13	18	19	(85)	13	15	17	13	34	43	(85)

Note: Responses to the SDQ were factor analyzed with the commercially available SPSS program which presents correlations among the oblique factors in the matrix of factor pattern correlations (see NIE, et al., 1975). Values in the diagonal of the factor pattern correlation matrix (the values in parentheses) are coefficient alpha based on item responses and provide only a rough approximation of the reliability of each of the factors. All values are presented without decimal points.

older children. Taken together, these findings appear to support the assumptions of a multifaceted, hierarchical self-concept and the validity of interpretations of scores from the SDQ.

The analyses presented in Table 16.3 are based upon a common or exploratory factor analysis. While this type of factor analysis is widely used, it is not entirely suitable for testing assumptions of the model. A particular structure cannot be statistically tested against alternative structures (beyond setting the number of factors and, perhaps, their level of correlation). That is, there is no generally agreed upon way to compare the results of different exploratory-factor solutions. Moreover, there is no way to examine the structure of first-order and higher-order factors within the same analysis. These limitations, however, can be overcome with confirmatory factor analysis (CFS). The results of such analyses, using LISREL V (Joreskog & Sorbom, 1981), are described below.

First-Order Factor Structures

In the basic CFA model, we hypothesized that: (a) the responses to the SDQ can be explained by seven factors, (b) each item-pair loads on only the factor that it is designed to measure, (c) the seven factors are correlated, and (3) the error/uniqueness terms for the measured variables are uncorrelated.[1] In Model 1, the goodness-of-fit of the seven-factor model to the data was examined for each grade level separately. That is, we did not require that any of the parameter estimates (e.g., factor loadings) at each grade level be the same (i.e., invariant). The chi-square goodness-of-fit test for the sum across the four grade levels and for each grade level separately appear in Table 16.4. The ratio of the summed chi-square to the summed degrees-of-freedom is small (1.85), indicating a good fit to the data. An examination of the fit for each grade level, though complicated by the different sample sizes (see Table 16.4), also indicates that each of the chi-square/df ratios is small. These re-

---

[1]For purposes of this study, each of the different models was defined with reference indicators where the factor loading for one of the measured variables (item-pairs) designed to measure each factor was set to 1.0, and the diagonal of the factor variance-covariance matrix was free to be estimated. Every model in Table 16.4 was tested in the correlation metric. The use of the correlation metric is justified in that one purpose is to compare these findings with those obtained with a common or exploratory factor analysis which was also performed on a correlation matrix, and also because models in the correlation metric are easier to construct and interpret. For models which do not involve any invariance constraints, the metric is arbitrary and the chi-square values for analyses performed on the covariance matrices are identical to those shown in Table 16.4. In only two of the 26 analyses are the values based upon the covariance matrices different from those reported in Table 16.4; 2569 for Model 2, and 2802 for Model 3. The choice of metric has not been resolved when there are invariance constraints. Logically, hypotheses can be stated in either metric. However, the LISREL program has been developed specifically to test hypotheses about covariance matrices, and the consequences of performing analyses on correlation matrices when there are invariance constraints is not well understood.

TABLE 16.4
The Goodness-of-Fit: Confirmatory Factor Analytic Models

Model	Description	Chi-Square (df)	Ratio
	First order Factor Models & Invariance Tests		
1	Basic model with no invariance constraints summed across all four grade levels	2430 (1316)	1.85
1A	Basic model in Grade 2 ($n = 174$)	689 (329)	2.09
1B	Basic model in Grade 3 ($n = 103$)	573 (329)	1.74
1C	Basic model in Grade 4 ($n = 134$)	517 (329)	1.57
1D	Basic model in Grade 5 ($n = 251$)	651 (329)	1.98
2	Basic model with factor loadings invariant	2507 (1379)	1.82
	Model 1 vs. Model 2	77 (63)	1.13
3	Basic model with factor variance-covariance matrix invariant	2732 (1463)	1.87
	Model 2 vs. Model 3	255 (84)	2.68
	Goodness of Fit Indicies for Higher-Order Models		
4	One general second-order factor summed across all four grade levels	2862 (1372)	2.09
4A	Model 4 in Grade 2 ($n = 174$)	799 (343)	2.33
4B	Model 4 in Grade 3 ($n = 103$)	646 (343)	1.88
4C	Model 4 in Grade 4 ($n = 134$)	617 (343)	1.80
4D	Model 4 in Grade 5 ($n = 251$)	799 (343)	2.33
5	Two second-order factors (4 nonacademic factors on one, 3 academic on other) summed across all four grade levels	2621 (1368)	1.92
5A	Model 5 in Grade 2 ($n = 174$)	749 (342)	2.19
5B	Model 5 in Grade 3 ($n = 103$)	634 (342)	1.85
5C	Model 5 in Grade 4 ($n = 134$)	547 (342)	1.60
5D	Model 5 in Grade 5 ($n = 251$)	691 (342)	2.02
6	Two second-order factors (same as Model 5 but with parents on both factors) summed across all four grade levels	2593 (1364)	1.90
6A	Model 6 in Grade 2 ($n = 174$)	744 (341)	2.18
6B	Model 6 in Grade 3 ($n = 103$)	620 (341)	1.82
6C	Model 6 in Grade 4 ($n = 134$)	547 (341)	1.60
6D	Model 6 in Grade 5 ($n = 251$)	682 (341)	2.00
7	One 3rd-order & three 2nd-order factors summed across all four grade levels	2478 (1348)	1.84
7A	Model 7 in Grade 2 ($n = 174$)	704 (337)	2.09
7B	Model 7 in Grade 3 ($n = 103$)	584 (337)	1.73
7C	Model 7 in Grade 4 ($n = 134$)	532 (337)	1.58
7D	Model 7 in Grade 5 ($n = 251$)	658 (337)	1.95
	Model 4 vs. Model 1 (target model)	432 (56)	7.71
	Model 5 vs. Model 1 (target model)	191 (52)	3.67
	Model 6 vs. Model 1 (target model)	163 (48)	3.40
	Model 7 vs. Model 1 (target model)	48 (32)	1.50

sults demonstrate that the factor structure hypothesized on the basis of self-concept theory to underlie responses to the SDQ is supported at each of the four grade levels.

The purpose of Model 2 is to determine whether the data can be explained by a model which constrains the factor loadings to be the same at each grade level. This constraint defined a much more restrictive model than Model 1, and is normally considered to be the minimal condition for factorial invariance (see Alwin & Jackson, 1982). The difference in chi-squares between Model 1 and Model 2 is small and not statistically significant. These results provide strong evidence that the factor structure is invariant across the four age groups (see footnote 1).

In the third model, we restricted both the factor loadings and the relationships among the factors to be the same across the four age levels. The added restriction is one of constant correlations among factors across grade levels. The chi-square, goodness-of-fit test for Model 3 indicates that this model does not fit the data as well as Model 2. (The difference in chi-squares is statistically significant, and the ratio of the chi-square difference to the difference in degrees of freedom is 2.68).

These results support both the SDQ factor structure and the self-concept model hypothesized in Figure 16.1. The factor structure hypothesized to underlie the SDQ provides a good fit to the data in each of the four age groups. The factors are well defined in that every factor loading at each grade level is large and statistically significant, and invariant over grades. The relationships among the factors, as hypothesized, were not invariant. This finding is consistent with the self-concept model in that the factors become more distinct with increasing grade level (age).

The Higher-Order Factor Structure

The correlations among the factors (self-concept facets) differed systematically with age, but no special assumptions about the pattern of correlations were made. However, both the model in Figure 16.1 and the design of the SDQ assume that there is a systematic hierarchical ordering of the facets of self-concept. The SDQ measures four nonacademic dimensions and three academic dimensions of self-concept. Thus, one reasonable hypothesis would be that the seven first-order factors form two second-order factors, a finding which would be consistent with Figure 16.1. However, the results of previous research and the correlations among the factors shown in Table 16.3 suggest several complications to this hypothesis. First, the parents factor is as highly correlated with some of the academic factors as with the nonacademic factors (perhaps this should not be surprising). Second, while the math and reading factors are each substantially correlated with the general school factor, they are not substantially correlated with each other. These findings suggest that the higher-order structure underlying the SDQ factors may be more complicated than previously assumed.

A series of analyses tested the structure proposed in Figure 16.1 against alternative models based on these observations at each of the four grade levels. In the higher-order factor models, the seven SDQ factors are defined as before. However, unlike the previous analyses, the relationships among these factors are explained in terms of a higher (second) order structure of self-concept. That is, the second order factors merely try to explain the covariation among the first-order factors. This second-order model is more parsimonious than the first order model which contains 21 correlations among all pairs of first-order factors. The goodness-of-fit for the higher-order model, however, will never be better than that for the corresponding first-order model, and would only be as good if the second-order factors completely accounted for all the covariation among the first-order factors. The first-order factor model (i.e., Model 1 described earlier), then, provides a target or optimum fit for the higher-order model, and we refer to it as the target model in the remainder of this chapter. A higher-order model that fits the data as well as the target model and uses fewer degrees of freedom will be preferred, while any higher-order models which do not fit the data as well as the target model will be rejected.

Since the higher-order factors are designed to explain these first-order relationships, and the relationships among the first-order factors vary systematically according to grade level, the higher-order factors must also differ according to grade level. For this reason, the higher-order factor models (Models 4-7 in Table 16.4) are tested separately for each grade level, and these results are compared with those based upon the target models determined for each grade level (Models 1A-D).

More specifically, in order to examine the hierarchical structure of self-concept, we tested four competing models. In the first competing model (Model 4 in Table 16.4), a single, general self-concept factor attempts to explain the relationships among the seven first-order factors. This model, however, did not provide an adequate fit at any of the grade levels, and thus can be rejected (Table 16.4). Model 5 proposed two factors — one defined by the four nonacademic factors and one defined by the three academic factors. Model 5 fit the data better than Model 4, but not as well as the target model (Table 16.4). In Model 6, we examined the observation that the parents factor is related to both academic and nonacademic factors by allowing this factor to load on both second-order factors in Model 5. Models 5 and 6 differ by only one degree-of-freedom, reflecting this "dual" loading of the parents factor at each grade level. But the improvement is statistically significant and supports the earlier observations about the parent factor.

Model 7 incorporates previous research with the SDQ that has shown self-concepts in reading and math to be (nearly) uncorrelated. Here we posit two second-order, academic factors — reading/academic and math/academic self-concepts. Consistent with the results in Model 6, the parents factor is allowed to load on each of these second-order factors. As well as the nonacademic factor, Model 7 also proposed that the three second-order factors were correlated (equivalent to saying that they combined to form a [third-order] general self-concept). This model fit the data significantly better than any of the previous second-order models (Model 7 versus Models 4-6). In fact, it fits nearly as well as the target model at each grade level and for the sum of these models (Model 7 versus Model 1).[2]

We proposed four competing models to explain the hierarchical ordering of the seven SDQ factors. In separate analyses of data at each grade level, the same model was shown to provide the most accurate description of responses to the SDQ. This model is consistent with Shavelson's assumption that self-concept is hierarchically ordered, but the particular form of this higher-order structure is more complicated than previously proposed.

THE STRUCTURE OF SELF-CONCEPT: LATE ADOLESCENTS

Most of the research on self-concept structure is based on data from preadolescents. Does the multifaceted, hierarchical structure posited in Figure 16.1 and as modified above hold for adolescents as well? Versions of the SDQ have been developed for both early adolescents (SDQ II) and late adolescents (SDQ III). This section briefly summarizes two studies based upon the SDQ III and explores their implications for the structure of self-concept.

The SDQ III is based upon the model shown in Figure 16.1 and research done with the SDQ. The initial version of the SDQ III contained items representing the seven factors from the SDQ, except that the peer scale was divided into relations with same-sex peers and relations with opposite-sex peers. Additional scales were constructed to represent emotional stability, problem solving/creative thinking, and general self (similar to the Rosenberg self-esteem scale; Rosenberg, 1965). In pilot research, subjects were asked to complete an early version of the SDQ III (which contained 180 items) and to indicate areas important to them which had been excluded from the scale.

---

[2]It should be noted that while we talk about fitting a third-order model, the third-order factor is in fact just-identified (i.e., the three factor loadings required to define the third-order factor use the same number of degrees-of-freedom as would three correlations among the second-order factors). Consequently, this model cannot be tested against a similar model where the three second-order factors were merely allowed to be correlated (i.e., the chi-square values and degrees-of-freedom are identical). Since it takes at least three second-order factors to "just-identify" a third-order factor, third-order factors could not be tested in Models 5, 6, and 7.

Preliminary statistical analyses confirmed empirically the conceptual structure of the original 11 scales; the best items were selected for inclusion on the current version of the SDQ III. The open-ended responses indicated the need to add scales related to religion/spirituality and honesty/dependability. Additional items were written to measure these two areas, piloted with a separate sample of subjects, and also included on the current SDQ III.

The first study examines responses from a sample of 296 girls in Grade 11 (mean age = 16.2 years) who attended one of two Catholic senior high schools in Australia. (Details and other aspects of the study are presented in more detail by Marsh & O'Neill, 1984, including the wording of the items.) The 10 (or 12) items from each of the 13 scales were divided into five (or six) item-pairs, and an oblique factor analysis was performed on the total scores for these 68 item-pairs (see Table 16.5). In this traditional factor analysis, each of the 13 SDQ III dimensions emerged with remarkable clarity. The factor loading for every item-pair is high on the factor it is designed to measure and low on other factors. The small correlation (mean r = 0.09) among the 13 SDQ III factors (see Table 16.6) demonstrates that the factors are quite distinct. None of the 78 factor correlations is greater than .37 and a majority fail even to reach statistical significance. Surprisingly, not even the general self factor is substantially correlated with the other factors. These findings argue that, while self-concept is multifaceted, there is no strong underlying hierarchical structure. The SDQ III appears to measure relatively distinct facets of self-concept.

Shavelson et al. (1976) posited increasing differentiation of the self-concept facets with age, but not to the degree of independence that was found here. This suggests possible problems for the model or with the data reported here (particularly given the highly selective nature of the sample.) However, the results of a subsequent study provide further support for the findings.

In the second study with the SDQ III, students from two Australian universities and one teachers' college were requested to complete the questionnaire and to ask "the person in the world who knew them best" to complete the questionnaire as if he or she were responding as the subject. Thus, the significant other was asked to predict the responses of the person who gave them the questionnaire and had already completed it. Subjects were explicitly instructed not to discuss their responses with their chosen other, not even after both had finished. A stamped envelope was included with the questionnaire given to the significant other, and they were also explicitly instructed not to discuss their responses with the subject.

A total of 151 paired responses were obtained where both the subject and the significant other completed the survey. Separate factor analyses of both sets of responses identified clearly the 13 SDQ factors.

A multitrait-multimethod matrix (see Table 16.7) was formed using the 13 factors as traits, and self and other as two different measurement methods.

TABLE 16.5
Factor Analysis of SDQ III Item Pairs

Self-Concept Facets		Math	Verb	Acad	Prob	Phys	Appr	SSPr	OSpr	Prnt	Sprt	Inst	Emot	Genl
Mathematics	1	74	-12	03	15	04	02	00	-13	03	-05	09	03	-08
	2	87	-09	-01	00	03	-04	-03	03	00	05	01	05	-03
	3	91	07	07	-03	01	05	-03	-02	-02	01	00	05	-04
	4	86	04	10	06	02	00	04	02	06	-06	-10	-04	-01
	5	76	-06	14	08	-06	02	05	-10	-08	02	01	-02	04
Verbal	1	-11	57	09	19	-01	10	02	08	02	-02	05	06	-01
	2	-05	64	09	00	-01	-04	-04	-10	-03	01	11	-03	04
	3	-03	39	15	33	-01	02	09	09	05	-03	00	04	17
	4	-04	66	-05	25	-03	09	01	12	-04	07	08	15	00
	5	-02	71	05	00	-03	-02	08	-03	07	-05	-02	-01	04
Academic	1	-06	-13	68	22	-08	01	08	-09	-02	-04	11	09	07
	2	09	11	80	07	03	-02	00	-02	05	-14	10	21	-01
	3	15	15	72	02	-05	04	-04	-04	13	-16	05	07	07
	4	19	23	65	08	-02	04	06	-05	13	-11	-01	18	03
	5	19	30	45	05	-04	04	05	04	-03	-05	-12	08	14
Problem Solving/	1	11	13	07	59	06	03	-03	11	-01	10	01	03	-04
Creativity	2	10	00	09	59	04	07	-01	04	00	-10	00	02	03
	3	21	14	11	55	07	-07	-01	-04	-08	09	-02	-10	14
	4	-12	17	-09	62	-01	02	11	10	05	01	-01	-04	11
	5	00	05	-01	52	04	-02	03	01	00	02	00	-08	09
Physical Abilities/	1	-02	-04	-02	06	85	15	04	-01	00	06	-03	03	01
Sports	2	-02	-09	-03	07	87	01	06	-01	01	00	05	08	-02
	3	03	05	-06	00	90	02	08	04	01	-05	00	04	01
	4	00	-03	03	00	89	01	03	05	04	-06	03	-01	00
	5	03	02	01	-01	86	-08	08	11	-02	04	-01	-04	01

Physical Appearance													
1	02	00	03	-01	-01	77	06	08	00	02	-02	01	08
2	06	00	05	05	12	75	-17	08	01	00	08	09	05
3	03	-07	04	00	09	68	-03	11	00	-05	10	12	11
4	-10	05	06	00	-05	74	09	-09	03	01	-07	-08	07
5	04	09	-11	04	-01	75	11	07	04	-02	-11	-09	07
Relations With Same Sex Peers													
1	-01	08	03	00	-01	02	40	08	-08	-02	-06	04	04
2	04	01	01	01	07	-09	42	23	-08	03	09	-04	19
3	04	03	-01	08	09	02	59	07	-05	05	00	-05	02
4	-07	-08	11	09	07	12	76	09	-06	-08	05	07	-19
5	03	00	-03	-07	06	-06	70	01	-01	02	-02	-02	13
Relations With Opposite Sex Peers													
1	-09	-04	08	02	-01	22	08	66	-01	00	-05	07	04
2	-01	-04	-06	09	03	03	11	79	00	-05	-01	-01	01
3	-03	02	01	04	05	-04	06	85	-06	-04	00	09	05
4	-07	03	-01	00	05	07	11	77	00	-02	01	07	08
5	00	07	-09	-01	09	02	09	75	03	-11	-02	02	10
Relations With Parents													
1	00	-01	-09	04	04	05	-05	-01	70	04	-02	-07	01
2	05	04	10	-08	04	-03	02	01	68	00	13	-02	13
3	-01	01	06	04	-01	13	05	-01	67	08	08	-03	04
4	-16	07	01	-02	03	-06	-01	06	79	-02	01	10	00
5	04	-05	-01	03	02	-01	03	-03	81	-05	12	01	08
Religion/ Spirituality													
1	00	03	27	00	09	03	-01	-05	-24	47	-02	-27	02
2	05	01	08	-02	-02	-02	-06	05	-02	81	12	-24	04
3	07	-02	19	-01	01	02	-05	-06	05	73	13	-26	02
4	01	03	18	07	-04	04	-04	02	06	74	09	-23	-06
5	-01	08	08	-02	01	-05	06	-12	03	35	-05	-22	03
6	-03	-01	21	03	03	02	01	-03	01	58	07	-15	06

(continued)

323

TABLE 16.5 (continued)

Self-Concept Facets		Math	Verb	Acad	Prob	Phys	Appr	SSPr	Ospr	Prnt	Sprt	Inst	Emot	Genl
Honesty/Reliability	1	-05	02	02	12	-03	00	-02	-05	10	08	42	04	-05
	2	07	-05	-06	-04	12	-04	06	-05	16	02	57	00	11
	3	04	15	07	-03	-01	00	-04	03	06	-04	64	-05	-06
	4	-05	13	03	00	07	-03	00	-05	-01	07	56	11	10
	5	-05	-12	12	13	-10	-02	-04	00	-08	11	51	-12	-02
	6	07	17	12	-09	-01	09	16	00	-02	-15	39	-07	07
Emotional Stability/ Physical Abilities/	1	-01	00	-06	01	01	06	05	-03	-09	23	-02	75	19
	2	02	06	-03	-08	08	-04	08	01	09	24	-05	53	13
	3	03	-03	-11	07	08	-04	16	06	20	15	01	60	11
	4	01	07	-09	03	01	12	20	-01	14	22	-05	70	01
	5	03	04	02	09	06	-03	12	12	01	23	-15	52	23
General Self-Concept	1	00	-02	12	10	-01	02	00	24	02	04	-03	10	62
	2	-06	-01	04	-01	-01	16	10	-05	02	04	12	-05	73
	3	-08	-01	02	18	02	08	05	11	00	04	03	10	61
	4	-02	13	00	05	00	09	08	11	11	05	01	05	65
	5	-03	07	06	01	-04	23	13	05	09	06	-06	15	65
	6	00	11	-02	08	03	17	18	05	10	00	05	04	56

Note: The oblique factor analysis was conducted (SPSS, NIE et al., 1975).

TABLE 16.6

Exploratory Factor Analyses of Responses to the SDQ III: The Factor Pattern Correlation Matrix

SQ III Factors Self-Factors	S1	S2	S3	S4	S5	S6	S7	S8	S9	S10	S11	S12	S13
S1 Math	(93)												
S2 Verbal	-04	(86)											
S3 Gen Academic	24	32	(90)										
S4 Prob Solve	14	37	27	(77)									
S5 Phys Ability	05	-04	-07	09	(95)								
S6 Appearace	00	10	09	11	06	(88)							
S7 Same Sex	00	16	07	13	21	12	(81)						
S8 Opp Sex	-10	08	-08	19	15	18	34	(93)					
S9 Parents	01	07	20	03	05	09	06	-03	(87)				
S10 Religion	-01	01	18	10	04	-02	03	-09	15	(89)			
S11 Honesty	00	15	24	09	04	00	00	-08	27	11	(75)		
S12 Emot Stable	03	10	-06	04	10	09	22	18	09	-07	-12	(88)	
S13 Gen Self	-03	24	17	26	06	30	34	26	18	16	08	29	(94)

Note: Correlations (presented without decimial points) greater than .12 are statistically significant ($p < .05$). Values in parenthesis are coefficient alpha estimates of reliability based on responses to item pairs.

TABLE 16.7

Multitrait-Multimethod Matrix: 13 SDQ III Factors Rated by Self and Significant Other (N = 151)

SDQ III Factors	Self												
Self-Factors	S1	S2	S3	S4	S5	S6	S7	S8	S9	S10	S11	S12	S13
S1 Math	100												
S2 Verbal	-03	100											
S3 Gen Academic	09	40	100										
S4 Prob Solve	08	17	30	100									
S5 Phys Ability	01	-14	-17	-03	100								
S6 Appearance	07	09	25	15	09	100							
S7 Same Sex	14	13	16	09	08	16	100						
S8 Opp Sex	06	24	03	05	03	11	21	100					
S9 Parents	05	14	-02	-14	-08	-04	18	16	100				
S10 Religion	-01	00	-02	-06	02	-08	10	-05	10	100			
S11 Honesty	00	06	13	-01	02	01	11	13	05	09	100		
S12 Emot Stable	03	12	10	05	12	08	27	27	14	-09	07	100	
S13 Gen Self	16	07	12	10	08	14	31	28	08	01	06	28	100
Other Factors													
O1 Math	(77)	-05	03	03	-08	-06	05	-03	07	05	-09	-06	05
O2 Verbal	-07	(51)	31	12	-19	18	-01	06	22	04	-10	08	-06
O3 Gen Academic	23	15	(31)	09	-00	07	-04	-13	-02	14	-06	-11	00
O4 Prob Solve	08	20	17	(52)	04	12	-03	-03	-07	-08	-01	18	01
O5 Phys Ability	04	-17	-10	-04	(78)	09	-01	-11	06	08	-01	18	08
O6 Appearance	04	-03	-06	10	06	(50)	05	11	15	07	06	08	19
O7 Same Sex	01	00	-12	-11	03	06	(45)	12	22	09	11	27	31
O8 Opp Sex	01	-02	20	07	12	00	12	(51)	08	00	-03	30	20
O9 Parents	07	00	-07	-10	02	-08	17	08	(76)	14	01	15	06
O10 Religion	05	-08	00	06	06	-13	04	-08	02	(79)	09	-09	01
O11 Honesty	-07	-05	05	-01	04	00	-04	-02	10	25	(44)	08	-02
O12 Emot Stable	02	18	-11	03	11	-01	12	23	24	05	00	(62)	12
O13 Gen Self	07	-08	-00	15	12	15	21	17	15	09	04	22	(41)

(continued)

SDQ III Factors Self-Factors	S1	S2	S3	S4	S5	S6	S7	S8	S9	S10	S11	S12	S13
S1 Math	100												
S2 Verbal	00	100											
S3 Gen Academic	22	32	100										
S4 Prob Solve	13	37	19	100									
S5 Phys Ability	04	00	15	15	100								
S6 Appearance	02	14	-05	17	20	100							
S7 Same Sex	01	11	-01	02	09	23	100						
S8 Opp Sex	00	02	-03	19	16	34	37	100					
S9 Parents	11	14	10	-01	15	08	32	09	100				
S10 Religion	05	-06	11	03	10	04	-02	-05	08	100			
S11 Honesty	-01	17	24	15	12	15	15	03	17	27	100		
S12 Emot Stable	-04	12	01	19	15	19	32	41	24	-01	08	100	
S13 Gen Self	02	13	11	22	16	41	29	36	21	08	16	33	100
Other Factors													
01 Math													
02 Verbal													
03 Gen Academic													
04 Prob Solve													
05 Phys Ability													
06 Appearance													
07 Same Sex													
08 Opp Sex													
09 Parents													
010 Religion													
011 Honesty													
012 Emot Stable													
013 Gen Self													

Note: Correlations (presented without deciminal points) greater than .19 are statistically significant.

327

Table 16.7 presents correlations of factor scores among the 13 "self" factors (the upper-left triangular submatrix), correlations among the 13 "other" factors (the lower-right triangular matrix), and correlations between the self and other factors (the square matrix). Correlations among the 13 "self" factors (median $r < |0.10|$) are small and represent approximately the same pattern and magnitude of relationship among the factors as observed in Table 16.6. Correlations among the 13 "other" factors (median $r < |0.15|$), though somewhat higher, are also modest. Correlations in the diagonal of the square submatrix (values in parentheses) are correlations between self and other response to the same factors. These convergent validity coefficients are quite high (median $r = 0.52$), and substantially higher than the off-diagonal correlations (maximum $r = 0.31$) in this square submatrix.

The results of this second SDQ III study substantially strengthen the conclusions based upon the first study. The clear identification of the SDQ III factors was again found with self-ratings, and was also demonstrated with responses by significant others. Correlations among the self factors and among the other factors are small. Most significantly, the self-other agreement is quite high, demonstrating strong support for the validity of interpretations of the SDQ III dimensions.

CONCLUSIONS

The findings from a number of data sets support the hypothesis of a multifaceted structure of self-concept. This structure appears to be hierarchical in nature, at least for children up to late adolescence. The structure, however, may be slightly different from that originally posited by Shavelson et al. (1976, Figure 16.1). The academic facet may actually be divided into two subfacets, reading and mathematics. And self-concept of parental relations not specifically considered in Shavelson et al.'s formulation, appears to be associated with the two academic subfacets and the nonacademic facet of self-concept. Perhaps most surprising is the finding of independence among self-concept facets for late adolescents. While Shavelson et al. posited increasing independence of self-concept facets with age, they did not envision independence. Further research, especially on this last finding, is clearly warranted.

REFERENCES

Alwin, D. F., & Jackson, D. J. Applications of simultaneous factor analysis to issues of factorial invariance. In D. D. Jackson & E. F. Borgotta (Eds.), *Factor analysis and measurement in sociological research: A multidimensional perspective.* Beverly Hills, CA: Sage, 1981.

Bentler, P. M., and Bonett, D. G. Significance tests and goodness of fit in the analysis of covariance structures, *Psychological Bulletin,* 1980, *88,* 588–606.

Brookover, W. B., Le Pere, J. M., Hamachek, T. S., & Erickson, E. *Self-concept of ability and school achievement.* II (Final report of Cooperative Research Project No. 1636). East Lansing: Michigan State University, 1965.

Fernandes, L. "The Factorial Validity of the Dimensions of Self Concept Measure for Each of Three Samples of Elementary, Junior High and Senior High School Students," *Dissertation Abstracts International,* 1978, 38, 6009.

Fernandes, M. W., Michael, W. B., and Smith, R. "The Factorial Validity of Three Forms of the Dimensions of Self-concept Measure, *Educational and Psychological Measurement,* 1978, *38,* 537–545.

Fleming, S. J., and Watts, W. A. "The Dimensionality of Self-esteem: Results for a College Sample," *Journal of Personality and Social Psychology,* 1980.

Fitts, W. H. *A manual for the Tennessee self concept scale.* Nashville, Tenn.: Counselor Recordings and Tests, 1965.

Jöreskog, K. G., and Sörbom, D. *LISREL V: Analysis of Linear Structural Relationships by the Method of Maximum Likelihood.* Chicago: International Educational Services, 1981.

Jöreskog, K. G., and Sörbom, D. *LISREL IV: Analysis of Linear Structural Relations by the Methods of Maximum Likelihood,* Chicago: National Educational Resources, 1978.

Kokenes, B. M. "A Factor Analytic Study of the Coopersmith Self Esteem Inventory," *Dissertation Abstracts International,* 1974, *34,* 4877-A.

Marsh, H. W., Barnes, L., Cairnes, L., and Tidman, M. "The self description questionnaire (SDQ): Age effects in the structure and level of self-concept for preadolescent children," paper presented at the Annual Meeting of the American Educational Research Association, Montreal, Quebec, Canada, 1983.

Marsh, H. W., and O'Niell, R. Self description questionnaire III (SDQ III): The construct validity of multidimensional self-concept ratings by late-adolescents. *Journal of Educational Measurement,* 1984, *21,* 153–174.

Marsh, H. W., Parker, J. W., and Smith, I. D. Preadolescent self-concept: Its relation to self-concept as inferred by teachers and to academic ability. *British Journal of Educational Psychology,* 1983, *53,* 60–78.

Marsh, H. W., Relich, J., and Smith, I. D. Self-concept: The construct validity of interpretations based upon the SDQ. *Journal of Personality and Social Psychology,* 1983, *45,* 173–187.

Marsh, H. W., Smith, I. D., and Barnes, J. Multitrait-multimethod analysis of interpretations based upon the SDQ: Student-teacher agreement on multidimensional ratings of student self-concept. *American Educational Research Journal,* 1983, *20,* 333–357.

Marx, R. W., and Winne, P. H. Construct interpretations of three self-concept inventories. *American Educational Research Journal,* 1978, *15,* 99–108.

Michael, W. B., Smith, R. A., and Michael, J. J. "The Factorial Validity of the Piers-Harris Children's Self-concept Scale for Each of Three Samples of Elementary, Junior High and Senior High School Students in a Large Metropolitan School District," *Educational and Psychological Measurement,* 1975, *35,* 405–414.

Nie, N. H., Hull, C. H., Jenkins, J. G., Steinbrenner, K., and Brent, D. H. *Statistical Package For the Social Sciences.* New York: McGraw-Hill, 1975. Rosenberg, M., *Society and the adolescent self-image.* Princeton, NJ: Princeton University Press, 1965.

Piers, E. V., and Harris, D. A. "Age and Other Correlates of Self-concept in Children," *Journal of Educational Psychology,* 1964, *55,* 91–95.

Rosenberg, M. *Society and the adolescent child.* Princeton: Prince Shavelson, R. J., and Bolus, R. Self-concept: The interplay of theory and methods. *Journal of Educational Psychology,* 1982, *74,* 3–17.

Shavelson, R. J., Hubner, J. J., and Stanton, J. C. "Self-concept: Validation of Construct Interpretations," *Review of Educational Research,* 1976, *46,* 407–441.

Shepard, L. A. "Self-acceptance: The Evaluative Components of the Self-concept Construct," *American Educational Research Journal,* 1979, *16,* 139–160.

Winne, P. H., Marx, R., and Taylor, T. D. A multitrait-multimethod study of three self-concept instruments. *Child Development,* 1977, *48,* 893–901.

Wylie, R. C. *The Self-Concept (Vol. 2): Theory and Research on Selected Topics.* Lincoln: University of Nebraska Press, 1979.

Author Index

Subject Index